Major Psychological Assessment Instruments

CHARLES S. NEWMARK, *Editor*
University of North Carolina School of Medicine

Allyn and Bacon, Inc.
Boston   London   Sydney   Toronto

To Steven, Beth, and Erica:
my three children whom I deeply love

Production Coordinator: Louise A. Lindenberger

Library of Congress Cataloging in Publication Data
Main entry under title:

Major psychological assessment instruments.

Includes bibliographies and index.
1. Psychological tests. I. Newmark, Charles S.
[DNLM: 1. Psychological Tests. WM 145 M233]
BF176.M35 1985   150′.28′7   85–753
ISBN 0–205–08457–5

Printed in the United States of America.

10 9 8 7 6 5 4 3   90 89 88 87 86

Contents

Contributors and
Their Affiliations

Jeffrey T. Barth   Director of the Neuropsychology Assessment Laboratories, Department of Behavioral Medicine and Psychiatry, University of Virginia Medical School, Charlottesville, Virginia

Arthur Canter   Chief, Division of Clinical Psychology, Department of Psychiatry, Unviersity of Iowa Hospitals, Iowa City, Iowa

Richard H. Dana   Diplomate in Clinical Psychology, Department of Psychology, University of Arkansas, Fayetteville, Arkansas

Philip Erdberg   Diplomate in Clinical Psychology, Private Practice in Greenbrae, California

Emanuel F. Hammer   Diplomate in Clinical Psychology, Practicing Psychoanalyst in New York, New York

Leonard Handler   Associate Director of the Clinical Psychology Training Program, University of Tennessee, Knoxville, Tennessee

Alvin Enis House   Department of Psychology, Illinois State University, Normal, Illinois

Randy W. Kamphaus   Coordinator of the School Psychology Program, Eastern Kentucky University, Richmond, Kentucky

Alan S. Kaufman   Professor of Psychology, California School of Professional Psychology, San Diego, California

Nadeen L. Kaufman   Director of the Psychoeducational Clinic, California School of Professional Psychology, San Diego, California

Annette M. LaGreca   Coordinator of Clinical-Child/Pediatric Training, Department of Psychology, University of Miami, Coral Gables, Florida

Marjorie L. Lewis   Department of Psychology, Illinois State University, Normal, Illinois

Stephen N. Macciocchi   Assistant Director of the Neuropsychology Assessment Laboratories, Department of Behavioral Medicine and Psychiatry, University of Virginia Medical School, Charlottesville, Virginia

Victoria Shea   Clinical Psychologist in the Division of Development and Learning, University of North Carolina Medical School, Chapel Hill, North Carolina

Sharon A. Stringer   Department of Psychology, University of New Orleans, New Orleans, Louisiana

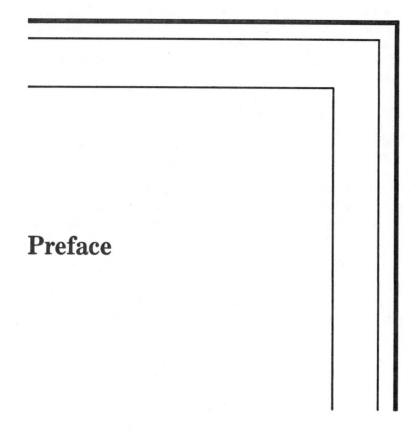

Preface

There are literally hundreds of psychometric instruments focusing on personality, intellectual, and neuropsychological assessment. In general, the literature devoted to these instruments falls into one of two categories: it either provides a cursory examination of numerous instruments or focuses solely on one test. The former approach is impractical and thus has very limited appeal, and the latter more utilized approach can be quite costly.

This text offers in a single source an in-depth examination of the most widely used tests in current psychological assessment practices. More than just a compilation of how to manuals, this book provides the reader with easy access to information concerning the introduction, construction, administration, interpretation, and status of these major tests. The tests are discussed in terms of their basic underlying assumptions, strategies, and issues. In addition, an illustrative case example is presented for each. The intent of this text is to present the core clinical knowledge and foundation necessary for the competent use of these instruments. As such the book can be used as a core text for courses in both personality and intellectual assessment, thereby sparing the student the expense of purchasing two books. The work is also intended to serve as an invaluable reference for both school and clinical psychologists.

I am extremely appreciative of the authors' significant contributions. Working with such a dedicated, responsible, and reliable group of professionals has been a rewarding experience. All the authors have published extensively and are nationally recognized authorities in their respective areas.

In particular, I would like to thank my former professor at the University of Alabama, Dr. Michael Dinoff. His personal and professional guidance throughout my graduate study and subsequent career has proven invaluable. He has been greatly missed since his death in 1982. Thanks also must be given to Mrs. Debbie Davis for her assistance in typing and proofreading the manuscript.

Finally, I am most fortunate to have worked with Mr. Bill Barke, managing editor at Allyn and Bacon. His confidence, encouragement, and many helpful comments and suggestions are testimony to his dedicated and responsible publishing expertise.

Overview of the Assessment Process

Victoria Shea

There was a time when the public thought testing was all that psychologists did. One stereotype consisted of a narrow-minded scientist in a lab coat, holding a stopwatch, and observing the hapless client struggle with a variety of puzzles, buzzers, and blocks. Another image was the faceless, anonymous psychologist, gleaning secrets from projective tests and passing them to the therapist, the *real doctor* who would use the results in some magical, therapeutic manner. Finally, there was the psychological expert working with children, who periodically had to confront anxious parents with confirmation of their child's cognitive limitations on an IQ test.

Eventually psychologists rebelled against these stereotypes, and fought political and public relations battles enabling them to engage in a wider variety of professional activities. Even within the profession, testing became devalued as a low-level, mechanical function which a technician could perform, leaving the psychologist free for more important and interesting activities such as psychotherapy, consultation, and research.

There are many fascinating and valuable areas within the field of psychology including the theme of this chapter: assessment. Most psychologists now distinguish between testing and assessment. Testing is seen as one segment of the assessment process; one which consists of evaluating a referral question, selecting appropriate procedures and tests, administering and scoring tests, interpreting and synthesizing findings, and communicating these effectively to the appropriate persons (e.g., client, referral source, other professionals). Clearly, these procedures require training, skill, and judgment far beyond the technician level. Issues related to each of these segments of assessment will now be reviewed.

EVALUATING REFERRAL QUESTIONS

Most psychologists have rejected the concept of a standard test battery being administered to all clients. Instead, assessment procedures are selected in order to answer specific questions. Thus, the first step in assessment is to clarify the referral question, but this is not always simple.

Sometimes clients are referred for testing by another professional simply for a psychologist's opinion with regard to diagnosis or treatment. The request for testing is merely a vehicle for getting the psychologist involved. In such situations, it may be appropriate for the psychologist to interview or observe the client, review previous test data, or consult with the referring professional, to save the patient the expense and time of retesting.

Other referrals may require testing, but only after the question is clarified. For example, the initial referral might be for overall evaluation, personality assessment, or developmental testing. An exploratory telephone call to the referring professional may result in a more manageable question (e.g., How disturbed is this person? How well-adjusted is this person? Would it be an effective course of action for this person to be hospitalized, toilet-trained, treated psychoanalytically, medicated, incarcerated, mainstreamed into regular classes?). Once such concrete questions are asked, the psychologist can plan the assessment.

SELECTING ASSESSMENT PROCEDURES

Above all, psychologists involved in assessment should hold as a solemn credo that *There is no clinical question for which a set of test scores is a sufficient answer*. Referral questions can be answered only within the context of information about the client's whole life. For example, what medical conditions may be affecting the client's behavior? What social and environmental factors have influenced the client in the past? If a specific recommendation is made, is anyone available to carry it out?

Sometimes the psychologist's responsibility is only to provide test scores, while someone else integrates the results with information from other sources. This arrangement is often reasonable and efficient. But someone must obtain and incorporate information about the client's history and setting into which the assessment results will be received.

The following chapters will describe the most widely-used and well-known psychological tests. Important as these instruments are, however, they are a minute sample of the standardized psychological tests available today. It is easy for psychologists to restrict themselves to the major tests as specifically taught in graduate school. For some clinical populations this is perfectly appropriate, but psychologists who work with specialized populations (e.g., developmentally delayed, physically handicapped, geriatric, non-English speaking) must be more knowledgeable and flexible in their selection of test instruments.

Psychologists should be familiar with references such as the *Mental Measurements Yearbook* series and *Tests in Print* (Buros, 1961). These sources provide evaluations of tests in terms of psychometric properties and clinical value. Psychologists must also be aware that the American Psychological Association has developed standards for tests, dealing with the technical information available in the test manual. Some tests are commercially available and do not conform to these standards. The mailboxes of most psychologists are replenished weekly with numerous pamphlets from test publishers offering tests that measure and predict all human skills and traits, with near-perfect reliability, often in 15–20 minutes!

In deciding to use a test as part of the assessment, the psychologist must maintain some degree of skepticism about the role of testing. A test instrument is simply "an objective and standardized measure of a sample of behavior" (Anastasi, 1976). Because psychologists have developed tests with standardized administration procedures, large normative samples, and empirically-derived behavioral correlates, psychologists can now give a test to an individual client and have some assurance that results will be more than merely clinical intuition. Thus, valid administration of a psychometrically sound test often makes an important contribution to a complete assessment. No test is magic, however, and all tests are subject to random variability and human error. Tests should be used to augment understanding, rather than form the basis of it.

Two vital additional sources of assessment information are interviews and behavioral observations. In many situations, it is the client who seeks psychological services, thus the client should be interviewed. Topics include: What kind of help/information is the client seeking? What kinds of experiences/problems has the client had in the past? What is the client's age, occupation, education, religion, health status, living arrangement, income? In other situations the client is referred for assessment by someone else such as a parent, teacher, physician, judge, adult child (of an elderly parent), etc. Usually the referring professional will contribute information about the client's difficulties and current status.

Behavioral observations provide an important complement to test performance (and some psychologists argue the reverse: tests are a supplement to behavioral observations). As mentioned previously, the client's test performance is merely a *sample* of behavior. Because this sample is usually obtained while sitting in a room alone with a psychologist, being asked unfamiliar questions or working on novel tasks, it can be argued that this sample of behavior is less representative and predictive of the client's daily functioning than direct observation of his or her behavior in the natural environment. The rebuttal argument is that well-validated tests do predict behavior outside of the testing situation and are a more efficient and practical means of obtaining information. In addition, psychologists can compare an individual's performance to a large normative sample tested under the same conditions. Still, tests are not infallible. Clients may give responses thoughtfully, impulsively, randomly, deceitfully, or erroneously. Only when test performance is integrated with careful observation and skillful interpretation of the client's behavior can appropriate conclusions be drawn.

ADMINISTERING TESTS

Administering psychological tests requires both attention to detail and flexibility. Many tests have standardized directions that must be followed precisely if tests results are to be valid. Thus, for example, if a question on an intelligence test is reworded, it may become either simpler or harder, so a client's response could not legitimately be compared to the test norms. Similarly, on some tests, demonstrations are allowed while on other tests they are not. The psychologist should be carefully trained in the administration of each test. Many psychologists appropriately continue to rely on the test manual for details of administration. Only in specialized settings will a psychologist administer a particular test so frequently that the minutiae of administration are fully memorized.

Attention to the details of administration must be accompanied by attention to the client. Inexperienced test administrators often focus so intently on the test procedures that they lose track of the client. This is where the importance of clinical skills and flexibility becomes evident. Testing in a clinical setting often requires the client to answer questions or work on tasks that are uncomfortable or difficult. Sometimes clients understand the anticipated benefits from the testing, or are willing to comply with the procedures simply because they are asked to do so. Often, however, the client's cooperation depends on some degree on rapport or relationship with the psychologist. In order to develop this rapport, the psychologist must convey a sense of respect for the client, interest in obtaining the client's most valid responses, and empathy for whatever discomfort the client feels as a result of testing. Simple courtesies such as comfortable seating and temperature, the availability of tissues and an ashtray, and the opportunity to use the restroom should be provided by the psychologist. In addition, while test procedures must be carried out according to standardization, it is still perfectly appropriate to make eye contact, smile, and/or converse briefly between tests items, etc. A discussion of specific techniques for establishing relationships with clients is beyond the scope of this chapter; suggested readings include *The Psychiatric Interview* (Sullivan, 1954) and the chapter on "Interviewing Strategies in Child Assessment" in Walker and Robert's *Handbook of Clinical Child Psychology* (1983).

When certain populations are administered certain tests, it is necessary for the psychologist to be quite directive in managing the client's behavior to complete testing. Examples of such clients include young or hyperactive children, depressed or agitated adults, and mildly rebellious adolescents. The psychologist may need to convince the client to sit down, answer one or two more questions before taking a rest, listen carefully before answering, etc. With such clients the psychologist's goals concern the client's attention to the test task and ability to give reasonable, valid responses. Occasionally psychologists explicitly reward clients, especially children, for paying attention. Typical rewards include praise, the opportunity to engage in a favorite activity, or more concrete reinforcers such as food, small toys, or tokens that can be traded for a larger reward at the end of testing.

When using rewards, the psychologist must be careful to make them contingent on cooperation and attention, rather than on correct answers. In both personality and ability testing there is a danger that the client's responses will be influenced by the psychologist's reactions. Thus, the psychologist must convey the message, both verbally and non-verbally, that "I will accept any response you give as long as you pay attention to the task and respond thoughtfully."

In some situations clients are disturbed or handicapped, therefore, valid and standardized testing cannot be obtained. In these cases the psychologist must rely on clinical observations and interview data to answer the referral questions as accurately as possible.

SCORING TESTS

Most tests have a test blank or protocol to record the client's responses (the major exceptions include the Thematic Apperception Test, the Rorschach, and other drawing tests, which use plain paper). It is important to record the client's responses fully and accurately, so the data can be reviewed, scored, and analyzed. Ideally, additional notes about the client's behavior and performance are made on the test protocol, so the psychologist can see which test items were associated with which behaviors (e.g., when the client saw pictures of a boxing match he or she became agitated and began talking very fast). Some test protocols do not have sufficient room for taking notes, so the psychologist must have additional paper available.

Some clients are oblivious to the psychologist's writing, while others are extremely sensitive to it and attempt to read the notes or scores. The psychologist usually handles these situations by using shorthand, keeping the protocol on a clipboard in his or her lap, and reassuring the client by saying, "I'm just making a note of what you said (did), to help me remember."

In many tests, the psychologist's job includes a sizeable amount of clerical work, e.g., assigning scores to responses, computing ratios, transforming raw scores into standardized scores, obtaining composite scores, etc. Every step in this process is vulnerable to human error, particularly when the psychologist has time constraints. It is always advisable to double-check arithmetic. When unexpected or inconsistent results are obtained, the psychologist's first reaction is to check the scoring prior to hypothesizing about possible reasons for the client's unusual performance.

INTERPRETING RESULTS

When the client has left and the mechanics of scoring are completed, the psychologist needs time to contemplate the wealth of data that has been collected.

The first question, "Are these test scores valid?" must be recognized. Even if the scores are not, valuable observations have been made about the client's behavioral style. The psychologist's responsibility is further complicated when the validity of the results is questionable, e.g., scores seem inflated because of guessing, diminished because of sleepiness, or bizarre because of an attitude of rebelliousness. Sometimes the psychologist decides that test results are essentially accurate, but must be interpreted with more caution than usual. This interpretation must be carefully explained and prominently displayed in the psychologist's report. The lay public and other professionals take psychological testing extremely seriously—sometimes too seriously. Often they place more faith in the test results than the psychologist does. It is the psychologist's ethical responsibility to ensure that test results are interpreted correctly, released only with appropriate and informed consent, and used in the client's best interest.

The second question that must be answered when interpreting test results is, "What does the testing add to the understanding of the client?" This question implies, appropriately, that the psychologist's initial understanding of the client is based on history, interview data, and the referral question. The testing, the face-to-face structured contact between psychologist and client is an adjunct supplying additional information. Test results may, for example, identify areas of emotional conflict, illustrate a thought disorder, measure a cognitive deficit, or suggest a pattern of ideas associated with behaviors such as violence, somatizing, depression, etc. This may be helpful for understanding the client's past behavior, predicting future behavior, or current needs. Thus, the psychologist uses test data to develop a more complete understanding of the client.

The third question to be answered is "How should the referral question be answered?" This is a two-part question: the reasons why testing was requested and what other needs or issues identified during the assessment process need to be addressed. For example, a client referred for disability assessment may have significant marital difficulties; a child referred for intelligence testing might display serious emotional and behavioral problems; a woman being evaluated for depression might show evidence of an undiagnosed learning disability. In all cases, the referral question must be answered clearly and fully. The assessment is not considered complete until this is done. In addition, the psychologist must make arrangements for the newly-identified issues to be addressed, whether by further exploration with the client or referral source, additional testing, or referral to another professional. Here again, it is clear that assessment requires high levels of clinical judgment and professional responsibility.

COMMUNICATING RESULTS

Psychologists are usually asked to prepare written reports of assessment results and recommendations. Over the years a standard format for these reports has developed. Like all traditions, this format is usually convenient and helpful, but occasionally counterproductive. The psychologist must remember that the purpose of the report is to communicate *effectively* with the reader. If standard format is an obstacle to communication in a particular case, then it must be modified.

Generally then, a psychological report should have the following components:

1. identifying information (e.g., client name, date of birth, date(s) of assessment, name of examiner),
2. background information and referral concerns,
3. behavioral observations,
4. interview data (e.g. from client, family members, other professionals),
5. test results,
6. interpretation/formulation,
7. recommendations and follow-up plans.

The report should be able to stand alone, as a coherent whole, so the reader can understand who the client is, why the assessment was performed, what was found, and what recommendations were proposed.

Two frequent flaws in psychological reports are the overuse of jargon and the inadequate interpretation of findings. Psychologists spend years in graduate school learning technical terms and studying complex theoretical concepts. Although these may help the psychologist identify, understand, predict, or modify human behavior, they do not belong in psychological reports. The report should be written for the reader, who almost never is a psychologist. Thus, technical terms (e.g., "gratification should be displaced from the id to the ego," or "employ a moderately aversive stimulus contingent on inappropriate behavior in combination with a DRO program") become a barrier rather than an aid to communication.

The other frequent problem in psychological reports is the failure of the psychologist to fully explain the results. There are two common reasons for this problem: the psychologist either does not fully understand the results, or understands them so well that the reader's point of view is forgotten. For example, sometimes behavioral observations are noted but not explained (e.g., the client frequently looked around the room; the client did not make eye contact; the client spoke in a loud voice). Without further explanation in the report, these observations are open to a wide variety of interpretations, and thus misinterpretations (e.g., the client was distractible/anxious/paranoid/alert; the client was visually impaired/schizoid/depressed; the client was angry/hearing impaired/manic). If the psychologist has a hypothesis about the meaning of the behavior, it should be stated in the report. If the significance of the behavior is not clear, and it is merely being included for future reference, this too should be explained.

Sometimes tests results are contradictory, or inadequate and do not enable the psychologist to answer the referral question. For example, one test may reveal average cognitive skills, while significant deficits are found on a similar test. Similarly, an interview may suggest significant psychopathology, while test results are benign and within normal limits. In these situations, it is important for the psychologist to describe all findings, acknowledge contradictions, and offer reasonable, alternative explanations. This is highly preferable to the practice of merely reporting results and leaving the reader to struggle with the interpretation.

A different problem occurs when the psychologist is so familiar with the test results that the reader's naiveté is overlooked. For example, a report might state "the client's WISC-R score was 74." The psychologist knows that the average IQ on the test is 100 and the standard deviation is 15, so the client's performance is almost two standard deviations below average. Furthermore, the psychologist finds the standard error of measurement of the test for the client's age, and knows that chances are 95 out of 100 that the client's true score lies within the range of 67–81. Most readers will not know or understand this, and must have the score put into perspective. For example, the report could state that the client's "cognitive skills are in the borderline range between average intelligence and mild mental retardation. The client can probably be expected to have difficulty with schoolwork, and require more practice and explanations than an average child in order to master academic skills." This principle of explaining and interpreting test scores applies when presenting an MMPI T-score, a Wechsler scaled score, a Rorschach F+ percentage, etc. The meaning of the test results must be made explicit, or readers will either draw their own conclusions (often erroneously) or remain uninformed.

SUMMARY

Psychological tests enable psychologists to measure and predict some human behaviors. By undertaking to assess and make judgments about clients, psychologists assume a major professional and ethical responsibility. They must recognize the limitations of even the finest measurement instruments, and the pervasive influence of chance and error. In performing assessments, psychologists must attend to details, reason carefully, write clearly, and at all times consider the client's best interests. Thus, psychological assessment is an exciting, professional challenge, that can make a significant contribution to the welfare of the clients.

REFERENCES

Anastasi, A. (1976). *Psychological testing* (4th ed.). New York: Macmillan Publishing Co.

Buros, O. (1961). *Tests in print.* Highland Park, NJ: Gryphon Press.

Buros, O. (Ed.). (1978). *The eighth mental measurements yearbook.* Highland Park, NJ: Gryphon Press.

Kanfer, R., Eyberg, S., & Krahn, G. (1983). Interviewing strategies in child assessment. In C. Walker & M. Roberts (Eds.), *Handbook of clinical child psychology* (pp. 95–108). Somerset, NJ: John Wiley & Sons, Inc.

Sullivan, H. (1954). *The psychiatric interview.* New York: W. W. Norton & Co., Inc.

1

The MMPI

Charles S. Newmark

Development *The Minnesota Multiphasic Personality Inventory* (MMPI) is the most widely used objective personality assessment instrument and the most widely researched of all psychological tests. Construction of the MMPI began in the late 1930s by Starke Hathaway, Ph.D., and Jovian McKinley, M.D. from the University of Minnesota Hospitals who recognized the need for an objective multidimensional instrument to assist in the identification of psychopathology. They were interested in developing an instrument that would provide a comprehensive sampling of significant behaviors to psychiatrists, yet would involve a simple format to be used with the majority of adult psychiatric patients (Lanyon & Goodstein, 1982).

The authors initially compiled a pool of more than one thousand items from various psychiatric textbooks, personality scales, and their own clinical experience, and prepared them in a self-report format. By deletion of duplicates and those items seeming to have relatively little significance for the intended purpose, the inventory was reduced to 504 items.

An empirical approach to scale construction was used. First, appropriate criterion groups were identified. Then, the test was administered to groups of normals and also to patients in a particular psychiatric diagnostic category, using the traditional system of diagnosis which, at that time, was based on Kraeplinian terminology. For each of the clinical groups, separately, an item analysis was conducted to identify those items in the pool of 504 that differentiated significantly between the clinical group and the group of normals. Individual MMPI items identified by this procedure were included in the resulting MMPI scale for that clinical group. Each clinical scale was developed in this manner and was cross-validated by comparing scores of new groups of normals, general psychiatric patients, and patients in the corresponding diagnostic group. Every effort was made to utilize responses only of psychiatric patients whose symptoms were obvious and who were relatively free from psychiatric signs other than those qualifying them for their particular diagnostic category.

The eight clinical scales that emerged originally were named for the syndrome identified. These include: *Hypochondriasis, Depression, Hysteria, Psychopathic Deviant, Paranoia, Psychasthenia, Schizophrenia* and *Hypomania*. Later, the *Masculinity-Femininity* scale and the *Social Introversion* scale were constructed and included as standard clinical scales. Finally, because earlier personality inventories were subject to criticism that they could easily be faked or distorted, the authors developed four validity indicators to detect deviant test-taking attitudes. Table 1.1 lists the fourteen validity and clinical scales as well as their number and abbreviation.

The construction of the MMPI thus proceeded independently of any theories about the structure of personality. It is intentionally an atheoretic test, and its development was based on a thoroughly empirical methodology. Consequently, it is not always possible to discern why a particular item distinguishes the criterion diagnostic group from normal groups.

Thus, the MMPI consists of 550 different items requiring the client to answer either true or false as it applies, although the client may indicate some items do not apply. The relatively unambiguous stimuli and the structured response format qualify the MMPI for classification as an objective technique of personality assessment. Originally published in 1943 by the Psychological Corporation, the test copyright was returned to the University of Minnesota Press in 1982.

ADMINISTRATION AND SCORING

A major positive feature of the MMPI is the ease of administration and scoring. Little professional time is required as the MMPI can be administered and scored by any individual with minimal training.

Table 1–1 MMPI Validity and Clinical Scales

Traditional Scale Name	Abbreviation	Scale Number
Validity		
Cannot Say	?	
Lie	L	
Frequency	F	
Correction	K	
Clinical		
Hypochondriasis	Hs	1
Depression	D	2
Hysteria	Hy	3
Psychopathic Deviant	Pd	4
Masculinity-Femininity	Mf	5
Paranoia	Pa	6
Psychasthenia	Pt	7
Schizophrenia	Sc	8
Hypomania	Ma	9
Social Introversion	Si	10

Nevertheless, the test should be presented to the patient as a serious and important task. In order to maximize cooperation, instructional set is critical. Patients should be informed why the MMPI is being administered. For example, in a psychiatric inpatient setting the clinician may explain that the psychotherapist specifically requested psychological testing to learn more about the patient so appropriate treatment strategies can be formulated. Effectively explaining to the patient that the testing is for his or her benefit will help immeasurably in enlisting full cooperation. If additional reassurance or further clarification of the intended use of the results is needed, a frank approach should be used. Furthermore, it is crucial the patient receive feedback regarding the results.

Some patients seek advice or request clarification of the items. Since the success of the instrument in documenting personality differences is based on the different ways patients interpret and answer the statements, the clinician should avoid providing direct help. For example, patients may have concerns regarding the word frequently, such as in the item "I frequently have headaches." The clinician must emphasize a response to this item based on the patient's interpretation of frequently. That is, if a patient has one headache a week and thinks that is frequently, then *True* should be checked. On the other hand if the patient has ten headaches a week, but does not view this as frequently, then *False* should be checked.

Because of the way the MMPI is scored, any item not answered either true or false is eliminated from the test. Therefore, the clinician must make every effort to keep the number of unanswered items to a minimum. Instructions to the patient before the test begins helps prevent this form of evasion. When items are omitted, carefully phrased requests to reconsider the unanswered items usually are effective in reducing the number significantly.

The MMPI can be administered to patients sixteen years of age or older who have at least six years of formal education. Patients as young as thirteen years of age and with less education may be able to take the MMPI if their reading level is adequate and their IQ is above 80. In such cases, attention and motivation become crucial variables. Psychiatric impairment rarely precludes taking the MMPI even though in some cases, such as mania or severe depression, the test cannot be completed in one session. In general, though, the test can be completed by patients in approximately 90–120 minutes.

Test Forms

The MMPI can be administered either as a group or individual instrument in a variety of ways. The most common form is the group booklet form which permits convenient administration to groups. Items are presented in a reusable test booklet, and a separate answer sheet is used for responses. The booklet presents the inventory in 566 items, sixteen of which are repeated for scoring purposes. Several answer sheets can be used with this form, most of which are designed for machine scoring, but hand scoring is possible if individual templates are developed. A major advantage of the group booklet form is that, by convention, all discussion of individual items in the MMPI literature follows the numbering system of this form.

The Form R booklet is a slightly modified version of the group booklet form. Hard covers enclose the pages that are spirally bound so this form can serve as a lapboard when no table or desk space is available. Form R consists of the same 566 items but in a different order so all items on the validity and clinical scales occur within the first 399 items. This is a major advantage of this form as only these first 399 items need to be administered to score all the standard scales.

A box form is available for patients of limited intellectual abilities and/or severely disturbed or confused patients who might have difficulty completing the booklet. The box version consists of 550 MMPI items on individual cards. The patient is asked to read each card and then place it in a pile labeled true or false. The test is scored by transferring the answers to an appropriate answer sheet.

A tape recorded version of the MMPI is also available for those patients who are blind, illiterate, or semi-literate, and with various disabilities that preclude completion of other MMPI test forms.

Scoring can be accomplished either by hand or any of several computer services. A thorough evaluation of computerized interpretation systems is discussed by Butcher and Owen (1978). Before any of the MMPI answer sheets are hand scored, they must be separated by sex since the Mf scale has separate keys for males and females. Next, the answer sheet must be carefully examined for omitted items and for doubly marked items which cannot be scored. The total of the number of items omitted and double-marked is the raw score for the ? (Cannot Say) scale.

The L (Lie) scale is scored next simply by counting the number of statements endorsed false among fifteen items (#15, 30, 45, 60, 75, 90, 105, 120, 135, 150, 165, 195, 225, 255, 285) on the group booklet form. The number of false responses is recorded as the L raw score.

The two other validity and ten clinical scales are scored by placing over the answer sheet a template with a hole punched at the scored (deviant) response for each item on the scale. The total number of such items endorsed by the patient is the raw score for that scale.

The first step in constructing the profile is to transfer the raw scores from the answer sheets or record form to the blanks at the bottom of the appropriate profile form. Before plotting the profile, it should be noted that beneath the row of raw scores entered on the profile form is a row of blank spaces labled K *to be added*. It has been found that adding the appropriate proportion of the K factor to five of the MMPI scales increased the discriminatory power. The proportion of the K scale raw score to be added to each of these scales is indicated on the profile form.

Once total raw scores are obtained, the profile can be plotted. The raw data from the MMPI now are transformed into T-scores directly on the profile sheet. T-scores are based on the response of the Minnesota normal group and have a mean of 50 and a standard deviation of 10. Thus, a T-score of 70 indicates the score is two standard deviations above the mean. T-scores are printed on each side of the profile sheet so raw scores can be visually converted. Using T-scores instead of raw scores enables the various scale scores of the same patient to be compared. For example, for a female patient, raw scores of 15 on scale 6 and 36 on scale 8 have no implications. However, corresponding T-scores of 70 on scale 6 and 77 on scale 8 permit scale comparisons that are crucial in profile interpretation.

Once scores are plotted, the profile is constructed by drawing a solid line to connect the three major validity scales (L, F, K), and another solid line to connect the ten clinical scales. The raw score on the ? (Cannot Say) scale is not plotted since any raw score less than or equal to 30 has a T-score value of 50, and comparison with other scales is not necessary.

Coding the Profile

After the profile has been plotted on the MMPI sheet, the profile needs to be coded. This coding offers a shorthand to be used to describe the profile in an efficient, systematic manner. In such codes the sequence and arrangements of scale numbers (Table 1.1) show at a glance the high and low points in the profile. Coding also permits easy grouping of similar profiles using all or parts of the code.

The major profile coding system was developed by Welsh (1948). In his system, the symbols are utilized as follows: scales with T-scores greater than or equal to 90 are followed by *, 80 to 89 by ", 70 to 79 by ', 60 to 69 by -, 50 to 59 by /, 40 to 49 by :, 30 to 39 by #, and scores below 30 appear to the right of #. Thus, a profile with these T-scores (1 = 90, 2 = 86, 3 = 86, 4 = 70, 5 = 29, 6 = 61, 7 = 69, 8 = 64, 9 = 39, 0 = 49) would be coded as such: 1* 23" 4'786- /0:9#5.

Since scales 2 and 3 have equal T-scores, they are underlined. This procedure is also followed when scores are within one T-score point of each other. For example, scales 4 and 7 are underlined even though they fall in different ranges since they are only one T-score point apart. When a 10-point T-score range contains no scale, the elevation symbol for the missing range is still included. In the example above, no scale score falls within the 50 to 59 range so scale 0 (T = 49) is preceded by the symbol / representing this range.

The validity scales also should be coded and placed separately to the right of the clinical scales code. In the profile above, if ? = 50, L = 60, F = 76, K = 46 (all T-scores) then F'L-?/K: is the remainder of the code.

INTRODUCTION TO INTERPRETATION

As noted above, the MMPI is scored according to ten clinical scales and four validity scales. The validity scales contain items designed to detect test-taking attitudes and attempts to distort test responses in favorable or unfavorable directions. The validity scales are referred to by scale name or abbreviation. While the clinical scales initially were referred to by scale name, it became evident that the actual behavioral correlates of the scales did not always match the originally applied scale name. Consequently, scale numbers now are used rather than the traditional scale names. The use of these numbers to refer to the ordinal positions of the scales on the profile sheet eliminates the necessity of using antiquated psychiatric labels and the associated psychopathology.

The definition of a high score on the clinical scales has varied considerably in literature. For most purposes, a T-score of 70 or more is considered a high score. When this is not the case, more precise information will be presented. In general, the higher the scores, the more likely the behavioral correlates discussed will apply to a patient. It is generally acceptable to consider T-scores below 45 as low scores. Unfortunately though, limited information is available concerning the meaning of low scores on the clinical scales. In most cases, low scores are characterized by the absence of the behavioral correlates that are present for high scores; exceptions will be noted.

The following section discusses basic validity and clinical scales, while the subsequent section will address these scale relationships. In all cases, the information provided refers to psychiatric patients. To present this information in a cogent yet parsimonious manner, specific references for each statement will be omitted. Instead, the following sections are an extraction and distillation of materials presented in Dahlstrom, Welsh, and Dahlstrom (1972), Fowler (1966), Golden (1979), Graham (1977), Greene (1980), Lachar (1977), Meyer (1983), and Webb and McNamara (1979), and are based on the author's extensive experience interpreting over 7500 MMPI profiles of psychiatric patients.

VALIDITY SCALES

(?) Cannot Say Scale

The ? scale is not actually a scale, but merely the number of items either omitted or answered as both true and false. In standard scoring procedures, omitted or double-marked items are considered answered in the non-deviant direction since only items answered in the deviant direction are counted. Thus, the potential effect of omitted or double-marked items is to lower the elevation of the overall profile and of any scales on which the items were omitted. Despite instructions to complete all of the answers, patients will fail to answer some. The easiest way to rectify this situation is to return the answer sheet to the patient and request that all items be answered.

It is generally assumed when thirty or more items are omitted or double-marked that a profile is invalid. However, the crucial question is where did these omitted or double-marked items come from? That is, even though the MMPI contains 550 different items, only 399 of these items are scored on the basic validity and clinical scales. The other items are scored on the various research and/or special scales. Therefore, a patient could omit or double-mark thirty or more items that are not scored on the basic validity and clinical scales and still obtain a valid profile.

Thus, it is crucial to examine the origin of the omitted or double-marked items. If the source of the items is from the basic validity and clinical scales, then the profile should not be scored unless the patient is willing to complete the MMPI. Note that in most cases, the omitted items are randomly distributed. The distribution of scores on this scale is highly skewed, with most patients scoring 0 to 5.

Some reasons for omitted or double-marked items and the resultant elevations on this scale include:

1. Insufficient reading level.
2. Carelessness.
3. Confusion and/or the presence of psychotic manifestations.
4. Severe obsessive-compulsive tendencies or ruminative components so the patient is indecisive regarding an answer.
5. The patient does not possess the information or experience necessary for a meaningful response.
6. The question does not apply to the patient. For example, on the question "I love my father," the patient may never have known his or her father.

It is Newmark's experience, that items are usually not omitted as a defensive ploy. Omitting or double-marking draws attention to those items. Therefore, it seems logical that if a patient wants to be defensive, he or she will just deny rather than omit.

L (Lie) Scale

The L Scale originally was constructed to detect a deliberate and rather unsophisticated attempt to present oneself in a favorable light. Fifteen items were selected on a rational basis to identify individuals who were deliberately attempting to avoid answering the MMPI frankly and honestly. The scale assesses attitudes and practices that are culturally laudable, but are actually found only in the most conscientious individuals. Examples of L scale items with the deviant answer in parentheses include:

"I get angry sometimes." (F)

"I do not like everyone I know." (F)

"I gossip a little at times." (F)*

Over 95 percent of the population, if they were being honest, would answer true to these items. Although most L scale items are not answered in the scored direction (false), many normals do endorse several of these items. The average raw score for the MMPI standardization group was four.

Subsequent research has revealed the better educated, brighter, more sophisticated patients from higher social classes tend to score lower on this scale. Therefore, such variables must be considered when deciding if a score is high. For example, a borderline IQ, rural, low socioeconomic black female from North Carolina with a sixth grade education may score high on this scale in order to present herself in a favorable light, so she will be accepted by those evaluating her. This denial does not necessarily mean the profile is invalid. In fact, an elevation on scale L rarely invalidates the profile. This is simply a measure of denial.

Various individuals have been known to score high on this scale. These include the clergy and those who understand the culture, but only on a superficial level. High scores also can be obtained from job applicants with limited social awareness who are naive enough to think a good impression can be made by answering negatively.

High scores on this scale are T-scores greater than or equal to 60, as scores above 70 are rare. Patients scoring above 60 are attempting to present themselves in an improbable yet favorable light concerning their self-control, moral values, and freedom from commonplace human frailties. A generalized lack of flexibility, limited insight, denial, and a poor tolerance for stress and pressure are strongly suggested. Low scores on this scale (less than 45) suggest the patient responded frankly to the items and was confident enough to be able to admit to minor faults and shortcomings.

F (Frequency) Scale

Unlike most other scales, the F scale was not derived by comparing item endorsement between criterion and normal groups. Instead, this scale consists of sixty-four items that were answered in the deviant direction by fewer than 10 percent of a normal adult population. Initially, F stood for feeblemindedness with the implication

*The Minnesota Multiphasic Personality Inventory. Copyright The University of Minnesota 1943, renewed 1970. All rights reserved.

that individuals scoring high on this scale were unable to read the items. While this may be one reason for an elevated F, it is best to view this scale as reflecting the frequency of seriously psychopathological items endorsed.

The scale taps a wide variety of obvious and unambiguous content areas, including bizarre sensations, strange thoughts, peculiar experiences, feelings of alienation, and a number of unlikely or contradictory beliefs, expectations and self-descriptions. Examples of F scale items with the deviant answer indicated in parentheses are:

"My soul sometimes leaves my body." (T)

"Everything tastes the same." (T)

"Someone has control over my mind." (T)*

There are at least six reasons for elevations on this scale. These include:

1. Clerical or scoring error.
2. Reading difficulty.
3. A deliberate attempt to look bad by endorsing those items reflecting significant psychopathology (F usually greater than 100).
4. Confusion, delusional thinking or other psychotic processes.
5. A plea for help by a patient who is exaggerating symptoms.
6. In adolescents an elevated F may signify the expression of defiance, hostility, and negativism.

T-scores in the range from 75–100 generally reflect the most significant psychopathology. When the T-score is above 100 on this scale, the profile must be examined carefully as this may indicate an invalid profile due either to an inability to read or to understand the questions, random responding, or deliberate attempts to look bad. These attempts to exaggerate psychopathology generally involve patients who have something to gain from a poor impression, such as those involved in court cases, disability applicants, patients attempting to prove an insanity plea, or patients who want to use hospitalization as an escape from life. Most psychotics score in the range of 75–100. Patients scoring a T-score over 110 rarely are diagnosed as psy-

*The Minnesota Multiphasic Personality Inventory. Copyright The University of Minnesota 1943, renewed 1970. All rights reserved.

chotic as their awareness of those items that reflected significant psychopathology suggests some lucidity which tends to preclude a psychotic diagnosis.

Low scores on the F scale suggest either an absence of bizarre and unusual thinking or may reflect an attempt to look good (see Determining Profile Invalidity). Normals answer only two to five items in the scored direction.

K (Correction) Scale

The K scale was added to the MMPI in an attempt to detect more subtle instances of denial than were measured by the L scale. This scale consists of thirty items that were empirically selected to assist in identifying patients who displayed significant psychopathology yet obtained profiles within the normal range. Thus, K is a measure of defensiveness as a test-taking attitude. Examples of K scale items with the deviant answer indicated in parentheses are:

"I think nearly everyone would tell a lie to keep out of trouble." (F)

"What others think of me does not bother me." (F)

"I certainly feel useless at times." (F)*

Items on this scale were selected empirically by comparing the responses of a group of patients who were known to be clinically deviant, but who produced normal MMPI profiles and for whom there was no indication of psychopathology. The resultant thirty items cover several different content areas in which patients can deny problems (e.g., hostility, suspiciousness, family turmoil, lack of self-confidence, worry). The items tend to be much more subtle than items on the L scale so it is less likely a defensive patient will be able to avoid detection.

High K scores are not associated with specific behaviors, but reflect a reluctance to admit psychopathology. Patients obtaining a T-score greater than 70 are extremely guarded and defensive and show a marked resistance to psychiatric inquiry accompanied by a need to remain inaccessible. They tend to minimize and overlook faults in their family, themselves, and their circumstances. Therefore, in most cases, an elevation greater than 70, results in an invalid profile due to excessive defensiveness. A major exception includes the various types of hysterical patients, especially the conversion reaction, where an elevated K is expected.

Low scores on the K scale, when not the result of a deliberate attempt to *fake bad,* suggest either the defenses are down or deteriorated. When the defenses are down, the patient is being self-effacing and self-critical and is likely to over-endorse pathological items, but usually not those reflecting psychotic manifestations. These patients rarely score over 100 on any of the clinical scales, but will obtain significant elevations on scales 2 and 7. Patients who are psychotic usually obtain elevations between 80 and 100 on scales F, 6, and 8. More specific criteria for the presence of psychotic manifestations will be discussed under Special Issues.

K scale scores may be associated with the setting, socioeconomic status, and educational level. For example, an elevated K is the norm in child custody cases and in personnel selection, while patients with high education and high socioeconomic status tend to obtain elevations on this scale also. In a normal population this scale is not a measure of defensiveness, but of personality integration and adjustment, with high scores reflecting healthy adjustment.

The K scale was later utilized to develop a correction factor for some of the clinical scales. Hathaway and McKinley reasoned that if the effect of a defensive test-taking attitude as reflected by a high K score is to lower scores on the clinical scales, perhaps they could determine the extent to which the scores on the clinical scales should be raised in order to reflect more accurately a patient's behavior (Graham, 1977). By comparing the efficiency of each clinical scale with various portions of the K scale added as a correction factor, these authors and colleagues determined the appropriate weighting of the K scale score for each clinical scale to correct for the defensiveness indicated by scale K. Scales 1, 4, 7, 8, and 9 have proportions of K added ranging from .2 to 1.0, while scales 2, 3, 5, 6, and 0 are not K-corrected because the simple raw score on these scales seems to produce the most accurate prediction.

Determining Profile Invalidity

In addition to the behavioral correlates associated with various elevations, the configuration of the validity scales provides an important source of information regarding test-taking attitudes, response sets, and biases. In many cases, there is no obvious difference between valid and invalid profiles. As a result, the determination of profile invalidity can be difficult and requires close scrutiny, not only of the validity scales but also of the clinical scales.

Traditionally, any profile with a T-score greater than 70 on scales F, K or L or with a ? scale greater than thirty items is viewed as invalid. However, such an extremely conservative approach represents an oversimplified view of profile validity and results in the discarding of many valid profiles. For example, as discussed earlier, if the number of items omitted is greater than thirty, it must be determined whether these items were from the basic clinical scales or from the research and special scales. If they were from the latter scales, then there is no justification for invalidity. Similarly, most psychotics score greater than 70 on the F scale, while patients with hysterical disorders may score above 70 on the K scale, and the clergy and unsophisticated low socioeconomic individuals may score above 70 on the L scale.

The only one of these invalidity criteria that is generally accepted is that in most cases when the K scale is greater than a T-score of 70, the profile is invalid. This does not necessarily imply an attempt to look good, but indicates the patient was too defensive and uncooperative. It must be emphasized that before stating a profile is invalid, the clinical scales should be examined to determine if the configuration and elevations are compatible with other demographic, historical, and diagnostic impressions. If so, regardless of the validity criteria, the profile may be interpreted as valid.

In determining profile invalidity, it is important to be aware of and recognize typical response patterns associated with invalid profiles. For example, it is easy to detect an all true or all false pattern simply by examining the MMPI answer sheet. However, a random response set cannot be readily determined from looking at the profile, but should be considered when both scales F and 8 have T-scores at approximately 110 and all other clinical scales and the L scale are elevated above a T-score of 60. Such a profile is easily distinguished from a highly psychotic profile having T-scores on scales F and 8 between 80 and 100 and usually a low score on K.

Two other typical response patterns associated with invalid profiles should be discussed. First, are those patients endorsing the majority of items reflecting the most serious psychopathology as applicable to themselves? They are attempting to *fake bad* with the resulting profile initially appearing to be suggestive of a severe disturbance. In a *fake bad* profile, F is usually greater than 100, scales 6, 7, and 8 are usually greater than 90, and L and K scales are usually less than 50. Also, a significantly high number of critical items (see Critical Items) are endorsed.

In contrast, patients may attempt to deny and minimize their differences. This *fake good* profile is characterized by a K score greater than 70 and most clinical scales and F scale with a T-score below 50. The score on the L scale will be inversely related to education and psychological sophistication. In detecting both *fake good* and *fake bad* responses, the motivation for responding in such a manner should be determined, if possible.

An additional method of determining *fake good* and *fake bad* profiles was developed by Gough (1950). He suggested taking the difference between the raw F and the raw K scores (F − K), with a score greater than 9 indicating *faking bad* and a score less than −9 indicating *faking good*. Unfortunately, using these rigid cut-off scores excludes a significant number of valid profiles. For example, most schizophrenics obtain an F − K greater than 9. An F − K ratio only seems applicable in a forensic setting. That is, if the F − K index is 15 or greater the statement can be made in court that only about 2 percent of these protocols were not deliberately faked (Ziskin, 1981).

Special mention should be made of another measure of test-taking attitude that has received little attention, but has shown promise in pilot studies (Greene, 1980). This measure is the test-retest (TR) index which is the total number of the sixteen repeated items in the group booklet form of the MMPI that the patient has endorsed inconsistently. In possible *fake bad* profiles, scores on this index might prove helpful. For example, if scores on F, 6, and 8 scale are all greater than 100, a high TR index score of at least 4 could suggest either confusion or random responding, but it is doubtful this is a deliberate *fake bad* profile. In the *fake bad* profile the TR index will be less than 4 reflecting a more consistent response pattern.

THE CLINICAL SCALES

There are ten basic clinical scales on the MMPI, although many tend to exclude scales 5 and 0. Golden (1979) emphasizes that several factors must be kept in mind when evaluating the importance of each scale. First, in discussing high scores on a scale, the meaning is relative to the profile. A score which is both high (greater than 70) and high relative to all other scales has much more significance than a high score that is only the fifth or sixth highest in the profile. Similarly, a score in the upper 60s assumes greater significance if it is the highest score in the profile. The significance of the lowest score or scores in the profile also must be noted.

A second significant factor is to recognize that several scales have a number of items repeated on one or more scales. Thus, two scales like 1 and 3 or F and 8 will tend to move up or down together. The degree to which one is high and the other low often suggests specific interpretations important to the scale and pattern analysis. Third, the rule of the validity scales must be considered. Interpretations should be adjusted according to whether a patient minimizes, exaggerates, or tends to be open and honest in responding. Finally, the relation of various crucial demographic variables and the clinical scales needs to be considered in modifying the interpretation. For example, the effects of age and race will be discussed under Special Issues, while other important demographic variables will be discussed within each clinical scale.

Scale 1 (Hs) Hypochondriasis

This scale, containing thirty-three items, is a direct measure of the degree of concern regarding body functioning. The items are obvious in content and the complaints embedded are not specific. Scale 1 seems to be the most clearly unidimensional of all the clinical scales and is characterized by the denial of good health and the admission of a variety of somatic complaints. Examples of scale 1 items with the deviant answer indicated in parentheses are:

"I do not tire quickly." (F)

"I feel weak all over much of the time." (T)

"I have very few headaches." (F)*

High scorers on this scale endorse an excessively large number of somatic complaints and show a prominent concern with body functions. In addition to indicating the presence of somatization defenses, such elevations strongly suggest these defenses are not working effectively. These patients often appear to be rather contradictorily asking, even pleading for care, while at the same time rejecting the possibility of treatment. There is an increasing probability of a rather sour, whiny, and complaining attitude, and a great deal of hostility and cynicism being expressed in this indirect manner. The sourness and cynicism may approach a rather paranoid posture whenever such patients are threatened.

When the scale elevations are over 80, such patients will manifest complaints for virtually every organ system. Indeed, some of these patients have developed truly remarkable skills for frustrating physicians. Passivity is rather pronounced, dependency readily apparent, and there is the almost child-like expectation that others should take care of them.

Medical patients with legitimate physical problems generally obtain somewhat lower elevations on scale 1 (T = 60–70) than psychiatric patients with somatization reactions. These medical patients will endorse their legitimate physical complaints, but they will not endorse the entire gamut of vague physical complaints tapped by this scale.

Low scorers on this scale tend to be much the opposite of high scorers, but they are a heterogeneous group as their only common characteristic is the non-endorsement of somatic complaints.

Scale 2 (D) Depression

This scale contains sixty items measuring symptomatic depression, a general attitude characterized by poor morale, lack of hope in the future, and general dissatisfaction with life. Many of the items deal with various aspects of depression such as denial of happiness and personal worth, psychomotor retardation, lack of interest, withdrawal, physical complaints, and excessive worry. Scale 2 tends to be more of a state measure and thus usually reflects situational depression. Examples of scale 2 items with the deviant answer indicated in parentheses are:

"My sleep is fitful and disturbed." (T)

"I certainly feel useless at times." (T)

"I brood a great deal." (T)*

Patients who score high on scale 2 are described as depressed, worried, pessimistic, and are likely to show a great deal of indecision, doubt, and vacillation as well as some withdrawing behavior. The depression is likely to be expressed as feelings of hopelessness and futility and may be accompanied by suicidal ideation. Marked feelings of insecurity, inferiority, and inadequacy exist. The depression may not be confined to subjective experiences and may extend to a motor retardation accompanied by a loss of interest, initiative, and involvement. These patients have difficulty expressing emotions in a modulated, adaptive way, and instead will internalize many of their feelings to the point that overcontrol is likely. They will attempt to avoid unpleasantness and will make concessions in order to avoid confrontations.

The exact interpretations on scale 2 vary markedly depending on which other clinical scales also are elevated (see Code Types). When scale 2 is the only elevated scale in the profile, usually this reflects a reactive depression in an individual who has experienced some type of situational stressor such as death in the family. In such circumstances an elevation on this scale is usual.

Low scores on this scale generally reflect a lack of depression, worry, pessimism, and a tendency to feel comfortable with life. These patients show an absence of the traits and behaviors characteristic of high 2 patients.

In order to provide some consistency in describing depressed patients, Newmark tends to follow his own subjective labeling. That is, a T-score between 65 and 75 is labeled mild depression, 75–85 is

*The Minnesota Multiphasic Personality Inventory. Copyright The University of Minnesota 1943, renewed 1970. All rights reserved.

moderate depression, while over 85 is severe depression. A depression of psychotic proportions can only be inferred based on the entire profile (see Special Issues). Also, a low score on scale 9 tends to accentuate the amount of depression indicated by scale 2.

Scale 3 (Hy) Hysteria

Scale 3 is comprised of sixty items tapping two overall constructs: items reflecting specific somatic complaints and items involving a general denial of psychological or emotional problems and of discomfort in social situations. Although these items are either unrelated or negatively correlated in normals, they are closely associated in patients utilizing hysterical defenses. Examples of scale 3 items with the deviant answer indicated in parentheses are:

"It takes a lot of argument to convince most people of the truth." (F)

"I think most people would lie to get ahead." (F)

"What others think of me does not bother me." (F)*

Patients who score high on this scale are generally immature, egocentric, and demanding with hysteroid characteristics and repressive defenses. They tend to be rather vain, labile, insightless, and dependently demanding in social interactions. When they do not receive the necessary attention and affection desired, hostility and resentment occur. However, these feelings will be denied and not expressed overtly. While usually gregarious, interpersonal relations are maintained on a rather shallow, superficial level. These patients may act out sexually, often acting seductive toward those of the opposite sex.

When an elevation on scale 3 is also accompanied by an elevation above 70 on scale 1, then the scale is tapping more of the hysterical conversion reaction. These patients are described as prone to develop any of a variety of circumscribed conversion symptoms. While the symptoms may be based in some actual organic pathology, they generally arise after protracted periods of tension in patients with a history of insecurity, immaturity, and a well-established proclivity to physical complaints. Thus, before a conversion reaction can be noted, some evidence of somatic complaints is needed. Additionally, it is crucial never to state that the somatic complaints are totally functional in nature. Even if an organic cause has been ruled out, it is best to emphasize this may be based in some actual organic pathology.

*The Minnesota Multiphasic Personality Inventory. Copyright The University of Minnesota 1943, renewed 1970. All rights reserved.

Low scorers on this scale are described as being constricted, conforming, suspicious, and with a narrow range of interests. Nevertheless, they are realistic, logical, and level-headed in their approach to problems and are not likely to make impulsive decisions. They seem to be content with what others judge to be a dull, uneventful life situation.

Scale 4 (Pd) Psychopathic Deviate

The fifty items on scale 4 seem to reflect a primary dimension ranging from constricted social conformity to antisocial, acting out impulses. In this respect, it is directly related to the tendency to express or inhibit aggressive and hostile impulses. Scale 4, like scale 3, is a characterological scale and tends to assess general social maladjustment, the absence of strongly pleasant experiences, a failure to appreciate the interpersonal side of life, complaints about family and authority figures in general, social alienation, and an emotional shallowness toward others. Examples of scale 4 items with the deviant answer indicated in parentheses are:

"I believe that my home life is as pleasant as that of most people I know." (F)

"I have never been in trouble with the law." (F)

"I have used alcohol excessively." (T)*

Patients scoring high on scale 4 are characterized by angry disidentification with recognized conventions and norms. Impulse control problems are prevalent as they exhibit an apparent inability to plan ahead, if not a reckless disregard of the consequences of their actions. They may justify their disregard of convention on the basis of being above mere propriety, reflecting the high values that many place on themselves. They are likely to show a poverty in affective reactions and have difficulty sustaining an affectionate relationship due to their inability to express tender feelings as well as their inability to empathize and put others first. Consequently, marital and/or family turmoil are evident. While quite visible socially, such relationships are used to exploit others. They are unwilling to accept the responsibility for their behaviors and tend to use projection as a primary defense. Sexual acting out and substance abuse are not uncommon. Frustration tolerance is likely to be limited, judgment poor, and they do not seem to benefit from past experiences. Immaturity and narcissism are rather pronounced.

*The Minnesota Multiphasic Personality Inventory. Copyright The University of Minnesota 1943, renewed 1970. All rights reserved.

Patients who score low on this scale tend to be overly conventional, conforming, and moralistic with low levels of drive and heterosexual aggressiveness. They feel uncomfortable in situations demanding anger, originality, or strength and tend to eschew vigorous and self-assertive behaviors. They are quite concerned about how others will react to them, tend to avoid competitive situations, and may have strong guilt feelings over minor infractions.

The specific interpretation of scale 4 in any particular profile is dependent upon relations with other scales as well as the incorporation of demographic data, especially age. For example, accompanying elevations on scale 3 appear to inhibit the potential for direct impulse expression suggested by scale 4, whereas accompanying elevations on scale 9 often provide increased impetus to acting out, antisocial behaviors (see Code Types). Also, elevations on this scale are typical for teenagers (see Special Issues).

Scale 5 (Mf) Masculinity-Femininity

Scale 5 is comprised of sixty items measuring a dimension of identification with culturally conventional masculine or feminine interest patterns as well as vocational choices, aesthetic interests, and an activity-passivity dimension. Most of the items are of obvious content and the scale can easily be faked without detection. Examples of scale 5 items include:

"I would like to be a florist."

"I like science."

"I enjoy reading love stories."*

Note that responses to these items are scored as deviant when they reflect femininity in men and masculinity in women. Five of the scale items which deal with sexually deviant behavior are scored in the same direction for both sexes. Scale 5 is the only MMPI scale scored differently for males and females. That is, the T-score conversions are reversed as a function of sex. On the profile sheet, a high raw score for males is transformed to a high T-score whereas a high raw score for females is transformed to a low T-score. The result is a high T-score for both sexes that is indicative of deviation.

By itself the scale is an inadequate estimate of tendencies toward overt or latent homosexuality. Male patients who are so overtly homosexual as to show extreme elevations on scale 5 could just as easily be identified by asking them directly. Nevertheless, the possibility of

*The Minnesota Multiphasic Personality Inventory. Copyright The University of Minnesota 1943, renewed 1970. All rights reserved.

homoerotic trends, homosexual behavior, and/or effeminate qualities should be considered when extreme elevations are obtained, particularly if the scores deviate markedly from expectations based on various demographic variables. That is, brighter, better educated, and higher social class male patients obtain higher scores. Male college students and male college-educated patients often obtain T-scores in the 65–75 range.

There is absolutely no relationship between scores on scale 5 for female patients and either homosexual ideas and behaviors or various demographic data, such as intelligence, education, and social class. Most female patients usually obtain a T-score less than 55 on this scale.

Males who score high on scale 5 tend to be rather passive, dependent, ambitious, sensitive, and interested in cultural and aesthetic pursuits. They lack interest in typically masculine pursuits and may be experiencing fundamental and disturbing questions concerning their own sexual identify.

Males who score low on scale 5 tend to adhere to the cultural stereotype of masculinity and place great emphasis on traditionally masculine behaviors. They are likely to appear somewhat crude, coarse, and even vulgar and may need to demonstrate their virility in order to camouflage underlying doubts about their masculinity.

Females who score high on scale 5 (greater than 60) are rare, but seem to have rejected many of the aspects of their traditional feminine role. They are described as active, aggressive, assertive, competitive, uninhibited, and domineering. They have strong interests in the so-called masculine areas of sports, work, and hobbies. Many of these women see themselves in active competition with men, attempting to prove they are equal or better.

Women scoring low on scale 5 are described as being passive, submissive, yielding, and demure, sometimes to the point of being caricatures of the cultural stereotype of femininity. They are highly constricted, self-pitying and may have significant doubts regarding their own adequacy as females.

Scale 6 (Pa) Paranoia

Scale 6 contains forty items ranging from obviously psychotic content, such as delusions of persecution and ideas of reference, to interpersonal sensitivity, suspiciousness, and moral self-righteousness. This is one of the weaker scales on the MMPI because the obvious content of many of the items makes it easier to deny paranoid thinking. Thus, there are very few false positives (patients obtaining elevations on this scale who do not manifest paranoid ideation), but some false negatives (patients obtaining low scores on this scale who do manifest paranoid ideation). Examples of scale 6 items with the deviant response indicated in parentheses are:

"I am sure I get a raw deal from life." (T)

"I belive I am being followed." (T)

"I have no enemies who really wish to harm me." (F)*

Patients who score high on this scale can be divided into two groups. The first involves T-scores in the range of 65–75 and even approach 80. This indicates sensitivity to criticism, a basic mistrust of the motives of others, a tendency to brood and harbor grudges, feelings of being discriminated against, a tendency to use rationalization and projection as primary defenses, and considerable anger and hostility regarding their difficulties. In other words, these are traits and behaviors suggesting paranoid tendencies and/or a paranoid personality. As the T-score becomes elevated over 75 and 80 (the second group), the possibility of psychotic manifestations should be considered. These include ideas of reference, feelings of influence, feelings of persecution as well as a variety of delusions resulting in impaired reality testing. Anger, hostility, and resentment are readily apparent and likely to be expressed overtly.

The T-score ranges listed above are general guidelines and it is sometimes quite difficult to differentiate the paranoid personality from the paranoid psychosis. Occasionally the paranoid personality will obtain a T-score greater than 80 while the patient with paranoid delusions may obtain a T-score less than 75. Therefore, it is important to examine the profile for other information. First, the elevation on the F scale can prove enlightening. If the F scale is elevated over 75, there is an increasing possibility the items reflecting more serious psychotic psychopathology were endorsed, while if F is below 75 there is an increasing possibility the nonpsychotic paranoid items were endorsed. Additionally, examination of the critical items (see Critical Items) can prove informative. If several critical items reflecting paranoid psychotic ideation are endorsed, this lends support to an interpretation reflecting the psychotic thinking. If few or none of these items are endorsed, this increases the likelihood the elevations on scale 6 reflect paranoid tendencies.

Three groups of patients obtain low scores (less than 35) on scale 6. The first and most common are those described as self-centered, stubborn, easily irritated, unaware, and insightless in their dealings with others. The second group of patients blatantly deny any inter-

*The Minnesota Multiphasic Personality Inventory. Copyright The University of Minnesota 1943, renewed 1970. All rights reserved.

personal sensitivity and attempt to present themselves as rather cold and callous. This appears to be a reaction formation against extreme interpersonal sensitivity and a basic mistrust of the motives of others. The paranoid symptomatology is well ingrained and there is sufficient reality testing to avoid endorsing the obvious content items on scale 6. Also, a T-score that is less than 35 on this scale may indicate a patient who is overtly paranoid, delusional, defensive, and evasive. It is these latter qualities which result in their denying symptomatology.

Scale 7 (Pt) Psychasthenia

Scale 7 contains forty-eight items reflecting chronic or trait anxiety, general dissatisfaction with life, indecisiveness, difficulty with concentration, self-doubt, rumination and agitated concern about self, and the obsessional aspects of the obsessive-compulsive personality. More compulsive patterns of coping may not be reflected in high elevations if such compulsive mechanisms are functioning effectively to reduce stress. This scale is a good index of psychological turmoil and discomfort. The original diagnostic label is antiquated and the scale now seems more related to obsessive-compulsive traits. Examples of scale 7 items with the deviant responses indicated in parentheses are:

"Life is a strain for me much of the time." (T)

"Almost every day something happens to frighten me." (T)

"I have more trouble concentrating than others seem to have." (T)*

Patients who score high on this scale are described as rigid, meticulous, moralistic, and intensely dissatisfied with their present life situation. Anxiety is rather pronounced and likely to be manifest clinically. They tend to be ruminatively introspective, self-analytical, and are over-ideational in their approach to solving emotional problems. However, their ideas are rarely translated into constructive behavior. Indecision, doubt, and vacillation as well as inefficiency in living are likely as these patients rely heavily on intellectualization, isolation, and rationalization as primary defenses. They may show some difficulty in concentration and thinking, and in recognizing environmental cues that could rationally reduce their anxiety. They are guilt ridden, intropunitive, and seem to have established for themselves unattainable goals and high levels of aspiration. Generalized physical complaints, such as fatigue, are common.

Patients who obtain low scores on scale 7 show an absence of the traits and behaviors characteristic of high 7 patients.

Patients in an emergency room having just experienced a crisis situation appear overtly anxious accompanied by motor tension and heightened autonomic activity. However, administration of the MMPI may not result in an elevation on scale 7. This occurs because the anxiety precipitated by a crisis situation is usually situational in nature, and thus there is no reason for an elevation on scale 7. A scale to measure situational anxiety will be discussed under Special Scales.

Scale 7 often is viewed as the *obsessional glue* that keeps potential psychotic patients relatively intact. Whenever scale 7 is equal to or greater than scale 8, it is rarely a psychotic disorder, but more likely a patient whose defenses are tenuous, and under stress will deteriorate into a psychosis. Following the deterioration there usually is a decrease in the elevation on scale 7.

Scale 8 (Sc) Schizophrenia

Scale 8, the longest scale on the MMPI, contains seventy-eight items. The items tap into dimensions of schizoid mentation, feelings of being different, feelings of isolation, bizarre thought processes and peculiar perceptions, poor family relationships, sexual identity concerns, and the tendency to withdraw into wish-fulfillment fantasies. Consequently, the scale appears to measure a general dimension of ego intactness to ego deterioration. Examples of scale 8 items with the deviant response in parentheses are:

"I have strange and peculiar thoughts." (T)

"No one seems to understand me." (T)

"I often feel as if things were not real." (T)*

As with scale 6, patients who score high on this scale can be divided into two groups, not necessarily mutually exclusive. One group shows disturbances in thought that are marked by alterations of concept formation, loose associations, and poor judgment which may lead to misinterpretations of reality. Corollary mood changes include ambivalent, constricted, and inappropriate emotional responsiveness and loss of empathy with others. These patients almost always receive a diagnosis of schizophrenia. The other group, who are not psychotic, tend to feel lonely, alienated, isolated, misunderstood, and not a part of the general social environment. They have fundamental and disturbing questions concerning their own sexual identity and worth and appear somewhat confused about how to cope with everyday stresses. Therefore, under stress they are likely to withdraw and occupy themselves with wish-fulfillment fantasies. This usually reflects a rather schizoid lifestyle.

When interpreting the MMPI, it is crucial to differentiate the schizophrenic from the more schizoid adjustment. This differentiation process is quite similar to what occurred with scale 6. That is, if scale F is equal to or greater than a T-score of 75, then it is likely there is some bizarre and unusual thinking and the possibility of a schizophrenic disorder should be further explored. But if F is less than a T-score of 75, then it is not likely psychotic manifestations are evident and the other interpretation is applicable. Another way to differentiate is to examine the critical items. Schizophrenics tend to endorse many critical items, especially those relating to thought disturbance, feelings of derealization, and other psychotic processes. If only a few or less of these items are endorsed, this increases the likelihood that elevations on scale 8 reflect the more schizoid adjustment rather than the schizophrenic process.

A more specific approach for differentiating these two groups is to utilize the MMPI criteria for diagnosing schizophrenia developed by Newmark and colleagues (1978). These will be discussed in detail under Special Issues but briefly include: T-score on Sc greater than or equal to 80 less than or equal to 100; T-score on F greater than or equal to 75 less than or equal to 95; T-score on 7 less than or equal to 8; and the total raw score on 8 cannot consist of more than 35 percent K items. The latter means that an elevated 8 due primarily to the addition of K items is different from an elevation on scale 8 when K is low.

The latter criterion lends support to the notion that scale 8 is the single most difficult scale to interpret in isolation because of the variety of factors that can result in an elevated score (Greene, 1980). Since the total number of K scale items endorsed in the deviant direction is added to the raw score on scale 8 to plot a K-corrected profile, approximately twenty of the seventy-eight scale 8 items endorsed in the deviant direction are sufficient to produce a T-score greater than 70 when the patient has an average score on the K scale.

As elevations on scale 8 increase over 100, several possibilities occur. These include an attempt to look bad, a plea for help, or an acutely disturbed patient. It is unusual for most schizophrenics to obtain such an elevated score. The fact the patient was aware that those items reflected the most serious psychopathology, and as such was able to endorse them as applicable, tends to preclude a psychotic diagnosis as this awareness implies lucidity and most likely reality contact.

Patients who obtain low scores on scale 8 show an interest in people and practical matters to the exclusion of theoretical and philosophical concerns. Nevertheless, interpersonally they appear compliant, submissive, and overly accepting of authority. They rarely devise creative solutions to difficulties as pragmatic and concrete thinking is likely.

Scale 9 (Ma) Hypomania

The forty-six items on scale 9 are a direct measure of energy level and may be thought of as a continuum ranging from low energy through a range of optimum energy with further elevations suggesting hypomanic behavior, including flights of ideas, elevated mood, increased motor activity, expansiveness, and grandiosity. Examples of scale items with the deviant response in parentheses are:

"Once a week or oftener I become very excited." (T)

"I do not blame a person for taking advantage of someone who lays himself open to it." (T)

"I have had periods of such great restlessness that I cannot sit long in a chair." (T)*

T-scores on scale 9 greater than 90 may be suggestive of a manic disorder in a patient who is characterized by expansiveness, easy distractibility, hyperactivity, flights of ideas, and delusions of grandeur resulting in impaired reality testing. However, most manics are too hyperactive and agitated to sit still to take the test. Therefore, psychotropic medication frequently needs to be administered before the MMPI is administered. As a result of this medication, the majority of manic patients obtain scores between 75 and 90 on scale 9.

A group of nonpsychotic patients also obtain T-scores between 75 and 90 on scale 9. They are described as restless, enthusiastic, impatient, energetic, gregarious, and with an exaggerated sense of self-worth and importance. They are competitive, have difficulty in any enterprise requiring sustained effort, and often show irritability and ready anger at minor obstacles and frustrations.

Unfortunately, the MMPI in most cases is not sensitive enough to differentiate between a manic psychosis, a hypomanic, and a high energy level patient. Most manics though are readily identified behaviorally.

Some manic patients obtain MMPI profiles that are essentially within normal limits except for an elevated scale 9. This is a reflection of the manic's grandiosity and implies that everything is fine. Most notable on the profile will be low scores on scales 2 and 7, reflecting both a lack of psychic distress and of concern regarding their actual difficulties.

There is one group, however, where the elevation on scale 9 has another implication. These are women between the ages of forty and fifty who are experiencing what is referred to as the empty nest syndrome. They have dedicated their lives to raising their children and now that the children have left home, these woman become depressed and lonely. They rechannel their energies and become overly involved in a variety of activities, such as civic or church groups, or community endeavors, in order to distract themselves from their depression and loss. This sudden change in behavior is readily apparent to friends and family who are likely to request a psychiatric consultation. The elevated scale 9 thus reflects the over-involvement and efforts to distract themselves from their distress. Brief psychotherapeutic intervention usually proves extremely effective.

Patients who obtain low scores on scale 9 (especially below 40) are described as being listless, lethargic, low in drive, and difficult to motivate. They lack interest, initiative, and involvement and are likely to show chronic fatigue and even physical exhaustion. In many cases, this reflects the psychomotor retardation seen in some types of depressive disorders. A low score on scale 9 tends to accentuate elevations on scale 2 as this reflects the more behavioral manifestations of depression, while scale 2 is a reflection of the mood or affective state. Low scorers on scale 9 also tend to be somewhat reserved, withdrawn, overly controlled, and reluctant to express emotions overtly.

Scale 0 (Si) Social Introversion-Extroversion

Scale 0 was developed later than the other scales and has not attracted much research interest. Consequently, the clinical lore for this scale is somewhat limited. The seventy items on this scale assess the social introversion-extroversion dimension with high scores reflecting introversion. The scale also may tap psychomotor depression, particularly when associated with social insecurity. Examples of scale items with the deviant response in parentheses are:

"I find it hard to make talk when I meet new people." (T)

"I like to be in a crowd who plays jokes on one another." (F)

"I seem to make friends about as quickly as others do." (F)*

*The Minnesota Multiphasic Personality Inventory. Copyright The University of Minnesota 1943, renewed 1970. All rights reserved.

Patients who score high on this scale tend to be introverted, shy, socially inept, and have a tendency to withdraw from others as well as from competitive situations. They lack self-confidence, are threatened by intimacy, feel uncomfortable around members of the opposite sex, and are overly sensitive to what others think of them. Their approach to problem solving tends to be rather cautious, conventional, and unoriginal. Elevations above 75 may reflect a schizoid withdrawal from interpersonal relationships, especially when combined with an elevated scale 8.

Patients who obtain T-scores in the range of 60–69 tend to be slightly introverted and may prefer to be alone or with a small group of friends. While they do have adequate social skills, they generally prefer to keep their interactions to a minimum. Patients who obtain T-scores in the range of 50–60 tend to have an average balance between extroverted and introverted attitudes and behaviors.

Patients who obtain low T-scores on scale 0 appear quite adept at making initial social contacts and are viewed as extremely gregarious, extroverted, confident, and the life of the party. However, close examination of their behavior reveals superficial and flighty social techniques and relations that are maintained on a rather shallow, insincere level. They are reluctant to discuss emotionally-laden topics, are quite threatened by intimacy, and may manipulate others for their own advantage. The potential for engaging in self-indulgent behaviors is high.

TWO-POINT CODE TYPES

In the last section interpretive data were provided for each of the validity and clinical scales. It should be obvious though that the original scales were grossly deficient as measures of the diagnostic categories their scale names implied. In fact, the test manual and related publications now caution against literal interpretation of the clinical scales. Instead, it is believed the relationships between the various scales provide extremely important information. This led to the development of profile analysis (i.e., code types) as the main interpretive mechanism of MMPI data.

Furthermore, on many occasions, especially with psychiatric patients, more than one scale is elevated. The standard procedure is to interpret profiles according to the two highest clinical scales above a T-score of 70, provided both scales are within ten T-points of each other. A code type is referred to by writing the number of the two scales involved with the most elevated one first. For example, if the patient obtained a T-score of 85 on scale 4 and a T-score of 81 on scale

8, then you have a 4–8 code type. There are 110 possible two-point code types on the MMPI following this procedure.

Behavioral correlates of the twenty-two most prominent (most frequent and most investigated) code types will be presented in this section. Please note that the individual scale correlates still may apply, but combining into code types yields some unique interpretive materials. The order of scales within the code type will not be differentiated unless empirical evidence indicates the correlates of the code type change depending on which scale is elevated higher. Also, it must be emphasized that each interpretive statement, while applying to most patients, does not apply to every patient who obtains that code type. Each interpretive statement is a probabilistic statement that may or may not apply to a specific patient.

When multiple code types are interpreted in a single profile, the highest two-point code type receives more weight than any lower pairs if there are any contradictions. Another difficulty may occur when three scales are all elevated above 70 and all are within a few T-points of each other. In such situations it is best to break the profile into as many two-point code types as possible. For example, if scales 2, 6, and 7 all were elevated at approximately a T-score of 80, it would be best to break this down into a 2–6 and 2–7 code type. This is done because a 6–7 code type occurs infrequently and little is documented regarding the behavioral correlates other than the information that can be obtained by individual scale interpretations.

1–2/2–1

These patients tend to experience depression, worry and pessimism, and endorse a large number of somatic complaints accompanied by a marked preoccupation with body functions. Symptoms are likely to involve pain, weakness, and easy fatigability and are most pronounced during periods of stress. They may present multiple somatic complaints or the symptoms may be restricted to one particular system. There is difficulty externalizing emotions and therefore they feel uncomfortable in situations demanding anger, originality, or strength. Many of their angry and hostile feelings become introjected resulting in an increase in heightened physiological reactivity. They tend to be passive-dependent in relationships and may harbor hostility toward others who are perceived as not offering enough attention or support. A history of drug and/or alcohol abuse should be considered. A rather sour, whiny, and complaining attitude is likely accompanied by skepticism and a great deal of cynicism regarding treatment. Their motivation for change is quite weak as they have learned to tolerate high levels of discomfort and because they refuse to consider physiological symptoms as signs of psychological stress. These patients consistently will seek medical attention in order to substantiate their somatic concerns. While insight is likely to be quite limited, judgment usually is intact.

1–3/3–1

These patients are generally immature, egocentric, and demanding with hysteroid characteristics and repressive defenses. If there are elevations on scale 2, then this implies these repressive defenses are not working effectively. They are prone to develop any of a variety of circumscribed conversion symptoms. While these symptoms may be based in some actual organic pathology, they generally arise after protracted periods of tension in patients with a history of insecurity, immaturity, and a well-established proclivity of physical complaints. They are likely to be quite demanding of attention and affection and will attempt to receive this through unobtrusively manipulative means. Rarely are such patients seen as psychotic. Denial is a major defense as they manifest an overly optimistic and pollyannish view of their situation and of the world in general, and they may not show appropriate concern about their symptoms. Overcontrol is likely as they will go to great lengths to inhibit the expression of hostile and aggressive feelings. This internalization of impulses occurs in almost every area except with the possibility of sexually acting out behavior. Many of these patients are especially vulnerable to narcissistic injury in heterosexual relationships. In psychotherapy they want immediate concrete solutions to their difficulties and will terminate prematurely when the therapist fails to respond to their excessive demands for attention. They lack insight into the nature of their behavior and are very resistant to interpretations that could imply psychological explanations of their physical difficulties.

1–8/8–1

When there is an elevated F associated with this profile, one possible diagnosis is schizophrenia. These patients are described as having difficulty handling stress and may show clearly delusional thinking regarding bodily functions and bodily illness. They harbor feelings of anger and hostility, but are unable to express these overtly for fear of retaliation from others. They either inhibit expression almost completely resulting in the feeling of being "bottled up" or they are overly belligerent, abrasive, and caustic in speech. Internalization of the feelings may be represented via numerous somatic complaints and heightened physiological reactivity. Trust appears to be a crucial issue resulting in limited social contacts and subsequent feelings of loneliness, alienation, isolation, and rejection. These patients have fundamental and disturbing questions concerning their own sexual identity and worth, and feel generally misunderstood and not a part of the general social environment. The possibility of some type of pre-psychotic disorder also should be considered.

1–9/9–1

These patients are described as being rather tense, anxious, and experiencing a great deal of emotional turmoil. They expect a high level of achievement from themselves but lack clear and definitive goals. Much of their frustration occurs due to their inability to obtain their rather high levels of aspiration. The elevation on scale 1 may be considered an indicator of basic passivity and strong needs for dependency which are being struggled against in counterphobic denial fashion by hyperactivity and tremendous efforts to produce. They are basically passive-dependent individuals who are trying to compensate for their perceived inadequacies. This code type also may be found among brain-damaged individuals who are experiencing difficulty coping with their limitations and deficits. However, the diagnosis of cerebral dysfunction never should be made based on MMPI code types.

2–3/3–2

Somewhat similar to the 2–1 code type, these patients typically show greater immaturity, feelings of inadequacy and insecurity, and inefficiency in living. Depression as well as lowered activity levels, feelings of helplessness, and self-doubt are evident. Initiative is lacking and they are likely to rely on others to take care of them. These patients are viewed by others as rather passive, docile, and dependent. Feelings of social inadequacy are evident resulting in a tendency to keep social contacts to a minimum. They especially avoid competitive situations where failure might occur. They are also quite uncomfortable with members of the opposite sex and sexual maladjustment, including frigidity and impotence, is common. Nevertheless, they do elicit nurturant and helpful attitudes from others. Overcontrol is pronounced as there is difficulty expressing angry and hostile feelings in a modulated, adaptive way. Instead, they deny experiencing these unacceptable feelings, but feel anxious and guilty when this denial fails. Somatic symptoms are present but often are inconsistent and changing. The prognosis in psychotherapy is guarded as these patients have learned to adjust to their somewhat chronic problems and have continued to function at low levels of efficiency for prolonged periods of time. Thus, their motivation for change typically is weak.

2-4/4-2

This code type is characteristic of two different types of patients. The most common is the psychopathic individual who has been caught in some illicit or illegal behavior and is subsequently being evaluated. The depression is a reaction to the constraints being placed upon their behavior, such as being put in prison or in a hospital. This depression abates when escape from stress is effected or when the constraints are removed. Nevertheless, the presence of even this situational depression results in a slightly better prognosis than for individuals in similar circumstances who do not admit to this affect. The most valid interpretation for this psychopathic patient would use primarily the correlates of scale 4.

Other patients obtaining this code type are described as being extremely hostile, angry, and resentful. Marital and/or family turmoil is rather prevalent resulting in intense dissatisfaction with their present life situation. They are immature, dependent, egocentric, and often vacillate between pitying themselves and blaming others for their difficulties. Impulse control problems are quite prevalent as they exhibit an apparent inability to plan ahead, if not a reckless disregard of the consequences of their behavior. They may react to stress by excessive alcohol consumption and/or drug abuse. They experience a failure to appreciate the interpersonal side of life, have difficulty showing warmth, tend to resent authority figures and demands imposed upon them, and may misinterpret the meaning of social events and relationships. Psychotherapeutic intervention will prove difficult as numerous characterological difficulties exist, and the depressive features are chronic in nature and deeply ingrained into the character structure.

2-6/6-2

This code type suggests the probability of an early stage of a psychosis in patients who may be experiencing more serious emotional difficulties than the profile would ordinarily suggest. There is a reservoir of anger and hostility present which is not entirely masked by the depressed feelings. Unlike most depressed patients who are unable to express their anger overtly, these patients usually are openly hostile, aggressive, and resentful toward others. They adopt a chip on the shoulder attitude in an attempt to reject others before they are rejected. Also, they usually read malevolent meaning into neutral situations and jump to conclusions on the basis of insufficient data. Paranoid trends are rather pronounced sometimes to the point where paranoid ideation is psychotic in nature.

2–7/7–2

This code type is the most common among psychiatric patients and suggests depression, worry, and pessimism with accompanying anxiety, tension, and nervousness accompanied by a pervading lack of self-confidence. Psychic conflicts may be represented in hypochondriacal tendencies and somatic complaints. These patients are guilt ridden, intropunitive, generally fearful, and obsessively preoccupied with their personal deficiencies. The latter is in disturbing conflict with their typically perfectionistic and meticulous attitude and their strong motive for personal achievement and recognition. They have high expectations for themselves and feel rather guilty when they fail to achieve their goals. They respond to frustration with considerable self-blame and guilt. They worry excessively, are vulnerable to both real and imagined threat, and anticipate problems before they occur. Socially, they tend to be rather docile and dependent, and find it difficult to be assertive when appropriate. The prognosis in psychotherapy is excellent as they appear motivated for help. However, if the elevation on scale 2 or 7 is greater than a T-score of 85, then the distress may be incapacitating. In such cases psychopharmacological treatment should be instituted before psychotherapy is initiated. The most likely diagnosis is some type of depressive and/or anxiety disorder.

2–8/8–2

This code type suggests depression with accompanying anxiety and agitation leading to a fear of loss of control of hostile and aggressive impulses. Suicidal ideation is likely and the potential for self-destructive behaviors is high. These patients exhibit a marked psychological deficit as evidenced by a general loss of efficiency, periods of confusion, a retarded stream of thought, a stereotyped approach to problem solving, and noticeable difficulties with concentration. Occasionally the clinical picture may include hysterically determined somatic symptoms of an atypical variety. Unlike the hysteric, however, these patients typically are unsociable, interpersonally sensitive, and suspicious. They complain of concentration and thinking difficulties and may show a formal thought disorder consistent with a schizophrenic disorder. The potential inherent in intimacy for subsequent rejection results in their reluctance to become involved with others. This lack of meaningful involvement increases their feelings of despair, worthlessness, and low self-esteem. This code type represents a chronic level of adjustment of marginal quality so the prognosis for intervention and subsequent change is poor. Most of these patients receive a diagnosis of either major depressive disorder, schizophrenia, or schizoaffective disorder.

2–9/9–2

This code type often reflects an agitated depression in which tension is discharged through heightened motor activity. These patients are overly expressive affectively, are extremely narcissistic, and ruminate excessively regarding their self-worth. Although they may express concern about achieving at a high level, it often appears that they set themselves up for failure. Another interpretation is that these patients are denying underlying feelings of inadequacy and worthlessness and may be attempting to use a variety of manic mechanisms, such as hyperactivity, denial of poor morale, and over-involvement with others to avoid focusing on their depression. In other words, these patients are experiencing a hypomanic process that is no longer sufficient to obscure their depressive features, at least on the MMPI. Both types of patients will appear tense and restless, and show irritability and ready anger at minor obstacles and frustrations.

In younger patients, this code type may be suggestive of an identity crisis characterized by lack of personal and vocational direction as well as numerous existential concerns. In older patients, this code type may be a reaction to physical disability or reflect an involutional depression.

3–4/4–3

Patients with a 3–4 code type have been found to display different behaviors from patients with a 4–3 code type. The relationship between scales 3 and 4 serves as an index of whether patients will overtly express or inhibit their socially unacceptable impulses, particularly anger, aggression, and hostility. If 3 is higher than 4, then a rather passive-aggressive expression of anger is likely. When aggressive actions do occur, these patients deny hostile intent and show a striking lack of insight. If 4 is higher than 3, these patients are likely to appear over-controlled and bottle up their anger for long periods of time. They then explode in rage periodically committing violent behaviors.

The 3–4/4–3 code type reflects patients experiencing a chronic and stable character disorder and tending to be extrapunitive in their reaction to stress and frustration. They handle conflicts by utilizing provocation, manipulation as well as blame, projection, and attempts at domination. Some of these patients are free of disabling anxiety and depression, but somatic complaints may occur. These patients typically experience marital disharmony, sexual maladjustment, and alcoholism. Interpersonal relationships are usually tenuous, though many establish enduring, though turbulent, relationships with marginal, acting out individuals, thereby vicariously gratifying their own antisocial tendencies. Psychotherapeutic intervention usually proves futile because such patients are apt to use psychotherapy for voicing complaints about others instead of concentrating on their own problems. Their motivation for help is typically weak and of questionable sincerity. Personality disorder diagnoses are most commonly associated with this code type.

3–6/6–3

Patients with this code type are seen as angry, hostile individuals who are repressing their own hostility and aggressive impulses. They tend to deny any suspicious attitudes and comfort themselves with a naive and rosy acceptance of things as they are. They perceive their relationships in positive terms and have difficulty understanding why others react to them the way they do. This no doubt contributes to significant marital turmoil. Their chronic feelings of hostility usually are directed toward members of the immediate family. Whenever this anger and hostility is recognized, these patients tend to rationalize so that it appears reasonable, warranted, and justified. They are hypersensitive to criticism, experience considerable anxiety and tension, and frequently have somatic complaints. When scale 6 is higher than scale 3 by five or more T-points, such patients strive for social power and prestige even to the point of ruthless power manipulation. The possibility of paranoid or psychotic features should be evaluated in this latter group, even though such traits are relatively unusual for this code type. The prognosis for significant change is poor.

3–8/8–3

Patients obtaining this code type typically have major thought disturbances (if F is greater than or equal to 75) to the point of disorientation, difficulty with concentration, and lapses of memory. Regression and autistic overideation may be present, and thinking may become delusional in nature. Feelings of unreality and emotional inappropriateness are likely. Also evident is a moderate degree of psychic distress that may be discharged into somatic complaints, especially headaches and insomnia. These patients are generally fearful, emotionally vulnerable, immature, and possess schizoid characteristics. They have an exaggerated need for attention and affection from others, but are quite threatened by intimacy and dependent relationships. They display intropunitive reactions to frustration and approach problems in a stereotyped manner. The most common diagnosis is schizophrenia, but an hysterical disorder should also be considered.

4–5/5–4

This code type is most common among men and suggests a chronic character disorder in patients appearing to experience minimal psychic distress. Any occurring distress is usually situational in nature. These patients can be expected to have nonconforming and defiant attitudes and values as well as aggressive and anti-social tendencies. They exhibit emotional passivity and poorly recognized desires for dependency. Dependency conflicts may be acted out and may create masculine protest types of behaviors as well as a variety of conduct disturbances. The guilt feelings and remorse about such behavior may temporarily prevent further expression. However, their strong tendency to narcissistically indulge themselves and their lack of frustration tolerance will probably determine their behavior. They have serious sexual identity concerns and may, in fact, be preoccupied regarding homoerotic impulses. Females obtaining this code type usually are rebelling against the feminine role and although they have strong needs for dependency, fear domination by significant others.

4–6/6–4

Patients obtaining this code type are likely to accentuate their complaints by a tendency to be self-dramatic and hysteroid. They can be expected to be chronically hostile and resentful and to use projection and acting out as preferred defense mechanisms. Impulse control is likely to be deficient and ineffective, and difficulty will be encountered in any enterprise requiring sustained effort. These patients tend to be narcissistic, dependent, and quite demanding of attention and sympathy, yet they will not reciprocate and resent demands imposed on them. They are extremely sensitive to criticism, mistrust the motives of others, tend to brood and harbor grudges, and feel they are not receiving the appropriate treatment they deserve. A history of social maladjustment is likely. They are often seen as irritable, sullen, argumentative, and obnoxious. Serious sexual and marital maladjustment is likely as well as excessive alcohol consumption and/or drug abuse. While the most likely diagnosis is some type of character disorder, the possibility of a borderline or psychotic disorder should be considered especially if scale 8 also is elevated. These patients have difficulty in psychotherapy as denial is pronounced and their basic mistrust of the motives of others precludes their acceptance of constructive criticism and attempts to help them. Furthermore, they will be reluctant to discuss emotionally-laden topics for fear that dire consequences will follow if they reveal themselves in any way.

4–7/7–4

Patients obtaining this code type show numerous characterological difficulties as well as cyclical patterns of acting out followed by periods of guilt, regret, and remorse for having done so. The guilt is usually out of proportion to the actual acting out behavior and frequently is accompanied by somatic complaints. While these patients appear to be overcontrolled, these controls are not sufficient to prevent recurrences of acting out behaviors and gross insensitivity to the consequences. Episodes of acting out may include excessive alcohol consumption, drug abuse, and sexual promiscuity. These patients find rules, regulations, and limits imposed by others quite irritating and anxiety-provoking. Though quite concerned with their own feelings and problems, they are markedly callous and indifferent to the needs and feelings of others. Psychotherapy initially may prove effective as these patients seek help when guilt is most pronounced. However, the long-term prognosis is guarded.

4–8/8–4

Patients obtaining this code type are experiencing considerable distress in addition to irritability, hostility, suspiciousness, and even possibly ideas of reference. Projection and acting out in asocial ways are primary defenses. Whenever they commit crimes they tend to be vicious, senseless, poorly planned, and poorly executed. The personality type is schizoid and these patients appear socially isolated and avoid close relationships because of fear of emotional involvement. Social intelligence is likely to be limited and serious difficulties can be expected in the areas of empathy and communication abilities. They are moody, emotionally inappropriate, and cannot express emotions in a modulated, adaptive way. In their behavior they are unpredictable, changeable, and nonconforming. Their educational and occupational histories are noted by underachievement, marginal adjustment, and uneven performance. Serious sexual identity concerns are present and excessive alcohol consumption and/or drug abuse likely. Judgment is likely to be poor and insight extremely limited. Suicide attempts are relatively common in these patients who are viewed by others as rather odd, peculiar, indifferent, and who do not seem to fit into the environment. The diagnostic possibilities include a borderline disorder, schizoid personality, or schizophrenia. The latter is most likely when scales 4 and 8 become elevated above a T-score of 80.

4–9/9–4

Patients with this code type show numerous characterological difficulties and are described as being impulsive and irresponsible in their behavior, untrustworthy, shallow, and superficial in relations to others. They have easy morals, are narcissistic and hedonistic, but may temporarily create a favorable impression because they are internally comfortable and free from inhibiting anxiety, worry, and guilt. However, they are actually quite deficient in their role-taking ability. Judgment is likely to be poor and they do not seem to benefit from past experiences. Their limited ability to intuitively sense the feelings of others persistently handicaps their development of an effective adult role. They have fluctuating ethical values and are prone to continue activities so long that they exceed proprieties, neglect other obligations, and alienate others. They possess a marked disregard for social rules and convention and engage in behaviors with little or no forethought. Alcoholism, legal trouble, marital problems, and sexually acting out behavior are common. They appear unwilling to accept the responsibility for their own behavior, and often construct emotionally satisfying, but irrational explanations of their difficulties. Such patients will rarely become involved in psychotherapy. The most likely diagnosis appears to be some type of character disorder with antisocial personality the most common.

6–8/8–6

Patients obtaining this code type usually show evidence of a formal thought disorder and paranoid ideation compatible with a paranoid schizophrenic reaction (if F is greater than or equal to 75). These patients can be expected to suffer from moderate distress, to be prevadingly hostile and suspicious, and to experience delusions of persecution and/or grandeur, and hallucinations. Regression, disorganization, and autistic associations are likely. Such patients are often preoccupied with abstract or theoretical matters to the exclusion of specific concrete aspects of their life. General apathy may be pronounced, affect seems blunted, and established defenses are lacking. Under stress they are likely to withdraw and occupy themselves with secretive autistic fantasy accompanied by loss of capacity to recognize reality. They are quite resentful of demands imposed upon them and are described as moody, irritable, unfriendly, and negativistic. Inner conflicts about sexuality are evident. When this code type does not fit the MMPI criteria for schizophrenia, then the most likely diagnosis involves paranoid state or schizoid personality.

6–9/9–6

Patients with this code type are tense, anxious, and usually react to even minor obstacles and frustrations with irritability, jumpiness, and ineffective excitability. They respond to environmental stimuli in an emotional way and have difficulty with thinking and concentrating. Grandiosity is a prominent feature and disorientation, feelings of perplexity, and confusion are noted. They suffer from ideas of reference and a pervading suspiciousness, which at times, may take the form of paranoid mentation and even delusions. These patients tend to ruminate and obsess, but rarely translate their ideas into constructive behaviors. Also evident is considerable difficulty externalizing their obvious anger and hostility in a socially acceptable way. Periodic undercontrolled emotional outbursts will alternate with excessive restraint and control. If scales F and 8 also are elevated, then a schizophrenic disorder is a possibility. Otherwise, some type of manic disorder or acute psychotic episode should be considered.

7–8/8–7

Patients obtaining this code type show chronic personality difficulties characterized by excessive worry, introspection, and over-ideational rumination. Passivity is pronounced and difficulty will be encountered in situations demanding anger, originality, and strength. Dependency is evident and they suffer from feelings of inferiority, insecurity, and inadequacy. They lack established defense patterns and tend to be quite nervous around others. A history with few rewarding social experiences is evident as they lack poise, assurance, and dominance. Judgment is likely to be poor and some confusion evident as their actions and planning reveal a lack of common sense. Rich fantasy lives are suggested, especially with regard to sexual matters, and they may spend much time daydreaming. Serious sexual identity concerns exist as patients feel inadequate in the traditional sex role and in heterosexual relations. They complain of concentration and thinking difficulties, suffer from excessive indecision, doubt, and vacillation, and may show a formal thought disorder. Psychological interventions are difficult because of the chronic ingrained nature of the conflicts and because of their difficulty in forming interpersonal relationships. As mentioned earlier and reiterated later under Special Issues, the relative elevations of scales 7 and 8 are crucial in differential diagnosis especially with regard to schizophrenia.

8–9/9–8

The majority of patients with this code type show evidence of paranoid mentation and a formal thought disorder. Onset is typically acute and accompanied by excitement, disorientation, and general feelings of perplexity. Well-established autistic trends, delusions, and hallucinations are likely. Regression is manifested by retarded and stereotyped thinking and by emotional inappropriateness. They tend to be narcissistic and infantile in their expectations of others and become extremely resentful and hostile when their demands for attention are not met. They may appear hyperactive, easily excitable, labile, and show grandiose thinking. They are quite unpredictable in their behavior and may act out unexpectedly. Psychotherapeutic intervention may prove extremely difficult as these patients are rather vague and evasive and tend to shift rapidly from topic to topic, so that addressing a specific issue is difficult. While the modal diagnosis is schizophrenia, manic disorders and drug-induced psychoses should also be considered.

SPECIAL SCALES AND CRITICAL ITEMS

In addition to the three validity scales assessing test-taking attitude and ten clinical scales identifying common types of abnormal behavior, numerous specialized MMPI scales have been constructed. Some of these specialized scales have been constructed to measure common personality dimensions such as dependency and prejudice; while others have been developed to identify specific patterns of abnormal behavior, such as alcoholism, that are not assessed directly by any of the standard clinical scales. While there are over six hundred specialized scales, most are too limited in scope for widespread use. However, the use of some specialized scales is quite common and will be discussed below. Scoring keys for the scales discussed are available either in Graham (1977) or Dahlstrom et al. (1975). A brief discussion of critical items will conclude this section.

Welsh's Anxiety (A)

High scorers on this scale tend to be anxious, tense, nervous, uncomfortable, unemotional, unexcitable, overcontrolled, accepting of authority, conforming and conventional in their behavior. These patients have a slow personal tempo, lack self-esteem, and lack poise in social situations. Constructive coping abilities are limited in stressful situations. The anxiety assessed by this scale reflects situational (state) anxiety rather than chronic (trait) anxiety as assessed by scale 7.

Welsh's Repression (R)

High scorers on this scale tend to be rather submissive, unexcitable, conventional, and have adopted a rather careful and cautious lifestyle. Affects are internalized and not expressed directly for fear of initiating a conflict situation that subsequently could overwhelm them. These patients are unwilling to discuss emotionally-laden topics which may reflect conscious suppression or actual repression and denial. Any difficulties will be rationalized. While their thinking is clear, insight is quite limited.

Ego Strength (Es)

The Ego Strength scale was developed to predict the response of neurotic patients in individual dynamically-oriented psychotherapy. However, it is not useful for predicting response of other kinds of treatment or for other kinds of patients. The scale seems to be related to emotional adjustment and may indicate strength of psychological resources available for dealing effectively with stress. Many patients scoring high on this scale possess the capacity to initiate deliberate and constructive actions in most coping situations. Patients who score low on this scale lack established defense patterns and experience serious psychopathology. Coping devices and emotional resources probably are limited and they suffer from marked feelings of insecurity, inferiority, and inadequacy.

Overcontrolled–Hostility Scale (OH)

This scale was developed to detect patients with the potential for committing extreme physical aggression. They have a history of chronic overcontrol and rigid inhibitions against the expression of any form of aggression. Most patients scoring high on this scale do not respond appropriately to even extreme provocation, but tend to let their angry hostile feelings accumulate to the point that an unexpected violent and destructive outburst may occur. These patients are described as rigid, socially alienated, and reluctant to admit to any forms of psychological difficulties. The OH scale is highly correlated with the 3–4/4–3 code type.

The MacAndrew Alcoholism Scale (MAC)

Initial research with this scale has shown consistently that the MAC will differentiate alcoholics from nonalcoholic patients in a variety of psychiatric settings. Subsequent research, however, has documented that the MAC is much more a measure of addiction proneness to either alcohol or other types of drugs rather than just a specific measure of alcohol abuse. High scorers on this scale are described as having a significantly high potential for substance abuse and other addictive problems. They are impulsive, energetic, non-conforming, inhibited, and gregarious. However, social relationships are usually maintained on a shallow, superficial level.

Dependency (Dy)

High scorers on this scale are experiencing unfulfilled dependency needs. They feel inadequately prepared to handle stress situations on their own and thus are most comfortable in situations where structure is provided and someone stronger than themselves is available to rely on. A general psychological maladjustment is suggested that can lead to feelings of dysphoria and unhappiness. Passivity is evident as well as extreme sensitivity to the reactions of others, a lack of self-confidence, indecisiveness, and feelings of being misunderstood.

Prejudice Scale (Pr)

Patients who score high on this scale are extremely rigid, intolerant, and prejudiced in their opinions and beliefs. A generally cynical, distrustful attitude toward others and the world is readily apparent. They are extremely dissatisfied with their current status, believe they are not receiving the appropriate treatment that they deserve, tend to belittle the achievements of others, and have a dogmatic style of thinking. High scores are more common among patients of lower socioeconomic status with less intelligence and less formal education.

Low Back Pain Scale (Lb)

High scores on this scale from psychiatric patients complaining of chronic low back pain that has not been substantiated by physical findings suggest the pain may be partially functional in nature. Such patients have difficulty integrating angry affects into the rest of their experiences. Therefore, such feelings become introjected resulting in heightened physiological reactivity and somatic symptoms. Low scores on this scale may be contraindicative of a functional disorder in psychiatric patients who complain of chronic low back pain. As mentioned earlier, the MMPI should only be used to suggest whether a functional component could be contributing to the physical complaint, but never to rule out an organic cause.

It should be emphasized that any interpretive materials derived from the use of these special scales should be viewed as tentative and validated against other clinical, psychometric, and demographic data. The reliability and validity of many of these scales has yet to be adequately documented.

CRITICAL ITEMS

Critical items are a list of items frequently used as *stop items* in screening patients. They are items which might have face validity for the presence of significant psychopathology. Endorsement of any of the critical items may indicate areas of major concern to the patient, but due to their obvious face validity the failure to endorse may not indicate the absence of these concerns.

The original set of items was developed intuitively by Grayson (1951) and included a number of blatantly psychotic behaviors and attitudes as well as items reflecting substance abuse, antisocial attitudes, family conflict, sexual concerns, and somatic complaints. While no empirical validation of these items has occurred, they have been accepted as an important source of content information on the MMPI. Since these original thirty-eight items, various others have developed their own set of critical items, either on a rational (Caldwell, 1969) or on an empirical (Koss & Butcher, 1973; Lachar & Wrobel, 1979) basis to identify severe psychopathology. It has not been determined empirically which of the critical item lists are most useful for which populations. In any case, these items supposedly have the greatest degree of discriminative validity as the endorsement frequencies for normals are usually less than 10 percent.

Examples of critical items appearing on several of the lists mentioned above include:

"I commonly hear voices without knowing where they come from."

"At times I have a strong urge to do something harmful or shocking."

"There is something wrong with my sex organs."

"Evil spirits possess me at times."

"Someone has been trying to poison me."

Endorsement of any one of the critical items should not be accepted as valid because an error or misunderstanding could have occurred. Therefore, the general consensus is to use the endorsement of the critical items as an entré for an interview with the patient, and then to obtain clarification.

Finally, as mentioned throughout this chapter, examination of the critical items list can be helpful in determining whether the interpretations on scales F, 6, and 8 reflect psychotic manifestations, since many of the items reflecting bizarre and unusual thinking on the critical items also appear on these scales. If these three scales or some combination are elevated, and numerous critical items from this area are endorsed, then scale interpretations reflecting psychotic manifestations are most applicable. On the other hand, if none or only a few of these critical items are endorsed, then alternative interpretations for these scale elevations should be considered. In all cases, caution should be exercised when using critical items since single items are extremely unreliable indicators of psychopathology.

SPECIAL ISSUES

A number of specific concerns generally arise in the interpretation of an MMPI profile. This section will attempt to address some of the more prominent as well as the utility of this instrument with adolescents, blacks, and the aged.

Acting-Out Behavior

Acting-out behavior refers to those behaviors which range from verbal hostility to physical assault. It is the latter that obviously is most important to predict. As Graham (1977) has emphasized, it is crucial to differentiate two types of potentially physically assaultive patients. First, there is the undercontrolled patient who has failed to learn to inhibit the expression of hostile and aggressive impulses, and reacts impulsively in response to external forms of provocation. Second, there is the overcontrolled patient who rigidly defends against the expression of hostile and aggressive impulses irrespective of the provocation, until finally these affects accumulate resulting in acting out in an extremely destructive manner. The 4–3/3–4 code type and the OH scale which recently have been associated with violent, assaultive behaviors tend to reflect those patients described as overcontrolled.

Scales on the MMPI can be divided into exciter or lack of impulse control scales, namely, 4, 6, 8, and 9, or inhibitor or control scales, namely, 1, 2, 3, 5, 7, and 0. Depending upon whether the exciter or inhibitor scales are elevated, problems with impulse control can be predicted. When both are elevated, then passive-aggressive behaviors are likely.

While the 4–9/9–4 code type typically has been associated with difficulties with impulse control problems, it should be noted that such a code type is also the most common for college students and psychologists. The crucial variable in determining acting out in such cases is level of intellectual functioning (Heilbrun, 1979). That is, the 4–9/9–4 code type is predictive of impulse control problems including violence, but only with less intelligent patients. The higher the intelligence, the less likely there will be overt acting out behaviors.

Suicide

Clopton (1979) in his comprehensive review of the literature on the MMPI and suicide concluded that neither standard MMPI scales, MMPI profile analysis, nor specific MMPI items are reliable in predicting suicide at significant levels. Attempts to develop a special MMPI suicide scale or to validate the accuracy of particular MMPI items as suicide predictors also have been unsuccessful. However, elevations on scale 2 and 7 are suggestive of depression and dissatisfaction with life that can precipitate suicidal ideation. When elevations on these two scales are accompanied by elevations on the excitor scales, then the likelihood of a suicide attempt increases. This occurs because an elevation on scale 4 suggests poor impulse control, an elevation on scale 8 suggests poor judgment, while an elevation on scale 9 implies adequate energy level to act on the suicidal ideation. However, this data must be integrated with all of the demographic variables and related situational variables in order to increase the predictive accuracy.

Two critical items, namely, "Most of the time I wish I were dead," and "The future seems hopeless to me," while not necessarily correlated with suicide attempts, may reflect desperation and a plea for help. It is often quite beneficial to interview these patients and discuss with them their reasons for endorsing these items.

Psychotic Manifestations

Attempts to use the MMPI to diagnose schizophrenia via individual scale elevations, especially on scale 8, have proven futile. Consequently, emphasis shifted from interpretation and diagnosis based on a single high point scale to a careful examination of more complex patterns of scales in the standard profile. These subsequent approaches ranged from coding of pattern and elevation data and constructing sets of profile rules to using various regression analyses for discriminant functions. Unfortunately, these approaches are either quite cumbersome and time-consuming or have not proven particularly accurate.

Newmark and colleagues (1978) developed a set of criteria for the detection of schizophrenia that include: T-score on scale 8 greater than or equal to 80 less than or equal to 100; total raw score on scale 8 consisted of not more than 35 percent K items; T-score on scale F greater than or equal to 75 less than or equal to 95; T-score on scale 7 less than or equal to scale 8. Approximately 72 percent of patients reliably diagnosed as schizophrenics were detected on the MMPI via this set of criteria. Thus, a crucial relationship emerged between scale 7 and scale 8. If scale 8 is greater than scale 7, a psychosis is more likely than if the reverse is true. When scale 7 is greater than or equal to scale 8, the patient may be prepsychotic or experiencing some type of borderline state. In any case, scale 7 is viewed as the obsessional glue that is maintaining the integrity of the patient's defense system.

Thus, the MMPI has some utility in diagnosing functional psychoses due to cognitive impairment. A major weakness of this instrument involves diagnosing functional psychoses due to major affective states. As mentioned earlier, it is difficult to diagnose a manic disorder because most manics are not able to sit still long enough to complete the test. Therefore, the test results will be confounded by the effects of psychotropic medication, usually lithium. This obviously will reduce the elevation of scale 9 making it difficult to differentiate a manic disorder from a hypomanic state from an energetic, exuberant, and restless individual.

Diagnostic difficulties also occur with the major depressive disorders. Meaning, it is often difficult to determine if a depression is of psychotic proportions. In many cases, accompanying elevations on scales F and 8 will occur suggesting some cognitive disturbance due to the presence of depression. However, some depressive reactions may be severe and incapacitating, yet cognitive functions remain relatively intact. Unfortunately, there are not sufficient indicators on the MMPI to detect these psychoses. The lack of research in this area is surprising.

Alcohol and Drug Abuse

The MMPI item pool has been used to develop a number of scales for identifying alcoholics. Most of these scales effectively discriminate alcoholics from nonalcoholic controls, but do not differentiate alcoholic from nonalcoholic psychiatric patients. However, one alcoholism scale discussed earlier, developed by MacAndrew (1965), can make this distinction. Subsequent investigations found this scale to more accurately reflect a general measure of addiction proneness.

Substance abuse, in general, is discussed as if there were a single personality type or trait common to all. Composite MMPI profiles presented by Penk (1981) contradict this notion. Instead, it appears that many different types of personality organizations contribute to substance abuse. Such heterogeneity in MMPI profiles not only is revealed when well-defined groups are compared with averaged composite profiles, but also is evident when frequency distributions of individually coded profiles are compiled. Various code types that have been associated with alcoholism and/or drug abuse include the 2–7–4, 2–4, 4–7, 4–8, 4–9, 6–8, 8–9, 1–3–9, and elevated 4 or 9. The 4–9, 4–8, and 8–9 code types are the most frequent of drug addicts. This suggests that addicts tend to be impulsive, socially nonconforming, rejecting of traditional values and restrictions, and show poor judgment.

The 8–9 code type deserves special mention. College students who appear in an emergency room with some confused and delusional thinking, feelings of perplexity, and even hallucinations may obtain this profile. Because psychotic manifestations are readily apparent, it is often assumed that this profile reflects a schizophrenic disorder. However, a drug-induced psychosis should be considered. The 8–9 profiles reflecting drug-induced psychoses often are accompanied by elevations on scale 1. This may be due to the physical effects induced by the drugs.

Prognosis

Many of the code types discussed earlier have prognostic statements associated with them. In this section, prognostic implications will be presented for each scale as discussed by Graham (1979). It is assumed each scale is elevated above a T-score of 70. Scale 5 has no prognostic significance.

Scale K   These patients may be reluctant to discuss emotionally-laden topics and will censor their answers for fear of too much self-disclosure. They become rigidly defended and threatened when their inadequacies are pointed out. They respond best to a pragmatic, problem solving type of psychotherapy which focuses on changing behavior to solve current problems and avoids exploration of underlying feelings, motivations, and dynamics.

Scale 1   These patients are not responsive to traditional psychotherapy. They lack insight into the nature and causes of their difficulties and are reluctant to accept the psychological interpretations of their problems. Instead, they will focus on the soma and will refuse to consider these physiological symptoms as signs of psychological stress.

Scale 2   When the elevation on this scale is between a T-score of 70 and 85, these patients show a good prognosis and usually are motivated for therapy. However, as the elevation on this scale increases over 85, then the depression may be overwhelming and incapacitating. Some type of psychotropic medication is needed before psychotherapeutic intervention can be effective. Some elevation on this scale with any diagnostic group improves the prognostic picture.

Scale 3   These patients initially are quite enthusiastic about psychotherapy because of strong needs for acceptance and affection. However, they are slow to gain insight into the underlying causes of their behavior and will resist psychological interpretations of their problems. Therefore, the prognosis is guarded.

Scale 4   Many of these patients are perceived initially as good candidates for psychotherapy due to smooth social skills. However, they are unwilling to accept the responsibility for their difficulties as projection is a primary defense. Most enter treatment in order to avoid something more unpleasant (e.g., jail, divorce, etc.). Their propensity to abuse medication is well documented so caution should be exercised in recommending psychotropic medication.

Scale 6   These patients are likely to show a basic mistrust of the motives of others precluding their acceptance of constructive criticism and attempts to help them. They have difficulty forming trusting relationships and will set up obstacles in order to assess the therapist's acceptance. The prognosis is quite guarded.

Scale 7   As with scale 2, when the elevation on this scale is between a T-score of 70 and 85, these patients usually are motivated for therapy and show a good prognosis. However, as the elevation on this scale increases over 85, the anxiety may be overwhelming and incapacitating. Some type of psychotropic medication is needed before psychotherapeutic intervention can be effective. These patients tend to rationalize, intellectualize, and ruminate a great deal in response to solving emotional problems. While they usually remain in psychotherapy longer than most, they show steady but slow progress.

Scale 8   These patients show poor judgment, a schizoid adjustment, and will have difficulty relating to the therapist in a meaningful way. The long-standing, chronic nature of their problems results in a rather guarded prognosis.

Scale 9   These patients tend to terminate psychotherapy prematurely because they are impatient, want immediate concrete solutions to their difficulties, and do not want to become dependent on the therapist. The relationship with the therapist usually will be maintained on a shallow, superficial level resulting in only minimal progress.

Utility with Adolescents, the Aged, and Blacks

Adolescents   The previous information with regard to behavioral correlates of individual scales and code types applies to patients of approximately nineteen to fifty-five years of age. The most extensive research with adolescents has been conducted by Marks, Seeman, and Haller (1974) who derived norms and obtained behavioral correlates of twenty-nine code types for this population. However, because these correlates have not been cross-validated and because some code types were based on a sample as small as ten, the utility of their findings is questionable. Therefore, it is generally recommended that both an adult and adolescent normed profile be plotted. It is probably best to use the already cross-validated behavioral correlates of the adult interpretative system to determine which norms yield the most accurate information for the adolescent patient.

To construct a profile from adolescent norms, it is critical to locate the correct table for the age and sex of the adolescent in the Appendix of the Marks et al. (1974) book, and determine the T-score equivalent of the raw score on each scale. Note that these tables are not K-corrected. These T-scores are plotted directly on the standard MMPI profile sheet. It is important to indicate on the sheet that the profile was plotted using adolescent norms.

When compared with adult norms, adolescents generally score at least ten T-points higher on scales F, 4, and 9, at least five T-points higher on scales 6 and 8, and at least five T-points lower on scales 1, 2, and 7. Note that these are rough estimates. Thus, an adolescent who obtains a 4–9 code type with both scales elevated at a T-score of 75 using adult norms is scoring within normal limits for this age group.

The Aged   Only a paucity of investigations have assessed the performance of the normal aged on the MMPI. It seems the aged score at least ten T-points higher on scales 1, 2, and 3, at least five T-points higher on 8 and 0, and at least five T-points lower on scale 9. Additionally, males tend to score at least five T-points higher on scale 5. The rationale for many of these norms is fairly obvious; for example, the higher scores on scale 1 reflect appropriate preoccupation with body functions and legitimate physical concerns.

Unfortunately, there is no published research on how to interpret an MMPI profile based on aged norms. Greene (1980), therefore, advocates plotting both the standard and an aged norm profile. The standard profile should be interpreted according to adult norms, with the aged norm profile used only to supplement this interpretation.

Blacks   The controversial issue of racial bias in the MMPI remains unsolved. Numerous methodological difficulties are apparent in many investigations tending to preclude any definitive results. Although black-white differences on the MMPI may be statistically significant, they have limited clinical applications because of the small mean differences. Nevertheless, it is generally assumed that blacks are overpathologized using standard MMPI interpretive criteria. In general, blacks tend to score at least 5 T-points higher on scales F, 4, 6, 8, and 9. The validity and subsequent utility of the MMPI with black patients have yet to be accurately determined.

CASE EXAMPLE OF PROFILE INTERPRETATION

Several issues need to be emphasized before attempting to interpret an MMPI profile. First, the interpretive process never should be done blind, that is without any additional source of data about the patient. It is important to consider a wide range of demographic data having some potential influence on the test profile. These data include age, education, occupation, race, socioeconomic status, religion, marital status, and cultural background. For example, similar profiles obtained from a forty-five-year-old black male in rural Alabama and a seventeen-year-old white male in New York City obviously have different implications.

Second, a thorough knowledge of psychopathology definitely is needed. For example, a sixty-five-year-old white female admitted to a psychiatric hospital for the first time obtains criteria compatible with schizophrenia on the MMPI. Because this is her first psychiatric admission and because there is no previous history of mental illness, it is doubtful this is a schizophrenic process. Alternative interpretations for these scales should be considered. Finally, while patients may endorse items that reflect significant psychopathology, such as "I believe I am being followed" or "I constantly hear things that others don't hear," it is important whenever possible to assess the accuracy of these statements. For example, this latter item was endorsed by a sixty-year-old farmer in North Carolina who lives in an isolated rural area. Information obtained from a subsequent interview verified real noises did occur at night that are typical for isolated and wooded rural areas.

Therefore, it is important to integrate all available demographic data, historical data, presenting complaints, interview, and observational behavior with the MMPI data. Such a procedure will increase significantly the accuracy of the interpretation.

The following MMPI profile is presented along with the corresponding numbers of the critical items. The patient is a thirty-two-year-old white male high school graduate from Charlotte, North Carolina. He is single, classified lower middle class, is an atheist, and works as an orderly in a general hospital. He received outpatient psychiatric treatment approximately four years ago for depression,

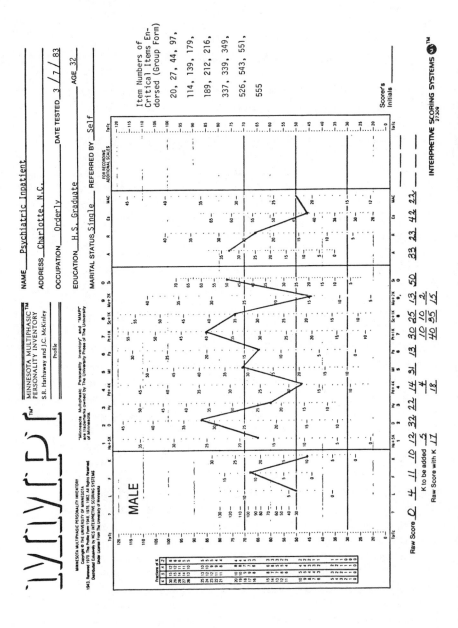

Figure 1–1 Minnesota Multiphasic Personality Inventory of a thirty-two-year old psychiatric inpatient.

Minnesota Multiphasic Personality Inventory. Copyright The University of Minnesota 1943, renewed 1970. This profile form, 1948, 1976, 1982. All rights reserved.

anxiety, and fear of engaging in self-destructive behaviors. His pre-senting complaints are quite similar for this first psychiatric hospi-talization.

In order to make the interpretive process more readily under-standable, each statement or group of statements will be followed in parentheses by the individual scale numbers and/or code types from which the statements came. If there are several successive statements without identifying numbers in parentheses, the next identifying scale numbers and/or code types then apply to that entire group of state-ments.

The patient was open and honest in his approach to the test and seemed to be making a sincere effort to cooperate (K). Although he was somewhat self-critical in responding, there is no evidence that he exaggerated (F, K). His raw score on the L scale is what would be expected for someone of his educational and socioeconomic back-ground. There is a moderate degree of emotional discomfort present in this male, who may be able to cope with some aspects of his life situation, but who generally lacks the capacity to initiate deliberate and constructive actions in coping situations (F).

The predominant symptom picture is likely to include moderate depression, worry, and pessimism with accompanying anxiety, ten-sion, and nervousness (2, 7, A). The depression does not seem confined to subjective experiences and may extend to a motor retardation ac-companied by a loss of interest, initiative, and involvement (9). The depression is likely to be expressed as feelings of hopelessness and futility and will be accompanied by suicidal ideation (2, Critical Items). However, his excessive overcontrol and low-energy level tend to reduce his suicide potential at present (4, 9, R).

The patient apparently has established rather unrealistic levels of aspiration for himself and becomes self-effacing when he is unable to attain these goals. Therefore, he is obsessively preoccupied with his personal deficiencies, which is in disturbing conflict with his typ-ically perfectionistic and meticulous attitude and his strong motive for personal achievement and recognition (2–7 code type). Strong ob-sessional characteristics are evident as the patient is likely to deal with his problems through self-analysis, ruminative introspection, and intellectualization. However, such ideas are rarely translated into concrete, constructive behaviors (7). While he complains of concen-tration and thinking difficulties and may suffer from excessive in-decision, doubt, and vacillation, there is no evidence to suggest a formal thought disorder (F, 7, 8). Nevertheless, some mildly uncon-ventional, bizarre, and unusual thinking is noted (F, 8).

Control is so excessive that the patient tends to eschew vigorous and self-assertive behaviors and deals with his difficulties in a rather vague, unrealistic fashion (4, 7, R). The patient has adopted a rather careful and cautious lifestyle, feels uncomfortable in situations demanding anger, originality, or strength, and is easily dominated by others (4, R). Many of his angry and hostile feelings become introjected resulting in heightened physiological reactivity and numerous somatic complaints (1, 4, 7, R). Symptoms are likely to involve pain, weakness, easy fatigability, and are most pronounced during periods of stress. Unfortunately, he does not realize that his somatic symptoms have a functional base (1, 3).

Socially, this patient is likely to be seen as rather shy, timid, reserved, and probably has few close friends. His limited abilities to intuitively sense the feelings of others persistently handicaps his development of an affective adult role (8, 0). While dependency is pronounced, he is likely to withdraw from social interactions, especially those involving competition, so others cannot become aware of his perceived inadequacies and subsequently reject him (2–7 code type, 8, 0). These limited social contacts result in intense feelings of loneliness, alienation, isolation, and rejection. The patient has fundamental and disturbing questions concerning his own sexual identity and worth and feels uncomfortable in his masculine role (8). Mature heterosexual relations may prove difficult as he probably feels uncomfortable, and at times intimidated, around women (8, 0). He is inclined toward solitary, aesthetic, and cultural pursuits and may show a somewhat feminine interest pattern (5).

The patient is extremely sensitive to the reaction of others, is easily hurt by even minor criticism, may personalize the actions of others toward himself, and often reads malevolent meaning into neutral situations (6). He is a somewhat skeptical, cynical, easily disillusioned male who feels misunderstood by others (1, 8). Because he depends on extrinsic achievement for his self-esteem and because he often fails to attain his high levels of aspiration, the patient is likely to suffer from marked feelings of insecurity, inferiority, and inadequacy (2–7 code type, Es).

Patients obtaining similar profiles usually receive a diagnosis of some type of depression or anxiety disorder accompanied by numerous characterological difficulties including passivity, dependency, obsessiveness, and schizoid tendencies. While cognitive functions appear intact and reality testing seems adequate, psychotic manifestations related to a major affective disorder, while unlikely, cannot be totally ignored.

Due to the presence of moderate psychic distress the patient is likely to be motivated for change and receptive to psychotherapy (2–7 code type). However, if the depression and anxiety appear to be incapacitating then psychotropic medication may be needed to reduce this distress to a more tolerable level. Meanwhile his basic mistrust of the motives of others may preclude his acceptance of constructive criticism and attempts to help him, while his tendency to use intellectualization and rationalization retard the psychotherapeutic process (6, 7). Psychotherapy initially should focus on reexamination and reevaluation of the patient's expectations and the development of more realistic standards and goals. Such a focus needs to occur within the context of a supportive, non-threatening atmosphere where trust can be developed and the patient will not fear becoming emotionally involved. As therapy progresses, the patient may respond best to a goal-directed approach which de-emphasizes further introspection, self-analysis, and general preoccupation with himself and encourages him to take a more active role in solving his difficulties. Gradual, but slow improvement can be expected and the prognosis is favorable.

SUMMARY

The original intent of the authors of the MMPI, namely to diagnose psychiatric patients, has not proven particularly successful. Nevertheless, subsequent construct validity studies have yielded a wide array of correlates for the original MMPI scales and various code types. Unfortunately though, some clinicians assume that interpretation is a rather simplistic routine procedure. Anyone familiar with this instrument has realizations to the contrary. The MMPI is an excellent tool for the skilled clinician who has mastered its intricacies and has a due appreciation of the relevant statistical concepts. However, it can be highly dangerous in the hands of the casual user who has seized upon it as one of the most reputable personality tests and one free of the problems of subjective scoring (Adcock, 1965).

REFERENCES

Adcock, C. J. (1965). Review of the MMPI. In O. K. Buros (Ed.), *The sixth mental measurement yearbook*. Highland Park, NJ: Gryphon Press.

Butcher, J., & Owen, P. (1978). Objective personality inventories: Recent research and some contemporary issues. In B. J. Wolman (Ed.), *Handbook of clinical psychology*. New York: Plenum Publishing Corp.

Caldwell, A. D. (1969). *MMPI critical items*. Unpublished mimeograph. (Available from Caldwell Reports, 3122 Santa Monica Boulevard, Santa Monica, California 90404.)

Clopton, J. R. (1979). The MMPI and suicide. In C. S. Newmark (Ed.), *MMPI: Clinical and research trends*. New York: Praeger Publishers.

Dahlstrom, W. G., Welsh, G. S., & Dahlstrom, L. E. (1972). *An MMPI handbook. Vol. 1. Clinical interpretations (rev. ed.)*. Minneapolis: University of Minnesota Press.

Fowler, R. D. (1966). The MMPI notebook: A guide to the clinical use of the automated MMPI. Roche Psychiatric Service Institute, Nutley, NJ.

Golden, C. J. (1979). *Clinical interpretation of objective psychological tests.* New York: Grune & Stratton, Inc.

Gough, H. G. (1950). The F-K dissimulation index for the MMPI. Journal of Consulting Psychology, 14, 408–413.

Graham, J. R. (1977). *The MMPI: A practical guide.* New York: Oxford University Press, Inc.

Graham, J. R. (1979). Using the MMPI in counseling and psychotherapy. In *Clinical notes on the MMPI.* Nutley, NJ: Hoffmann-LaRoche.

Grayson, H. M. (1951). A psychological admission's testing program and manual. Los Angeles: VA Center, Neuropsychiatric Hospital.

Greene, R. G. (1980). *The MMPI: An interpretive manual.* New York: Grune & Stratton, Inc.

Heilbrun, A. D. (1979). Psychopathy and violent crime. *Journal of Consulting Clinical Psychology, 47,* 509–516.

Kleinmuntz, B. (1982). *Personality and psychological assessment.* New York: St. Martin's Press, Inc.

Koss, N. P., & Butcher, J. N. (1973). A comparison of psychiatric patients' self-report with other sources of clinical information. *Journal of Research in Personality, 7,* 225–236.

Lachar, D. (1977). *The MMPI: Clinical assessment and automated interpretation.* Los Angeles: Western Psychological Services.

Lachar, D., & Wrobel, T. A. (1979). Validating clinician's hunches: Construction of a new MMPI critical item set. *Journal of Consulting and Clinical Psychology, 47,* 277–284.

Lanyon, R. I., & Goodstein, L. D. (1982). *Personality assessment* (2nd ed.). New York: John Wiley & Sons, Inc.

MacAndrew, C. (1965). The differentiation of male alcoholic outpatients from non-alcoholic psychiatric outpatients by means of the MMPI. *Quarterly Journal of Studies on Alcohol, 26,* 238–246.

Marks, P. A., Seeman, W., & Haller, D. L. (1974). *The actuarial use of the MMPI with adolescents and adults.* Baltimore: Williams & Wilkins.

Meyer, R. G. (1983). *The clinician's handbook.* Boston: Allyn and Bacon, Inc.

Newmark, C. S., Gentry, L., Simpson, M., & Jones, T. (1978). MMPI criteria for diagnosing schizophrenia. *Journal of Personality Assessment, 42,* 366–373.

Penk, W. E. (1981). Assessing the substance abuser with the MMPI. In *Clinical notes on the MMPI.* Nutley, NJ: Hoffmann-LaRoche.

Webb, J. T., & McNamara, K. M. (1979). Configural interpretation of the MMPI. In C. S. Newmark (Ed.), *MMPI: Clinical and research trends.* New York: Praeger Publishers.

Welsh, G. S. (1948). An extension of Hathaway's MMPI profile coding system. *Journal of Consulting Psychology, 12,* 343–344.

Ziskin, J. (1981). Use of the MMPI in forensic settings. In *Clinical notes on the MMPI.* Nutley, NJ: Hoffmann-LaRoche.

2

The Rorschach

Philip Erdberg

Introduction   Find some typical people, show them the term *psychological test,* ask them to tell you their first thought, and many would answer something about the Rorschach or inkblots. The Rorschach is an old and widely used instrument, and in the popular mind, it is often synonymous with psychological testing. If the subjects turned the tables and asked the question, many would be curious about how the Rorschach works, how psychologists are able to take a person's responses to some inkblots and formulate an extensive personality description. The purpose of this chapter is to answer that question. In the process, discussion will include many aspects of the Rorschach, but the emphasis throughout will be on understanding how the test accomplishes its goal of providing descriptions of psychological operation.

SOME RORSCHACH BASICS

The Rorschach is a test of personality function that can be used with children as young as five through aged adults. The test consists of ten inkblots: five of which are black or some shade of gray and five which have color; each are displayed on a white background. The blots were developed by a Swiss psychiatrist, Hermann Rorschach, during the second decade of this century, and were first described in his monograph, *Psychodiagnostik,* in 1921. Earlier researchers used inkblots to study imagination, but Rorschach moved far beyond a focus solely on the content of the response to form a unique concept—the idea that the way a person produces responses to the inkblots is representative of behavior in similar situations and thus forms the basis for a description of general psychological operation. As an example, if a person brought a great deal of action into the Rorschach percepts (two ladies dancing around a Maypole with streamers flying and capes blowing in the wind, as opposed to two ladies sitting down), psychologists hypothesize that the person would take an active approach in other parts of his or her world. Validity studies, in which this sort of approach to the Rorschach was shown to be associated with findings about behavior in other situations, provide support for this hypothesis.

Rorschach died in 1922, at the age of 38, only a year after the test was published, and, regrettably, he was never able to develop many of the ideas he had outlined in his monograph. Some of his colleagues kept interest in the test alive, and after it was brought to the United States in 1925, five American psychologists each developed systems for its use. From 1936 to 1957, these five systematizers—Samuel Beck, Marguerite Hertz, Bruno Klopfer, Zygmunt Piotrowski, and David Rapaport—produced overlapping but independent approaches to the test. Although there were often arguments among proponents of the various systems, the research studies and training of new psychologists, which resulted from each of the five systemizers, insured the Rorschach's survival. More recently, Exner and his colleagues (1974, 1978; Exner & Weiner, 1982) have developed a Comprehensive System based on the most clinically useful aspects of earlier approaches and enhanced by a series of new research findings.

The following example uses the Comprehensive System of the Rorschach. The clinician, who is seated by the patient's side to minimize body language communication, begins the *free association phase* by presenting the first blot with the question, "What might this be?" If the patient asks for more information about how to approach the test ("May I turn the card sideways?"), the clinician responds in a non-directive way ("It's up to you").

When all ten blots have been presented, the clinician starts the *inquiry phase* by explaining to the patient that they both will go back through the blots. The clinician will ask questions to discover the exact blot location of each percept and to ascertain which variables, such as the form or color of the blot, played a part in the creation of the response. The data developed during the free association and inquiry phases allow the clinician to *code* the patient's responses, a process that involves reducing the codes to a series of symbols. As examples, the use of the entire blot for a percept is coded W (whole), and the use of the shape features of the blot to produce a response is coded F (form). After all the responses have been coded, a group of summary scores are calculated. An example of such a score is *Lambda,* which is the ratio of times the patient uses only the shape of the blot (form) in constructing his or her responses against the number of times he or she uses other variables, such as color or texture. These scores, as well as the actual content of the patient's verbalizations, are then analyzed to formulate a personality description.

What is known about the mechanisms by which the Rorschach works? It is a *perceptual-cognitive task,* in which the patient is given a series of problems consisting of ambiguous visual stimuli. With few guidelines provided by the clinician, the patient is asked to solve the inkblots by using first perceptual and then higher-level operations to form a response. The process used by the patient is representative of the way he or she operates in other situations that require making judgments in the face of ambiguous data. The perceptual portion of the task occurs quickly (eye movement studies indicate that each of the blots can be scanned in less than a second). The next several seconds before the response is verbalized are devoted to a complex process in which both the patient's preferred style of handling problems and his or her psychological needs come together to determine how the individual will structure his or her response. As examples, there is a good deal of variation in how much organizational function is used by different people in producing their responses and depressed inpatients report much greater use of the gray-black features of the blots than non-depressed individuals. These findings reflect styles of problem solving and psychological need states. Coding these ways of processing the Rorschach and then, through a network of validity studies linking Rorschach elements with experience and behavior in other settings or with independently determined diagnostic categories, a hypothesis of how our patient is operating throughout the world is derived. The following section is a survey of these various Rorschach elements.

THE RORSCHACH ELEMENTS

Previously, the process of how the ambiguous visual stimuli of the Rorschach blots elicited psychological operations was explained. As mentioned, analysis of this process is made by coding various elements of the person's Rorschach responses, and this section will describe each of these elements. The first section describes how each element is identified and then discusses the ways of generalizing the Rorschach finding to hypothesize about the person's behavior in other settings. The statistical and validity data presented in this section can be studied in detail in the works by Exner as cited previously.

Location

The first element the clinician codes in analyzing a Rorschach percept is its location, how much of the blot is used to produce the response. If the person utilizes the entire blot, the location is W (whole). If he or she chooses a part that normative tables indicate is frequently seen, the location is D (common detail). If the client uses an area not often reported, the location is Dd (uncommon detail). If the white background space (S) is used as part of the percept, the scoring is WS, DS, or DdS, depending on whether the overall location is the entire blot, a common, or uncommon detail area.

The use of the entire blot (W) is associated with the ability to interact actively and efficiently with the environment, particularly if these percepts involve organization or if they occur to some of the more fragmented blots whose configurations make such responses difficult. Adults have more of these superior Ws than do children, and within the adult population, individuals with no psychiatric history have more superior Ws than do schizophrenics or neurotics. The superior W finding is associated with other measures of problem-solving ability, and both the amount and quality of W is associated with the presence of anxiety and depression.

Common details (D) are also related to efficient function, and they are by far the most frequent location choice made by non-psychiatric adults. They involve a less energy-consuming and integrative approach than does W, reflecting instead a more conservative, matter-of-fact response to the obvious aspects of the environment. Non-psychiatric adults have about half as many Ws as Ds (32 percent versus 62 percent), and this balance suggests ability to both reach out to organize the world and skill in handling its details in a practical way. D decreases under stress or time pressure, indicating that the production of this response is associated with the ability to operate in a measured, thoughtful way. D goes up significantly in the successful treatment of schizophrenia, and this finding is correlated with a variety of indicators which suggest the recovering individual is demonstrating more concern about social appropriateness.

Uncommon details (Dd) account for about 6 percent of the location choices non-psychiatric individuals make in their Rorschachs, and if the percentage goes much higher, it is likely to be associated with significant difficulties with operation in the society. Inpatient schizo-phrenics, for example, have notably higher proportions (22 percent) of Dd percepts in their records, as do individuals who may have some sort of organic brain dysfunction. If there is a high percentage of Dd in the record, normative data explains that the patient has responded to one aspect of the test quite differently from the majority. If other test findings also suggest this sort of distance from the norm, a question arises about whether the patient is finding it difficult to remain in the mainstream of other parts of the environment.

Rorschach and other systematizers viewed the use of the white space (S) areas as associated with an oppositional or negative style, although it was suggested this attribute could also have adaptive aspects in contributing to autonomy and uniqueness. There are S areas in 5 percent of the location choices for the adult non-psychiatric sample, while S occurs over three times more frequently (16 percent) in the Rorschachs of individuals who have been hospitalized with a variety of behavior disorders. Suicidal and paranoid individuals also have more S in their records than the non-psychiatric sample. It would appear that, in low proportions, S represents a healthy ability to differentiate oneself from society, while higher percentages of this finding tend to be associated with a variety of syndromes characterized by a sense of alienation.

After coding the percept's location on the blot, the psychologist next turns his or her attention to the question of what aspects of the blot have been used in producing the response. This element is known as the *determinant,* and may involve color or shading, some attribution of movement, the shape of the area chosen, or a combination of these possibilities. These determinants provide a major source of interpretive data, and each will be discussed in some detail.

Chromatic Color

The first determinant to be described is chromatic color, involving the use of the reds, blues, greens, or other non-gray, black, or white colors to form the percept. When this happens, the clinician must ascertain whether the shape of the blot was also involved, and this is done during the inquiry phase of the test. For example, if an individual reported the percept blood, in the free association, during the inquiry the clinician would ask the individual to explain what about the blot made it look like that, and if the individual said, "It's all red, just like blood," the coding would be C. The percept flower, explained during the inquiry as "It has that reddish color and here are the petals and here is the stem," would be scored CF, indicating that color was the primary determinant, but there was also some use of the shape or form (F) features. If the same percept was explained as "Here are the petals and the stem with a shape like a rose and it has a pinkish color," the coding would be FC, indicating that form was the primary determinant, but color was secondarily involved. This decision as to whether form is totally absent, secondary, or primary is made in coding determinants which involve achromatic color and shading as well.

There are a number of validity studies linking chromatic color on the Rorschach with findings of responsiveness to and interest in other parts of the environment. Individuals giving more chromatic color are more easily hypnotized, more apt to alter their judgments in the face of persuasion, and more likely to give words related to the environment in a free association task. Chromatic color appears to be associated with interaction with the environment, and the next question concerns how well controlled and adaptive is this interaction. The balance of FC to CF and C provides some data about this question, with FC associated with better control. Normative studies indicate children have more CF and C in their records than they do FC, with this balance shifting at about age twelve, as their ability to mediate interaction with society increases. Adults who are able to delay their responses in a problem-solving task have more FC than CF and C in their records, and this distinction also separates assaultive from non-assaultive individuals. A shift from CF and C to FC is associated with ratings of treatment progress and lowered probability of relapse for a variety of patient groups.

Human Movement

The second deterinant to be discussed is human movement, and M is the symbol used to code this percept. It is used for any sort of human activity, either active, "Two people dancing," or passive, "A man sitting and thinking."

The presence of the M determinant appears to reflect the use of internal resources as a way of solving problems. M is associated with findings of abstract thinking, intellectual operations, and a less action-oriented, more thoughtful style. When a problem arises the client with a good deal of M in the Rorschach is more likely to go for a walk and think it through rather than seek out a friend and talk it through.

The two problem-solving styles reflected by chromatic color and human movement are quite different stylistically. Rorschach called this contrast the *erlebnistypus* (EB), the *preferred response style*. Clients with a preponderance of chromatic color in their Rorschachs *(extratensives)* tend to deal with stressful situations by interacting with the environment in some way, while clients whose EB is in the M direction *(introversives)* are more apt to utilize internal resources as a way of solving problems. Clients having about the same amount of the two components are called *ambitents,* and often they oscillate between the two styles with no clear preference.

Although the introversive and extratensive problem-solving styles are often different behaviorally, they are equally effective in formulating solutions. For example, in one problem-solving study (Exner, Bryant, & Leura, 1975), introversives, extratensives, and ambitents were compared on a logical analysis task in which they received feedback after each move. The extratensive group made more moves with shorter times between, while the introversives made fewer moves with longer intervals, but both groups reached the solution in the same amount of time. Interestingly, the ambitents took significantly longer to reach solutions than either the introversives or the extratensives. The results suggest both dramatic differences in problem-solving style—with the extratensive group using more environmental feedback and the introversive group depending more on internal processes—and similar efficiency of both styles. These approaches are associated with effectiveness in dealing with problems and most people are able to use both, with the direction of their *erlebnistypus* predicting the more likely style. Clinicians can cumulate the total of a client's introversive and extratensive potential to provide a measure, EA (the *experience actual*), which provides an estimate of the client's overall ability to operate in organized, task-oriented, productive ways.

The next several determinants to be discussed are associated with less well-organized psychological processes than those described thus far. While chromatic color and human movement both involve efficient, although different approaches to solving problems, the next several determinants appear to reflect an experience in which ideation or affect impinges on the client in unpredictable, non-volitional ways making it difficult to deal with problems effectively.

Animal Movement

This determinant is coded FM and is reserved for animals in activity common to their species. "A bear poised to leap" or "A seahorse swimming through the water" are examples of FM.

Interpretively, it appears FM is associated with some sort of drive state experience that has the ability to intrude into consciousness, disrupt concentration and task-oriented activity, and sometimes provoke behavior. While M involves the deliberate decision to utilize ideation as a way of solving problems, FM is need-state ideation impinging in non-predictable ways. Two studies have indicated that if FM is higher than M, the probability of relapse after hospitalization is much greater for several kinds of psychiatric patients. FM may drive inappropriate and sometimes impulsive behavior, while M is associated with the ability to delay and carefully think through stressful situations. Two other interesting studies suggest FM is increased in juvenile offenders faced with indeterminate sentences and in overweight individuals hospitalized on a liquid-only diet, two groups one expects to be in high need states.

Inanimate Movement

The coding for this determinant is m, and it involves objects in motion that are neither human nor animal. An example of m would be "A rocket ship blasting off."

While FM appears to be associated with internal need states, m is linked with the awareness of outside pressure. Clinicians know m increases significantly in individuals under situational stress in settings where circumstances are beyond control. Trainees the day before their first parachute jump, patients the day before surgery, and Navy personnel during severe storm conditions all show increases in the amount of m in their records. As expected, m is one of the variables on the Rorschach which shows much fluctuation over time, reflecting day-to-day variations in how much situational stress the client is experiencing.

Shading

This is the first of the determinants discussed in which variations in hue (ranging from light to dark) are used. The coding for the use of this shading variation is Y. If the shape of the percept is primary and the use of the light-dark variation is secondary, the coding would be FY. An example would be the free association of "An x-ray of an arm bone," with an inquiry that explained the percept by noting, "It's sort of long like an arm and some parts are darker and other parts are lighter like in x-ray film." If the light-dark variation is primary with form secondary, "It has darker and lighter parts like a storm cloud, and it has that shape too," the scoring would be YF. If there is no use of form at all, "It's just lighter and darker smoke," the scoring would be Y.

From an interpretive standpoint, the presence of shading in a record is associated with the unpleasant experience of being helpless in dealing with stressful situations. Like m, the Y determinant also varies to some extent over time as a function of situational stress. Although anxiety may be involved, Y deals more specifically with the feeling of not having the *psychological equipment* to deal with problem situations, a sense of helplessness in the face of stress. This determinant occurs with greater frequency in depressed individuals, alcoholics, children, and teenagers described as withdrawn, and in

individuals that other Rorschach variables suggest are apt to be feeling helpless. People able to terminate psychotherapy at eighteen
months show decreases in the amount of shading in their Rorschachs,
while those not ready to make termination have about the same amount
of shading as they did in their pretreatment records.

Texture

This determinant involves the use of variation in the light-dark
features of the blot as a way of giving a sense of texture. An example
would be a free association percept of a "bearskin rug" which was
explained during the inquiry as "Some parts are lighter and some
parts are darker, and gives the impression that it's furry, like a bearskin rug." The coding is FT, TF, or T, depending on whether the shape
of the blot is the predominant determinant with texture secondary,
whether shape is secondary, or whether there is no use of shape features at all.

Texture is associated with the experience of need for emotional
contact with others. It appears with greater frequency in individuals
who have recently lost important interpersonal connections, such as
widows and widowers, children of deceased parents, and individuals
who have just been separated or divorced. However, if interpersonal
resources are taken away early or are never present, as in children
who have never had a foster home placement longer than fourteen
months, there may be no texture in the record at all, a finding suggesting a *burnt child syndrome*. Most non-psychiatric adults have
approximately one texture response in their records, while studies of
a variety of patient groups suggest they are charaterized either by
more texture responses or records containing no texture responses at
all. What is appearing in these groups is either an inordinate need
for emotional contact and dependency or the denial of any need for
this sort of experience.

Vista

This determinant, which is coded V, occurs when variations in
the hue of the blot are used to give a sense of depth or dimensionality.
As with the other shading determinants discussed, the coding is FV,
VF, or V, depending on whether shape is primary, secondary, or not
used at all. An example of an FV percept is the free association of "a
tunnel," which was explained during the inquiry as "The lighter part
makes it look like it goes back into the distance."

Vista is a relatively infrequent determinant, and is associated
with the experience of thinking about oneself and concluding with
negative evaluations. It is related to painful, unrealistic introspection

and has a tendency to maximize and distort problem areas often in a guilt-ridden way. This determinant occurs more frequently in the Rorschachs of chronically depressed and suicidal individuals.

Achromatic Color

The coding for the use of the gray, white, or black features of the blot is C′, and a particular percept would be scored FC′, C′F, or C′ depending on whether form is primary, secondary, or not utilized at all. The free association "a black bat," explained during the inquiry as "Here are the wings and the antennae and it's black like a bat," is an example of FC′.

From an interpretive standpoint, it is the presence of significant amounts of achromatic color in a client's Rorschach that is associated with constraint or internalization of emotion as opposed to the person's being able to express his or her feelings. This holding in of emotion is a painful process, and depressed individuals, patients with psychosomatic problems, obsessive-compulsives, and schizoid individuals have higher amounts of achromatic color in their records than those who are better able to express their emotions.

Although animal and inanimate movement, shading, texture, vista, and achromatic color are representative of widely different experiences, they commonly involve non-volitional, non-productive psychological processes. Each reflect ideas or emotions that impinge on the person in unwanted ways, interfering with his or her task-oriented function. The ep *(experience potential)* is a measure developed to quantify the client's disruptive psychological processes, and is calculated as the total of these *intrusive* determinants. Comparing a person's EA, the total organized psychological resources, with the client's ep, clinicians can predict how the client will be able to operate in a task-oriented, productive fashion. If the EA is greater than or about the same as the ep, it is likely the client will direct his or her behavior toward identified goals. If the unorganized material reflected by ep is significantly greater, the potential for disrupted behavior is frequently controlled by need states and intrusive emotionality increases.

Pure Form and Lambda

All the determinants discussed thus far, whether reflective of task-oriented or intrusive psychological processes, have involved the individual's bringing significant aspects of his or her own psychology into the production of the percept. Another determinant, pure form (F), is qualitatively different in that it reflects more emotion-free operation, and with a derivative measure, *Lambda,* can provide useful data about the person's rational versus emotional operation.

From a coding standpoint, clinicians assign the determinant F whenever the individual uses only the shape or form of the blot in creating the percept. An example is the free association "butterfly" with an inquiry that explained the percept by saying, "Here are the wings, and here is the head, and here's the tail which has a shape just like a swallowtail butterfly." The person used only the form aspects of the blot, with no articulation of movement, color, or shading. This is the most common determinant on the Rorschach, and our non-psychiatric adult sample gives pure form as the only determinant for approximately 45 percent of their responses.

As noted above, pure form is thought to be the most emotion-free determinant on the Rorschach, with the individual responding to the inkblot by searching through remembered data about the shapes of objects and forming a best fit answer in the same way a computer does. Pure form keeps the individual's psychological role to a minimum in the formation of the percept, emphasizing instead rational, affect-free operation. For example, schizophrenics have less pure form in their records during acute periods than during times of remission and recovery.

One important issue concerns the time the individual operates in the affect-free way reflected by pure form, and *Lambda* provides a useful measure in this regard. The time is calculated as the number of pure form determinants in the record divided by all other determinants. Some examples will be helpful in understanding the use of this index. In a twenty-response record, if the person had only five pure F determinants and 15 of any other type of determinant, the *Lambda* would be 5 divided by fifteen or .33. Using normative data, which indicates the mean *Lambda* for the adult non-psychiatric group is .82 with a standard deviation of .3, indicates that this individual has substantially less pure form in his or her record than most adults and he or she is likely to find his or her own psychology frequently impinging, making it difficult for the individual to operate in affect-free ways. On the other hand, if the person has fifteen pure form determinants and only five of any other kind, the *Lambda* would be fifteen divided by five or 3.0, far above the non-psychiatric norm. This person would be characterized as having too severe control over his or her affect, and would be described by others as operating in a computer-like manner, rarely allowing his or her own feelings to be involved in the function. If *Lambda* goes much above or below the norm, the finding is associated with a less adaptive ability to maintain a balance between rational and emotional operation.

Blends

If the client uses more than one determinant in producing the percept, the response is called a *blend,* and all of the determinants are coded in the order in which they occur. An example is "A coat with black stripes on a blue background." The coding would be FC´ FC. Most adults produce blends in about 23 percent of their responses, and these more complicated percepts are thought to reflect psychological energy and complexity. If the percentage is much below the norm, questions arise about the client's ability to give more than bare minimum responses. If the percentage goes much above the norm, the clinician might suggest that the client is employing an over-ideational style. Most blends have two determinants, and if the individual uses three or more determinants in many of the blends, questions ensue about what is the immobilizing amount of complexity in the operation.

Form Quality and Special Scorings

After the clinician has coded the response's determinant or determinants, the clinician next evaluates it for perceptual accuracy or form quality. This will illustrate how much the particular blot area looks like what the client says it looks like by utilizing tables providing data about other clients' perceptions. The definition of reality on the Rorschach thus becomes a normative one. If many people have seen a particular percept for a particular blot area, it is good form; if the percept is infrequently seen or if it involves gross distortions, the form quality is poor. By calculating percentages for the amount of good form quality in a person's Rorschach (X + %), clinicians make suggestions about how accurately the client is testing reality in other parts of his or her environment. For example, schizophrenics have lower form quality percentages than non-psychiatric controls. The mean X + % in the non-psychiatric controls' records is 81 percent, while the mean X + % for inpatient schizophrenics is 57 percent.

There are several indicators called *special scorings* whose presence suggests the person may be processing the data received in unusual and inaccurate ways. The first of these is the *incongruous combination* (INCOM), a percept in which the person has difficulty integrating all the parts into a consistent whole. An example is "a grasshopper with the head of a butterfly." Here, the individual has operated too concretely, not allowing the overall percept to account for minor inconsistencies.

Another difficulty of this type is the *fabulized combination* (FABCOM), a special scoring category in which the client juxtaposes two elements which should have been seen as separate percepts. An example is "Two bears repairing an airplane." In the FABCOM, the individual produces a strained and unrealistic synthesis instead of being able to view discrete elements as separate and unrelated.

The *contamination* (CONTAM) is a serious special scoring category that is most often associated with significant thought disorder.

Here, the individual is unable to keep two separate percepts from blending into each other "It looks like coal and it could also be a monster so it must be a coal monster."

Other special scoring categories include the *deviant verbalization* (DV), which is an unusual use of language and *austic logic* (ALOG), in which the client forms an unusual cause-and-effect relationship. An example of a deviant verbalization is "The disseverance of this picture makes it look like an image-foot," and autistic logic might involve a percept such as "It seems to be reddish-pink so it probably would be able to fly for long distances."

Each of these special scoring categories suggest the person's ability to process data may be compromised, and, not surprisingly, their presence can be of value in the assessment of thought disorder.

Self-Focus Measures

There are several Rorschach elements that provide data about the amount and quality of time the person spends in self-focus activities. These indicators provide data about the proportion of self-focus to externally-oriented attention. The use of pair responses, "Two ladies dancing," and reflection responses, "A bear looking at his reflection in the water," is related to self-focus. These responses occur more frequently in individuals who give self-focus answers on incomplete sentences tests, than those who engage in mirror-looking behavior while waiting for an interview, and those who make use of the pronoun "I" during interviews. Reflection responses appear to be associated with a particularly intense sort of self-focus. Depressed and suicidal individuals are characterized by fewer pair and reflection precepts. Clinicians calculate a measure, the *egocentricity index*, which provides the proportion of the client's responses involving pair or reflection percepts. Findings that are much higher or lower than the norm (37 percent for the non-psychiatric adult sample with a standard deviation of 6 percent) tend to be associated with a variety of maladaptive syndromes. High findings are indicative of an egocentric stance, and low findings suggest the person isn't sufficiently self-centered. Psychologists hypothesize that one aspect of a healthy psychological function is a moderate amount—not too much and not too little—focus on self.

Another element associated with self-focus is a determinant not yet discussed, called *form dimensionality* (FD). This is coded when the client uses the different sizes of various parts of the blot to give a sense of perspective. An example is a free association of "A monster looking down at you," explained during the inquiry by "His head looks small, like it's a long way away, and his feet are gigantic, like they're very close." A number of studies suggest this determinant is associated with productive introspective activity—the ability to evaluate both the positive and negative aspects of one's function.

Active-Passive Ratio

All of the movement determinants—human, animal, and inanimate—can be coded according to whether the movement involved is active or passive. An example of active movement is "A man banging on a drum," while "A bear lying down and resting" is passive. By cumulating the number of active movement percepts and the number of passive movement percepts occurring in the record, clinicians produce an index called the active-passive ratio. The non-psychiatric sample is characterized by a mix of about twice as many active as passive answers. Acute schizophrenics, character disorders, and individuals whose behavior involves assault show significantly more active percepts in their records, whereas chronic schizophrenics and depressives are characterized by more passive percepts. Clients having more passive than active percepts tend to show a variety of passive behaviors on ratings done by those people who know them well.

It is important to note that a wide variety of patient groups tend to show skewed active-passive ratios, either with three or more times as many active as passive responses or vice versa. This skewed profile is associated with a cognitive rigidity, making it difficult for the person to be flexible in his or her coping style. Patients rated as improved show a movement toward a more balanced active-passive ratio during their treatment, while those clients not rated as improved tend to keep about the same active-passive ratio.

Organizational Activity

Another element which the clinician codes is the amount of organizational activity that the client uses in generating a Rorschach response. In the percept "Two people standing over a large kettle and deciding what kind of soup to make," the individual has initiated major organization, forming a relationship between various segments of the blot. This is a different approach than the percept "two people" given to the same blot area; a response that does not involve the process of organizing the material by postulating a relationship between the different parts. Percepts involving organization and those including the whole blot are more energy-consuming than single detail percepts with no formulation of relationships. Adult normative samples show about 43 percent of these more complex responses. If the client is much higher or lower than that figure in his or her organizational attempts, the clinician questions whether the client organizes his or her environment too much or not enough. Clinicians use an index called Z Frequency (Zf) to indicate the actual number of organizational attempts the client has made.

Regardless of how much a person organizes his or her environment, another important question concerns how efficient is each organizational attempt. For any given number of organizational attempts, clinicians know approximately how many details a non-psychiatric sample brings and can compare any particular individual's responses against that norm. If a client has provided many more details than most people do for a given number of organizational attempts, clinicians say the client is an *over-incorporator*. Over-incorporators deal extensively with their world, needing to account for every detail before acting. Sometimes this cautious style can immobilize behavior, since it is often necessary to act with less than complete data. On the other hand, *under-incorporators* bring in fewer details per organizational attempt than most others. Under-incorporators tend to miss important elements in their environment because they scan too quickly, and their approach on a variety of tasks is characterized by speed but inaccuracy. Under-incorporators may behave inappropriately because they have not accounted for all the elements necessary to make a thoughtful decision. Clinicians use an index called the Z difference (Zd) to indicate whether an individual's organizational performance has differed from the expected norm. If the Zd is high and positive (+3.5 or more), it means the individual has involved more elements per organizational attempt than expected, therefore the individual is an over-incorporator. Zd scores of −3.5 or below are associated with under-incorporators, people who use fewer elements than expected.

Affective Ratio

The last three Rorschach inkblots (cards VIII, IX, and X) are fully chromatic, with many shades of blue, green, yellow, pink, and brown. The other seven cards are either solely gray and black (I, IV, V, VI, and VII) or only partially chromatic (II and III), with some red areas in addition to the black. The ratio of responses the person gives to the three fully chromatic cards compared to the number of responses to the other seven cards provides some data about his or her responsiveness to the emotional aspects of the world. Most people give about 40 percent of their responses to the last three chromatic cards. If the individual's percentage is much higher or lower than that, a number of studies suggests the individual may be either receptive to the emotional aspects of the world or someone who backs off from emotionally-charged situations.

It is also interesting to note extratensives give more responses to the fully chromatic cards than do introversives, even though there is a good deal of overlap between the two groups. This finding is consistent with the characterization of extratensives as people tending to interact more readily with their environment. As has been the case with some of the other Rorschach elements discussed, patient groups tend to be at the extremes in terms of their affective ratios, suggesting either too much or too little willingness to process the emotional parts of their experience. A shift toward a more balanced affective ratio frequently accompanies ratings of treatment progress.

Content

The final element which the clinician evaluates while analyzing someone's Rorschach is the actual content of the percepts: what the individual sees, and the exact words the individual uses to describe them. Normatively, animals and humans are frequently seen, and on the average about 40 percent of a person's responses will involve animals and about 20 percent will involve humans. Some responses are normatively so frequent (a bat or butterfly on card I, for example) that they are called *Populars,* and these responses constitute about 30 percent of most records. When an individual's percentages deviate significantly from these averages, the findings are analyzed in terms of conventionality and interest in interpersonal activities. Inpatient schizophrenics, for example, give fewer Popular responses than the non-psychiatric controls.

Another group of content categories—plant life, clouds, maps, nature, and landscape—has been associated with a distant, superficial, interpersonal style. If these responses constitute more than one-quarter of the client's Rorschach, the correlation between various measures of social isolation is significant.

Percepts describing the object as dead, destroyed, injured, broken, damaged, or as having a dysphoric characteristic such as sad are coded as *morbid* (MOR) content. These percepts appear more frequently in depressive syndromes. *Aggressive* (AG) content involves people, animals, or objects in clearly aggressive or destructive activity, and initial work suggests these responses are associated with acting-out behavior in a variety of settings.

Finally, the clinician seeks content or descriptions that seem unique to the client. As an example, if the client tends to describe many of the percepts as menacing, scary, or frightening, the clinician may hypothesize whether the client also sees other parts of the world as threatening.

Element Clusters

An important new direction in Rorschach research involves the discovery that clusters of the elements discussed so far can be associated with specific behavioral or diagnostic categories. As an example, Exner and Wylie (1977) identified a group of eleven elements occurring more frequently in the Rorschachs of suicidal individuals than for non-suicidal psychiatric patients or non-patients. Other clusters have been developed that are of value in differentiating schizophrenic and chronically depressed individuals.

RORSCHACH INTERPRETATION: A CLINICAL EXAMPLE

Using all of the Rorschach elements discussed, the psychologist is able to provide a comprehensive description of personality operation. The process involved—and the opportunity to review the elements— will be examined by using a set of sample Rorschach data to produce a personality description. Discussion of the various elements will appear in the same order they were presented in the last section, using the normative adult statistics provided by Exner (1978) as reference data to guide interpretation. The example involves the Rorschach of a man in his late forties, Mr. N, who had sought psychotherapy for himself and his family because of family problems. A summary of findings, using the format developed for the Comprehensive System, is shown in Figure 2–1.

Location

The most noteworthy finding in Mr. N's choice of locations for his percepts is his use of many more wholes (W) than expected. He has twice as many Ws as common details (D), whereas normative data expects just the opposite. This finding has both positive and negative aspects. Mr. N's use of the whole location, particularly since many of his Ws involve complex organizational activity, is reflective of an active, reaching out approach to the environment. The relative scarcity of D in the record suggests he may incur difficulty when he must shift from his energetic, integrative style to a more matter-of-fact, detail-oriented style.

His one uncommon detail (Dd) location is normative, indicating that Mr. N has dealt with the test the same way most people do in terms of choice of blot location for his percepts. Do not over-interpret Mr. N's complete absence of white space (S) locations, since such a finding is not normatively unusual, but suggests some tendency toward a conventional style.

Determinants

Analysis of the determinants Mr. N chose to formulate his percepts begins by noting his use of chromatic color and human movement

STRUCTURAL SUMMARY*

R = 16   Zf = 12   ZSum = 42.5   P = 7   (2) = 4

Location Features	Determinants (Blends First)	Contents	Contents (Idiographic)

Location Features

W = 10
D = 5
Dd = 1
S = 0
DW = 0

Determinants (Blends First)

FV·FM   M·FY
FC·FY   FM·FC
m·FC·FC'   FM·Fr
M·C   M·FY·FC
FM·FY·FD   FM·M·CF
FM·FY·FT

M = 1
FM = 1
m =
C =
Cn =
CF =
FC = 1
C' =
C'F =
FC' =
T =
TF =
FT = 1
V =
VF =
FV =
Y =
YF =
FY =
rF =
Fr =
FD =
F = 1

Contents

H = 1   Bl =
(H) = 1   Bt =
Hd =   Cg =
(Hd) = 1   Cl =
A = 6   Ex = 0, 1
(A) =   Fi =
Ad =   Fd =
(Ad) =   Ge =
Ab =   Hh =
Al =   Ls = 1
An =   Na =
Art =   Sx = 2
Ay =   Xy =

Contents (Idiographic)

lipstick .... = 1
missile .... = 1
monster .... = 1
rug .... = 1
.... =
.... =
.... =

DQ	M Quality
+ = 9	+ = 0
o = 7	o = 3
v = 0	w = 2
— = 0	— = 0
	NO FORM = 0

Form Quality

FQx	FQf
+ = 0	+ = 0
o = 13	o = 1
w = 3	w = 0
— = 0	— = 0
NO FORM = 0	

S-CONSTELLATION (Adult)

.... FV+VF+V+FD > 2
.X. .Col-Shd Bl > 0
.... 3r+(2)/R < .30
.X. .Zd > ± 3.5
.X. .ep > EA
.... CF+C > FC
.... X+% < .70
.... S > 3
.X. .P < 3 or >8
.... H < 2
.X. .R < 17
5 ...... TOTAL

Special Scorings

DV =
INCOM =
FABCOM =
ALOG =
CONTAM =
———
CP =
MOR =
PER =
PSV =
AG =

RATIOS, PERCENTAGES, AND DERIVATIONS

ZSum-Zest = 42.5 - 38.0

Zd = +4.5

EB = 5:5   EA = 10

eb = 8:9   ep = 17

(FM= 7 m=1 T=2 C'=1 V=1 Y=5)

Blends:R = 11:16

a:p = 7:6

Ma:Mp = 2:3

FC:CF+C = 5:2

W:M = 10:5

W:D = 10:5

L = .07

F+% = 100%

X+% = 81%

A% = 38%

Afr = .33

3r+(2)/R = .44

Cont:R = 8:16

H+Hd:A+Ad = 1:6
(H)+(Hd):(A)+(Ad) = 2:0

H+A:Hd+Ad = 8:1

XRT Achrom = 7.1"

XRT Chrom = 11.2"

Figure 2–1 Represents the structural summary of Mr. N's Rorschach using the format developed for the Comprehensive System.

are equal (his EB is 5:5), making him an ambitent. He does not have a straightforward problem-solving style, and his approach when faced with stressful situations may involve some oscillation between interacting with the environment and spending time by himself thinking the problem through. The approach ambitents use appears to be less efficient than either a clearly extratensive or introversive style, both of which allow more decisive resolutions in shorter time periods.

Next, analysis involves the sum of Mr. N's human movement and chromatic color (his EA is 10) in comparison with the sum of his shading and achromatic color determinants (his ep is 17). The EA is thought to represent the total of a person's organized coping strategies, while ep reflects unorganized, disruptive psychological material. At present, Mr. N has substantially more unorganized material impinging on him than he has resources available to cope with this overload (he is about two standard deviations below the adult mean in this regard).

In order to understand the specific nature of the disruptive overload Mr. N is experiencing, the psychologist examines the actual determinants making up his ep. He has more than twice as much animal movement (FM) as expected, suggesting Mr. N is experiencing substantial ideational intrusion, often associated with need states, which has the ability to disrupt his concentration. His m determinant indicates awareness of external stress, and he has about five times the normative amount of shading determinant (Y), suggesting he currently is feeling helplessness about dealing with the situational pressure he is experiencing. He has perhaps one more texture (T) determinant than expected, possibly indicating greater than usual current need for emotional contact with others. The presence of his one vista (V) determinant is of concern because it raises the possibility that Mr. N is spending time in painful introspection, thinking about himself, and concluding with negative material. Although not far from normative, the presence of an achromatic color (C´) determinant in the record suggests Mr. N is attempting to contain some of the emotion he is experiencing as opposed to telling others.

Pure Form and Lambda

Mr. N's *Lambda* of .07 is far below the adult mean (.82), a finding that indicates he has used the pure form (F) determinant much less frequently than most. F is associated with relatively affect-free operation, in which the individual is able to deal with situations in an objective manner, and when *Lambda* is as low as Mr. N's is, psychologists say his emotions are involved in much of his behavior.

Blends

Mr. N is a complicated person. Some 69 percent of his responses involve blends, as opposed to the 23 percent expected normatively. Five of his blends are particularly involved, with three determinants instead of the more usual two. Although blends do reflect psychological energy and richness, the excessive number and complexity of Mr. N's responses suggests an over-ideational style with potential for becoming immobilizing.

Form Quality and Special Scorings

Mr. N's form quality (X + %) of 81 percent is normative, and he has no special scorings. In other words, his perceptual accuracy and processing efficiency are entirely adequate, with no indications of reality testing difficulties or thought disorder.

Self-Focus Measures

Mr. N's egocentricity index is .44, one standard deviation above the adult mean, and includes a reflection (Fr) response, which is normatively infrequent. Mr. N appears to spend somewhat more time in self-focus activities than most people and some of this activity is quite intense. Mention has already been made that he has a vista response in the record, suggesting some of his introspection may be painful. The presence of a *form dimensionality* (FD) determinant suggests he also has the ability to view himself in a more balanced way.

Active-Passive Ratio

Mr. N's overall active-passive ratio of 7:6 and his human movement active-passive ratio of 2:3 are somewhat more passive than the 2:1 ratio that is approximately normative. A hypothesis arises that sometimes Mr. N has difficulty taking an active role in the implementation of solutions.

Organizational Activity

Mr. N has introduced some sort of organization for 75 percent of his percepts, substantially more than the 43 percent expected normatively. This is consistent with other findings, suggesting he devotes more energy than most when attempting to synthesize and integrate the various elements of his world. His Zd of +4.5 suggests Mr. N is an over-incorporator, a person who scans his world extensively, sometimes not acting because he has not accounted for all the details. It is possible this overly thorough style may be immobilizing for Mr. N in situations which require a reasonable best guess with less than total data. As an example, over-incorporators often have trouble with situations involving deadlines.

Affective Ratio

The affective ratio measures how responsive a person is to the affective components of the external world. Mr. N's affective ratio is .33, well below the adult mean of .69. He tends to screen out emotionally-charged material coming from external sources.

Content

Mr. N has more Popular percepts than expected (44 percent of his responses were Populars in contrast to the normative 30 percent), again suggesting the possibility of conventional style. Only one of his percepts involves a whole person, a finding substantially lower than expected normatively and suggestive of some interpersonal distancing. He does not have the sort of content findings associated with themes of extreme social isolation, morbidity, or aggression.

Element Clusters

Mr. N does not have the clusters of findings associated with suicidal, chronically depressed, or schizophrenic individuals.

Summary and Treatment Implications

Integrating the various Rorschach elements, Mr. N emerges as a man who is presently experiencing an overload of intrusive ideas and emotions, with more disruption than his organized resources can handle. It is not surprising that he is seeking outside help at this time. His concentration and his ability to handle situations in a task-oriented, emotion-free manner are significantly compromised. He is unclear about selecting a problem-solving style, and he often feels helpless in knowing how to better his situation. A complicated and thoughtful man, he sometimes has difficulty arriving at decisive solutions and in actively implementing those solutions in his world. He is spending much time in rather intense self-focus, ending sometimes with painful results.

Since his presenting problem involves family difficulties, it will be helpful to think about some of Mr. N's Rorschach findings in the context of their interpersonal meaning. His broadly conceptual style sometimes makes it difficult for him to deal with the day-to-day necessities of family life. Other family members may see him as impractical, perfectionistic in his expectations of them, and perhaps as overly conventional and stereotyped in his values. When a family member wants to talk with him about emotional issues, his response may be to back off, making him appear cold and disinterested. At the same time, he is experiencing need for more satisfying interpersonal contact and support, although he finds it difficult to talk about those desires with the people who are most able to satisfy them.

How do these Rorschach findings help in planning an intervention approach for Mr. N? The current state of overload in which Mr. N finds himself must be the first treatment target, since the stress he is experiencing is substantial. Immediately, it is crucial to speak with Mr. N about his present situation to help him develop some short-range techniques for dealing with these problems. In addition to individual counseling, treatment may involve some brief conjoint therapy with family members who are significant within the current situation. This will temporarily bring the difficulties into manageable proportions.

On a more long-range basis, Mr. N will need to deal with at least two important constellations of issues. From a purely individual standpoint, the conflict between his highly conceptual ideational style and the difficulties he is having in actively pursuing his ideas to successful resolution must be addressed. From an interpersonal standpoint, it is likely Mr. N is having serious difficulties meeting the needs of the members of his family. There is some indication he feels some of his own important needs are not being satisfied. It will be crucial to talk about family interactions—how the other people in his family see him and how he sees them—and here, couple and family therapy is the most appropriate approach. Personality testing for the other significant members of Mr. N's family will be helpful to better understand the interactions. Using the Rorschach to help identify a variety of important issues and place them in perspective, it is suggested that a combined individual, couple, and family approach involving immediate, short-term intervention and then longer-range therapy would serve Mr. N and his family best.

THE RORSCHACH IN PERSPECTIVE

The sample case just reviewed provides a good starting point for considering the strengths and weaknesses of the Rorschach. What the test effectively accomplished was a broadly comprehensive description of Mr. N's current personality operation, culminating in an intervention approach. It was less helpful in providing detailed data about specific areas of concern. Conjecture allows, for example, that sexual issues may be of some importance, but anything more definite is not known. No specific data from the Rorschach explains how Mr. N sees his role as husband, father, or worker. The clinical interview and the Thematic Apperception Test would supply details about the uniquely personal aspects of the disruption that the Rorschach described in general terms. What the Rorschach does best is provide a comprehensive picture of present personality function, while interview, drawing, and apperception techniques elaborate idiographic material and investigate the developmental history of problem areas.

Just as the Rorschach is not the best test for describing the unique details of a particular problem area, it is also not the appropriate test for evaluating intellectual operation or neuropsychological difficulties. Although the presence of highly organized W responses and blends in Mr. N's record suggests more than adequate intellectual function, cognitive and neuropsychological instruments such as those developed by Wechsler and Reitan would be more helpful in describing the specifics of his intellectual operation.

Another consideration of the strengths and weaknesses of the Rorschach explores its psychometric properties: Is it reliable and valid in its measurement of personality attributes? The answer to this question is an increasingly positive one. Exner (1974) has shown that interscorer reliability in coding the various Rorschach elements is quite good, and his 1978 work indicates these elements remain consistent over time in adults. As an example, when non-patient adults were retested thirty-five to thirty-eight months after an initial Rorschach, seventy-five of the seventy-seven who had been clearly introversive or extratensive on the first testing continued to have the same preferred response style. Although more research is needed regarding the reliability of conclusions when two interpreters evaluate the same Rorschach, speculation allows that as psychologists utilize the quantitative material as described thus far, instead of focusing solely on content data, the inter-interpreter reliability of their reports will improve markedly. More research is also needed in the area of the Rorschach's applicability across demographic variables and cultures, but Exner and Weiner (1982) report data suggesting the test taps a level of function that is strikingly stable over such variables as sex, socioeconomic status, and cultural background.

The validity question focuses on how consistently Rorschach findings can be associated with diagnostic category membership or with behavior. In the already mentioned study by Exner and Wylie (1977), a cluster of variables was used to differentiate suicidal from non-suicidal individuals. This approach identified 75 percent of the suicidal individuals while describing only 20 percent of depressed, but non-suicidal inpatients and no non-patient as suicidal. The clusters associated with chronic depression and with schizophrenia also appear quite accurate in their ability to identify individuals who can be placed in those diagnostic categories on the basis of comprehensive clinical evaluation.

Throughout this chapter, validity studies have been associated with the various Rorschach elements with internal experience and external behavior and emphasized it is these studies that allow the psychologist to generalize from test findings a description of what a person is feeling and how he is operating. The ability of the Rorschach to continue its history of clinical usefulness, now extending back more than half a century, depends on the acquisition of more validity data that links test findings with experience and behavior in the world.

REFERENCES

Exner, J. E. (1974). *The Rorschach: A comprehensive system.* (Vol. 1). New York: John Wiley & Sons, Inc.

Exner, J. E. (1978). *The Rorschach: A comprehensive system.* (Vol. 2: *Current research and advanced interpretation.*) New York: John Wiley & Sons, Inc.

Exner, J. E., Bryant E. L., & Leura, A. V. (1975). *Variations in problem solving by three EB types.* Workshops study No. 217 (unpublished). Bayville, NY: Rorschach Workshops.

Exner, J. E., & Weiner, I. B. (1982). *The Rorschach: A comprehensive system.* (Vol. 3: *Assessment of children and adolescents.*) New York: John Wiley & Sons, Inc.

Exner, J. E., & Wylie, J. R. (1977). Some Rorschach data concerning suicide. *Journal of Personality Assessment, 41,* 339–348.

Mortimer, R. L., & Smith, W. H. (1983). The use of the psychological test report in setting the focus of psychotherapy. *Journal of Personality Assessment, 47,* 134–138.

3

THEMATIC APPERCEPTION TEST (TAT)*

Richard H. Dana

Introduction   The Thematic Apperception Test (TAT) was developed in the 1930s to provide a vehicle for applying Henry Murray's (1938) need-press theory of personality to individuals. Murray assumed the TAT elicited fantasy as a result of a projection of past experience and present needs in response to ambiguous picture stimuli. The TAT differs from the Rorschach by providing less ambiguous stimuli with clear structure in the directions to tell a story, a familiar task to most clients. As a result the client can exercise control over the story and choose to include and emphasize particular contents and/or minimize, distort, and even omit other contents.

While there has been abundant research literature on Murray needs and over two thousand studies listed in the *Eighth Mental Measurements Yearbook* (Buros, 1978), there has been almost no use of

*Grateful acknowledgment is made to the three anonymous persons who contributed their TAT data for this chapter and graciously permitted the working notes and written reports to be included.

this literature for TAT interpretation (Dana, 1968; Klopfer & Taulbee, 1976). Unlike the Rorschach, which was created with a scoring system and has prevailed with only minor modifications, the original Murray scoring system has not been used by personality assessors. Nor has any other scoring system achieved any consensus as a means of coding the potential data of the stories, or permitting valid prediction of clinical diagnosis. Nonetheless, the TAT is the second most frequently recommended projective technique by clinical psychologists (Wade, Baker, Morton & Baker, 1978), and the most frequently mentioned projective technique by clinical psychology programs (C. Piotrowski & Keller, in press).

The absence of accepted, formal scoring procedures has deprived students and practitioners of a modus operandi for learning interpretation. As a result, TAT interpretation has become a clinical art form. This chapter will be primarily concerned with interpretation of the TAT for personality description since there are objective tests that are much more useful for clinical diagnosis. First, the nature of the picture stimuli will be considered in detail using story examples from one male client. Construction, administration, and scoring will be briefly described. A section on principles of interpretation will synthesize the literature to provide a panorama against which to examine TAT stories from a well-functioning woman. These stories will be presented verbatim, with working notes, and a completed report. This report was discussed with the client as part of informed consent and her comments and reactions are included. Providing clients with complete feedback, including the report, is an essential ingredient of responsible practice with the TAT. TAT stories provided by a well-functioning native American woman are included in the same format. A discussion of the use of the TAT with minority persons follows this example. Finally, an enumeration of assets and liabilities of the TAT as a personality assessment device will lead to some conclusions concerning present and future usage.

CONSTRUCTION

There are thirty-one pictures in this instrument that includes eleven for adult men and women over fourteen years of age (1, 2, 4, 5, 10, 11, 13, 14, 15, 19, 20), seven for adult males and boys from seven-to-fourteen years (BM cards) and adult women and girls from seven-to-fourteen (GF cards) (3, 6, 7, 8, 9, 17, 18), one for adult males (12M), one for adult females (12F), one for children of either sex (12BG), one for male children (13B), one for female children (13G), and a blank card (16) for all clients. Each picture contains a dramatic event or critical situation and a person with whom the client can identify (Morgan & Murray, 1935). The cards are intended to be comprehensive in the sense of including the gamut of life situations and to compose a standard set although no systematic selection procedures are used. Murray was concerned with the evocation of fantasy by picture stimuli and believed that the first ten cards constituted an everyday series while the second ten were more unusual, dramatic, and bizarre.

Murray (1943) noted that pictures 12BM, 13G, and 20 were suggested by Dr. R. N. Sanford; 4, 6GF, 8BM, 9GF, and 19 by Dr. F. Wyatt; 2, 4GF, 8GF, by Dr. J. Fuesch. Mr. Samuel Thal drew 3GF, 5, 7BM, 8BM, 9BM, 10, 12M, 13BM, 17BM, and 18GF to specifications while Mrs. C. D. Morgan drew 1, 3BM, 6BM, 12F, 14, and 18BM. Picture 20 is a reproduction of an unknown original.

ADMINISTRATION

Murray instructed clients to sit with their backs to the clinician presumably to facilitate free association as in early psychoanalysis. Clients are now seated in a convenient manner, either face-to-face across a table or at the corner of a desk. The original directions stressed that the TAT was a test of fantasy, of creative or literary imagination, and as a form of intelligence (Murray, 1943). All twenty cards for males or females were administered in standard one through ten and eleven through twenty order during two separate sessions. Verbatim recording was used. An inquiry was provided for omitted parts of the directions. However, the majority of clients were not Murray's Harvard undergraduates and the directions were soon altered to exclude referents to imagination or intelligence.

Currently, a typical set of directions asks for a story that includes describing the card, explaining what the characters are doing, what they have done in the past or what led to the situation, and what they may do in the future. Feelings and thoughts of the characters are requested. An outcome is also asked for whenever there is one.

Unlike the Rorschach which apparently tolerates varied directions, it does make a difference in the TAT whether or not standard directions are used. Blatant directions with loaded words produce distress in a variety of studies. Similarly, the traditional oral response by an individual client differs markedly from a written response, or from a response dictated into a recorder. Group responses also differ from responses in an individual administration (see Dana, 1982, pp. 113–115 for review).

STIMULUS CHARACTERISTICS

While there are thirty-one cards to be administered in standard order during two sessions, assessors have consistently used short forms composed of selected cards (see Dana, 1982, pp. 120–121, 139–149,

380, 383). The practice of using short forms can only be justified when stimulus and response characteristics are known to be equivalent between the short form and entire set of cards. In fact, whenever the TAT is the only assessment instrument used, it is unwise if not unethical to omit cards in the standard series. However, unless the clinician can anticipate court proceedings involving testimony based on the use of the TAT, a short form as part of a test battery may be acceptable practice. Whenever short forms are used, it is preferable to have cards in their originally numbered order, although Murstein (1963) has suggested on the basis of several studies that stimulus properties overshadow order effects.

There has been considerable agreement among studies using a variety of interpretive criteria that cards of medium ambiguity are most useful in eliciting relevant personality data from college students. Short forms including 2, 3BM, 4, 6 (BM or GF), and 13MF are desirable. In addition, 11, 19, and the blank card 16, are strong contenders in spite of their relative ambiguity for any short form set composed of less than ten cards. Short forms have seldom been developed for psychiatric patients (Newmark & Flouranzano, 1973).

The remainder of this section will discuss each TAT card used for both male and female clients and for male clients, exclusively. Each card description begins with the original Murray (1943) description in parentheses after the card number. Description of the cards used for female clients will be contained in parentheses following the card numbers later in this chapter. For each card, reference is made to Eron (1950; 1953) norms for major themes. Verbatim TAT stories from a twenty-three-year old male college senior with three male sibs from a small town and a working-class family are provided for each card. These stories are compared with stimulus characteristics and normative expectations. Interpretive hypotheses are included that are the equivalent of working notes. While a report is not included due to space limitations, the content of a report can be readily extrapolated from the discussion.

Card 1 (A young boy is contemplating a violin which rests on a table in front of him.)   This picture is the prototype for all achievement dramas, at least within middle-class culture. The violin and learning to play it to whatever criterion is symbolic of achievement in anything. The fact that it is a child in the picture means that clients may project a personal childhood achievement dilemma. The absence of others in the picture permits the client to include early family surroundings, especially as pertinent to the atmosphere of support, indifference, or censure for the child's efforts. A story is expected that relates to achievement. The child plays or does not play the violin, and the reasons for this behavior are usually stated. There is generally both an immediate and long-term consequence of the child's involvement with the violin. Nearly 50 percent of normal males produce aspiration themes while women and hospitalized males are less likely to do so. Parental pressure for achievement for both sexes is a dominant theme. Occupational concern for women, perhaps due to Eron's selected samples, is salient.

In the story that follows, the achievement theme and the parental investment are presented.

> OK. This boy is taking violin lessons and he's been taking them for a couple of weeks and he's tried and tried to get this thing down—and he's realized that this is not for him—and he's pondering how to tell his folks that he's not cut out to be a violinist. And he's pretty right to be worried about it because his parents are not going to be happy when they hear what he has to say.

It should be noted that many stories recognize years or a lifetime of practice as necessary for achievement. Here the decision is made quickly by the child. There is an awareness of responsibility to the parents and an awareness of their feelings. Internalized values and insight in the client may be inferred from such awareness by the character in the story. While there is no active or long-term conflict with parents as a result of the decision, there is anticipation of their negative reaction, even though this prediction does not change the outcome. At another level, the client may be suggesting that conventional achievement of any kind is not for him.

Card 2 (Country scene: In the foreground is a young woman with books in her hand; in the background a man is working in the fields and an older woman is looking on.) The farm scene usually evokes a story concerning family relationships and quality of life. The young girl in the foreground may be leaving home for an independent life with whatever emotions this change entails. One-third of the males assessed focus on occupational concern and aspiration while aspiration is the dominant theme for women. What is being relinquished and the belief in what is coming to pass are salient.

In the example, this card is almost rejected and pressure from the clinician is required to elicit the following story.

> (I don't get any clear sense of what's happening with these people or where they might be headed.) (Wants to go to next card) (? to stretch imagination) I can see man and woman in foreground as maybe newlyweds—woman against tree . . . mother-in-law. Three of them trying to eke out an existence. Woman is schoolteacher, man with horse getting ready to plow this field. Woman against tree looks pretty grim—wondering where their sustenance is going to come from—maybe own a mortgage on their farm or something.

Instead of the usual focus upon the girl in the foreground, the emphasis is on the couple who are designated as newlyweds, a unique label in this instance. The quality of family life is depicted as bleak and marginal. The grimness may stem from turmoil, poor family relationships, lack of love—all potential equivalents of sustenance. Somehow the picture has confused the client and the result is a reversal of the usual relationships perhaps because the client sees himself as mired in the family drama and unable to extricate himself. These hypotheses stem from departures from normative expectations.

Card 3BM (On the floor against a couch is the huddled form of a boy with his head bowed on his right arm. Beside him on the floor is a revolver.) This card is considered to pull for central value, or whatever is sufficiently important to account for the posture of the figure and the implied dysphoric affect. Most stories may be analyzed in this manner, so the central value becomes whatever provided the impetus for suicide or emotional disturbance in normatively high frequency stories. Inclusion or omission of the gun on the floor is indicative of acceptance and/or denial of hostile feelings. The gun may also be (mis)perceived as scissors, knife, or even an innocuous object such as keys. The figure is reported as male or female with equal frequency by males and females and no special interpretation is made from the sex of this figure.

The following sample story labels the condition of the central figure, notes the cause, attributes to others insensitivity and neglect, but accepts ultimate responsibility.

> This is a woman just in existential despair—she's just on the brink of suicide. . . . I don't know why she wants to commit suicide, but she feels like an abject failure, defeated by everything she has tried. She feels nobody has any empathy for situation or true understanding of her internal life. Object on floor is a knife. Weeping against this piece of furniture because she feels deep contempt for herself because she lacks the courage to end her own misery.

In telling this story, the client feels sorry for himself, simultaneously blames others for lack of understanding and himself for conspicuous lack of courage. The intensity of feelings is betrayed by the use of words and phrases like "brink," "abject," and "deep contempt." The story seems to follow from Card 1 in which the hero does not really try to persevere. Here "defeated in everything she has tried" evokes the idea that she has dabbled with life opportunities in search of meaning, probably with notions of some self-fulfilling career objective. While there is anger turned inward and directed out at significant others, these feelings are also dissipated by being intellectualized. As a result, there is a portrait of despair in which the lament is louder than any destructive action so that failure of resolve is experienced once again in an unending cycle of ontological guilt, anger, and self-immolation. These interpretive statements stem from the vividness of language, the intensity of feeling, and the reiteration of existential process. After three stories, there is already an impression of a young man who is enmeshed for personal reasons with family and loved ones. He struggles half-heartedly with vocation as a purveyor of meaning and/or purpose, but is not steadfast either in goal definition or means-end process for reasons as yet undisclosed.

Card 4 (A woman is clutching the shoulders of a man whose face and body are averted as if he were trying to pull away from her.) This card usually evokes themes pertaining to the balance of power in male-female relationships. Attitudes towards oneself and toward the opposite sex are displayed prominently. For males, pressure from partner is the major theme, while women provide themes of succor from partner. However, such themes for women may now differ markedly from these norms of the 1950s. In addition, there are opportunities for a romantic triangle by inclusion of the poster content in the background.

The following male story provides distance from the client and a tongue-in-cheek vision of stereotyped male and female roles.

> This reminds me of a 1940s movie of some sort with swashbuckling hero—Rhett Butler character—Dietrich or somebody saying, "Don't go! Don't go!" "But I have to." Sort of like *High Noon* or something. So he'll go take care of the bad guys coming in on the train and he and she will go off in the sunset together and live happily ever after.

The question of why an honest, sincere, self-searching young man deals with this critical card in such casual terms is raised. The matters portrayed here appear to be of central importance and it is possible to wonder whether or not he feels that relationships and romantic love are beyond his grasp.

Card 5 (A middle-aged woman is standing on the threshold of a half-opened door looking into a room.) This seldom used picture yields themes of curiosity and parental pressure from both sexes. It may also tap attitudes of suspicion and distrust, of parents toward children, and of children toward parents. The central issue concerns what is discovered when the woman opens the door. Since the card is essentially innocuous, themes that are extravagant in presenting a blatant situation are potentially more interpretable than themes more congruent with the neutral picture. The male client provides a neutral story.

OK. This is a lady—a mother—peeking into the parlor where her daughter and her date are necking on the couch. Kind of a comical situation, but mother is not able to see the humor of the situation, but she probably will later on—a few years later on. Right now she'll just tell the kid to go home and she'll speak to her daughter for a few minutes, but it's not going to be a major blow-up.

There are two notable exceptions to expectations here. First, the mother is intruding upon a daughter rather than a son. This reversal is similar to the focus upon a couple in Card 2 rather than the young girl with books in the foreground. The second matter pertains to the understanding of mother—the absence of humor and perspective now is replaced by future understanding. As in Card 1, there is acute awareness and acceptance of parental displeasure over the daughter's behavior.

Card 6BM (A short elderly woman stands with her back turned to a tall young man. The latter is looking downward with a perplexed expression.) Parental pressure and departure from parents are frequent themes while marriage of child, succorance from parents, and aggression occur less often. The mother-son relationship is the primary focus. The emotional reactions to communication or attempted communication, often provide clear evidence of the quality of relationships. The male client again seeks distance in the following story.

This one also makes me think of 1940s era movie. . . . Something where father has died, lost mortgage on house. Mother staring out window saying, "Where will we go? What will we do?" Young man thinking we'll find a way somehow. Man makes good for himself and sends a check to saintly, gray-haired mother. Usually meets a girl behind counter in candy store in process. Even though things seem bleak for them just now, I feel confident that they are going to come out all right.

This story is reminiscent of Card 4. The tragedy is presented by juxtaposing the father's death with a lost mortgage as if to minimize the importance of the father or to relegate him to a financial resource for the family. The happy ending not only includes making good and supporting the mother financially, but also almost gratuitously a girl is introduced to further the fantasy.

Card 7BM (A gray-haired man is looking at a younger man who is sullenly staring into space.) Normatively this card evokes themes of succorance from a father or older man. In addition, the quality of their relationship may suggest attitudes towards authority. The sample story has a succorance theme.

This fellow on the right side with dark hair—looks a little like Jimmy Stewart—Mr. Smith goes to Washington—when Jimmy Stewart is waging a one-man filibuster against a piece of corrupt legislation—been up for forty-eight hours without sleep. Mentor comes and gives me, "Win one for the Gipper speech." Even though looks dragged out, essentially young and healthy, will draw on his resources and support from elder statesman. He'll pull it off because he did in the movie.

While the extravagant tone is similar to earlier stories, the content differs. There is probably identification with ideology of a Jimmy Stewart liberal politician, hence the use of "me." There is balance between external support and inner resources, although the outcome is marred by the reason for success—"because he did it in the movie." The bravado falters because the sources of motivation may be insufficient to the task of implementing idealism. At least there is a doubt concerning his own wherewithal.

Card 8BM *(An adolescent boy looks straight out of the picture. The barrel of a rifle is visible at one side, and in the background is the dim scene of a surgical operation, like a reverie-image.)*   Although the norms suggest that aspiration is a frequent theme, more often there is an interplay of violence directed toward father or a father-surrogate. As in Card 3BM there are opportunities to recognize or deny the gun and the knife, although recognition is more usual here since the stimulus is blatant.

. . . This seems almost surrealistic—sort of an effeminate-looking young boy in foreground seems to be remembering sort of brutal battlefield surgery—doesn't seem to have much of effect on him—remembers it with indifference. Man on table looks to be in exruciating pain even though they hadn't made the incision. Perhaps his father. Father killed in battle—remembers in abstract way what it must have been like for his father to have been killed in battle when he was still young boy or infant.

This is a complex story beginning with the unusual and again gratuitous description of an "effeminate-looking" boy. The indifference of the boy to the trauma and the mention of extreme pain suggest both anger and distance toward father, although the personal pain may be in the remote past. Father has had little impact on his life for many years, but older males (Card 7BM) are seen as helpful and mentors.

Card 9BM *(Four men in overalls are lying on the grass taking it easy.)*   Probably the least frequently used card of the first ten, the range of themes is narrow. While normatively retirement is suggested, a work break with a boy on the periphery who does not quite fit in may be more frequent.

> This is a WPA work team and they've been planting trees all afternoon, taking a little break about three o'clock. Probably been planting trees since about 7 A.M. Probably a jug of iced tea around somewhere out of field of view.

Here expectations are met with a curious precision about time, how long the men have worked, and the nicety of iced tea. The fact of a "WPA" (Works Progress Administration) work team in 1983 suggests a social consciousness and bolsters that hypothesis for Card 7BM.

Card 10 (A young woman's head against a man's shoulder.) Themes of contentment from both sexes are frequent especially in the context of an older couple holding each other closely or dancing and reminiscing about their good life together. Tenderness, sensitivity, and responsivity in a heterosexual context may also occur. However, the male client reverses the age expectations.

> . . . This could be a young couple, just embracing in an intimate moment, or could be a young couple after a moment of tragedy, some disaster, trying to console one another. They're not terribly young—probably late thirties early forties, but seems kinda like an ambiguous picture—I have a hard time deciding what is going on.

It is possible that he does not perceive old people—parents—as having a harmonious relationship and thus younger persons are described. That the picture is difficult and ambiguous questions what is disturbing—the heterosexual intimacy, the young and/or old figures, or the hint of tragedy?

Card 11 (A road skirting a deep chasm between high cliffs. On the road in the distance are obscure figures. Protruding from the rocky wall on one side is the long head and neck of a dragon.) Impersonal aggression is the normative theme. However, the ambiguity of the figures permits either human or animal figures to be recognized. Clients of higher abstract and conceptual intelligence are more likely to discover human figures. Often the figures are fleeing across the bridge to sanctuary with the dragon in pursuit. The embellishment, process, and outcome all provide cues that often pertain to a present life crisis. Expression may be in symbolized form such as a struggle between good and evil. The dragon is an aggressive figure akin to the weapons in Cards 3BM and 8BM. The male client impaired a great distance that is linked to the present by the game situation.

OK. This is a medieval quest. This is a band of journeyers on their way into a castle—swords and sorcery situations—dragon just made a pass at them, trying to get over bridge into cover before dragon makes a second pass. There's a variety of travelers in this band. In addition to the usual knights, elves, I can see a roc and cloak of a magician whose magic is probably going to be critical to the success of the travel.

The client carefully spelled "roc" for the clinician in order to emphasize the significance of this special journeyer. To say that magic is critical to the success of life's voyage is to place a premium on the unknown and unexpected while negating the impact of conventional means-end sequences of events. When juxtaposition is made with the ready abandonment of the drudgery of achievement in Card 1, it is clear that it is not whimsey, laziness, or impulsivity, but merely a matter of belief in the credibility of other routes to desired outcomes.

Card 12M (A young man is lying on a couch with his eyes closed. Leaning over him is the gaunt form of an elderly man, his hand stretched out above the face of the reclining figure.) While hypnotism is the most frequent normative theme, religion, emotional disturbance, and death or illness also occur with some frequency. Stories to this card have been used to predict responses to psychotherapy as well as susceptibility to hypnosis.

OK. This is a physician leaning over a male in his twenties. Physician is recoiling a little bit, just taken hand away from lad's neck where he was feeling his pulse. Just realized boy is not breathing—unexpected—didn't realize that the kid was dead.

Without fanfare, without overstatement, this story describes the loss of faith—in physicians, in psychologists, in authoritarian healers and gurus of all persuasions. The tone is matter-of-fact and the hypothesis is that he has lost faith in conventional goals, conventional explanations, and conventional resolutions to life's problems.

Card 13MF (A young man is standing with downcast head buried in his arm. Behind him is the figure of a woman lying in the bed.) For males guilt, remorse, death, illness, and illicit sex top the list of normative themes while females produce death and/or illness themes more frequently and remorse themes less frequently. There is opportunity also for projection of relationship characteristics and sex-role stereotyped attitudes or behavior. The male client produces an almost conventional story.

. . . OK. I see this being about 6 A.M.—sun's just coming up and the fellow is wiping brow—whew! What a night. And the woman in the bed is still asleep. I think they are probably college students—hardly any furniture in there—bed looks like made by putting your mattress on the floor. This is a fairly strapping young man—can see muscles—pecs—through shirt. These two people have some affection for each other but I don't think their relationship is going to last any length of time.

The departure from conventional storytelling here is the physical description of the young man. The "Whew. What a night!," and the emphasis on physique may constitute a protest that the storyteller is really a lusty, robust male—even macho in the sense of proving or demonstrating male prowess. The other side of this coin, however, is recognition that satisfying a woman sexually (and otherwise as well) is no easy task. The fragility of the relationshsip in this story and the potential independence of affection from sexuality, suggest that in his own perceptions at least, the necessary conditions for an enduring relationship are not present.

Card 14 (The silhouette of a man (or woman) against a bright window. The rest of the picture is totally black.) Frequent themes for both men and women include curiosity and aspiration. There is opportunity for looking out or looking in as well as for accompanying feelings of joy or despair. The silhouette figure may be interpreted as male or female. However, the male client chooses two versions of looking outward.

AH—this could equally well be right at dawn on farm—fellow throws up window and looks out—here's the promise of a new day. I can just about hear all animal noises on a farm. Or else could equally well be fellow in urban setting—city—looking out window at night-time sky. Looking at sky—cold, clear winter's night. First I thought he was standing with foot up on stool—window section—decided he's not by himself in the room—person sitting in chair in foreground—two images have combined to make a single silhouette. (Points to corner of chair and other person's head.) Line of stomach not fall like that. So he's probably sitting up late at night talking to somebody—philosophical meaning of life talk.

Contrasts are presented, contrasts perhaps for himself, vistas on alternative futures, but these perspectives are immediately short-circuited by focus and preoccupation on what is happening in the room. Since these events and the other person are literally conjured up from the dark ink, they serve to forestall any further planning. In addition, since the stimulus does not yield these story components, there is distortion required to produce them. The action has been transferred (again) from a possible means-end sequence to an internal dialogue—

a present problem—a perennial conflict that interferes with planning for the future. The elaborate transition to the conjured figure in the darkness, the combination of images into a single silhouette, and the apparently innocent "philosophical meaning of life talk" strongly suggest the ingredients for something that is actively inhibiting future plans.

Card 15 (A gaunt man with clenched hands is standing among grave-stones.)   Normative themes for both sexes include death and/or illness of partner or peer, religion, or some supernatural event. Additionally, women produce themes of emotional disturbance, loneliness, guilt, and acquisition. In fact, the stimulus is so foreboding that the story should reflect gloom, despondency, or reactive depression. The male client finds distance by evoking an historic fiction writer to personify the central character.

> This makes me think of Charles Dickens—not any particular story. This man is a very rigid, inflexible, austere person. Probably a miser—never really done anybody much harm but has never done much good for anybody either. He's come to visit the grave of a business partner—who's also the only person he had any real dealings with. He's beginning to wonder if he's lived his life in a proper way. I think as a result of this visit that he's going to undergo a character change and turn over a new leaf.

There is a hint of the Scrooge theme, repentance upon confrontation with the grave occupied by the only person "he had any real dealings with." The message is that just getting along is not sufficient for a proper life. Notice the description is not of an evil man, but simply an average citizen who could even be anyone's father. The client wants to achieve a different kind of life, one that makes a difference to others and one that is described in other stories, particularly 7BM. Although there is a hint in his most ebullient and secret fantasy that themes in Cards 4 and 6BM are not as repugnant as their casual presentation suggests.

Card 16 (Blank Card)   (Administered as last card after 20.) This card evokes themes of either the ideal life situation or a current problem. Most stories can be classified in these two categories. Usually the ideal life situation contains either family or loved one sharing some pleasant activity or depicts a person alone contemplating nature or otherwise enjoying some solitude. The male client carefully provides distance by labeling his story as a short story idea.

> OK. (This is—not sure fair or not—short story idea. Can't decide how it's going to come out.) There's this character named Atman

and she's kinda of a maverick—not very conforming kind of person and she's trying to figure out—kinda struggling with questions of theology—whether or not God exists—if exists is good, or even actively evil and she's either training in psychology or undergoing psychological services—haven't decided yet. Keeps coming up against this philosophy that psychologists are always doing things to people saying it is in their own best interests—wonder whether for convenience of perpetrators. Begins to wonder whether that same thought applies to God—because religions say world is made as is because eventually have best result for human beings—really made for human beings or for God and his convenience? Eventually strain and strife of all of her conflicts with psychological establishment leads her to be hospitalized—electro-shock therapy and all sorts of violent things, repugnant to her and person she is being made into. Throws herself out of tall building—commits suicide—when dies discovers she never was person at all—a computer simulation created by team of psychologists to try to solve questions about approaches to therapy. Rationale: More humane than trying out this on flesh and blood people. "What about me? Ethical to use me this way? How many times do I live the life you have made for me just so you can find answers to your questions?" Psychologist says, "As many as it takes."

In fact, this is a capsule presentation of an idea for a short story, but its emergence here at this time suggests strong personal significance in addition to the novelty of testing the idea itself. If the interpretation is focused upon a current problem, then identification of the problem is the first task. The client related that Atman was from the Hindu word for self or ego, so the personal relevance is unmistakable. The central character is female. In Cards 2, 3BM, and 5 there was also some alteration in sex of the character with whom identification is expected. In Card 16 psychologists are manipulating Atman and their motives are suspect. The client—at one level—is impugning the motives of the clinician by suggesting the feedback is of less consequence than the data to include in this chapter. This notion is generalized to a loss of faith in all authorities including God. There is a cynical core to this convoluted tale that begins with the self (Atman), and progresses to include psychologists, the clinician, and ultimately God. The client can be separated from his story by labeling the conflict as obsessive concern with the ramifications of all actions. This hypothesis accounts for the absence of means-end, enduring, goal-oriented behaviors in spite of the requisite intelligence, internalized values, and adequacy of work habits to be a coherent person. In addition, there is a nagging doubt with regard to identity, and the question "Who am I?" is further broken down into sexual identity, work identity, religious identity, and even human identity. Such rumination, even when attenuated by fictional plots that might well become cogent short stories in their own right, does dampen, inhibit, and restrain decision-making in the present and for the future.

Card 17BM (A naked man is clinging to a rope. He is in the act of climbing up or down.)   This card elicits themes of self-esteem, exhibition, competition, and escape. Hidden in these themes are achievement, narcissism, adulation, and physical prowess concerns. The male client provides a usual theme, but one with a personalized and recurrent source of interference.

> Olympics coming up next spring—hard not to think of Olympics. I see it as gymnast training for Olympics—probably worried whether or not they're going to find the steroids in his blood.

This story begins as the normal combination of achievement and/or athletic prowess, but it does not include any future or any outcome. The gymnast apparently becomes bogged down by rumination and the story ends at this point. There is also concern that a secret may be discovered which will vitiate his masculinity and/or his social acceptability.

Card 18BM (A man is clutched from behind by three hands. The figures of his antagonists are invisible.)   While themes of drunkenness predominate, peer succorance, pressure, and emotional disturbance are also frequent. This card is not often used in short form sets. The male client related another movie plot.

> These all make me think of a 1940s movie. Denouement where Edward G. Robinson has been nabbed and police lieutenant is saying, "The gig is up, Rockey" going to take him off to the pokey. Probably standing on roof top in city where he has been chased and there is nowhere left to run.

The distance permits a story without a positive outcome, even though the chief character is probably not an idealized folk-hero for the client. There are none of the extravagant statements present in other renditions of movie plots. This one is serious and it is possible to infer that the storyteller believes there is literally "nowhere to run."

Card 19 (A weird picture of cloud formations overhanging a snow-covered cabin in the country.)   Impersonal aggression is the predominant theme for both sexes. Forces of nature threaten whoever is within the cabin. Contentment within the dwelling is a secondary theme as are invocation of supernatural forces for both sexes. The critical content of these stories has to do with whatever happens within the house and there may be description of family dynamics in response to an external danger. The male client makes the threat into a game and thereby neutralizes it.

> OK. There's a video game called DONKEY KONG* and these little tiny flames that look like spooks chase your character around the screen. Just like the top of his head peeking out from behind. Looks kinda like a snowstorm—igloo—peeking out from behind. Igloo has chimney and a couple of little windows. Might be got tired of being spook—decided to go live on North Pole.

There is a playfulness to this story, a rapid alternation of focus, a lack of sustained effort that results in abandonment of the game. The client has produced a second computer simulation person (Card 16 for the first one) who instead of being trapped in an unending succession of manipulated lives has the option of leaving for distant and unknown places. The transformation of video game flame into "spook" with the capacity for voluntary, self-directed action is noteworthy here. The difference between these two stories is that in Card 16 the grim reality of the client's life is presented—the entrapment of a pseudo-person in unending manipulations by others—while in Card 19 the hope of breaking out of the diurnal ritual appears. Only by assuming control of his own destiny can the client do what he wants to do with his own life.

Card 20 (The dimly illumined figure of a man (or woman) in the dead of night leaning against a lamp post.)   For males the predominant theme is vacillation with economic pressure being secondary. For females, vacillation and loneliness occur with moderate frequency. Themes of waiting for someone or something to happen are also frequent. This card is rarely used on short forms. The male client chooses an ordinary theme but embellishes it.

> OK. This is equally one or two things. Could be Humphrey Bogart hanging out in front of Rick's Place in *Casablanca* or could be Jimmy Stewart leaning against his street lamp in *Harvey* waiting for his rabbit to come visit.

The embellishment is the presence of two movie characters who presumably represent separate but equal sides of the fantasy. The tough honest guy who takes what he wants is contrasted with the idealistic social reformer (see also Card 7BM) who attends an imaginary companion (Card 14) albeit a companion whom he loves and cherishes.

*DONKEY KONG is a trademark and © of Nintendo, 1981.

This section primarily serves to provide relevant detail for the relationships between card stimuli and interpretive hypotheses using one sample of stories. A report follows that was shared with the client.

TAT Report, Male Client

These TAT stories depict a young man with an exacerbated awareness and sensitivity to himself and to others. He is still enmeshed in a family drama containing turmoil, a certain bleak perdurability, and little appreciation for his differentness from other family members. He harbors some anger at his father for being distant and unable to provide him with emotional support and any reaffirmation of his own identity. His love and understanding of family members prevents him from any extrication from the family or his own feelings about them.

He is engaged in a quest for meaning that will enable him to understand who he is. When he implicitly asks, "Who am I?", he is querying with regard to identity—sexual, religious, work, and even human identity. This quest falters because he has experienced a loss of faith and only intermittent and unsteady motivation. He has lost faith in the credibility of conventional goals, conventional explanations, and conventional resolutions to life problems. He has lost faith in the traditional sources of knowledge—both in persons and institutions. As a result of being aware of the great disparity between institutional goals and human needs, he often feels alienated and manipulated in a series of life experiences he cannot control.

His reiterated question "Who am I?" is especially poignant in areas of work and love. He struggles with vocational choice and with the means-end preparation for any career. He dabbles with opportunities and avenues for meaningful occupation that are consonant with his values, ideals, and a creative, unorthodox approach to problem-solving, but he cannot persevere in any sustained direction.

He has a strong inclination toward romantic love and idealized love relationships. He yearns for an enduring relationship with a woman who is intelligent, sensitive, compassionate, and shares his view of the world, but discovers only momentary sexual liaisons and disappointment.

Because he is so attuned to an inner landscape and nurtured by his own fantasy, he wonders if he is insufficiently masculine, perhaps as an explanation for failure to maintain a love relationship with a woman. He experiences an awareness of his own submerged femininity (anima) almost as a secret part of himself that he is hesitant to share with others. He fears not only social censure for being more human than macho and feels incursions upon his self-concept as well. His masculinity is an issue.

While he accepts responsibility (albeit with a little squirming and self-pity), he experiences conflict and paralysis of action as a direct result of his internal dialogue. He knows resolution of his dilemma ultimately requires will (and guts) and voluntary self-initiated, self-directed, and self-sustained actions. However, he cannot act in a self-consistent goal-directed manner in order to affirm individuality, assert integrity, and confirm identity. Instead, he experiences ontological guilt, anger, self-immolation, and a short-circuiting of action. His acute awareness enables him to foreclose on all possible outcomes before they can be translated into behavior. Since knowledge is not sufficient and the sources of the continuing human support which he sorely needs are suspect, he struggles to maintain equilibrium. In this process, he presents himself as an honest, engaging, idealistic person who usually displays good cheer and belief in the positive outcome of his quest. However, when it is hardest to cope with the immensity and apparent futility of his dilemma, he expresses genuine distress in the form of uncontrolled anxiety that sometimes interferes with daily activities.

The client expressed concern about two departures from verbatim recording during the administration of TAT cards. Verbatim recording is the only safeguard for the probity of the data. Clinicians are usually convinced individually that they seldom (if ever) lapse from the professional propriety of this deceptively simple task. Nonetheless, veridical recording often does not occur and in teaching projective techniques, it is helpful for students to have audio and/or video recordings of TAT administrations to compare with their own verbatim recordings.

In Card 7BM the client affirmed that while he recalled an m sound, he did not use the word me which signaled the literal nature of this story for the clinician. Although there are other cues in this story from the idealistic nature of the original movie, this slight variation in recording could have led to accepting a story at face value as being highly personal that did not, in fact, reflect the client's own motives and behaviors.

In Card 14, a potentially more serious difference in perceptions pertained to the client's memory that the two versions were looking out in daytime and looking into the room at night. The difference here is between an either/or construction of alternative themes and a reversal of figure-ground which would document a facile creativity in dealing with card stimuli and an important addition for subsequent interpretation. The likelihood and extent of possibly faulty recording can be evaluated by reexamining the story provided for Card 14.

Finally, a more substantive matter pertaining to the interpretation of Card 16. Remember that the client had a previously formulated plot for a short story that was convenient to relate in this context presumably due to recency and saliency of content. To what extent does this fact of story origin mitigate the interpretive hypotheses? First, the choice of the name, Atman, refers additionally to *essence of youness* so that interpretation has a choice between the gender and self-revelatory implications, or both. Second, and more important, the feelings directed at psychologists (and attributed here as directed toward the clinician as well) were not experienced as emerging from this assessment proceeding, but from a recent suicide of a friend who had been consistently mistreated by the psychology establishment and ultimately was coercively socialized as a mental patient. These memories were still present, raw and unverbalized, persistently nagging at him, flooding him with feelings and unanswered questions. Thus, the choice of story was dictated by his own feelings of confusion and/ or helplessness and by anger at the ostensible failure of area mental health services to prevent a tragedy.

When the client read the report, he denied awareness of anger toward his father, although recognizing occasional anger directed at his mother. He was also concerned with the description "feels alienated and manipulated" and wanted to be clear that he did not experience a conspiracy or personalize his reactions. However, as an antidote for these feelings, he does choose to take issue, to stand up and be heard in jousts with the establishment over matters of ideology, morality, or humanity. In addition, he wanted to affirm that six months after the TAT administration, he is finding an ability to sustain endeavor, particularly in the academic arena, and is experiencing a productive and rewarding semester—the first one in several years.

SCORING

Prior to either scoring or interpretation, some form of coding the raw story data usually occurs. This may be done informally by notes, hypothesis, and themes, or more formally by writing a synopsis or restatement for each story. However, as Shneidman (1954) has indicated in his summary of interpretative methods, there are scoring systems that quantify the story data into psychograms, profiles, ratings, ratios, patterns, and scores to be compared with norms. Frequency and intensity of variables can be obtained. Some of these scoring systems have been used for clinical diagnosis (e.g., Dana, 1959). Scoring systems like Murray (1938), Tomkins (1947), and Henry (1956) are elaborate attempts to sensitize neophyte assessors to the richness of data provided by TAT stories and are valuable reading for this purpose. None of these systems have received any widespread usage for personality description or diagnosis of psychopathology.

INTERPRETATION

Interpretation is based on verbatim recording, a few mechanical steps to organize and render portions of the stories salient, an immersion in the stories by reading and rereading them, and an attitude requiring identification of hypotheses. Essentially, however, TAT interpretation is intuitive and creative. However, it is trained intuition and disciplined creativity. This training consists of a general clinicial exposure to procedures permitting systematic, empirically grounded, and normatively relevant use of stories as data. Prior experience with many clients having told stories to these same picture stimuli is required, but it is the use of implicit normative data within a hypothesis-testing frame of reference that contributes to consensus in interpretation.

Initially, the mechanical steps include a synopsis of each story as it stems from the particular card stimulus. There is subsequent cross-referencing for similar themes, conflicts, persons, settings, etc. Frequencies of occurrence and the particular cards involved are noted. Finally, recording is made of relative emphasis, importance, or personalization of thematic contents.

Each TAT analyst has a set of interpretive guidelines, usually implicit, but which can be applied systematically as a series of questions that are asked of the summarized story data. Several such guidelines will be suggested and will constitute a synthesis of literature and experience with interpretation. These guidelines include congruence of stories with picture stimuli and directions, distance of story content from client life experience, the presence and intensity of conflict, and the literalness of story content.

Congruence with Picture Stimuli

Typical and expected themes, at least for the early 1950s, were noted in the descriptions of separate cards. However, in the absence of published normative thematic data that is representative and of recent origin, departures from expectations are only notable whenever the theme is blatantly discordant with the stimulus, for example, a bland story to Card 13MF for a violent story to Card 5. Infrequent themes may be personally relevant. Some assessors will want to use

Arnold's (1949) classification for themes that include parent-child situations (Cards 1, 2, 3, 6, 7), heterosexual situations (Cards 2, 3, 4, 6, 7, 8, 9, 13, 17, 18), same-sex situations (Cards 5, 9), single-person situations (Cards 11, 12, 14, 15, 16).

Card hypotheses similar to Rorschach plate IV, father-authority, may also be evoked, for example, achievement (cards 1, 14, 17BM), central value (3BM for both sexes), ideal life situation versus present conflict (16), present conflict (11, 19), depression (15), response to psychotherapy (12M), etc. Caution must be exercised in using card hypotheses since only for 3BM and 16 are these hypotheses comparable in credibility to Rorschach plate IV.

Conformity with Directions

The ordinary seven-part directions constitute another framework of implicit normative expectations (Dana, 1959). The construct validity status of ego sufficiency (for review, see Dana & Cunningham, 1983) that embodies adequate representation of these directions in stories suggests that omissions of components of the directions not only relate to personality organization but to adequacy of functioning as well. Application is made by recording the relative conformity with directions across cards and noting what components are omitted by card. For example, if there are no endings in stories from cards stimulating achievement themes or if feeling is omitted from stories to cards relating to one or both parents, relevant hypotheses can be formulated.

Additional violations of directions are found in any attempt, successful or otherwise, to reject a card (for example, Card 2 for the male client herein), inconsistent latencies between card presentation and the beginning of a story (similar to Rorschach reaction times), or in the reactive length of stories across cards.

Distance

Physical, psychological, and geographical distance of the client from the story permits personal content to be revealed and these distance indicators should be related to specific cards. The issue is remoteness from awareness and Tomkins' (1947, pp. 78–82) discussion and Z. A. Piotrowski's (1950) rules should be consulted. While preoccupation with card description may mask genuine drives, Piotrowski has stated that whenever the client and TAT figures are similar, the action in the story is more acceptable. Less acceptable drives occur in stories that contain characters who differ from the client in age, sex, race, or social status. Social attitudes may be directly reflected by the behaviors and personality characteristics of TAT figures who differ from the client.

Conflict

Conflict in TAT stories may be similar across cards or varied from one card to another and may be rated for strength. Whenever conflict is similar and consistent across cards, energy expended in handling the conflict may be inferred from the percentage of cards used that express the same conflict (Tomkins, 1947). When conflicts are dissimilar across cards, but frequent in occurrence, poor functioning and anxiety may be inferred (Z. A. Piotrowski, 1950). In addition, the intensity of conflict or the accompanying emotionality, especially where expression is not congruent with the card demand or card hypothesis, may indicate presence of distress in a single instance.

Literal Story Content

Central to interpretation is the recognition of instances in which story content is considered to be a literal statement of the client's subjective experience and/or life events. It is known that TAT imagery stabilizes over long periods of time and is also correlated with behavior. The problem is to identify the portions of the TAT protocol that can be accepted at face value.

When stories are considered as free associations, then any alteration in the process of storytelling is evidence of personal relevance. Voice inflection, rate of speech, groupings of words, out of place phrases, changes in affect, misplaced concreteness, concurrent behavior, all become indicators.

CASE EXAMPLE

This example contains stories to twenty-one cards including all cards for women plus 3BM which is used for both sexes. The client is a twenty-two-year-old college senior from an upper middle-class family in a small southern city. She has one younger sister. After listening to the directions, she demurred with regard to inclusions of outcomes and with the presentation of Card 1 asked, "What if I have two stories?" This clinician's usual preference to omit any inquiry was not followed here and (?) indicates at what points in the stories requests were made for additional content or specific questions were asked. Table 3–1 presents the verbatim stories and the working notes and includes the original Murray descriptions for the eight cards which were not described earlier.

When the working notes are summarized, some dimensions of the final report become evident. For examples, five cards (1, 2, 5, 7GF, 12F) provide themes relevant to family. There are three references to

Table 3–1 TAT Stories and Working Notes: A College Woman

Card/Story	Working Notes
1. This looks like either wants to learn how to play the violin or he's frustrated—been participating—I can see in his eyes he doesn't hate it—or it could have belonged to someone who was very dear to him.	Either/or, dual themes, suggest quality of thinking—rapid fluctuation of ideas/feelings. Hint of family concern with achievement in past ownership of violin. May want achievement, but it does not happen, at least in context of family concern, therefore, frustration. Use of facial expression as indicant of affect.
2. Well, in one sense, I see this as kinda the development of man: have animal there, beast of burden used to plow fields—man very muscular—woman who is pregnant—development on to this girl who pursues intellectual things—holding the books. She looks like she is reflecting on all this—not sure if she sees herself different from woman who is pregnant—man in the fields. I think she might. All looking in this direction—may be toward future and this is past. Or could be parents—real simple—woman concerned with having babies and man out working—divided by this barrier of rocks because she's different dressed nicely (?) I would say that she's gonna take all this into account—anxious, apprehensive about the future—kinda cradling these books—knowledge—guess she's got that to back her up—guess she's just gonna go out in the world.	"Development of man" initially an intellectualized screen that prevents more personal story. Either/or. "Reflecting" constitutes anxious concern re own continuity, identity with family, especially mother. Not certain she is different from family, but she is isolated from them by barrier. Is barrier something tangible, an event, or is it a personal characteristic? Anxiety extends to personal future. Mother is simple—conventional sex-role stereotyped—she is not. "Cradling" books instead of being "pregnant"/"having babies." Knowledge may be "cradled" for her—handled tenderly, nurtured, loved, supported. Why?
3GF. (A young woman is standing with downcast head, her face covered with her right hand. Her left arm is stretched forward against a wooden door.) This woman—she's really—	"Upset" consistent with picture—use of physical cues. Second theme—religious. Almost fabricates cross. Own mental images are unremittingly vivid. Why "repetence?" For what rea- (continued)

Table 3–1 (continued)

Card/Story	*Working Notes*
she's upset—more than upset—can't exactly think what she's upset about—clutching the door—see muscles in right hand holding her face. Probably would be crying—I can't tell if she's gonna open the door—or just opened the door—and is seeing something that caused her great anxiety and she's turned around . . . also another interpretation might be panels on door form a cross, might be really repenting for what she's done—holding on to this door and her head is down. Also has on a long white dress—sort of formal (?) I don't know. Looks like someone might have died.	son, event, act? Followed by physical description. Death of someone as explanation (not voluntary) for position/upset. No real story, but alternation between story components and use of physical cues which do not necessarily cohere with story.
3BM. Hmm. This girl is either very very tired and she's resting on this bench or she's either contemplating suicide or she's already killed herself, gun under hand—might have dropped it. Not in position for someone who has shot herself—might have tried, threw herself in this position, dropped the gun. Don't know where she would be have a bench like that—have them in churches (?). She looks frustrated—may be she feels she can't do anything about her life situation—can't even kill herself—correlates to one of stories—probably has no control over life as she sees it.	Initially makes blatant stimulus innocuous—defensive, but then deals with suicide/gun theme. Follows intense affect by retreat to description, questions "bench"; again as in 3GF a religious infusion. Has she lost her religion? Frustrated as in Card 1, but here refers to "life situation" that may be beyond control. Use of "correlate" is intellectual support.
4. This woman wants this man's attention and well, she wants it in a physical way—not sure if necessarily sexual—might be because of eyes—half-closed, veiling. He's looking away not looking at anything in picture—fact of picture on wall behind	One theme, repeated. Sexual focus; again physical cues "eyes . . . veiling." Man rejects woman because of "thinking" about another woman/lack of responsiveness. Caring is unrequited. Loss of distance by use of "I."

Table 3–1 (continued)

Card/Story	*Working Notes*
head, he's thinking of another woman . . . I can't even think of situation that could lead up to this. He's not being very responsive to her, not doing it intentionally to get her to act that way. Doesn't care either way— what she does. She obviously cares more about him than he does about her from the picture—but you can't tell. Or think I've decided that she wants some kind of sexual contact with this man. That's why he's turned his head away— thinking of someone else, or doesn't know how to tell her that he doesn't feel the same way.	
5. This woman looks middle-aged, looking into this room, and she's either checking to see whether it's still there, or could be someone in there—past the table— that she's checking on, or they've called her. At first I thought she looked questioning—whatever drew her to the door. Doesn't look like she's gonna go in the room just because of way she's positioned— holding on to knob, looks like she's going to shut the door pretty soon. Not much in there (describes room) flowers don't really go—room looks old and very uninteresting—flowers mean someone goes in there— also a lyre—don't know if old phonograph or piece of furniture with lyre carved on it. Maybe really subtle—all objects in this room, subtle and vague, but part of her past.	Checking on "it"; suspicion and protectiveness. Lapses into card description, physical cues. Hint of family (as in Card 1), life (flowers) among the artifacts (old and uninteresting). Reaffirms family history as subtle and vague.

(continued)

Table 3–1 (continued)

Card/Story	*Working Notes*
6GF. (A young woman sitting on the edge of a sofa looks back over her shoulder at an older man with a pipe in his mouth who seems to be addressing her.) This woman looks like she might be in a bar-nightclub. She's dressed nicely, but yet not dressed immaculately—part of collar button, material over collar—handkerchief in pocket sideways. Kind of leaning—was sitting comfortably before man walked up—either a stranger who thinks a lot of himself— trying to persuade this woman to think a lot of him, too. Looks really comfortable, relaxed, in control of this situation—way he's leaning. Or else he's an old lover of hers—seeing her out— she's kind of surprised—not letting it be known. He's self-assured about the situation, but he's caught her in an awkward position—manipulative—said something to her—she turned around. He's using that to his advantage I think. Hard to say what their relationship was or how long it lasted—she doesn't look like she's a very caring person—at least not when someone approaches her like that. Could be she is youth and he is experienced—looking down on her. She doesn't look like she's very open to his suggestions—might be doing something and he can see right through it because he is experienced and she doesn't like that maybe.	Potential sexual content. Woman rejects self-assured man. Woman is not dressed "immaculately," critical, may be self-critical, or critical of woman who rejects man. Second theme: hides own reaction to ex-lover, tried to catch her off balance, "Manipulative." Woman uncaring under these conditions. Third theme: youth vs. experience. Fears her own transparency to experienced male— perhaps test/assessor; not being genuinely cooperative.
7GF. (An older woman is sitting on a sofa close beside a girl, speaking or reading to her. The girl, who holds a doll in her lap, is look-	Usual story except for cradling doll, rejecting it, rejecting mother, rejecting Bible (religion), rejects being told what to

Table 3–1 (continued)

Card/Story	*Working Notes*
ing away.) This looks like a mother and a daughter. I can't tell what the mother is holding. It looks like a book. Little girl looks like she'd rather be playing—rather be somewhere else. Holding doll—not cradling it—doesn't even want to play with it. Crowded room (furniture). Not giving full attention. Looks like Bible—maybe just doesn't like—some dogmatic type document—looks a little young. Doesn't like having something read to her that she knows she must believe. Mother's hair all the way up on top of head—in place—being restrictive/conservative. Girl's hair hanging wild, loose, out of face. Mother is aggressively trying to keep her attention—get her attention. Little girl very blatant—not interested—doesn't know how to get out of situation. Mother so intent doesn't know she's thinking about something else. Mother's eyes closed, little girl's eyes open—symbolized openmindedness and closemindedness to me.	believe (think). Mother is restrictive/conservative/demanding that child conform/unaware/closeminded. Girl is wild/loose (from mother?)/blatant (not deceptive?), but bound. Symbolism from physical cues.

8GF. (A young woman sits with her chin in her hand looking off into space.) Well, this girl could be posing for an art class. Struck a pose and something draped over chair so students won't draw the chair. Classic pose or could be thinking about something—reminiscing—not analysing it and not longing for it. Might be she's unenergetic—resting her head—might be tired—might be cleaning up her room, but I can't imagine her resting like that—must be posing—either that or so deep in thought can't feel the strain of it.

Posing plus physical description—enjoys center stage? Reminiscence is not analysis/longing or desire. Is "longing" frequent? Second theme: innocuous retreat—"so deep in thought." Though may be powerful, fixating, immobilizing.

(continued)

Table 3–1 (continued)

Card/Story	*Working Notes*
9GF. (A young woman with a magazine and a purse in her hand looks from behind a tree at another young woman in a party dress running along a beach.) (turns card) Well, first of all can't imagine what these two women are doing out—river, trees, rocks—not dressed for outdoors. Lower one looks like she's angry, trying to move fast, dress held up on one side, determined look on face. Other leaning on a tree looking down, might be had an argument— sees how angry other woman is—doesn't know how to deal with it—so irrational and strong. She's moving, too, going to go after her—not going to run—or totally different is that—way it's divided—same woman looking at self; calm on top—life just divided by black edge—looking at self—mild-mannered, somewhat passive— other side of her—exact opposite.	One theme: Physical description—critical—first, then invokes anger in irrational and strong woman (part of herself) versus calm, mild-mannered, somewhat passive person others see. Woman she will become when submerged self is united with present, surface self? "Black edge" is internal equivalent of barrier in story 2.
10. Well, I can't really tell—can't really be sure of their sex— lower one looks like woman but also looks like a man. Top one looks like a man could be a woman. What's going on—not sexual. I think it's affection— holding each other close. Nothing really has happened. I guess just comforting each other. Both got eyes closed. I think both thinking about other one.	Unusual ambivalence re gender of figures. Double denial of homosexual activity. Affection/comfort. Physical cues—thinking—as opposed to sexuality?
11. This looks like prehistoric times—all the rocks and the height of the walls. Well, it could be . . . this dinosaur looks like a phallic symbol—	Prehistoric—great distance. Equation of dinosaur with male sexuality and symbolized intercourse. Is male sexuality dangerous, archaic, primitive,

Table 3–1 (continued)

Card/Story	*Working Notes*
could be might be whole picture symbol of intercourse. Inside is inside of woman. It's vast and there is that one way to enter it which this dinosaur has—whatever the creature is. It's a whole other world in there. Dinosaur didn't expect it, even another little creature in there, too.	obsolete? Preoccupation with own sexuality. Why referent to "even another little creature in there?"
12F. (The portrait of a young woman. A weird old woman with a shawl over her head is grimacing in the background.) Well, this character on left could be man and could be a woman— real androgynous-looking person. Way eyebrow is—almost a smile—thinking about something pleasant. Woman behind is much older, doesn't seem to think about things . . . woman is kinds reproachful society manifestation in androgynous person's mind. Older woman doesn't know enough about it to understand—not very powerful about it—got so many male and female characteristics—so maybe—older one is not very intelligent. Could not say if younger person thinking about future, or older person thinking about when she was young— way positioned—first interpretation.	Sexual identity again confused (as in Card 10), labeled androgynous—physical cue. Older woman may be mother (society, too); negative/reproachful/dull/ not knowledgeable—not understanding. Thought re future does not stimulate any action (in Card 2, apprehensiveness = action).
13MF. Well, woman looks like she's nude. She's in a one-person, single bed. Man looks like he's turned away—sort of anxiety. He's fully dressed. Might be he walked in and saw her undressed. Maybe she wants to have sex with him. Maybe he doesn't want to with her. He's	Immediate—nude woman, anxious male. Woman wants sex, man rejects her. Physical description of card. Misinterpretaion: "touching his leg"—loss of distance. Criticism/bewildered/confused re picture and her interpretation.

(continued)

Table 3–1 (continued)

Card/Story	*Working Notes*

being very dramatic, looks away, putting his hands over his eyes. He's in a dilemma. I can't figure out why the bed is so close to ground. Looks like it's a single bed. Looks like she might be touching his leg with her hand. Might be he's telling her something that he's ashamed of—can't understand why she would be laying there nude if they were having such a serious conversation about something else.

14. Well, this man is looking upward and out this window and it's the only light. It could be symbolic of the future: looking upward, outward, and toward the light. Everything else about him could be dark, vague, ambiguous—window is only outlet to direct, clear, unambiguous situation.

Working Notes: Symbolism: present is dark, vague, ambiguous (in Card 5 past was vague as well as subtle). Only future is direct, clear, unambiguous. What aspect: sexual identity, androgyny?

15. It has on a dress, but I don't think it's a woman . . . in a graveyard, crosses, makes me think of religion and death. Hands on the figure are cuffed together. May be mankind chained to ideas about life and death and religion—Christianity.

Working Notes: Male is "it," has dress, but is not a woman. Religion (Christianity), death now associated with ambiguous sexual identity. Hands "cuffed" together—misinterpretation (see Cards 3GF, 5). What "ideas" result in being cuffed? Perhaps related to sex-role stereotyped activities instead of androgyny. Is she stifled, inhibited in movement, lost freedom (as is the conservative mother in 7GF and reproachful/negative society in 12GF)?

16. If I was going to make a picture—use symbols for all the general flux of things, all perceptions. Probably be just an entangled mess. Symbols for good, evil, knowledge, ignorance,

Working Notes: No people—unusual, infrequent. Symbols are safer? or primary? A Jungian entourage of opposites/dichotomies that are really continuous ("intricate connections"). Juxtaposes "mess" with

Table 3–1 (continued)

Card/Story	*Working Notes*
male and female . . . and love and hate, and warm and cold, mind and body, day and night. Then it would have all sorts of little intricate connectors—couldn't single out any one without having touched all the rest of them. I don't think I've named all symbols. Middle of picture have round symbol—like Platonic ideal of soul—where all these opposites come together. Don't think have a name—this center of picture. Would be some transcendent thing. Probably a mess.	"transcendent thing." Suggests that all her necessary intellectual armormentarium (her bravado, her defense against the world of conventional, middle-class standards, people, parents, etc.) is a "mess," a poor substitute for life, strong emotional attachments to males, to a personal future, etc., and not sufficient.
17GF. (A bridge over water. A female figure leans over the railing. In the background are tall buildings and small figures of men.) This looks like slavery. One guy in charge, all rest humped over carrying big packages of something—fruit or vegetable. Odd because sun is black, yet it is still shining. Might be black because of the slavery. Woman on top of bridge—looking other way—may mean slavery is common knowledge to her or ignoring it—looking into river.	Similar to 11 and 13MF is blatant label, "slavery." Misperception: "sun is black"—deals with paradox plus symbolism. No outcome for woman—looking without acting. She hides in the present tense, doesn't reach out and extrude herself and thus is neither recognized nor understood. Takes her social conscience for granted ("turns away") as part of developmental level.
18GF. (A woman has her hands squeezed around the throat of another woman whom she appears to be pushing backwards across the banister of a stairway.) Again there are two woman. One is really upset—can't see her face—fallen on floor—maybe talking . . . sobbing on floor. Other has picked her up. Disgust in face also compassion—leaning her on staircase. Might be other	Upset has no stated cause—See 3GF where interpersonal cause—death has to be elicited by (?). She does not tell the cause/reason for her distress. However, "disgust" is unusual reaction here to "fallen on floor" unless "fallen" means degraded by behavior/ideation that is unacceptable. Disgust is moderated by "compassion." No outcome—immobilized in present—"just looking at her."

(continued)

Table 3–1 (continued)

Card/Story	*Working Notes*
woman just really upset about something—really in pitiful state—other woman doesn't know what to do just looking at her.	
19. Either child's drawing of house . . . in a snow storm—or a submarine—or kinda looks like the Loch Ness monster, or a whale. If a house, there's a glow around the windows—kinda like eyes—inside very warm—outside it's cold, wind blowing. Looks like a dream image—not very well defined, sky got all those other objects (?) I think they'd be having a pleasant time—two or three people—sitting and talking—glad to be inside together because so windy and cold—almost scary.	Many stories—avoids house, but returns to it. Feeling reaction. Forced into house by assessor (?), finds three persons in it—unusual unless labeled as family. Avoids intimacy/family dynamics. She chooses not to be revealing, but wonder who people are, etc.
20. This looks like a soldier overseas standing under a street lamp—maybe in London—looks foggy. He's reflecting or thinking—it's not cold. He's just casually leaning. He's not waiting for anyone, looking for anyone. Maybe had a couple of beers, just walking around the street, just stopped to think.	Extended picture description—hero is alone, does not wait for anyone. Thinking may be more important (safer?) than people.

religion (3BM, 7GF, 15). Heterosexuality occurs in five stories (4, 6GF, 8GF, 11, 13MF), but unsureness regarding gender of TAT figures is found in three stories (10, 12F, 15). Frustration occurs twice (1, 3BM) and leads to lack of hate or follows a suicide attempt. Perturbation and/or anxiety in female (3GF) and in male (13MF), upset (18GF) in fallen female while deep thought is insulating (8GF), and thinking (19) satisfies aloneness. There is also anger (9GF), affection (10), and disgust plus compassion (18GF). Almost all stories have physical cues noted and used to account for behaviors and/or feelings. Explicit symbolism occurs in at least eight stories. Misperceptions are found in five stories: cross (3GF), lyre (5), touching his leg (13MF), hands cuffed (15), and black sun (17GF).

These frequencies are used to suggest relative importance of content. Family and sexual issues (heterosexuality and sexual identity) are primary. However, feeling states occur only infrequently while many unusual misperceptions are present and physical cues and symbolism are omnipresent. Almost all stories have two themes (exceptions are 4 and 9GF). The report should reflect all of these frequencies, consider their relevance and meaning, and try to sort out the thought processes, life experiences, and fantasies contributing to these TAT stories. This is a more complex set of stories than the other two sets contained in this chapter.

TAT Report, Female Client

In consenting to this TAT assessment and feedback you were curious, almost intrigued by the possibility of genuine self-scrutiny, but nonetheless your usual stance is to be somewhat guarded with other persons and to not reveal your emotions and reactions easily (as the woman in 6GF). As a result, few people know you well and intimately. You entered this situation nondefensively with no intention to dissemble or withhold yourself. However, the use of symbolism, the creative (albeit highly personal) misinterpretations or misperceptions of card stimuli, and the complexity of themes do provide some protection and this formidable intellectual display may serve to distance you from other persons. Thus, while you were comfortable during the assessment process, you did not really anticipate being understood.

You are still in process of emancipation from family, but it is not an easy transition in spite of long-standing differences between your values and behaviors and their expectations for you. It appears you are emerging from a family that has clear expectations for children, close working relationships, and a mother, especially, who has been a strong influence on your life. Your mother is depicted in these stories as family and child preoccupied. Your mother may share some of the characteristics of mothers in your stories: religious, conservative, dogmatic, restrictive, dominant, even suspicious, and to use your own word, close-minded. In your stories, the mother also symbolized society with reproachful and negative attitudes toward you, your behavior, and your differences.

While you feel frustrated by demands and/or expectations from family and recognize their waning power over you—especially for conformity to a middle-class lifestyle, conventionality, religiosity, and sex-role stereotypy, this is not the major source of concern. Rather, it is the person you are becoming that is the major focus of your attention, energy, and apprehensiveness. You want to become whole in the sense of putting submerged parts of your identity together. You want to integrate strength that is expressed in capacity for anger and irrationality with calmness, mild manners, and passivity. You would like to be able to be truly androgynous—able to express equally female and male archetypes in your behavior.

Sexuality is part of this internal pressure toward an androgynous lifestyle. Your sexual needs are strong. You see yourself as capable of being wild and even loose, and yet, you are critical (or ambivalent) toward a woman who actively looks for sex. In a sense, attention and sexual attention from males have not been clearly distinguished. However, you have had some rejection experiences with men who cared less than you did. As a result there is some derogation of males and male sexuality as if to suggest that—ultimately—males may be unnecessary for your sexual satisfaction and well-being.

However, you are remarkably uneasy about any transition toward androgyny. You deny active homosexuality and express disgust and compassion for a fallen woman. The result of this turmoil is crisis in the present, a muddle in which books are substituted for babies, for proper (expected) sex-role identity, and an intellectual sanctuary is erected to permit you control of your own thought processes and hence of your own life. But the present is dark, vague, ambiguous, even a mess while you have pious hopes that in the future you will be direct, clear, and unambiguous in your sexual identity.

Sometimes you are so deep in thought as to be oblivious of your surroundings (internal and external), and to even accept aloneness. You have been asking persistent questions about yourself that invade consciousness—questions pertaining to identity, sexuality, future—and are immobilizing. Some experience is intellectualized and you hope your intelligence will suffice and prevail and even substitute for genuine intimacy. Affection, sexuality, engagement of curiosity, and especially intellectual pursuits have become substitutes for intimacy and development of long-standing relationships. Nonetheless, at some level you do label this mess, this panoply of intellect, of symbol, of personal understandings as deficient and are aware that there can be no substitutes for loving, intimate, enduring relationships.

Some of this interpretation is dramatized and overstated in the attempt to capture the quality of experience. Nonetheless, the consequences of divesting yourself of a valuable family heritage in order to be a person in your own right—one who is whole and human and uses her intellect in constructive, growth-oriented ways—is certainly your preoccupation. There is no hint in these stories of what the future will bring since you are still looking over your shoulder at a subtle, vague, and confusing past while you attempt to forge a meaningful identity in the present.

During the feedback hours, the client was intent upon understanding the logic of the inference process as expressed in the working notes. She described the report as "very accurate," cited particular contents as examples, and did not take exception to any interpretive statement.

CROSS-CULTURAL TAT USE

The use of projective techniques with persons who are culturally different has a history in anthropological research (Lindzey, 1961). There was hope that the TAT, especially with modified pictures, would have equivalent impact on persons from various cultures and provide an adequate sample of personality data because of universal psychological determinants (Holtzman, 1980). However, provision of special cards for minority populations (e.g., Henry, 1947 for Navajos; Thompson, 1949 for Blacks) while necessary for easier identification with figures and contexts is not sufficient without special assessor knowledge and skills.

Sundberg and Gonzales (1981) have stated that the clinician should have considerable general knowledge about the client's culture, be aware of culture-related aspects of the assessor role and instruments, and have some special skills for addressing common culture-related behaviors. These kinds of learning are extraordinarily difficult for white middle-class assessors since most clinical programs do not provide adequate training. As a result, responsible assessors providing assessment services to minority populations are ethically obligated to avail themselves of information and special skills. The effect of not having an adequate perspective on the client's culture and the effect of the clinician's technology as applied to culturally different persons has been pathologization, caricature, and dehumanization of minority persons.

Since minority persons often expect the worst possible outcome from assessment and/or intervention provided by a white middle-class clinician, there is always a specific relationship issue that potentially complicates the service and is based upon the history of cross-cultural contact. For examples, native Americans may bring with them to assessment an implicit knowledge that genocide has been at issue historically while blacks bring residuals from slavery and economic exploitation. Thus, in addition to cultural differences, there are these less tangible issues that may be addressed by the attitude of assessor toward the client and by the quality of the climate created for the projective assessment.

As an example of the minimum background for the example to follow, this clinician had several summers of assessment experience with Sioux Indians for clinical and research purposes using intelligence and personality tests. Moreover, there had been time for getting to know Sioux people in a variety of social settings. Ethnographies and other tribe-relevant materials had been examined carefully. More specifically, several informal conversations with the client had preceded asking for her cooperation. The rule here is to relate to the client as a person first and at any available opportunity prior to assessment. Native Americans, Blacks, and Chicanos are less immediately task-oriented and willingly agree to assessment and/or intervention on the basis of the relationship rather than initial intrinsic interest (Gibbs, 1980; Roll, Millen & Martinez, 1980). When the assessment session begins, it is helpful to socialize before presenting test materials and to avoid direct eye contact at the onset. Expect slow response times and be prepared for the causal presence of other adults and children even in a professional agency setting. Once assessment is completed, time should be available for more talk, especially conversation that is related to the client's own life.

A TAT EXAMPLE

This TAT interpretation is based on stories obtained from a thirty-three-year-old Navajo-Sioux woman who is the eldest of four children raised by grandparents in a medium-sized midwestern city. She has also lived on two reservations and in several major cities in different parts of the country. She is married, employed by a mental health facility serving native Americans, and has three children. She completed high school and started junior college and beautician school. The TAT stories were obtained soon after a trip to a nearby city, an exciting fun-filled junket with a co-worker, and some of the let down experienced in the return to more mundane activities is apparent in these stories.

The TAT stories and working notes follow in table form to conserve space (Table 3–2). When these working notes are organized, ten stories have themes from movies or books (4, 6GF, 9GF, 11, 12F, 14, 15, 17GF, 18GF, 20), four stories contain themes of suffering, death, sorrow (3BM, 3GF, 8GF, 13), three stories contain grandparents or grandmother (5, 7GF, 10), and two stories demonstrate ambivalence (1, 2).

Table 3–2 TAT Stories and Working Notes: An American Indian Woman

Card/Story	*Working Notes*
1. (What does this look like?) Looks like a little boy looking at a violin. He doesn't look too happy about it. I don't know. (Directions repeated) Looks like he wants to play the violin—other side—looking at violin and just can't play it—wants to and doesn't want to—maybe thinking to self if he really tries he can play it. (Enough? Or do you want more?) (Continue spontaneously) Either taking lessons and can't master it or looking at violin wanting to play it—just sitting there wishing that he could—dreaming about him being one of those guys that really play real good.	Cautious repetition of directions to provide more structure. Very important to do what is expected. Card description and immediate brief emotional reaction, then elaboration. Ambivalent about achievement and own abilities. Does not achieve and uses fantasy-wish fulfillment. No future included.
2. That looks like a young girl, father, mother and background. Her mother looks pregnant—looks peaceful and happy. She doesn't want that kind of life—probably want to learn more—go on to school or college—got back turned to her father and mother. (That's about it.)	Card description. Siblings. Pregnancy associated with good feelings—contentment in being woman and mother. Rejects family lifestyle but does not leave, wants different life but cannot have it. No future—just desire. No good communication with parents—her choice.
3GF. That is a woman and she's not happy about something. Looks like she's in a lot of pain—hurts a lot. Looks like something on side—scissors or knife or something. Only way out—then couldn't go through with it—sitting there crying.	Pain-suicide solution not feasible. Hurt without surcease, without behavioral solution. Can only suffer and hurt, cannot avoid life.
3GF. Now this looks like a person just came through the door and she must be ashamed or something or something must have hurt her—crying—or got something in eye (laughs) or maybe somebody died that's what it looks like—somebody died and figure that she's feeling bad about.	Responsive to social pressure, sense of humor, tries to make light of tragedy but death must be dealt with and pain maybe experienced. Reaction to loss is internalization—solitude. Maybe heard going to her bedroom to figure out death—and that person.

(continued)

Table 3–2 (continued)

Card/Story	*Working Notes*
4. This looks like Gary Cooper movie—I don't know which movie though—then again looks like man that wants to do something and woman is holding him back. (That's about it.) Does look like Gary Cooper though and Ida Lupino.	More description: labeling. No outcome in male-female relations just stasis in present.
5. This reminds me of my grandma—coming in—tell us kids to go to bed. Then again reminds me of my mother when I had a boyfriend coming over—every now and then peek—to see if they are doing anything—peek in—check up on me.	Grandmother first influence in early life. Mother is controlling, suspicious.
6GF. Those look like old movie characters—seems like he's asking her some question and she's sorta drawing back—either that or looks like she's just been accused of something. He looks like a lawyer. Might be a movie where he is trying to find out if she had anything to do with murder. (That's all.)	Movie: description, murder as theme, accusatory.
7GF. That reminds me of grandmother! Playing dolls—got that doll in her hand. Looks like grandma trying to tell her how she should raise her baby—when she grows up. (My grandma did a lot of that—tell me how to raise babies and where they came from. My grandma did that—my mother didn't tell me that stuff.)	Grandmother instructs—very much personalized—contrast to mother.
8GF. That looks like a poor, married woman that's bored and just staring out the window (laughs) thinking of how things might have been—only if—for a lot of reasons. Either that or she's daydreaming about something	Poor—feels sorry for herself, but self-perspective in laughter. Nostalgia, romanticization, fantasy, daydream as substitute for empty existence.

Table 3–2 (continued)

Card/Story	*Working Notes*
that happened to her that she was happy about.	
9GF. (LP) (Geez) (Can I say it just looks like two women running to something?) Reminds me of a movie—don't know what the name of the movie is. (That's all I can think about this.) Maybe a boat just came in.	Movie: excitement-seeking, running toward and running away from. Wish fulfillment.
10. That looks like my grandma and grandpa—cause they're together for sixty-one years now still alive—always together. (That's all.) They love each other—they're old—either old or they're dancing. (Raised me until I was about eleven.)	Venerates age and own grandparents. Personalized (7GF)
11. That looks like a monster movie and some—what is name—Gargoyles or something like that—monster coming out of its hole—another monster on ledge—old monster movie—cause they don't make them anymore.	Movie: sheer threat without outcome.
12GF. That reminds me of Snow White and Seven Dwarfs. Older woman in back looks like the witch—looks evil—don't look very nice. Other woman looks like Snow White. (She don't look anything like my grandma.)	Movie: evil and personalization (loss of distance) and clear distinctions—dichotomous thinking.
13MF. (LP) Well, there's a naked lady laying there. There's this guy but he's got his clothes on. Maybe he came home and found his wife drunk and he feels bad for her being drunk. Either that or he's just killed her.	Sympathy with drunkenness, atypical theme, or murder. Drunkenness is frequent and forgiven on reservation.
14. That reminds me of a book I read—I read a lot of books. In	Personalization—books as escape. Solace for loneliness is (continued)

Table 3–2 (continued)

Card/Story	*Working Notes*
Italy—gone there to get training in art—peeking out at night—because he misses the United States—thinking about Big Apple, Hot Dogs, Baseball— probably his family and his friends. Then again he could be saying to himself, Italy is really a pretty place—look at street lights and water.	nostalgia and a sensuous enjoyment of immediate present.
15. Oh, reminds me of Christmas Carol—what's his name— Scrooge—graveyard. He looks evil. That's about it. Then again he might be a poor old man who is lonesome for someone who just died—probably wishes he was with them because he looks miserable.	Story: evil—either/or—two stories but what passes for evil is only someone lonesome and miserable.
16. I'd like to see real pretty mountains—like in Arizona—sand and desert, mountains and trees and a stream. I could just smell it—just animals and kids playing. Everything nice and clean. Like anymore all of the pictures you have—sorta wish it could be like it was a long time ago before all this civilization came, I guess. Everything was nice and clean—no bottles, no cars, nothing. When life was just simple—you see a house, hogan, teepee, whatever, no signs, beer bottles, Pampers. Kids playing, happy, everybody doing their own thing—father working in garden, mother—something. That's about it.	Ultimate wish-fulfillment: land is source for family-nostalgia for earlier times—with clean and simpler life. Theme: things were better in good old days. Nostalgia for Arizona—for Navajos.
17GF. (Tell a story about this?) This sorta reminds me of that one movie—*Escape from New York*—cause its got a big wall. Can't make up no story about	Movie: escape/suicide. Equivalent themes.

Table 3–2 (continued)

Card/Story	*Working Notes*
this—just plain. There's this guy—looks like he's waiting for this girl to come down. Maybe she's running off from someplace and they're gonna escape. Then again it looks like a girl standing on a bridge looking over—may be she wants to jump.	
18GF. This don't look like anything— except for woman that collapsed or something—other woman trying to help her, see if she's alright. Reminds me of movie— *Gone with the Wind*. Scarlet taking care of her—woman fainted, sick, or something.	Movie: helpful-non-judgmental—fainted or sick.
19. This looks like it's in Alaska— snowy—it's a blizzard. Looks like hogan—Navajo hogan in a way. That's it. I could look at it longer and longer and say something evil is trying to creep up on house (?). I don't know— probably like a big monster story—eat them up—or maybe get possessed by evil spirits. First guess—hogan in wintertime—something evil trying to get it, take over. Navajos are really superstitious.	Navajo origins: ambivalence. Hogan in Alaska not seen as inconsistent. She is also superstitious. Evil spirits are equivalent to being consumed/destroyed.
20. This reminds me of Thin Man movie—guy always standing on street and theme song comes on. That's all (repeats). He walks cross the street, stands in doorway, lights up a cigarette, looks into a camera, and they say "Thin Man" (Hams it up).	Loner tries to embellish the present.

TAT Report

Ms. C approached the story-telling cautiously, wanting to please and to do it exactly the right way. Life as experienced is extraordinarily difficult. Suffering and pain, hurt, alcohol, murder, death are everyday occurrences. Life can also be boring and lacking in excitement. Pleasant experiences are infrequent. She is ambivalent regarding her own ability and likelihood of achievement. She is also ambivalent regarding where she belongs—with her family or away from her family, on the reservation or elsewhere. She is literally frozen in day-to-day activities and can see little change over time. While she has a ready sense of humor, compassion for others and perspective on her life situation, she sometimes feels sorry for herself and uses fantasy to remove herself from the daily events of her life. Books and movies provide nourishment, but the salient content of these escapist activities is remarkably similar to her own life experiences: Themes of being bogged down in the present, threats, murder, sickness, and evil. She honors her grandparents as models for human relationships involving love, devotion, and caring for others. She imagines being like her grandmother, growing old, and experiencing the pleasure of her grandchildren. An ideal life for her constitutes a family in a rural setting before "all this civilization came." There is nostalgia but no real hope for change or surcease from the pain of living. She endures with good humor and good feelings for others, but she aches for a daily life that contains more than work, tragedy, and escapes into fantasy.

During the feedback process Ms. C expressed discomfort about the report. First, she noted that most of the pictures seemed designed to yield negative emotions and did not present scenes that are particularly relevant for native Americans. Second, she felt that there was some overstatement in the report. For example, her own life has not been "extraordinarily difficult." She had a good family life with the exception of alcoholism in the family. Nor are pleasant experiences necessarily infrequent. She cites time spent with her children, work, gardening, and visiting as examples of pleasant everyday experiences. In addition, her exposure as a counselor and mental health worker to the tragedy in human life may have served to select negative experiences for inclusion in these stories.

It should be emphasized, however, that reservation life is characteristically punctuated by a high incidence of the kinds of negative events occurring in her stories and reports of stress by many persons on this same reservation consistently emphasize an extraordinary concatenation of negative life experiences (Dana, Hornby & Hoffmann, 1984). Finally, she demurs regarding the final sentence in the report suggesting she desires more from life than work, tragedy, and escapist fantasy. Here the overstatement in the report may approach distortion because, in fact, her life is more tranquil and more rewarding than is typical for this reservation.

ASSETS AND LIABILITIES

The TAT provides a sample of oral behavior—storytelling—that is focused, time-limited, repetitive across picture stimuli, and structured by directions. The protocol data are presumed to provide an adequate representation of personality contents. However, these contents are also responsive to culture, the clinician, and the purpose for assessment.

Competent interpretation of the TAT requires an adequate sample of personality data from use of the entire set of Murray cards administered in standard order and recorded verbatim or from a short form set of cards administered as part of a test battery. An alternative set of pictures designed to provide more systematic representation of emotional tone, action, and energy levels is now available (Ritzler, Sharkey & Chudy, 1980).

The TAT is a more difficult instrument than the Rorschach to interpret competently due to the absence of consensual scoring and consequent vulnerability to eisegesis (i.e., faulty interpretation via projection of clinician-related contents, see Dana, 1966) that results from subjective approaches to interpretation. Interpretation requires caution, an adequate time commitment, and a systematic approach that includes feedback from clients as well as from more experienced assessors (Dana, 1982). Formal training for use of the TAT is generally inadequate (for a notable exception, see Coché, 1982), and requires supplementation by recognition that the logic of the clinical method as such for analysis of personality data (e.g., Rapaport, 1945) has relevance equal to the sensitization acquired from immersion in formal scoring systems (e.g., Henry, 1956; Murray, 1938; Tomkins, 1947).

The TAT is useful for personality description and for psychodiagnosis. Shneidman (1954) synthesized sixteen approaches to interpretation and found that 14.5 percent of the 802 concepts and statements contained in reports from one set of TAT stories were related to symptoms, diagnoses, etiology while the remainder of the content was germane to personality description. The personality areas elucidated were affects, feelings, emotions (13 percent), personality defenses and mechanisms (12 percent), interpersonal and object relations (12 percent), sexual thoughts and behavior (9 percent), and outlook, attitudes, beliefs (8 percent).

Interpretation of TAT records from culturally-different minority clients must be contextualized in a knowledge of the particular culture as well as those interactive social role/social etiquette behaviors that are specific to the assessment setting. Attention to ethical issues inherent in assessment of these persons is imperative (Sue, 1983).

SUMMARY

The TAT continues to be frequently used in assessment practice and is third among the top twenty tests in number of research publications, following the Rorschach and the Minnesota Multiphasic Personality Inventory (Buros, 1978). The major limitations of the TAT are unsystematic card stimuli, lack of standard directions and administration procedures, use of various short forms, an absence of consensual scoring, and a paucity of careful training for interpretation. These are formidable liabilities and it is only the potential richness of these data for personality research and intensive case study that sustains the TAT as a major projective technique.

The TAT does rival the Rorschach for description of personality. Such description is useful for differential diagnosis, planning for conventional long-term psychotherapy, and facilitating care of individual patients in medical settings. Sets of TAT-like cards designed for populations specified by age, minority status, or special condition will continue to be used since such cards acknowledge the impact of relevant card stimuli and make for easier identification with figures and settings.

In order for the TAT to become more competently used, a scoring system similar to the Rorschach that adequately and simply codes the response process is mandatory. Since the TAT protocol/response is a combination of structure and content, the fact that such scoring has not been accomplished is probably due to disinterest rather than magnitude of task. The immediate future of personality assessment lies in the development and validation of specific instruments with limited measurement purposes (Dana, in press). Such instruments will dovetail with and be predictive of success with particular interventions and be limited for use with carefully defined populations of medical or psychiatric patients and to segments of the general population presenting specific behavior problems. The TAT, as it has been used historically, occupies only a very small portion of this new assessment spectrum. TAT usage that is directed toward clearly articulated assessment purposes, preferably with a combination of objective and subjective modes of interpretation, should survive in the 1980s. The key to survival of the TAT, however, lies in the development of an empirical base that will document specific assessment purposes.

REFERENCES

Arnold, M. B. (1949). A demonstration analysis of the TAT in a clinical setting. *Journal of Abnormal and Social Psychology, 44,* 97–111.

Buros, O. K. (Ed.). (1978). *Mental measurements yearbook.* Highland Park, NJ: Gryphon Press.

Coché, E. (1982, March). *The structured use of the Thematic Apperception Test.* Workshop presented at the meeting of the Society for Personality Assessment, Tampa, FL.

Dana, R. H. (1959). Proposal for objective scoring of the TAT. *Perceptual and Motor Skills, 10,* 27–43.

Dana, R. H. (1966). Eisegesis and assessment. *Journal of Projective Techniques and Personality Assessment, 30,* 215–222.

Dana, R. H. (1968). Thematic techniques and clinical practice. *Journal of Projective Techniques and Personality Assessment, 32,* 204–214.

Dana, R. H. (1982). *A human science model for personality assessment with projective techniques.* Springfield, IL: Charles C Thomas, publisher.

Dana, R. H. (in press). Personality assessment: Practice and teaching for the next decade. *Journal of Personality Assessment.*

Dana, R. H., & Cunningham, K. M. (1983). Convergent validity of Rorschach and Thematic Apperception Test ego strength measures. *Perceptual and Motor Skills, 57,* 1101–1102.

Dana, R. H., Hornby, R., & Hoffmann, T. (1984). The Rosebud Sioux: Personality assessment using local normative data. *White Cloud Journal, 3*(2), 19–25.

Eron, L. D. (1950). A normative study of the Thematic Apperception Test. *Psychological Monographs, 64* (9, Whole No. 315).

Eron, L. D. (1953). Reponses of women to the Thematic Apperception Test. *Journal of Consulting Psychology, 17,* 269–282.

Gibbs, J. T. (1980). The interpersonal orientation in mental health consultation: Toward a model of ethnic variations in consultation. *Journal of Community Psychology, 8,* 195–207.

Henry, W. E. (1947). The Thematic Apperception Test in the study of culture-personality relations. *Genetic Psychology Monographs, 35,* 3–135.

Henry, W. E. (1956). *The analysis of fantasy.* New York: John Wiley & Sons, Inc.

Holtzman, W. H. (1980). Projective techniques. In H. C. Triandis and J. W. Berry (Eds.), *Handbook of cross-cultural psychology.* (Volume 2). Boston: Allyn and Bacon, Inc.

Klopfer, W. G., & Taulbee, E. S. (1976). Projective tests. In M. R. Rosenzweig and L. W. Porter (Eds.), *Annual Review of Psychology, 17,* 543–567.

Lindzey, G. (1961). *Projective techniques and cross-cultural research.* New York: Appleton-Century-Crofts.

Morgan, C. D., & Murray, H. A. (1935). A method for investigating fantasies. *AMA Archives of Neurology and Psychiatry, 34,* 389–406.

Murray, H. A. (1938). *Explorations in personality.* New York: Oxford University Press, Inc.

Murray, H. A. (1943). *Thematic Apperception Test manual.* Cambridge, MA: Harvard University Press.

Murstein, B. I. (1963). *Theory and research in projective techniques.* New York: John Wiley & Sons, Inc.

Newmark, C. S., & Flouranzano, F. (1977). Replication of an empirically derived TAT set with hospitalized psychiatric patients. *Journal of Personality Assessment, 37,* 340–341.

Piotrowski, C., & Keller, J. W. (in press). Psychodiagnostic testing in APA-approved clinical psychology programs. *Professional Psychology.*

Piotrowski, Z. A. (1950). A new evaluation of the Thematic Apperception Test. *Psychoanalytic Review, 37,* 101–127.

Rapaport, D. (1945). *Diagnostic psychological testing.* (Vol. II). Chicago: Year Book Medical Publishers, Inc.

Ritzler, B. A., Sharkey, K. J., & Chudy, J. F. (1980). A comprehensive projective alternative to the TAT. *Journal of Personality Assessment, 44,* 358–367.

Roll, S., Millen, L., & Martinez, R. (1980). Common errors in psychotherapy with Chicanos: Extrapolations from research and clinical experience. *Psychotherapy: Theory, Research, and Practice, 17,* 158–168.

Shneidman, E. S. (Ed.). (1951). *Thematic test analysis.* New York: Grune & Stratton, Inc.

Sue, S. (1983). Ethnic minority issues in psychology. *American Psychologist, 38,* 583–592.

Sundberg, N. D., & Gonzales, L. R. (1981). Cross-cultural and cross-ethnic assessment: Overview and issues. In P. McReynolds (Ed.), *Advances in psychological assessment.* (Vol. 5). San Francisco: Jossey-Bass Inc., Publishers.

Thompson, C. E. (1949). The Thompson modification of the Thematic Apperception Test. *Rorschach Research Exchange and Journal of Projective Techniques, 13,* 469–478.

Tomkins, S. S. (1947). *The Thematic Apperception Test.* New York: Grune & Stratton, Inc.

Wade, T. C., Baker, T. B., Morton, T. L., & Baker, L. J. (1978). The status of psychological testing in clinical psychology: Relationships between test use and professional activities and orientations. *Journal of Personality Assessment, 42,* 3–11.

4

The House-Tree-
Person Test*

Emanuel F. Hammer

The House-Tree-Person Projective Drawing Technique In the drawing of a house, a tree, and a person of each sex (the H-T-P Test) it is the client's inner view of himself or herself and the environment, the things considered important, and those items emphasized and those neglected that are of interest to the clinician. Symbolically, potent concepts such as house, tree, and person are saturated with the emotional and ideational experiences associated with the personality's development, and the drawing of these images compel projection on the part of the drawer.

*Material for this chapter is an extraction and update from two earlier Hammer presentations, namely: *The Clinical Application of Projective Drawings,* 1958, 1980, courtesy of Charles C Thomas, Publisher, Springfield, Illinois, and a chapter contributed to Buck, J. N., *The House-Tree-Person Technique: Revised Manual,* Copyright 1966, 1970 by Western Psychological Services. Reprinted and adapted by permission of Western Psychological Services, 12031 Wilshire Boulevard, Los Angeles, CA 90025.

Administration The H-T-P taps the stream of personality as it floods the area of artistic creativity. Certain restrictions have been placed upon completely free expression in the interest of standardization. The same concepts, for example, are requested from each subject, on the same size paper, with similar materials. A number-two pencil with eraser is employed on a four-page form sheet of white paper, each page 7 by 8½ inches in size (Buck, 1948). Only one surface is exposed at a time to the subject. The drawing of a house is requested with the longer axis of the sheet placed horizontally before the subject, and his drawings of a tree and person of each sex in turn are then obtained on separate sides with the longer axis the vertical way.

The subject is asked to draw as good a house (and later tree and persons) as possible. The subject is instructed to draw any house, erase as much as necessary, and take as much time as needed. The pencil and the pencil drawings are then taken away, crayons are substituted, and a chromatic set of drawings of a house, tree, and person of each sex is obtained. The subject is allowed to use the crayons in any way, as few or as many as desired, to shade in or draw only the outline as preferred, and all questions are handled non-directively.

THE PROJECTIVE ASPECTS OF THE HOUSE-TREE-PERSON DRAWINGS

Traditionally, a clinical technique qualifies as a projective device if it presents the subject with a stimulus or series of stimuli, either so unstructured or so ambiguous that their meaning for the subject must come, in part, from within himself or herself.

The structuring involved in asking the subject to draw a house, a tree, and a person is more ambiguous than one might think at first. Although the subject is asked to draw a house, a tree and a person, specifications are not provided. No clue is given from the examiner, it is from within the subject that the response flows: the size, type, placement or presentation of the house; kind, age, size, placement, or presentation of the tree; or sex, facial expression, body stance, age, race, size, clothing, presentation (side, three-quarter or full-view placement), or action of the person.

In addition, the inclusion or exclusion of the various details of a house, tree, and person is left wholly to the subject, as is the relative emphasis therein. To borrow an example from the Hammer's H-T-P study on sex offenders (Hammer, 1955), whereas normal subjects tend to draw an unnoteworthy (clinically) chimney on the house, sex offenders have been found:

> To display their feelings of phallic inadequacy directly by drawing a chimney in the following cluster of ways: with the upper part

missing as if sliced away on the diagonal; with the roof showing through the chimney that is presented as transparent (thus reflecting the subjects' feelings of flimsiness in regard to his phallus); with the chimney depicted as toppling or falling off the edge of the roof; or with a two-dimensional chimney presented on a house which is treated three-dimensionally (thus conveying the subjects' feelings that there is less substance to the phallic than to the other parts of the body-image).

Or to mask their feelings of phallic inadequacy under a cloak of compensatory virility strivings by drawing several chimneys (rather than the more conventional one) on a roof; an elongated oversized chimney; a chimney phallically shaped with a rounded tip; a chimney overemphasized by line pressure, shading or prominent placement (as a full-length chimney extending to the ground and in some drawings made the central focal point of the entire picture).

This does not, however, mean that the chimney must be a phallic symbol in drawings. In well-adjusted subjects, the chimney usually represents only a necessary detail in the depiction of a house. But if a subject suffers from psychosexual conflicts, the chimney—by virtue of its structural design and its protrusion from the body of the house— is susceptible to receive the projection of the subject's inner feelings about his phallus.

The house, as a dwelling place, has been found to arouse, within the subject, associations concerning home-life and intrafamilial relationships. In children, it has been found to tap their attitude concerning the home situation and relationships to parents and siblings. One drawing obtained with profuse and over-heavily shaded smoke pouring forth from the chimney of the house as a reflection of the hot and turbulent emotional atmosphere in the home situation, illustrates this relationship of the house drawing to the perceived home conditions.

For married adults, the drawings of the house may reflect the subjects' domestic situation in relationship to the spouse. With many married, adult subjects, however, the childhood relationship to parental figures is still apparent, as residual attitudes revealed in the house drawing. And the more neurotic, regressed, or fixated the subject, the more likely the latter, rather than the former, depiction is likely to occur.

As to the tree and the person, both these concepts touch that core of the personality which theorists, notably Paul Schilder (1935), have labeled the body image and the self-concept. The drawing of the tree appears to reflect the subjects' relatively deeper and more unconscious feelings about themselves whereas the drawn person becomes the vehicle for conveying the subjects' closer-to-conscious views of themselves and their relationship with the environment. In this manner, a picture of the conflicts and defenses as set in the hierarchy of the subject's personality structure is provided.

The tree, a more basic, natural, vegetative entity, has been found to be a more suitable symbol to project the deeper personal feelings, feelings about the self residing at a more primitive personality level than what is considered the norm. The latter, including the subject's methods of dealing with others and feelings toward them, is more apt to be projected onto the drawn person.

The view, that the tree elicits more basic and long-standing feelings, is supported by the fact that the tree is less susceptible to change on retesting. Psychotherapy of a non-intensive kind will frequently bring improvement as indicated in a decrease of the psychopathological signs in the drawn person. Only deep and extensive psychoanalytic collaboration (or highly significant alterations in a life situation, particularly of children whose personalities have enough resiliency to improve along with situational improvements) will produce minor changes in the tree.

Clinical experience also suggests that it is easier for a subject to attribute a more conflicting or emotionally-disturbing negative to the drawn tree than to the drawn person because the former is less close to home as a self-portrait. The deeper or more forbidden feelings can more readily be projected onto the tree than onto the person, with less fear of revealing oneself and less need for ego-defensive manuevering.

A subject may, for instance, more readily and unwittingly portray his feeling of emotional trauma by scarring the drawn tree's trunk and truncating its branches, than by a parallel mutilation of the drawn person's face and body and similar damaging of the drawn person's arms.

INTERPRETATION OF ELEMENTS WITHIN HOUSE, TREE, AND PERSON

It is the content of the drawings, more so than the expressive movements employed in the drawings, which reflects the more unconscious qualities existing at the center of one's personality.

House

Roof Empirical findings with the H-T-P indicate that the roof of the drawn house may be employed by subjects to symbolize the fantasy area of their life. Colloquial expressions such as bats in the belfry, something wrong upstairs, or a few shingles loose elicit the same symbolism of the roof area as equated with mental life. Thus, a condition whereby fantasy distorts one's mental functioning is spoken of in terms of an impairment in the individual's roof.

A house shown with an overly large roof, overhanging and dwarfing the rest of the house (see Figure 4–1), is drawn by patients overimmersed in fantasy and relatively withdrawn from overt interpersonal contact.

Occasionally schizophrenic or distinctly schizoid patients draw a roof and then place the door and windows within the roof outline, so that what is produced is essentially a house which is all roof (see Figure 4–2). The schizophrenic and markedly schizoid individual exists in a world which is largely fantasy. In a relative way, these subjects are more withdrawn into their fantasy life than the subjects who draw an overly large roof overhanging the walls of the house. In the latter group, there is an exaggerated emphasis on fantasy life that throws the personality structure out of balance, whereas patients who draw a house that is all roof live a predominantly fantasy existence.

The absence of a roof on a house or a roof consisting of only a single line connecting the two end walls so that there is no height to the roof (it is essentially one-dimensional rather than two-dimensional) occurs at the other end of the use-of-fantasy continuum. The group most noted for the single-line roof are mentally-retarded individuals who lack the capacity to daydream or fantasize in other ways. Within the normal intelligence range, the one-dimensional roof depiction is drawn by those with constricted personalities and concrete orientation. In clinical practice, it most commonly appears hand-in-hand with a coarctated Rorschach record.

Thus, extremes in the relative size of the roof tend to reflect the subject's degree of fantasy life.

A roof reinforced by heavy line pressure or by repeated retracing of the roof outline is drawn by subjects who are attempting to defend themselves from the threat of fantasy breaking away from control (see Figure 4–3). Its most frequent occurrence is in the drawings of prepsychotics, although it also occurs to a lesser extent with anxiety neurotics. At any rate, it represents heightened concern with the fear that those impulses presently discharged in fantasy will flood into overt behavior or distort the perception of reality.

Walls   The strength and adequacy of the depicted walls of the house have been found to be directly related to the degree of ego-strength in the personality. Crumbling walls have occurred in the drawings by patient's with overtly disintegrating egos. A reinforced boundary of walls is frequently offered by incipient psychotics who are employing an all-out, hypervigilant, and oftentimes conscious effort to maintain ego intactness.

The outline of the walls of the house drawn with a faint and

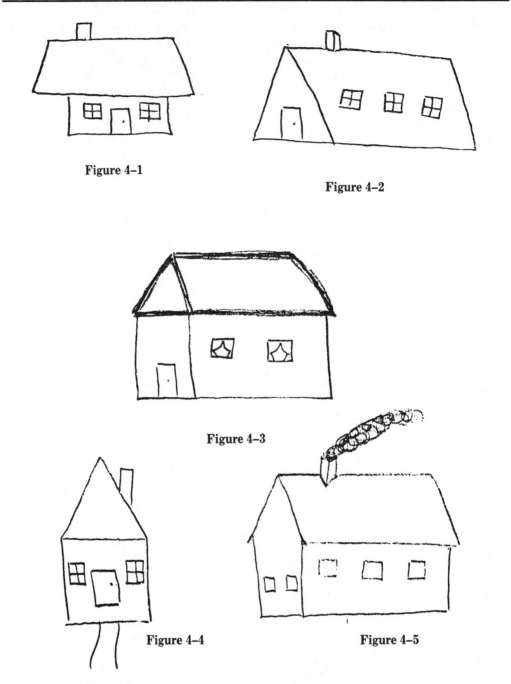

Figure 4–1

Figure 4–2

Figure 4–3

Figure 4–4

Figure 4–5

Figures 4–1, 4–2, 4–3, 4–4, and 4–5 are pencil representations of the interpretive significance of houses drawn by various subjects.

Reproduced from E. Hammer, *The Clinical Application of Projective Drawings,* 1958, 1980. Courtesy of Charles C Thomas, Publisher, Springfield, Illinois.

inadequate line quality connotes a feeling of impending personality breakdown and weak ego control without the employment of compensatory defenses. Patients offering this inadequate wall periphery are more reconciled to their impending pathology (they have accepted defeat as inevitable and have ceased to struggle) than patients who overly reinforce the outline of the walls. Instead of attempting to fend off the breakdown, the former group adopts an attitude of surrender toward the disintegrative forces which threaten.

Transparent walls in the drawings by adults are direct evidence of a reality-testing impairment. Young children frequently draw walls that are transparent (with objects within the house showing through the wall material), and in so doing, they merely indicate their immaturity of conceptual ability, taking a gross liberty with the presentation of reality. With adults, however, defects in reality testing of this magnitude occur, in Hammer's experience, only in drawings of mentally retarded and psychotic patients.

Door   The door is the detail of the house that, in actuality, allows direct contact with the environment. A door that is tiny in relation to the size of the windows and the house, in general, reflects a reluctance to make contact with the environment, a withdrawal from interpersonal give-and-take, and an inhibited capacity for social relations. Timidity and fearfulness in one's relationship with others are the behavioral correlates of the tiny-door depiction. Emotional exchange with others has been found to result in pain, and the subject is reluctant to expose himself or herself again.

The door placed high above the house's baseline and not made more approachable by steps (see Figure 4–4) is another way subjects indicate their attempts to keep their personality inaccessible. This depiction is common in those tending to make contact with others in the environment on their own terms.

The overly large door (here, as elsewhere in psychology, it is both extremes that are deviant) is drawn by those giving other clinical evidence of being overly-dependent upon others. The drawing of the door as open conveys an intense thirst to receive emotional warmth from without (if the Post-Drawing Inquiry reveals the house to be occupied). If the house is said to be vacant, the open door connotes a feeling of extreme vulnerability and a lack of adequacy of ego defenses.

Emphasis upon locks and/or hinges demonstrates defensive sensitivity, of the type found in paranoid subjects.

Windows   In the drawing of the house, windows represent a secondary medium of interaction with the environment. Emphasis upon window locks, as with parallel treatment of the door locks, occurs in drawings by those who are over-defensively fearful of danger from without—again found most frequently in paranoid orientations. Similarly, shutters or curtains added to the windows and presented as closed, also convey withdrawal needs and extreme reluctance to interact with others.

Shutters, shades, or curtains put on the windows but presented as open or partially open, mirror an attitude of controlled interaction with the environment. These subjects suffer a degree of anxiety, manifested as tact, in interpersonal relations. Social workers, examined in connection with a study of personality patterns of various groups, showed a predilection for depicting this attribute of controlled emotional give-and-take with others.

Windows completely bare, without curtains or shades nor crosshatching, occur in the drawings by subjects who interact with those in the environment in an overly blunt and direct fashion. The exercise of tact is minimal in their behavior, and they tend to be a bit of a bull-in-a-china-shop type of social participant.

Reinforcement of window outlines, if similar reinforcement does not occur elsewhere in the drawing, has most frequently been presented by subjects with oral fixations or oral character traits. Occasionally, however, the window outline is also emphasized by those with anal orientations; and frequently, the oral as opposed to buttock emphasis on the drawn person allows a differential interpretation.

In regard to size of the windows, convention decrees that the living room window be presented as the largest and the bathroom window as the smallest. Where deviations from this rule occur, an index of a strong emotional need pressing forward is available. A distinct distaste for social intercourse is exhibited by the attempts to minimize the importance of the associations to the living room by drawing the window of this room the smallest in the house.

Undue importance given to the bathroom by making the window in that room the largest of all the windows, tends to reflect experiences involving severe toilet training during childhood. It has also been found in those suffering masturbation guilt and those with compulsive handwashing as a symptom.

Placement of windows that does not conform from wall-to-wall (suggesting that the height of the floor as viewed from the front of the house is not the same as if viewed from the side of the house, as in Figure 4–5), directly reflects an organizational and perceptual difficulty, empirically found to be suggestive of early schizophrenia.

Chimney This was previously discussed in the introductory section of this chapter to illustrate the wide variety of treatments that might be accorded a single detail of the drawings.

Smoke A profusion of dense and excessive smoke pouring forth from the chimney reflects either considerable inner tension in the subject, or conflict and emotional turbulence in the home situation, or both, since the latter may well produce the former condition, and vice versa.

Smoke veering sharply to one side, as if indicating a strong wind, reflects a feeling of environmental pressure and has been frequently associated with children having reading disability problems where parental pressures, both causative and reactive, are strong. Adolescents experiencing undue parental pressure toward social conformity and/or scholastic achievement have also made use of this depiction, as have some adults examined shortly after their induction into the armed services.

Perspective   The house drawn as if the viewer is above and looking down upon it (labeled by Buck (1948) the "bird's-eye view") is produced by subjects who basically reject the home situation and the values espoused therein. Such subjects combine compensatory superiority feelings with a revolt against the traditional values taught at home. Iconoclastic attitudes accompany the feeling of being above the demands of convention and conformity.

The worm's-eye view, in which the house is presented as if the viewer is below and looking up at it, is a perspective employed by subjects who feel rejected and inferior in the home situation. Feelings of lack of worth mingle with low self-esteem and feelings of inadequacy; happiness in the home situation is considered unobtainable.

The perspective of the house presented as if far away, that is, as distant from the viewer, is employed by two groups of subjects: Those who project a self-portrait in the drawing of the house and thus disclose their feelings of withdrawal and inaccessibility; and those who convey a perception of the home situation—a home situation with which the subjects feels unable to cope. In this latter use of the far-away perspective, the subject is displaying a view that feelings of comfort and belonging are unattainable in relationship to those at home.

The absolute profile presentation of the house is another personally-meaningful deviation from the usual perspective. The term *absolute profile* refers to a house drawn with only the side presented to the viewer. The front of the house, including the door or other entrance, is turned away making it unseen and less accessible. Withdrawn, oppositional, or inaccessible subjects project these traits in this manner.

The house drawn from the rear, and particularly if no back door is indicated, mirrors the same withdrawal and oppositional tendencies as does the absolute profile presentation, but to proportions of greater pathology. The rare rear view depictions seen, have been in the drawings of early paranoid schizophrenics, when the need to protectively withdraw is most acutely felt.

Groundline The relationship of the drawn house, tree, or person to the groundline reflects the subject's degree of contact with reality. The same symbolic stream equating the ground with practical reality is also evident in colloquial speech: He has his feet firmly planted on the ground. Whether the contact with the ground is either firm or tenuous is of major diagnostic interest. Latent or borderline schizophrenics invariably have difficulty presenting their drawn whole in firm contact with reality (as represented by the groundline). They either offer a drawing resting tenuously on a choppy or sporadically-drawn groundline, on an amorphous, cloud-like groundline, or as being up-rooted (in the case of the tree) from the ground and toppling. A greater degree of schizophrenic pathology and fantasy-absorbing distance from reality is displayed by a drawing that hovers over, but nowhere touches, a groundline drawn beneath it.

Accessories Some subjects directly reveal their feelings of insecurity by having to surround and buttress their house with many bushes, trees, and other details unrelated to the instruction.

A walkway, easily drawn and well proportioned, leading to the door, is commonly added by individuals who exercise a degree of control and tact in their contact with others. A long and winding walkway, on the other hand, occurs in the drawings of those who are initially aloof in their interpersonal relations, but eventually warm up and establish emotional rapport with others. They are slow and cautious in making friendships, but when relationships with others develop, these tend to be of a deep quality.

A walkway excessively wide at the end toward the viewer and leading in a direct line to the door, but with the width of the walkway narrowing too sharply, so that it is considerably less than the width of the door where they meet, reveals an attempt to cloak a basic desire to remain aloof by employing superficial friendliness.

Fences placed around the drawn house are a defensiveness maneuver. A shy, eight-year-old boy recently offered a picture in which the most conspicuous elaboration of the drawing of the house was a fence "to keep everybody away." He was desperately trying to ensure that nobody could interfere with what little security he did feel.

Summary Thus, in an abbreviated way, one might say that the drawn house most frequently represents two major entities: a self-portrait with fantasy, ego, reality contact, accessibility, or problem areas (for example, phallic emphasis) as elements thereof; and the perception of the home situation—past, present, desired future, or some combination of all three.

The adult mind is capable of voluntarily assuming different attitudes in its perception and experience of the environment. The person can be at one moment the detached observer; the next moment be open receptively to all the impressions from the environment and the feelings and pleasures aroused by them; and in the next project himself or herself in emphatic experience with some object of the environment.

Looking at a tree, for example, a subject can at one moment be the detached botanist who observes, compares, and classifies what's seen; and in the next moment, surrender to the color of the foliage and bark, the sound of leaves rustling in the breeze, the fresh scent after a shower of rain; and in the next moment, attempt to feel, inside of himself, kinesthetically, how slight or solid the trunk stands and rises up, how calmly the branches spread, or how gracefully they move and yield to the wind.

In the drawing of a tree, the subject chooses from the memory of the countless number seen, the one with which he or she has the greatest empathic identification; and in drawing, the subject modifies and recreates the tree further in the direction of his or her own inner feelings.

It is no surprise to anthropologists that one's view of a tree is personally meaningful. In myth and folklore, and even everyday parlance, the tree has always symbolized life and growth.

The symbol-seeped meaning of the tree carries through to the twentieth century and is apparent in speaking of the family tree and in sayings like, As the twig is bent, so grows the tree.

In drawings of a tree, a subject will neglect the branches if the subject does not branch out, mingling with and enjoying other people. In this manner, the subject projects, during the process of drawing the tree, and makes it a veritable self-portrait.

Sometimes subjects will draw a tree that is tossed by the wind and broken by storms—a reflection of the effects of the damaging environmental pressures they have endured.

> The unconscious etching-out of the self-image via the tree drawing was most evident in a recent case of a woman who drew a basket under the tree with five shining fruits in it. She had five children, and the drawing quite clearly represented her basic pride in her maternal role.
>
> Her positive evaluation of her material achievements is in sharp contrast to that revealed in the tree drawn by a woman who was seen for a clinical evaluation in connection with the psychotherapy program of both her children, one a twenty-year-old overt

homosexual and the other an eleven-year-old boy with a severe remedial reading disability. The mother's unconscious rejection of her children and/or her negative evaluation of herself as a mother came through with graphic impact in her drawing of a fruit tree when a conspicuous comment, "These are two rotten apples that have fallen to the ground," brought this picture from her unconscious into sharp focus.

A tree drawing may be grasped as a whole, intuitively; even without investigation of the details, one can receive an impression of harmony, unrest, emptiness, baldness, fullness, or one may receive an impression of hostility and be warned. This, too, is the first stage in the learning of the method. One should passively submit oneself to the effect of a large number of tree drawings, contemplate them, simply look at them without any critical attitude. Thus, slowly, looking becomes seeing, distinctions are recognized, and the picture begins to differentiate itself.

The tree, a living or one-time living plant in an elemental environment (rain, wind, sleet, storm, warmth, or sunshine), is the most likely of the four drawings to convey the subject's felt image of himself or herself in the context of the relationship to the environment (Buck, 1948).

Buck (1948) adds to this the postulations that:

1. The trunk represents a subject's feeling of basic power and inner strength (in analytic terminology, the ego-strength);

2. The branch structure depicts the subject's feelings of ability to derive satisfaction from the environment (eliciting a more unconscious level of the same area tapped by the adequacy of the arms and hands on the drawn person) and;

3. The organization of the drawn whole reflects the subject's feeling of intrapersonal balance.

The dynamic significance of the subject's differential treatment of the details within the drawing of the tree:

Trunk   In support of the concept of the trunk serving as an index of the basic strength of the personality, reinforced peripheral lines in this area of the tree have been found to reflect the subject's felt need to maintain personality intactness. Here, the subject employs compensatory defenses to cloak and combat fear of personality diffusion and disintegration. Such heavily reinforced trunk lines reflect attempts to guard against this eventuality with all available resources.

On the other hand, faint, sketchy, or perforated lines employed for the tree trunk, and not elsewhere in the drawing, depict a more advanced state of feelings of impending personality collapse or loss of identity—a stage in which compensatory defenses are no longer looked to with any real hope of staving off the imminent breakdown. Acute anxiety is invariably present.

Holes have been placed in the trunk and animals shown peeping out of them by those who inwardly feel that a segment of the personality is pathologically free from control (dissociated) and potentially destructive. The most frequent instance of this depiction is offered by those wracked by obsessive guilt feelings. These subjects are identifying primarily with the animal within the tree trunk, rather than with the tree, and are thus depicting their regressive yearnings for a withdrawn, warm, protected, uterine existence. The former identification with the tree occurs more frequently with adult subjects, and the latter identification with the animal within is more usually employed by children. The safest guide, however, for making the differential interpretation is the Post-Drawing Inquiry, the other projective data, and the clinical history.

Roots   If the subject is unduly concerned about his or her hold upon reality, the subject may express this by an overemphasis upon the roots of the tree as it makes contact with, and takes hold of, the ground. A talon-like grasp (the roots depicted as if straining to hold onto the ground) was recently drawn by a male subject who subsequently suffered an overt psychotic breakdown and had to be institutionalized. At the time the H-T-P was administered, two weeks prior to his overt breakdown, the adhesive clutch of his tree roots reflected his hypervigilant clinging to reality and panic-like fear of losing contact with reality.

Roots drawn as showing through transparent ground serve as direct evidence of an impairment of the subject's reality testing ability. If the subject is of average intelligence, or better, and in the adolescent or adult age range, this reality testing impairment has been found to be an item that serves to alert the clinician to the possibility—but only the possibility—of other suggestions of a schizophrenic process.

Paper-Based Tree   Employment of the bottom edge of the paper as the groundline, with the drawn picture resting on that edge, is a favorite presentation of insecure subjects who suffer feelings of inadequacy. They cling to the bottom of the page for compensatory security. Depressed subjects dropping the placement of their drawing down to the lower section of the page may also allow it to come to rest on the bottom edge. The use of faint lines, reflecting the depressive's sapping of energy and drive, as well as the favorite tree content—a

weeping willow—may provide clues to aid in the differential interpretation.

Branches   The branches represent the subject's felt resources for
seeking satisfaction from the environment, for reaching out to others,
branching out, reaching upward, or straining upward achievement-
wise. The tree limbs represent a more unconscious parallel, in the
subject's self-concept, to the drawn person's arms. Joyce Kilmer, in
his epic piece, had a poet's finger on the pulse of symbolism in his
analogy: A tree who "lifts her leafy arms to pray."

Occasionally a subject will try to mask with superficial and compensatory optimism deeper feelings of inability to obtain satisfaction.
For example, the subject may draw his or her person with overly long
arms extending away from the body as if striving manfully, but the
tree will show clearly, by its truncated and broken branches, that
basically the subject feels no real hope of success.

Branch structures presented as tall and narrow, reaching unduly
upward and minimally outward to the sides, have been seen in tree
drawings of subjects who are afraid to seek satisfaction from, and in,
the environment and, hence, over-reach into fantasy (upward toward
the top of the page) for substitute gratification. These depictions are
employed most commonly by those in the introverted-to-schizoid range
when it is not the upward straining branches of the achievement-
pursuing subject. A better balance in the distribution of one's satisfaction-seeking pursuits occurs in those whose tree branches extend
laterally outward into the contemporary environment as well as upward into the fantasy area.

At times, a subject will emphasize the upward reaching of the
branch structure to the point where the top of the tree extends off
beyond the page's top. This is an extreme example of a subject over-
extended into fantasy. Whereas introverted and schizoid subjects both
tend to overemphasize the upward extension of their tree's branches,
only those subjects near the frankly schizoid end of the continuum
extend branches beyond the page's top. And certainly this is so when
the trunk itself goes above the page top.

Occasionally, a subject will abruptly flatten the top of the foliage
area or crown of the tree, as if attempting to deny or reject the fantasy
area entirely. This recently occurred in one patient who was panicked
by the emergence of homosexual fantasies, and in another patient who
was attempting to deny the site of his painful guilt produced by obsessive thoughts of killing his younger brother. Both wished to repress
their fantasy life and deny the threatening content forcing its way
into that area.

One-dimensional branches, that do not form a system and are
inadequately joined to a one-dimensional trunk (segmentalization),
make the presence of organicity suspect (see Figure 4–6). Whether or

not organicity is suggested by the concrete flavoring of the rest of the drawings, the other projective techniques, the case history, or the neurological findings, this type of tree reflects feelings of impotence, futility, and lack of ego-strength with poor integration of the satisfaction-seeking resources—all contributing to a graphic picture of feelings of inadequacy.

Flexibility of the branch structure, with the organization of the branches proceeding from thick to thin in a proximal-distal direction, is a favorable finding and bespeaks a feeling of a high ability on the part of the subject to attain satisfaction from the environment. This tends to be so, providing, of course, the branch structure is of adequate size in relation to the trunk.

Branches which appear club-like or look spear-like with excessively sharpened points at the ends, or appear to have barb-like thorns along their surface, underscore the presence of intense and ready impulses of hostility and aggression. If the behavioral picture indicates the subject is not acting out these impulses, but on the contrary appears to be a relatively mild and meek individual, rest assured that this surface adjustment is made at the expense of massive efforts at repression of anger with concomitant inner tension of considerable proportions. In such instances, the clinician might do well to inspect the drawings for indications of lack of control to appraise the likelihood of incipient and catastrophic acting-out of these impulses.

If the signs of control are overemphasized, they may of themselves be regarded as indicating an approaching impulse-eruption into overt behavior, since the subject may well be on the verge of exhausting his or her strained defensive potential.

Within the tree drawing, two-dimensional branches drawn and unclosed at the distal end, mirror a feeling of little control over the expression of one's impulses (see Figure 4–7). One schizophrenic, with the intuitive sensitivity of one whose formerly unconscious processes have flooded into consciousness, commented in reference to his drawn tree with its open-ended branches: "This is a picture of me, with no control over what comes out of me, the things that I do."

Branches that are drawn so that they actually look more phallic-like than branch-like, are offered by those with sexual preoccupations and/or virility strivings.

Broken branches and cut-off branches depict the subject's feelings of being traumatized and not a complete unit within himself or herself. Feelings of castration may also exist, whether on a psychosocial level resulting in feelings of inadequacy, helplessness, and passivity, or on a psychosexual level where feelings range from lack of virility to actual impotency.

If the tree trunk itself is truncated and tiny branches grow from the stump, it is the core of the self which is felt to be damaged. This type of drawing reflects stunted emotional growth, but with begin-

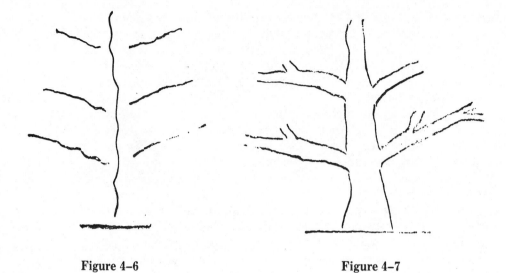

Figure 4–6   Figure 4–7

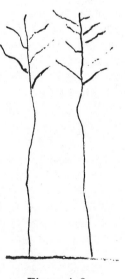

Figure 4–8

Figures 4–6, 4–7, and 4–8 are pencil representations of the interpretive significance of trees drawn by various subjects.

Reproduced from E. Hammer, *The Clinical Application of Projective Drawings,* 1958, 1980. Courtesy of Charles C Thomas, Publisher, Springfield, Illinois.

ning—although tentative and rather feeble—efforts at regrowth, stimulated, perhaps, by the beginning phase of the therapeutic relationship.

Branches that turn inward toward the tree instead of reaching outward toward the environment, reflect egocentricity, and strong introverted, ruminating tendencies. Thus far, this portrayal has been seen only in obsessive-compulsives and narcissistic patients.

An overly large branch structure placed on top of a relatively tiny tree trunk suggests an overemphasis on hungry satisfaction seeking. This was most recently seen in the drawing of a subject tested one weekday evening.

> The patient gave a rather rich and lengthy projective protocol, and it was midnight before we were finished with the entire battery. The patient asked if he might phone his wife, and I offered him my apologies to add to what I thought would be his own apologies for going home so late. It was with some surprise that I learned he was phoning his wife to discuss whether to meet at the Stork Club or the Twenty-One Club, at one A.M., to begin the evening. When I inquired as to the time of his business appointments the following day, he replied quite casually, "Nine o'clock." His frantic pleasure seeking, in his efforts to quiet or at least mask the inner voice of doubt concerning his essential feelings of worth and significance (the tiny tree trunk), supported the interpretation (over-emphasis on satisfaction seeking) that his overbalanced branch structure suggested.

If the opposite extreme occurs, i.e., a tiny branch structure topping an overly large trunk, it tends to imply that the subject experiences frustration due to an inability to satisfy strong underlying needs.

In children's drawings, particularly, branches are sometimes drawn reaching appealingly to the sun. This occurs in the drawings of those youngsters having marked and frustrated needs for affection. The tree stretches out its arms hungrily for the warmth from some significant authority figure above (in this case, represented by the sun), a warmth for which the subject is starved.

Occasionally, a child will draw a tree as bending away from a large and low-placed sun, drawn as bearing down upon the tree. This depiction is offered by subjects who shy away from domination by a parental or other authoritarian figure who makes the subject feel painfully subjugated, uncomfortable, and inadequate.

Before leaving the section devoted to the discussion of the branches, a relatively rare, but symbolically clear treatment deserves mention. Secondary branches are drawn spike-like and imbedded like thorns into the flesh of the primary branches. The points of the secondary branches, rather than being at the outer end, are at the point of contact with the tree trunk or with the branches from which they grow. These small branches appear to dig into, rather than grow from, the larger branches. The reader has correctly anticipated the interpretation of masochistic tendencies.

> One such instance was made in a drawing by a woman who at one time was complaining of the inconvenience resulting from the plumbing in her kitchen being out-of-order and the many times within a few days she had to call in the plumber. "If I have to call just once more . . ." (and the clinician expected to hear the sentence finished with some extrapunitively directed expression of her anger not far short of hitting the plumber over the head with the kitchen sink) . . . "I'll pull my hair out." The intrapunitive direction of the release of her aggression was consistent with the masochistic orientation apparent in her branch treatment.

Midway between an intrapunitive and extrapunitive role in life, a predominantly impunitive subject may portray his or her orientation by wrapping the ends of the branches in cloud-like balls. The hard expression of the branch is covered-up as though wrapped in a cushioning pad of cotton. Although aggression with this subject is not discharged inward, inhibitions prevent its discharge outward. Pleasant manners and a soft-spoken way frequently accompany this impunitive branch treatment.

In a general way, the overall impression conveyed by the branches correlates with the broad personality dimensions of the subject, whether the branch or foliage treatment is composed of lively, animated, and soft effects, or angular, harsh, and stern outlines, or jerky, irritable, anxious, and insecure treatment.

Keyhole Tree   The depiction of the trunk and foliage area, as if by one continuous line without a line separating the crown from the trunk, is so-called because of its resemblance to a keyhole. Actually the presentation is one of enclosed unrelieved white space, and like the space response on the Rorschach, has been found to be offered by oppositional and negativistic subjects. In drawing this type of tree, subjects are complying with the examiner's request, but only in a minimal manner. Such subjects do the least they can short of refusing outright to render the drawing.

Split Tree   The name for this drawing response comes from the fact that the sidelines of the trunk do not have any lines connecting them to each other; they extend upward, each one forming its own independent branch structure (see Figure 4–8). The impression is that of a tree split down the middle, giving the appearance of two one-dimensional trees side-by-side. It suggests a shattering of personality, a process of disintegration. It is as if the cohesiveness of the self has dissolved. If there is any single sign in the H-T-P that can be regaraded as pathognomonic of schizophrenia, it is this one.

Theme   The implications of a sense of doom in the drawing of a tree with a buzzard hovering over it; the utter lack of worth, abysmally low self-esteem and sense of degradation apparent in the drawing of a tree with a dog urinating on it; and the terror of a feeling of imminent mutilation conveyed by the drawing of a tree with a man identified as a father-figure chopping upon it are self-explanatory.

Pregnant women often offer fruit trees and depressed patients, as previously suggested, show a propensity for weeping willows.

Young children will frequently draw apple trees; the frequency is 35 percent at the kindergarten age, 9 percent by the tenth year of age, and close to none by the fourteenth year of life (Koch, 1952). With young children, the identification is apparently with the fruit of the tree, the tree itself representing the mother-figure, because children who suffer from feelings of rejection will draw one apple as falling (having been cast off) or having fallen, from the tree.

Age Ascribed to the Tree   The implications of feelings of immaturity apparent in an adult's drawing of a tiny sapling rather than a full-grown tree are clear. To get a more refined index, however, of the developmental level meant to be conveyed by the drawn tree, when the subject is finished he or she is asked how old the tree in the drawing is. Experience suggests that the age projected is related to the felt level of psycho-social-sexual maturity of the subject. This was supported by an experimental study by Hammer (1954).

Tree Depicted as Dead   Subjects who respond to the question, "Is that tree alive?" by indicting that the tree is dead have been found to be significantly maladjusted. This response is most prevalent in the withdrawn, schizophrenic, depressed, and severely neurotic who have given up hope of ever achieving a comfortable adjustment. Hence, its occurrence is of negative prognostic significance, as are all other signs suggesting feelings of futility.

In the Post-Drawing Inquiry, if the tree is said to be dead clinicians are interested in discovering whether the death is perceived as caused by something external or something internal. If the death of the tree is said to have been caused by such things as wind, elements, lightning, having been chopped down, etc., such subjects hold something in the outer environment responsible for their difficulties and usually suffer acutely from feelings of traumatization. If the death is said to have been caused by something internal such as rotting of the roots, trunk, or limbs, these subjects regard themselves as unwholesome and unacceptable. Generally, clinicians found much more intense pathology, often of schizophrenic proportions, to be present in those who perceive the tree as rotting away from the inside than in those who see the tree as killed by outside agents.

All else being equal, the prognosis is generally better when the damage is ascribed to external agents. If the tree is perceived as dead, the subject is asked how long ago it may have died. It has been found that the time said to have elapsed since the death of the tree can serve as a clue to the relative duration of the subject's feelings of such pathology and loss of hope.

Person

The person is that concept in the House-Tree-Person Test that is most often submitted incompletely or rejected entirely. Since it is at times the most difficult to draw, it may arouse in some subjects a fear of failure, particularly in subjects who feel they will not do adequately on this test. Hence, it is during the drawing of the person that these subjects may more frequently need emotional support from the clinician.

In regard to theme, the drawing of a person tends to elicit principally three types: a self-portrait, an ideal-self, and a depiction of one's perception of significant others (parents, siblings, etc.).

Self-portraits depict what subjects feel themselves to be. Body contours, whether obese or thin, physiological areas of sensitivity such as a hooked nose, cauliflower ear, pocked-marked skin, or club foot are often reproduced faithfully and exactly in the drawn person. Subjects of average or below average I.Q. will usually reproduce their own physical handicaps on their drawn persons in mirror image, i.e., if the subject has a withered right hand, he or she will reproduce this condition on the drawn person's left hand. Abstract ability allows the non-mirror image depiction (i.e., the subject's right side to be portrayed by the drawn person's right side) and is seldom found in subjects of less than high average intelligence.

It has been noticed that physiological flaws or physical disabilities are reproduced in the drawing of the person only if they have impinged upon the subject's self-concept and have created an area of psychological sensitivity.

Along with the projection of feelings of physical defects, the subject also projects assets: broad shoulders, muscular development, attractive physiognomy; this is done to the point where even with artistically incapable subjects, an amazing likeness frequently results.

In addition to the physical self, the subject projects a picture of the psychological self into the drawing of the person. Subjects of adequate or superior height may draw a tiny figure with arms dangling rather helplessly away from the sides and a beseeching facial expression. Here, the subject is projecting his psychological view of himself as tiny, insignificant, helpless, dependent, and in need of support, the physical self not withstanding.

> A helplessly compliant adult male, living at home and controlled by a domineering mother, drew for his person a puppet with strings attached.
>
> A nine-year-old boy drew a football dummy for his person. The social worker reported that as punishment, the boy was often deprived of food and severely whipped with a cat-of-nine-tails. When he was enuretic he was put into cold water to be taught a lesson. While his mother was at work, he was frequently beaten by his older brother. Hence, in his self-concept, he portrays his unconscious view of himself as a football dummy whose function, we may deduce, is to absorb punishment.
>
> The self-disdain of one subject was reflected by his drawing "a man asking for a handout" as his person. At the same time, his feelings of futility about matching up to the expectations of the male role were made apparent in the drawing of this man with clothes much too large for him, essentially hanging unfilled from his shoulders.

Other examples include the aggressive, simian-like person drawn by a rapist; the toppling person losing equilibrium offered by a pre-schizophrenic; the mannequin-like clothes dummy suggesting feelings of depersonalization; the adolescent's drawn person carrying a baseball bat in one hand, a tennis racket in the other, and wearing a mustache on his lip, revealed by his yearning for so many badges of virility, his underlying feelings of inadequacy in this area; the exhibitionistic female subject who managed to expose a good deal of her drawn female person by having a strong gust of wind blowing the drawn person's skirt up; the drawing of a clown as a fusion of the subject's attempts to depict the harmlessness of his instinctual impulses and his secondary use of this concept in an attention-getting maneuver; the reduced energy and drive suggested by a drawn person slumped into an arm chair rather than standing on his feet (as is statistically the norm) and the need for emotional warmth and security implied by the placing of this seated figure in front of a conspicuously-detailed roaring fireplace; the narcissism reflected by the drawing of a woman with her hands thrust ecstatically in her hair, while dancing alone to music (supported by the Rorschach response: "Animal looking at his reflection in the water"); and a patient's over-defensive state expressed in a drawing of a male with rigidly erect body, with the absolute side view presented, depicting both the subject's refusal to face others squarely and his rigid unadaptiveness. All these themes support the thesis that the drawn person may represent a psychological self-portrait.

An **Ego-ideal** is elicited rather than pictures what subjects presently feel themselves to be.

> A slender, rather frail, intensely paranoid male drew a boxer whose shoulders, before he was through, extended to the dimensions of a Hercules.
>
> An unmarried, pregnant, young girl, suffering feelings of terrible shame in regard to the stomach contour that was so revealing of her condition drew a lithe, graceful, slender dancer twirling unencumbered by any burden.

Adolescent boys frequently draw muscular athletes attired in bathing suits, while adolescent girls draw female movie star figures wearing evening gowns—the ideal states for which the adolescents of respective sexes long.

With patients who come into therapy with obesity as their presenting symptom, it has been found that those who still cling to their ego-ideal (i.e., draw a slim rather than an obese person) have a considerably better prognosis.

Depiction of a significant person is elicited in subjects' contemporary or past environments, usually because of either strong positive or negative valence for the subject.

The pressing forward onto the drawing page of the subject's perception of significant figures in the environment, in contrast to the perception of one's self, occurs more often in the drawings of children than of adolescents or adults. And the person children represent in their drawings are almost invariably a parental figure. The depiction of a parental figure more frequently in the drawings of children than of adults represents the importance of the parent to the child's life, and the child's need for a model to identify with and after whom to pattern himself or herself. Thus, the kind of perception of mother- or father-figure the child reveals in his or her drawing is frequently a prophesying element predicting the traits which retest drawings, years later, indicate the child incorporates.

> One eight-year-old boy, referred because of excessive bullying of his classmates, drew a man, menacing in every aspect: Bared teeth sharpened to a point, a club in one hand, and the other hand coming to an end not in conventional fingers, but in a clear depiction of what looked like the ends of scissors—a weapon which might shear off and do damage to vital parts of the subject. The social worker's investigation of the home revealed a father who was a despot in every way, cruel, punitive, and domineering. The

bullying attitudes the subject had picked up suggested that he had begun to defend himself against the threat of the destruction-invested father through the mechanism of incorporation. In a self-protective maneuver, he donned his enemy's cloak so that he could put himself out of harm's way. He became the bully, rather than the bullied. The process of incorporation became the bridge across which the subject sought to travel to comparative safety.

In this manner, projective drawings tend to reveal the felt self, the ideal self, and—the clinician is tempted to say—the future self (barring the intervention of psychotherapy or significant changes in the environmental situation).

At this point, the reader is referred to Chapter 5 by Leonard Handler for a discussion of the significance of various elements within the drawn person.

EVALUATION OF THE H-T-P AS AN ASSESSMENT INSTRUMENT

An assessment instrument has outgrown its beginning when the key question asked of it is no longer, "Is it good?" Nurtured on a rich clinical diet with the emergence of experimental studies to add substance to the fare, projective drawings have evolved and the question now is, "What are the strengths and weaknesses of the instrument?" Additionally, since even the most enthusiastic supporters of a projective instrument do not claim the technique does everything, it seems less tenable to prove or disprove a test than to find out what it can or cannot do, in what areas it has special applicability, and in what areas it is only marginally useful. Some of these issues will be addressed below.

1. The H-T-P, basically a non-verbal technique, has the obvious advantages of greater applicability to young children. A non-verbal projective test also has relative advantages with subjects of limited education, limited intellectual ability, low socioeconomic and/or culturally deprived backgrounds, as well as those who are painfully shy and withdrawn, do not speak English, or are mute.

2. The H-T-P requires little time and is simple to administer.

3. A research advantage of the H-T-P is that it is essentially a cultural-free technique for anthropological use in the investigation of other societies across the language handicap. The investigator need only possess a vocabulary of a few words (e.g., draw, house, tree, person, male, female) in order to administer this test.

Some of the disadvantages of the H-T-P include the following.

1. Verbal subjects generally are less responsive to graphic techniques than to the Rorschach and TAT. As verbally inarticulate subjects provide less richly nuanced Rorschach protocols, those who draw poorly provide less revealing H-T-P protocols.

2. Psychomotor difficulties, such as physical handicaps or tremulousness that may occur with many geriatric patients, often result in meager and spuriously hampered projection on the H-T-P. Their personality expression is held back by their motoric handicap.

3. Patients with a paucity of inner life, such as the schizoid, provide a comparatively still more barren personality portrait on the H-T-P. The empty sheet of paper does not stimulate their sluggish projection process as do at least, to a slightly greater degree, the inkblots or TAT pictures. These latter stimuli are something to which to respond. These patients need something external to stimulate their mental processes where their inner resources and imagination are so impoverished. The blank page leaves such patients blank.

CASE ILLUSTRATION

Masculine Character Posturing: A Man in the Clothes of a Clown, in the Clothes of a Man

The following case was seen in response to a challenge made over the telephone by a rather skeptical psychiatrist-colleague, who had been treating a thirty-seven-year-old man and wanted a psychological evaluation. But the psychiatrist wanted the evaluation done blindly so that he could be sure the results came solely from the psychological examination and were in no way the result of inferences made from data otherwise known about the patient. The psychiatrist, thus, did not want the psychologist to know anything about the patient or his symptoms other than what came through the projective examination.

This psychiatrist was putting projective techniques to the test, to determine whether or not anything of importance could be learned about the patient from the way in which he drew a house, a tree, and a person, composed stories related to pictures, and interpreted inkblots.

The psychologist explained to the psychiatrist that the most sound and effective use of projective technique evaluation is not one in which the procedure is attempted blindly. However, the psychiatrist remained firm.

When the patient Mr. C appeared for the psychological examination, he was well-dressed and had an air of assurance and poise. He was pleasant, cooperative, and readily participated in the psychological examination.

The patient had given a relatively full and extensive Rorschach and TAT; time was running out, and Mr. C had to catch a train. So after he had completed the achromatic house, tree, and person of each sex, the chromatic drawing phase was abbreviated to merely a tree and a person.

Mr. C's first drawing, that of a house, was drawn in a slow, meticulous manner. Compared to his other drawings, the house is small, constricted, and set way back from the viewer. Feelings of inadequacy, inferiority, constriction, and withdrawal in the home situation, past and present, are suggested.

The wide and conspicuous driveway implies a need to present himself as interested in social and interpersonal contacts in relation to others. Since the driveway does not reach the house and is U-shaped rather than merely leading to the house, it conveys the impression that this man's emotional accessibility is more apparent than real. The roadway leads people past him, rather than to him. The psychologist may then hypothesize, but not yet deduce, that a seemingly cordial and friendly exterior is used to conceal an underlying detachment and a need for retreat from others. In keeping with the merely token acceptance of the fact that society expects him to be reasonably accessible, the windows on the ground floor are placed well above the usual level in relation to the door, and all the windows have the shades half-lowered.

His drawings of trees, both achromatic and chromatic, emphasize the bark, a finding frequent in people hypochondriacally oriented with feelings of physical disjointedness and inadequacy.

Both the chromatic tree and the achromatic male person have the top of the drawing sliced away. Thus, the suggestion is offered that Mr. C attempts to deny that fantasy area, presumably because of the unacceptable content of his fantasy and the guilt it produces.

The first male drawing attempts to give an impression of virility and masculine prowess: the crew-cut hair, the bull neck, and the broadened shoulders. However, these are belied by the anxiety-indicating difficulty that Mr. C experienced with the crotch area, the flaccid droop of the toes and the apparently withered hands. As in his drawing of the house, with his withdrawal tendencies tucked away behind a superficially cordial front, reaction-formation again is used, this time combined with compensation, in an effort to conceal his feelings of sexual impotency behind a characterological parade of masculinity.

Following this unsuccessful attempt to present a virile front convincingly, Mr. C's next drawing is of a provocatively-posed, nude fe-

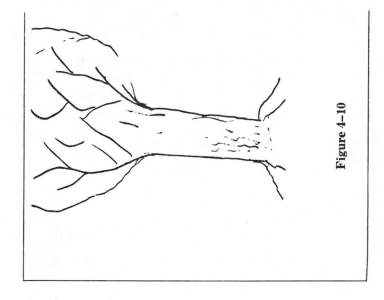

Figure 4–10

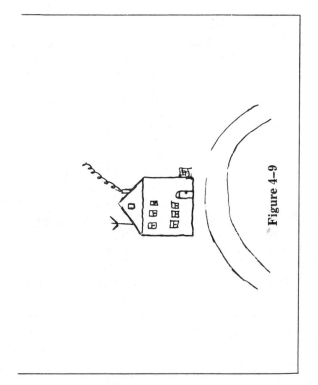

Figure 4–9

Figures 4–9 and 4–10 are case illustrations of achromatic drawings of a house and a tree completed by Mr. C.

From J. N. Buck, *The House-Tree-Person Technique: Revised Manual.* Copyrighted 1966, 1970 by Western Psychological Services. Reprinted and adapted by permission of Western Psychological Services, 12031 Wilshire Blvd., Los Angeles, California 90025.

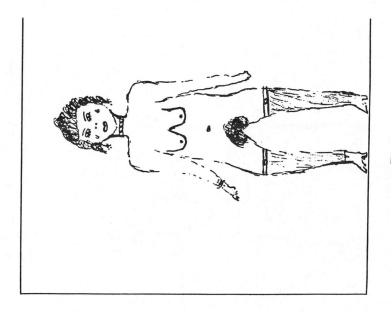

Figure 4-12

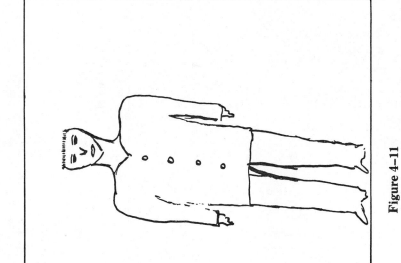

Figure 4-11

Figures 4–11 and 4–12 are case illustrations of achromatic drawings of the male person and the female person completed by Mr. C.

From J. N. Buck, *The House-Tree-Person Technique: Revised Manual.* Copyrighted 1966, 1970 by Western Psychological Services. Reprinted and adapted by permission of Western Psychological Services, 12031 Wilshire Blvd., Los Angeles, California 90025.

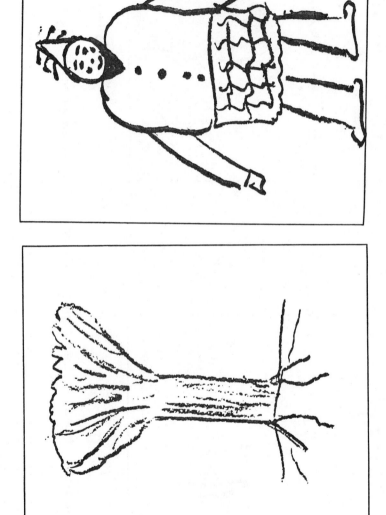

Figure 4–13

Figure 4–14

Figures 4–13 and 4–14 are case illustrations of chromatic drawing (crayon) phases of a tree and a person completed by Mr. C.

From J. N. Buck, *The House-Tree-Person Technique: Revised Manual.* Copyrighted 1966, 1970 by Western Psychological Services. Reprinted and adapted by permission of Western Psychological Services, 12031 Wilshire Blvd., Los Angeles, California 90025.

male. His attempt to present the female as sexually exciting also does not quite succeed. She has a cold, doll-like, immobile, uninviting expression made only superficially attractive with dabs of rouge and the absence of clothing. The body lacks feminine shape and grace with no hip curve nor waist delineation. The breasts appear sagging and devoid of youth and appeal.

Despite the profuse hair at the vaginal area, erotic emphasis actually is shifted to the legs. This is consistent with Mr. C's many eroticized Rorschach responses involving legs.

Following the attempt to draw a sexualized woman, Mr. C's next drawing of a person (chromatic) is of a male clown. Here Mr. C portrays graphically his major need to play a role which will amuse and disarm rather than antagonize. Thus, he attempts to indicate the harmlessness of his drives. On top of that, following his transgression of contemplating a female in raw sexual terms, he draws a skirt on the male clown and then places a cross-hatching of lines across the pelvic area as if further to protect the genitals. Hence, two defensive maneuvers are used by Mr. C to protect himself against genital damage: the harmless lack of assertion, and effeminacy.

In addition, a depressed and resigned quality comes through beneath the clown paint—i.e., shows through his unsuccessful attempts to use the reaction formations of cheerfulness, gaiety, and carefreeness.

The arms of the chromatic person are attached to the body well below the shoulder level: The subject may feel overwhelmed by the male role and massively inadequate in carrying it off.

Following Mr. C's stream of associations through his three persons, the psychologist thus finds that a particularly virile facade and an ambivalently-perceived sex object, produces massive fear within him and results in his presenting himself as an innocuous, passive, and female-like character.

After receiving the report, the psychiatrist called the psychologist to tell him something about the patient. It turned out that the patient had been married for six years but had never had intercourse. Impotency problems were at the core of his reasons for seeking psychiatric treatment. Along with this, he had frequent masturbatory fantasies of half-undressed women in which his attention was focused upon their legs and high heels.

The psychiatrist's material on his patient, thus, was consistent with the title of this section: Mr. C was a man who hid under the protective disguise of a clown over which, on a secondary level, he then placed the superficial varnish of being a virile, impressive male. Thus, who is this man? On one level, he puts up a bravado front. Below that he hides in cloaks of absurdity and damage. And still deeper, at the core, he crouches in fear, and has yet—hopefully with the assistance of therapy—to find himself.

REFERENCES

Buck, J. N. (1948). The H-T-P technique: A quantitative and qualitative scoring manual. *Clinical Psychology Monographs, 5,* 1–20.

Burns, R. C. (1982). *Self-growth in families: Kinetic family drawings (K-F-D).* New York: Brunner/Mazel, Inc.

Gardner, H. (1980). *Artful scribbles—The significance of children's drawings,* New York: Basic Books, Inc., Publishers.

Hammer, E. F. (1954). A comparison of H-T-P's of rapists and pedophiles. *Journal of Projective Techniques, 18,* 346–354.

Hammer, E. F. (1955). A comparison of H-T-P's of rapists and pedophiles: The dead tree as an index of psychopathology. *Journal of Clinical Psychology, 11,* 67–69.

Hammer, E. F. (1958). *The clinical application of projective drawings.* Springfield, IL: Charles C Thomas, Publisher.

Hammer, E. F. (1980). *The clinical application of projective drawings.* Springfield, IL: Charles C Thomas, Publisher.

Koch, C. (1952). *The tree test.* New York: Grune & Stratton, Inc.

Levick, M. (1983). *They could not talk and so they draw.* Springfield, IL: Charles C Thomas, Publisher.

Schilder, P. (1935). Image and appearance of the human body. London: Kegan Paul.

5

The Clinical Use of the Draw-A-Person Test (DAP)

*Leonard Handler**

Introduction Even members of the ancient societies consistently recognized that artists project themselves into their artistic productions. For example, the Paleolithic cave paintings in the Trois Frères cave in France depict a man wrapped in an animal hide, playing a primitive flute, as if he meant to put a spell on the animals or attract them to him. Jaffé (1964) describes another painting in the same cave: "... a dancing human being, with antlers, a horse's head, and bear's paws ... unquestionably the 'Lord of the Animals.' " (p. 235). Thus, the painting symbolizes the artist's control of the animals—by incorporating all their strengths.

It long ago became obvious that all art reflects some aspects of the artist's personality, his or her style of life, and his or her approach to the world. Hammer (1958) quotes Elbert Hubbard, an artist who

* The author would like to thank Dr. Barbara Handler, Robin Bishop, Darlene Copperfield, and Joseph Kot for assistance in various phases of preparation, typing, and editing of this chapter.

stated, "When an artists paints a portrait, he paints two, himself and the sitter," (p. 8) and another artist who stated, "The artist does not see things as they are, but as he is" (p. 8).

The creation of the artistic production involves the expression of the unconscious through symbolism as well as the expression of the artist's style and approach. A variety of conflicts may be symbolized in the artist's production; the style of approach to the paper or canvas may be typical of the approach to the world in general. One artist may draw with bold, colorful strokes on a large canvas, while another draws tiny, tight figures of muted colors, on a small canvas.

HISTORY

In 1926, Florence Goodenough developed and standardized an intelligence scale that was based upon the drawing of a man. This test, that came to be called the Goodenough Draw-A-Man Test (DAP), was based mostly on the quality of the drawing and the amount of detail in it. Clinicians (such as Hammer; Karen Machover, 1949; and even Goodenough herself) soon became aware that although the Draw-A-Man Test was supposed to be a test of intelligence, the drawings were also tapping a variety of personality variables.

Since 1926, the clinical use of the DAP has increased dramatically. Indeed, in 1961, Sundberg reported that the DAP was the second most frequently used psychological test in hospitals, clinics, and counseling centers throughout the country. Other surveys of psychological testing practices (Crenshaw, Bohn, Hoffman, Matheus & Offenbach, 1968; Lubin, Wallis & Paine, 1971) indicate that the DAP continues to be used with a majority of cases in a variety of clinical settings and it is among the five most frequently used projective tests in research situations.

Just what is there about the drawing of a human figure which makes it a good indicator of personality patterns and conflicts? Perhaps it is because graphic representation and drawing are early developmental skills. Indeed, Hammer (1958) emphasized that children draw before they can write. Drawings are therefore capable of tapping early, primitive layers of personality, set down before a great deal of intellectual control has taken over. The artist expresses symbolically many hidden aspects of personality which have typically come to control and modulate. Thus, Hammer (1958) states:

> The drawing page ... serves as a canvas upon which the subject may sketch a glimpse of his inner world, his traits and attitudes, his behavioral characteristics, his personality strengths and weaknesses including the degree to which he can mobilize his inner resources to handle his psychodynamic conflicts, both interpersonal and intrapsychic (p. 6).

ADVANTAGES OF THE DAP

1. The DAP is a simple, easy task for most patients. Children, especially young children, like it and will usually cooperate quite readily. They are often more fluent graphically than they are verbally.

2. The DAP is quick and easy to administer; it is typically completed within five or ten minutes, and it requires few materials.

3. The DAP is one of the few graphic tests in the test battery.

4. The DAP is the only test in the battery which has no external stimulus or structure. There are no designs to copy and no vague forms from which to produce associations. Therefore, the clinician has the opportunity to observe the patient's functioning on a relatively unstructured task; the structure must come completely from within. The patient's functioning under these task conditions should be compared with functioning on more structured tests in order to determine the degree to which he or she needs external structure in order to function, and to determine the qualitative and quantitative effects of functioning when external structure is absent. Is the internal structure (the self) sufficient to allow the patient to function well (i.e., the production of a well-integrated drawing)? The data generated from the DAP in comparison with other tests can frequently answer this question. In situations where there is not adequate functioning, an analysis of the style and content of the drawing will often offer clues concerning the specific conflict areas which might be responsible for poor self-integration. For example, a poorly integrated drawing which shows a greal deal of distortion in the sexual areas might indicate that the ego disturbance is focused around sexual conflict. If it was executed with the hands covering the genital area, the patient might be expressing conflict concerning sexual inhibition or intercourse.

5. The DAP often yields a great deal of information concerning self-concept, as well as information concerning personality style, orientation, and conflict areas.

6. The DAP has few age and intelligence limitations.

7. The DAP is often welcomed by inhibited and non-talkative patients. It is a relatively non-verbal test (the only verbal material is contained in the thematic associations to the drawings) and therefore, it is useful when language is a problem, e.g., with the poorly educated patient, the mentally defective patient, the non-English speaking patient, the mute patient, the shy or withdrawn patient, the patient from an underpri-

vileged background who feels insecure about verbal ability, the learning disabled or reading disabled patient who sometimes develops emotional blocks in verbal areas, all of which frequently interfere with productivity on the more verbal tests.

8. The DAP is a useful test with patients who are evasive and/ or guarded. These patients give barren verbal records in tests where they are able to exercise more control over their verbal expression. But in the DAP, the patient expresses himself in a more direct, primitive manner. Such guarded patients seem more aware of what they might be expressing in the verbal tests, but they are probably less certain of what their graphic expression might reveal about them and they perhaps can utilize less control over this more primitive mode of expression. Concrete, primitive personalities often produce richer DAP records, compared with their Rorschach records, while verbal, intellectual patients often produce richer Rorschach and TAT records compared with their DAP protocols. (Fox, 1952; Hammer, 1954).

9. Since the DAP is quick and easy to administer, it lends itself well as an instrument to measure change in psychotherapy. For example, Figure 5–1, taken from Harrower (1965), illustrates the before and after therapy drawings of a female pa-

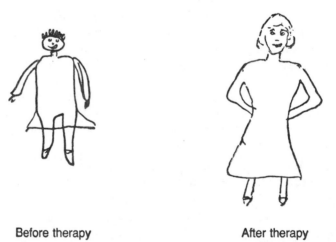

Before therapy   After therapy

Figure 5–1 Illustrates the before and after therapy drawings of a female patient rated as maximally improved.

From M. Harrower, *Psychological Testing: An Empirical Approach,* 1965. Courtesy of Charles C Thomas, Publisher, Springfield, Illinois.

tient rated as maximally improved. Note the improvement in overall drawing quality, the more sophisticated presentation of the head and body, and the disappearance of the transparency.

10. The DAP is often an excellent springboard for discussion of specific conflict areas. Here the patient may be asked to associate the drawing just completed. Repeated administration allows the clinician to see changes which have taken place, and to identify problem areas which still need attention. Hammer (1968) cites the case of a twenty-five-year-old school teacher who had a problem relating to men and a block against getting married. She sensed that her moderate obesity might be a defense against males:

> After a year-and-a-half of treatment, she was able to lose weight, had begun going out, and had established a "going steady" relationship with one young man. One day, she came to the therapy session, proudly showed an engagement ring, and announced jubilantly that she was to be married.
>
> Feeling that she had accomplished her goals in therapy, but also having some marginal doubts, she asked if she might re-take the H-T-P to compare it with the one she had taken upon entering treatment. The drawing of a female she now produced (Figure 5–2) was better integrated, prettier, more feminine and certainly no longer the representation of the obese woman it had been. The figure, like the earlier one, still stood on phallic feet and the hands were now drawn into a position of pelvic defense. Both hands, in spite of the ring now conspicuous on the third finger were drawn to a position of guarding the genital area. Whereas noteworthy gains in self-image were apparent, the drawing cried out with the problem of fear of intercourse and some underlying masculine identification still unresolved (pp. 369–370).

11. The DAP is more sensitive to psychopathology compared with other projective tests (Calden, 1953; Zucker, 1948). Zucker found that the DAP was the first test in the battery to show incipient psychopathology. Thus, it is a good prognostic indicator. However, Zucker also found that the DAP was the last test to show improvement.

12. A number of clinicians have begun to utilize the DAP as a measure of progress and outcome in therapy for sexual disorders (Hartman & Fithian, 1972; Sarrel & Sarrel, 1979). Sarrel, Sarrel & Berman (1981), in a remarkable paper, detail the major ways in which the DAP is useful in sex therapy: assessing the individual (including psychopathology, body image, sexual orientation and/or gender identity, sexual re-

Figure 5–2 Is a drawing by a twenty-five-year-old school teacher after becoming engaged, suggesting sexual panic at impending marriage.

From A. I. Rabin (Ed.), *Assessment With Projective Techniques,* page 156.
Copyright 1981 by Springer Publishing Company, Inc., New York. Used by
permission.

sponse and behavior, organic disease, motivation, and personality style), assessing interpersonal issues, and assessing
change during the course of sex therapy.

Concerning the use of the DAP in interpersonal issues, clinicians
use the drawing to determine feelings about the opposite sex and
feelings specific to the couple's relationships (an index of the psychological bonding between the couple), to assess interpersonal issues
and change during the course of sex therapy (changes in the individual
and in the couple's relationship). The DAP is also used to assess such
differences as global body image problems, body penetration anxiety,
body boundary problems, and anxiety about the genitals or other parts
of the body.

Figure 5–3 illustrates the initial drawings done by a twenty-six-
year-old woman who disliked sex and had never had an orgasm. The
patient felt rejected by her father, who told her at age sixteen that
she was "as sexy as a wet dishrag." Figure 5–4 was done at the
completion of therapy—note the dramatic change in body image.

Clinicians also illustrate the manner in which the DAP can be

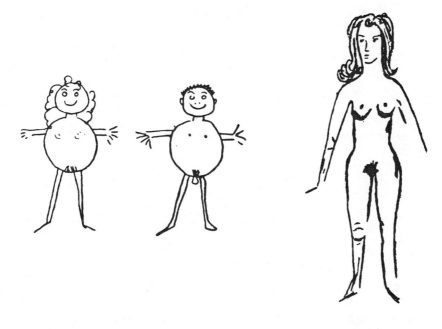

Figure 5–3   **Figure 5–4**
Before therapy   After therapy

Figure 5–3 and Figure 5–4 Are drawings by a twenty-six-year-old woman before and after sex therapy.

Reproduced from "Using the Draw-A-Person (DAP) Test in Sex Therapy" by P. Sarrell, L. Sarrell, and S. Berman. *Journal of Sex and Marital Therapy*, 1981, 7, 163–183. Human Sciences Press, 72 Fifth Avenue, New York, NY 10011, copyright 1981.

used to monitor changes in the individual as well as changes in a couple's interpersonal dynamics. Figure 5–5 was drawn by a thirty-two-year-old impotent male who was extremely fearful and severely disturbed. The first drawing was done before therapy, the second drawing was done when the patient began to have early successful erectile experiences, and the third drawing was done at the end of therapy. "The first drawing", the patient remarked, "was a hermaphrodite." Note the tiny size of the figure, the lack of definition of the body, and the discontinuity in the line, all indicators of severe pathology.

The last illustrations (Figure 5–6) are the drawings of a sexually dysfunctional, inhibited woman who began to emerge as an assertive, sexual woman. In turn, her initially confident husband became frightened and sexually dysfunctional. The woman's drawings are on the left and her husband's drawings are on the right. The clinician emphasizes the immature and child-like self-image projected by the woman

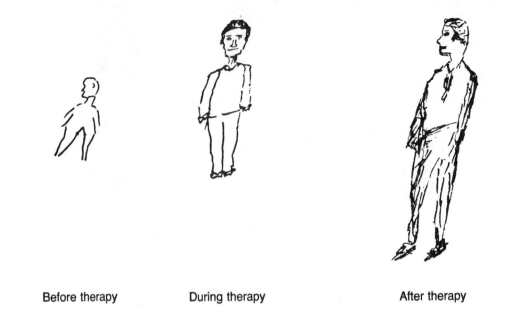

Before therapy	During therapy	After therapy

Figure 5–5 Are drawings by a thirty-two-year-old male before, during, and after sex therapy.

in the first drawing. The subsequent drawings show her increasing self-confidence and her husband's increasing anxiety. As therapy progressed, the husband could not ejaculate. He feared losing control of himself and hurting his wife. The authors note that his pictures indicate ". . . increasing levels of repressed anger . . . and genital anxiety" (p. 180).

INSTRUCTIONS

The clinician should have a supply of 8½ × 11 inch unlined paper and some well-sharpened #2 pencils with erasers. The drawing surface beneath the paper should be flat and smooth and there should be sufficient illumination. The patient should be seated comfortably with enough room for arms and legs. The patient should be able to rest his or her arms comfortably on the drawing surface.

One sheet of paper should be placed in front of the patient in a vertical position, with one pencil. The patient should be told: "I would like you to draw a picture of a person." The clinician should give the patient little more guidance than that, despite the fact that the patient often asks a variety of questions in order to get the examiner to struc-

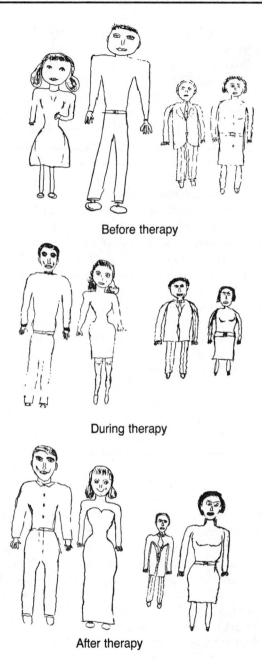

Before therapy

During therapy

After therapy

Figure 5–6 Are drawings of a sexually dysfunctional, inhibited woman and her husband before, during, and after sex therapy.

ture the situation more clearly. However, since this is a projective test, the clinician should resist adding any additional instructions which will interfere with unemcumbered, free performance. For example, patients often ask, "What kind of figure should I draw?", "Should I draw the head only?", "Should I draw the whole person?" or, "Is a stick figure ok?" In response to these and other such questions, the clinician should respond, "Do it any way you like; it's up to you." Sometimes the patient responds with comments indicating concern about his or her ability to perform adequately, such as "I was never a good artist," or, "I can't do this because I can't draw." To such comments as these, the examiner should respond, "This is not a test of artistic ability. I'm not concerned with how good an artist you are. Just do the best you can and don't worry." Should the patient draw merely the head, the head and shoulders, or a stick figure he should be given another sheet of paper and should then be told, "This time I'd like you to draw the entire person (or, a non-stick figure person)."

When the first complete drawing is finished, the clinician should put another sheet of paper in front of the patient and should be told, "Now I'd like you to draw a person of the opposite sex." If the patient being tested is a child, the clinician should say, "You drew a boy (man); now draw a girl or a woman," or, "You drew a girl (woman); now draw a boy or a man." When this task has been completed satisfactorily, the patient should be asked to sign each drawing. The clinican should then date each drawing, either on the front or on the back. In addition, the clinician should indicate which drawing was done first, which was done second, and so on.

The clinician should then present the first complete drawing to the patient and should request that the patient make up a story about the person drawn: "Now I'd like you to make up a story about the person you've drawn. Look at it and make up a story, and I'll write it down." The story should be recorded verbatim because interpretation often depends on the manner in which the words are phrased and expressed. Sometimes it is necessary to urge or encourage the patient. Should the patient be unable to make up a story, it will then be necessary to ask specific questions about the drawing. For example, "How old is the person?" "What does the person do for a living?" "How does the person feel?" "What is he thinking about?" "What will happen to him in the future?" "What fears does he have?" "What gets him angry?" "How does he get along with his wife (husband, mother, father), etc.?" For a more detailed set of questions for an adult and a separate set for a child, see Machover (1951). Any questions that the clinician feels will help the patient associate to the drawing should be used.

A third approach in obtaining verbal associations is to ask the patient to examine the drawings and associate to them. The patient should be asked to describe the person he has drawn, and to tell what comes to mind when the drawing is examined, or, the examiner might ask, "Tell me about this person; what is he like?" Sarrel, Sarrel & Berman (1981) ask the patient to "Look at the finished pictures . . . and write down any observations or feelings that occur to you as you look at the pictures" (p. 165).

Kissen (1981) describes an important modification of the verbal association phase which, he feels, enhances the "psychodynamic potentiality" of the DAP. He encourages the patient to "adopt an attitude of naiveté and curiosity toward his or her own figure drawings," and he invites the patient to "explore psychologically some of the salient expressive characteristics of the human figures produced" (pp. 43–44). The patient becomes a consultant, thereby joining the resistance. This role reversal "allows the patient to become spontaneous and open to inner experiential states" (p. 44).

After the patient completes both figures, the clinician states:

> I would like you to look at your first drawing as though it were drawn by somebody else. From the physical characteristics of the drawing, facial expression, posture, style of clothing—what sort of person comes through to you? What personal characteristics come to mind? (p. 45).

The clinician asks the patient to "describe how the male person in the drawing relates to other males, how the female relates to other females, and how the person in the drawing relates to peers of the opposite sex." Kissen also asks the patient to describe an animal that seems most like the person in the drawing, and then he draws a cartoon balloon coming from the mouth of the figure and asks the patient to "Write in the balloon a statement that you can imagine the person you have described making. Write a typical statement that is characteristic of this sort of person" (pp. 45–46). The same procedure is used for the second drawing.

During the drawing task itself, it is important for the clinician to observe the drawing sequence. For example, although the great majority of patients draw the head first, a recent patient began with the feet and ended with the head. Since this pattern is quite atypical and may indicate severe pathology, it is important that the clinician observe and record such variations in approach to the drawing task. In another example, a patient drew a mouth with a frown, erased it, and replaced it with a heavily overworked grin. An adolescent male first drew a male with small, narrow shoulders, only to erase them and replace them with extremely broad compensatory shoulders. In still another example, the patient went back over a light, tentative line and reinforced it to give the drawing a superficial look of confidence and adequacy.

Although the DAP is one of the easiest tests in the battery for most patients, the clinician should be aware that the task of drawing a person is difficult for some patients, especially in the anxiety-provoking testing situation. Although a good clinician will help the patient manage and deal with anxiety concerning the testing situation and the anxiety concerning personal self-revelation, the testing situation is sometimes tension-filled and the patient has little knowledge concerning the adequacy of the performance. Therefore, the remarks made by the patient, the style of approach to the task, and the adequacy of attempts to manage the task appropriately despite the pressure of the testing situation, should all be observed and noted. For example, does the patient stop to erase and fix a poorly drawn spot; does the patient verbalize any defensive responses (e.g., "I can't draw too well, I never studied art in school"); does the patient verbalize an evaluation of the drawing (e.g., "This man looks angry")?

It is important to note how the patient orients to the relatively unstructured drawing situation. Does the patient ask for direction, either verbally or non-verbally, or does the patient seem comfortable and self-assured? Is the patient's approach to the task quick and impulsive, careful, or overly cautious and uncertain? Does the patient express doubts about his or her ability? Each aspect of approach to the task tells the clinician a great deal about adaptation in the environment, self-concept, methods of dealing with stressful situations, conflicts, and personality style.

THE PATIENT'S EXPERIENCE

What is the experience of the patient when asked to draw a person? How does a patient begin to organize the task, to pick and choose what he or she will draw? Of course, previous drawing experience may provide a guide, but experience alone is probably not enough to produce an integrated drawing. The patient must in some way refer to all of the images of himself/herself and of other persons that crowd his/her mind. The patient draws upon visual perception of other people, both past and present, as well as the emotional experiences which go with these perceptions. There is also the patient's visual perception of his or her body image, which is a product of experience, indentifications, projections, and introjections. The composite DAP image is intimately tied to the self. In the process of creating the figure, conscious and unconscious determinants guide patients; images of cultural and social stereotypes contribute to body image conception. Thus, tall, thin, asthenic people are associated with certain psychological attributes in patients' minds, while other types of body builds are identified with other temperaments. Strong arms, thick necks, and long noses often have stereotyped social meanings. For example, Dick Tracy's square jaw symbolizes strength, virtue, and determination, while Elmer Fudd's short, round body, and bald head symbolize bumbling inadequacy and ineffectualness. Combined with these social images are those that arise from within private experience. Added to this are the more universal symbols of psychoanalysis and folklore. All of these images intermingle to produce the subtle and complex projections of the self.

It is clear, then, that the task of drawing the human figure is a creative one. The pencil is guided by unconscious forces asking for expression and by stylistic patterns of expressive behavior that are typical of the patient in a variety of situations. The figure the patient draws is himself or herself in many respects, and the page upon which the patient draws is his or her world. The end product is a drawing of self-experience in the patient's world.

THE DRAWING AS A REPRESENTATION OF THE SELF

Perhaps the paragraph above describes why human beings do not typically draw what they look like, or how they are built, but instead draw a figure which reflects how they feel about themselves, and how they feel as a person dealing within the environment. For example, a burly and powerful lumberjack or construction worker might draw a tiny, uncertain looking man, while a thin, frail, and effeminate-looking man might draw a large, virile male in an attempt to live out a fantasy. The body image projected on the paper may refer to deep, unconscious wishes, to a frank acknowledgment of physical or psychological impairment, to conscious or unconscious compensation for a physical or a psychological defect, or to a combination of all of these factors.

The drawing that a patient makes of a human figure represents the self in the environment. The actual presentation of the self may reflect the patient's deepest wishes; it may reflect and expose a painful physical or emotional defect; it may be a vigorous compensation for this defect; or a combination of all these factors. The drawing may represent an ego ideal or a hero figure, as, for example, the drawing of a fierce and muscular warrior drawn by a recent patient—a short, chubby eleven-year-old Philippino boy. However, this approach may be seen as an attempt to present the self in a more admired manner. The patient seems to be saying, "Right now I feel small in a much larger adult world, but when I grow up I'm going to be a big, strong, brave man like this!" Perhaps during the experience of drawing, which seemed quite pleasurable to the boy, he was also saying, "Right now I am big; I am that strong, brave warrior!"

While patients sometimes attempt to express an ideal self rather than the real self, the underlying basis for this expression may also be seen in the drawing, thereby giving the clinician a picture of both the real self and the ideal self. Occasionally, the patient draws in such a manner as to illustrate his or her attitudes toward life and society in general. The drawing may be a conscious expression of these feelings, or it may include deeply disguised and unconscious information, expressed indirectly through symbolism.

Some clinicians (Levy, 1950) feel that the drawing might also represent a projection of attitudes toward someone else in the environment (e.g., the patient's feelings about his or her father or mother), a projection of an ideal self-image, or an expression of the patient's attitude toward life and toward the world in general. Handler feels that these other possible representations constitute or relate to some aspect of the self-concept. For example, the patient's attitude about a parent or feelings about the world are directly related to how the patient feels about himself or herself.

Some observers have indicated that the DAP is invalid because people do not represent themselves as they appear physically and, therefore, the DAP does not represent a true picture of the self. These critics do not understand the principle of symbolic representation, where the material is presented in a disguised or symbolically-transformed manner. For example, Hammer (1958) illustrates a drawing produced by a man with a missing left arm and hand. The left arm and hand are present in the drawing, but they appear withered and much smaller than the right arm and hand.

Several other examples come from the work of Schildkrout, Shenker, and Sonnenblick (1972). The drawing (Figure 5–7) was done by a fifteen-year-old girl with exaggerated concern about a mild facial acne and irregular menses. She eradicates her acne by becoming totally faceless. The next drawing (Figure 5–8) was done by a twelve-year-old girl with a congenital heart defect about which she verbalized no concern. Notice that she symbolized her underlying concern about her heart problem by the heart-shaped body she drew.

NORMATIVE DATA

The typical drawing of a person consists of a head, that is drawn first, facial features (eyes, nose, mouth, ears, hair), legs, feet, arms, hands, fingers, neck, shoulders, and trunk. The typical drawing also includes such additional details as a belt and clothing of some type (skirt, dress, trousers, shirt, jacket). It is placed approximately in the middle of the page and is about six to seven inches in size.

Figure 5–7 Is a drawing by a fifteen-year-old girl with exaggerated concern
about mild facial acne and irregular menses.

Reprinted with permission from Schildkraut, M. S., Shenker, I. R., and Sonnenblick, M., *Human Figure Drawings in Adolescents*. New York: Brunner/
Mazel, 1972. Copyright held by the authors.

Figure 5–8 Is a drawing by a twelve-year-old girl with a congenital heart
defect about which she seemed unconcerned.

Reprinted with permission from Schildkraut, M. S., Shenker, I. R., and Sonnenblick, M., *Human Figure Drawings in Adolescents*. New York: Brunner/
Mazel, 1972. Copyright held by authors.

There are relatively few studies concerning the quality of the
typical adult drawing. Below is a short summary of these findings:
the head, trunk, arms, and legs are typically in proportion, with relative symmetry, spontaneity, movement, or animation. The line quality is typically consistent. The head is more oval than round, and some
attempt is made to draw the facial features in a realistic manner (e.g.,
eyes are almond shaped, not round circles or dots, lips are indicated
by a double line). The body is life-like, with a three-dimensional quality. The head sits well on the neck and shoulders. Secondary sex
characteristics are included, so that the male and female drawings
may be distinguished from each other (Jones & Thomas, 1964; Thomas,
1966; Urban, 1963; Wagner & Schubert, 1955).

Drawings by children must be judged by other criteria, since the
style and quality of the drawing will vary with age and with developmental status. Unless the clinician knows the developmental drawing norms, the clinician is liable to make an interpretation based upon
developmental or maturational issues. For example, the omission of
the neck or the feet on the DAP are not unusual for the typical five-
year-old boy, and therefore they do not have clinical significance. It

is also important to note that drawings done by children and adults from other cultures and other countries should not be evaluated with the same criteria, since cultural factors affect drawing style and quality in some dramatic ways.

Table 5–1, which summarizes the expected drawing items (present in 86–100 percent of the drawings) and the exceptional items (present in 15 percent or less of the drawings) for boys and girls, is taken from Koppitz (1968). The exceptional items are found only on drawings of children with above average mental maturity. This table may be used to rate the developmental quality of the drawing to distinguish developmental factors from emotional factors. For example, a five-year-old boy can be expected to include hands, eyes, nose, mouth, body, and legs in his drawing. Omission of one or more of these items is said by Koppitz to be clinically significant.

Koppitz has validated a series of emotional indicators, that are listed in Table 5–2, along with the ages at which they become clinically valid for boys and girls. Note, for example, that Koppitz finds shading of the body and/or limbs is normal for young children and therefore it does not become an indicator of conflict until the boy is nine and the girl is eight.

Machover (1960) offers normative DAP data from middle-class white boys and girls, ages five through twelve. She correlates the normative findings with sex, age, and stage-related psychodynamic patterns and cultural epochs (e.g., the Oedipal and latency periods). Handler has included selected illustrations (Figure 5–9) that show the beginning development of the body concept.

Schildkrout, et al. (1972) discussed the normal adolescent drawing. They emphasize that drawings done by normal adolescents typically reflect their predominant age- and stage-related problems and conflicts. For example, the early adolescent (ages twelve through fifteen) is said to have an overpowering urge to return to dependency on the infantile mother image. The teenager directs his or her efforts against this regressive tendency and towards an object of affection outside the family. They continue:

> ... The dependency upon the parent is seen commonly in drawings of both boys and girls in the form of obvious midline emphasis, numerous buttons, and belt buckles. Efforts to control impulses in the face of weakening superego and ego are reflected in the frequent use of stripes, plaids, dots, and other designs covering much of the body ... The use of body shading and emphasis in sexual regions, reflect(s) the ansiety experienced over the dramatic physical changes which are taking place (p. 6).

Schildkrout et al., discussed the typical conflicts of the middle and the late adolescent, and their reflection in the drawing. For ex-

Table 5-1 Expected and Exceptional Items on Human Figure Drawings of Boys and Girls Age 5 to 12

Expected Items	Age 5		Age 6		Age 7		Age 8		Age 9		Age 10		Age 11 & 12	
	Boys	Girls	Boys	Girls	Boys	Girls	Boys	Girls	Boys	Girls	Boys	Girls	Boys	Girls
N	128	128	131	133	134	125	138	130	134	134	109	108	157	167
Head	X	X	X	X	X	X	X	X	X	X	X	X	X	X
Eyes	X	X	X	X	X	X	X	X	X	X	X	X	X	X
Nose	X	X	X	X	X	X	X	X	X	X	X	X	X	X
Mouth	X	X	X	X	X	X	X	X	X	X	X	X	X	X
Body	X	X	X	X	X	X	X	X	X	X	X	X	X	X
Legs	X	X	X	X	X	X	X	X	X	X	X	X	X	X
Arms		X	X	X	X	X	X	X	X	X	X	X	X	X
Feet				X	X	X	X	X	X	X	X	X	X	X
Arms 2 dimension					X		X	X	X	X	X	X	X	X
Legs 2 dimension						X	X	X	X	X	X	X	X	X
Hair						X		X	X	X	X	X	X	X
Neck				X				X		X	X	X	X	X
Arm down											X		X	
Arms at shoulder												X		X
2 clothing items													X	X

Exceptional Items

Knee	X	X	X	X	X	X	X	X	X	X	X
Profile	X	X	X	X	X	X	X	X	X	X
Elbow	X	X	X	X	X	X	X	X
Two lips	X	X	X	X	X	X	X	X
Nostrils	X	X	X	X	X	X	X
Proportions	X	X	X	X
Arms at shoulder	X	X	X
4 clothing items	X	X
Feet 2 dimension	X	X
Five fingers	X	X
Pupils	X

From E. Koppitz, *Psychological Evaluation of Children's Human Figure Drawings.* New York: Grune and Stratton, Inc, 1968. Reproduced by permission.

Table 5–2 Emotional Indicators on Human Figure Drawings of Children

Poor integration of parts of figure (Boys 7, Girls 6)
Shading of face
Shading of body and/or limbs (Boys 9, Girls 8)
Shading of hands and/or neck (Boys 8, Girls 7)
Gross asymmetry of limbs
Slanting figure, axis of figure tilted by 15° or more
Tiny figure, two inches high or less
Big figure, nine inches or more in height (Boys and Girls 8)
Transparencies
Tiny head, head less than 1/10th of total figure in height
Crossed eyes, both eyes turned in or out
Teeth
Short arms, arms not long enough to reach waistline
Long arms, arms long enough to reach knee line
Arms clinging to sides of body
Big hands, hands as large or larger than face of figure
Hands cut off, arms without hands or fingers (hidden hands not scored)
Legs pressed together
Genitals
Monster or grotesque figure
Three or more figures spontaneously drawn
Clouds, rain, snow
Omissions: Eyes; Nose (Boys 6, Girls 5); Mouth; Body; Arms (Boys 6, Girls
5); Legs; Feet (Boys 9, Girls 7); Neck (Boys 10, Girls 9)

Note: All of the Emotional Indicators are considered valid for boys and girls age 5–12, unless otherwise indicated.

From E. Koppitz, *Psychological Evaluation of Children's Human Figure Drawings.* New York: Grune and Stratton, Inc., 1968. Reproduced by permission.

ample, the drawings of the middle adolescent often appear grandiose by depicting an idealized physical image because of the resolution of the Oedipus conflict through identification with the parent of the same sex and the establishment of a male or female role. The authors stated, "The sixteen-year-old girl may draw a seductive, fashionably dressed female while the boy may portray a male of obvious athletic prowess" (p. 7).

Saarni and Azara (1977) compiled two categories of anxiety indices—an aggressive-hostile category (scars, gross asymmetry of limbs, oversize figures, crossed eyes, teeth present, transparencies, disproportionately long arms and hands, omission of arms, genitals present) and an insecure-labile category (vertical slant more than 15 degrees; undifferentiated shading of face, neck; disproportionately short arms; arms clinging to sides of body; no hands, fingers, eyes, mouth, legs, feet, neck; tiny figure; baseline under figure; excessive midline detailing; and faint, scribbly-scratchy lines). They theorized that a de-

Figure 5-9 Are male and female drawings produced by children of various ages.

Reprinted with permission from Schildkraut, M. S., Schenker, I. R., and Sonnenblick, M., *Human Figure Drawings in Adolescents*. New York: Brunner/Mazel, 1972. Copyright held by authors.

velopmental comparison of adolescents, young adults, and aged adults would reveal different patterns of aggressive-hostile signs and insecure-labile signs. They found that relative to females, males revealed significantly more aggressive-hostile indices. The high school girls obtained a mean number of insecure-labile indices which were almost twice those of the young adult females. Insecure-labile indices were not sex typed, as the authors had predicted, but the incidence of bizarre figures appeared to be a male sex typed DAP characteristic, while ambiguous, childlike figures were somewhat more typical in the female DAP.

The results of this study strongly suggest that it is important, in the analysis of an individual DAP, to be aware of normative findings. There are apparently some DAP variables which are related primarily to personality factors, those that are primarily related to social-cultural factors, and those that reflect both personality and socio-cultural variables, as they interact. Gilbert and Hall (1966) indicate that as people get older, there is an increasing tendency for their drawings to become absurd, incongruous, fragmented, and primitive; they found a marked similarity between the drawings of young and middle-age schizophrenics and normal elderly people. If additional studies support such a surprising finding, it will be necessary to generate an extensive set of age-related norms.

THE PROBLEM OF ARTISTIC ABILITY

A major problem in the use of the DAP concerns the relationship between drawing signs and artistic ability. It has been determined that clinicians often make clinical interpretations based upon the artistic ability of the patient and not upon actual personality variables (Levy, Lomax & Minsky, 1963; Lewinsohn & May, 1963; Nichols & Stumpfer, 1962; Sherman, 1958; Stumpfer & Nichols, 1962; Whitmyre, 1953). This finding has been utilized by research-oriented clinical psychologists to discredit the clinical use of the DAP. However, more applied clinicians have continued to use figure drawings because they nevertheless believe that the test has clinical merit. While the researcher typically believes that the applied clinician is deluding himself or herself, the applied clinician believes that the researcher is being entirely too rigid and conservative. And so the battle continues with each side merely reaffirming what it already believes.

In an effort to resolve this controversy Handler decided to investigate the incorporation of research-oriented methodology into the clinical interpretive process. He reasoned that if the DAP interpreters confused artistic ability with emotional problems, a control figure was needed to determine, for each patient, how much of the variation in performance was due to artistic ability and how much was due to emotional problems as they were portrayed in the drawing. Handler reasoned that if artistic ability was a large factor in a patient's drawing, then a neutral control figure of equal task difficulty could be utilized in the interpretive process to partial out the differential effects of emotional factors and artistic ability.

Several different types of drawings were considered and were ruled out as possibilities for a variety of reasons. Handler finally decided to use the drawing of an automobile as the control figure. In a series of pilot studies with males and females who drew a man, woman, and an automobile, it was determined that drawing an automobile was equal in task difficulty, compared with drawing a man or woman; both men and women felt it was as easy (or as difficult) to draw an automobile as it was to draw a person. The automobile drawing was then subject to a series of validation studies to determine whether it could be used as a neutral control figure. In a series of studies, it was found that externally-induced stress significantly increased manifestations of anxiety on all three figures; the automobile drawing reflected significantly less anxiety compared with the male and female drawings (Handler & Reyher, 1964; Jacobson & Handler, 1967). In several other studies (Handler & Reyher, 1966; Nordquist & Handler, 1969) subjects were asked to draw a man, woman, and an automobile while autonomic measures (heart rate or GSR) were obtained. A huge difference was found in the degree of anxiety reflected in the three drawings; the automobile drawings had the fewest number of anxiety indices. Exactly the same results were obtained when the autonomic measures were analyzed. Since the automobile was found to be a relatively neutral drawing of equal task difficulty, Handler concluded that it was possible to use it as a control figure. If the automobile drawing is done poorly, and the people drawings are also done poorly, then an interpretation of poor artistic ability should be made. However, if the people drawings are done poorly and the automobile drawing is done well, the interpretation of poor artistic ability should not be made. Instead, the poor execution of the people drawings should be taken as an indication of either intrapsychic problems, an indication of the effects of external stress (emanating from the testing situation itself or perceived stress from other external sources), or both.

INTERPRETATION

Many tests lend themselves to both impressionistic interpretation or to more detailed quantified interpretation. The interpretation of the DAP is not an exception. For example, it is possible to inves-

tigate conflict and anxiety in a drawing by the use of a rating scale*
(Handler & Reyher, 1964, 1966) or the drawings may be interpreted
more impressionistically. In order to utilize the latter method, it is
important for the clinician to become intimately involved with the
drawing. The clinician must be able to become the person drawn to
some degree. The clinician should put himself or herself in the position
of the person drawn—to lose distance, so to speak. Kris (1952) has
described this creative experience as "regression in the service of the
ego." If clinicians can experience what it is like to be the person drawn,
then they will be able to feel and understand the artist. Since the
drawn person is believed to be representative of the personality of the
drawer, getting in touch with the drawing gives clinicians a valuable
method to understand the individual being studied.

In order to accomplish this task, it is often useful to put the
clinician's body in the same position as that of the drawing and to
imitate the facial expression as represented in the drawing. Sometimes asking the question, "What must be going on right now to
produce a drawing like this?", helps to experience the patient's world
as the patient experiences it.

Kris (1952) describes the reaction of a person viewing a work of
art that is probably quite close to the phenomenological process of
interpreting a drawing:

> Looking long enough, one tends to become aware of a kinesthetic
> reaction, however slight; it may be that one tries, at first imper-
> ceptibly and later consciously, to react with one's own body, or it
> may be that the reaction remains unconscious. We know that our
> ensuing emotional experience will still be colored by the reflection
> of the perceived posture, that our ego has in the process of per-
> ception utilized a complex apparatus, the body scheme, or ... the
> image of the body.... On the second stage of reaction we identify
> ourselves with the artist's model.... We change imperceptibly from
> identification with the model into the stage in which we "imitate"
> the strokes and lines with which it (the drawing) was produced.
> To some extent we have changed roles. We started out as part of
> the world which the artist created; we end as co-creators: We iden-
> tify ourselves with the artist (pp. 55–56).

In a series of five classroom demonstrations over a period of five
years, second-year graduate students who had no previous DAP ex-

---

* There is a conflict/anxiety scoring manual available for those who wish to score
drawings obtained from patients (Handler, 1967). Interrater reliability is quite high,
as indicated in a series of studies (Attkisson, Waidler, Jeffrey, & Lambert, 1974;
Handler & Reyher, 1964, 1966; Jacobson & Handler, 1967; Nordquist & Handler,
1969; Trestman, 1981).

perience were able to achieve 81 percent correct interpretations. The demonstrations followed essentially the following pattern: The students were given a drawing done by a patient who was in psychotherapy with a colleague who would verify the accuracy of the interpretations generated by the graduate students. The drawing was passed around and the students were presented the impressionistic process of interpretation as described above. The students were asked to become intimately involved with the drawing, to lose distance, and to then generate specific, detailed hypotheses concerning the patient. The specific hypotheses were recorded on a chalkboard. Once the students generated all the hypotheses they could (typically twenty to thirty), the therapist went down the list and verified each hypothesis.

Handler has done a number of blind interpretations convincing him that the DAP can yield important clinical information about a patient. For example, a student brought Handler a DAP done by a patient in a nearby state mental hospital who had applied for a weekend pass. Based upon a battery of test results, it was recommended that the patient be allowed to return home and visit his wife for the weekend. Handler urged the student not to recommend the pass: "This man is dangerous; he'll hurt his wife, and perhaps try to kill her." Unhappily, it was too late; he had been released the previous weekend and had slit his wife's throat and killed her! All indications of this tragic event were clear to Handler from the drawings. The male drawing reflected an angry, impulse-oriented person with sadistic tendencies and poor judgment; the woman he drew appeared frightened and helpless, and there was a strange line drawn across her neck, a clumsy exaggerated attempt to represent a collar. There, in the drawing, was even represented the method by which the patient was to kill his wife!

In another informal interpretive attempt Handler told a student that the person who did the female drawing he had presented was an assertive, sexually-manipulative woman who handled men in a rather domineering manner. In addition, Handler indicated that she was an artist, recently divorced from a weak and passive husband and was on the prowl. The student was quite surprised at first and then insisted that Handler knew the woman who had drawn the picture. When the student was finally convinced that Handler did not know the woman, the student requested an explanation. The same sex drawing was executed with rather large bold strokes. It was rather large, attractively clothed, with a smug look of self-assurance. The seated male was nude, rather small, and his head was pointed downward, facing away from the viewer. The automobile control figure was a phallic, sleek, late-model convertible sports car. Fifteen years ago, women typically did not draw such cars. Although artists typically draw the nude figure, this woman chose to draw the male without clothes rather than the female or both figures without clothes. The nude male in the seated position, turned away, certainly portrayed less adequacy and ability than the engrossing dynamic female.

Are clinicians to conclude that because of negative research findings the DAP should be abandoned as a clinical tool? How can so many clinicians using the technique so effectively, come to grips with these negative research findings, and on the other hand, how can researchers who view the DAP as unreliable and invalid, come to terms with its rich and creative use in the hands of many gifted clinicians? In response to these issues and questions, it is first necessary to understand the interpretive process. For example, Schmidt and McGowan (1959) found that clinicians with an affective orientation, who used an impressionistic or feeling approach to drawings could diagnostically sort drawings correctly, whereas a cognitive group, who evaluated the drawings in terms of specific signs, in a more scientific and intellectualized manner, could not sort the drawings correctly.

Hammer's observations concerning the differential ability of clinicians to use the DAP effectively is expressed quite picturesquely:

> My own experience is that in the hands of some students projective drawings are an exquisitely sensitive tool, and in the hands of others, those employing a wooden, stilted approach, they are like disconnected phones (1968, p. 385).

Burley and Handler (1970) attempted to determine whether there were individual differences among examiners in the accuracy of DAP interpretation. Introductory psychology students and graduate students were shown DAP protocols and were given a list of forced choice interpretations based on therapeutic contact with the patients. The students were asked to choose the interpretation that seemed most descriptive of the patient whose drawings they were studying. The most and least accurate undergraduate and all the graduate students were given the Remote Associates Test, as a measure of creativity and divergent production, the Myers-Briggs Type Indicator to provide a measure of intuition, and the Hogan Empathy Scale. There were significant differences for the good interpreters versus the poor interpreters on the Hogan Empathy Scale, the Myers-Briggs, and the Remote Associates Test. The good DAP interpreter was a person who could think creatively, who was able to connect loosely associated ideas, and who was socially sensitive to subtle nuances in interpersonal behavior. Subjects who were capable of putting themselves in their patients' shoes and in addition, were more able to utilize their preconscious and unconscious associations to the test data were found to be more accurate in their interpretations.

What are the elements that go into the accurate interpretation of the DAP? In addition to the variables mentioned above, a good DAP interpreter should understand the concept of symbolism from the psychoanalytic point of view, as well as understanding symbolization in culture and in folklore. It would help if the clinician studied art and understood the various approaches to symbolization used by various artists. Understanding symbolization in myth, the dream, and in other unconscious representations is of great help in allowing the drawing to communicate meaning. A thorough working knowledge of the dream work, along with an understanding of the mechanisms of substitution, displacement, and condensation would be of great help in allowing the clinician to see the manner in which the unconscious symbolization is transformed into graphic structures.

In approaching the interpretation of the DAP, a more impressionistic approach should be used at first. Attention should then be focused on the drawing details as they fit together to communicate a feeling tone, or message. The posture of the figure and the facial expression convey a mood and tone of the figure, perhaps active and vigorous, perhaps passive and bewildered. The type of line used by the patient and the strength conveyed by the arms and legs add a great deal to the overall impression. The figure may be rigid or tense or there may be undue emphasis on symmetry. Expansiveness, constriction, daydreaming, self-involvement, depression, or anger may be the major expressive element around which the impressions crystalize.

How Is Conflict Expressed

Conflict may be expressed in a variety of ways. First, the patient's approach to the task of drawing may indicate conflict. The patient may be reluctant to draw, he may omit body parts or perhaps even the entire body and may draw only the head, thereby avoiding one or more issues relating to the body. The patient may ask too many preliminary questions, attempting to delay or avoid coming to grips with the situation. Other observable conflict indicators include frequent erasure and reworking of one or more areas, usually with poor results; verbalized dissatisfaction with one or more drawn areas; random and feverish graphic expression.

It is important to emphasize that an interpretive approach that merely lists signs observed in the drawings, coupled with their specified meanings, is in the worst traditions of both clinical and experimental psychology. Such a procedure precludes an approach that attempts to find reason and coherence in the understanding of human personality functioning. All the reasoning surrounding the many implications of the presence of such a sign is curtailed when only one specific interpretation is generated for a specific test sign. There is no attempt to try and reconstruct how a patient is thinking or how the patient approaches a task. The clinician should not ask what it means that, for example, the hands are drawn behind the back. The clinician should instead ask what it *could* mean that the hands are drawn behind the back. Perhaps the patient is a poor artist, and he has difficulty drawing hands. Artistic ability is often a factor in the omission of hands or in hiding hands behind the back; many normal individuals indicate that drawing hands is difficult. It is therefore difficult to determine whether hands behind the back or hands otherwise hidden (e.g., in pockets) indicate a normal reaction to the performance of a difficult task under pressure (the testing situation) or whether it represents a tendency to withdraw. This hypothesis can be verified by examining the quality of the drawing and the quality of the control figure. Other data (from the DAP and other tests) can help differentiate among a number of hypotheses that include anxiety concerning interpersonal relationships, sexual anxieties, evasiveness, or guilt feelings.

A Note of Caution

Although many hypotheses may be generated concerning a patient's functioning, it is important to check these interpretations against other data in the test battery. There should be both a convergence of several sources of data and/or an integration of data from different sources to form a three-dimensional picture of the patient's functioning. Thus, for example, if a male patient's graphic production suggests an attempt to present himself as a smiling, friendly, and open person, but other aspects of the test battery (e.g., the Rorschach) suggest an angry agressive person, it would probably be best to combine these two observations and suggest that while the patient attempts to present himself in a positive light, as an open, friendly, and carefree person, the underlying personality pattern is one of anger and aggression. There are a variety of additional test signs, especially on the Rorschach or the TAT, that would indicate how likely and under what circumstances these underlying hostility patterns would surface and even the source of these patterns. A more detailed examination of the figure drawing for signs of hostility and aggression can also offer clues concerning the likelihood that these underlying and somewhat masked aggressive impulses would make themselves evident in a wide variety of interpersonal relationships and life situations. For example, Hammer (1968) notes:

> Generally, regarding acting-out, we may state that the stronger, the more frank, the more direct (and hence unsublimated) the

expression of impulses which break through in the projective drawings, the more the defensive and adaptive operations of the ego may be presumed to be insufficient in their assimilative function, and the more the likelihood of acting-out (p. 382).

This is an important principle in determining whether certain unconscious materials may become evident. An examination of the opposite sex drawing may also offer clues to these questions. For example, if the female is drawn in an aggressive, hostile, negative, and/or fearful manner, it might be possible to speculate that both the source of the problem as well as the object of the negative expression may be focused on the female. An examination of the style and content of the thematic material collected with the drawings may help to support these notions, as would other thematic materials in the battery (e.g., the TAT).

INTERPRETATION OF STRUCTURE AND CONTENT

Ogdon (1979) has produced a handbook of interpretive hypotheses for the evaluation of the DAP (along with other tests) derived from both the clinical and the experimental literature. Below is a selected list of figure drawing variables and some possible interpretive hypotheses. This section should not be used as a cookbook, and the signs should not be interpreted in isolation. Ogdon cautions the user of the manual that these are "suggested interpretive hypotheses," since few if any DAP indices "... have been found to be valid assessors and prognosticators when applied to individual evaluations of psychodiagnoses" and "... No single sign is conclusive evidence of anything" (p. 66). The reader is referred to Ogdon's book for the sources of these interpretations, as well as for a more detailed exposition of figure drawing variables.

Drawings may be analyzed utilizing structural and content variables. The structural variables concern the style in which the drawing was executed (size, pressure, line quality, placement on the page, degree of detailing, perspective, shading, erasure, and reinforcement). The content variables concern the type of person drawn, the facial expression, the postural tone, and the subtle nuances which communicate to the viewer the emotional tone of the patient who executed the drawing.

Size

Typically the size of the drawing tells clinicians something about the patient's self-esteem and the manner in which the patient deals with self-esteem. A patient who feels inadequate may draw a tiny figure, thereby directly indicating inadequacy feelings and perhaps responding to them by withdrawal. On the other hand, another patient may react with self-expansiveness and self-aggrandizement in order to cover up similar inadequacy feelings. The drawing may fill the entire page. Such a patient may compensate for feelings of inadequacy by resorting to compensatory action or fantasy. Other possible interpretations of small and large size are probably related to the issue of self-confidence. Unusually large drawings indicate aggressive and acting-out tendencies; expansive, euphoric, or grandiose tendencies; hyperactive, emotional, manic conditions; or anxiety/conflict. Unusually small drawings are said to indicate feelings of inferiority; inadequacy and low self-esteem; anxiety; withdrawal tendencies in inhibited, restrained, timid, shy, or constricted adults and children; depressive tendencies; regressive, dependent tendencies; construction under stress.

Pencil Pressure

Pencil pressure has been described as an indication of the patient's energy level. Heavy pressure has been said to indicate high energy level, whereas light pressure has been said to indicate low energy level. Heavy pressure may also indicate extreme tension or anxiety; an approach to life which is assertive and forceful (ambition); aggressive tendencies; anxiety and constrictive behavior, particularly under stress; and possible paranoid conditions. Unusually light pressure has been said to indicate a hesitant, indecisive, timid, fearful, inhibited, and insecure personality pattern; a neurotic condition, most often with anxiety symptoms; depressive conditions, or an expansive adaptation under external stress situations.

Stroke and Line Quality

Long pencil strokes indicate controlled behavior, perhaps even inhibition in the extreme; short strokes are said to indicate impulsive behavior and excitation. Horizontal movement emphasis may suggest fearfulness or self-protective tendencies; vertical movement could suggest assertiveness and determination. Curved line emphasis is said to suggest flexibility; straight line emphasis may indicate assertiveness, or rigidity. Line quality that is discontinuous (e.g., many breaks in the outside boundary of the figures) indicates anxiety and/or conflict, but in the extreme it suggests that the anxiety has overwhelmed the patient. Drawings, where the outline of the figure seems to be so discontinuous that it appears as a series of disconnected dashes, are often found in severely disturbed (psychotic) patients who have problems with reality contact, and who are overwhelmed by confused bizarre thoughts. Straight, uninterrupted strokes have been associated with a personality style that emphasizes a quick, decisive, and assertive approach to life.

Lack of Detail

Lack of detail indicates withdrawal tendencies with an associated reduction of energy; a typical reaction to stress experienced as external to the patient; or depression that is often associated with withdrawal tendencies and lack of energy to complete the figure. Excessive detailing is often seen in obsessive-compulsive patients. Some patients, under external stress conditions, deal with the stress by becoming increasingly obsessive; their drawings contain much detail, and they are carefully and meticulously drawn.

Placement

Placement roughly in the middle of the page is typical of most normal subjects. Placement on the right side of the page indicates stability and controlled behavior; willingness to delay satisfaction of needs and drives; preference for intellectual satisfactions compared to emotional ones; tendency to intellectualize; introversive tendencies; orientation to the future; negativism and rebellious tendencies. Placement on the left side of the page indicates impulsive acting-out behavior; a tendency toward immediate, frank, and emotional satisfaction of motives; extroversion; preoccupation with one's changing needs; a self-centered approach to life; orientation and concern with the past; possible feelings of uncertainty and apprehension.

Drawings placed high on the page indictes high-drive level; high level of aspiration; striving for achievement, or striving to achieve difficult goals. The higher the drawing is on the page, the greater is the possibility that the patient feels he or she is striving hard; that the goal is relatively unattainable; that the patient tends to seek satisfaction in fantasy rather than in reality; or that the patient is aloof and relatively inaccessible (Hammer, 1958). Some clinicians feel that drawings placed high on the page also indicate optimism, which is frequently unjustified, or an aloof orientation in a patient who is psychologically or socially inaccessible. Placement low on the page is said to be an indication of insecurity and inadequacy with resultant depression; an indication that the patient feels reality bound and tends to be concrete, rather than theoretical or abstract; or an indication of a defeatist attitude.

Placement in the upper left-hand corner may indicate regressive tendencies; feelings of insecurity and hesitancy; withdrawal; anxiety (except for children in the early elementary grades, for whom this is typical). Placement in the upper right-hand corner suggests a desire to suppress an unpleasant past or excessive optimism about the future, while placement on the bottom edge of the paper suggests the need for support associated with feelings of insecurity and low self-assurance; dependency; fear of independent action; anxiety; tendency to avoid new experiences or remain absorbed in fantasy; or depressive conditions.

Erasure

Excessive erasure indicates uncertainty; conflict-filled indecisiveness and restlessness; dissatisfaction with self; or anxiety/conflict. The latter is especially true if the erasure and subsequent redrawing does not improve the drawing. The area(s) erased offer(s) a clue to the content of the conflict.

Shading

Excessive shading indicates anxiety/conflict or agitated depression. However, Handler and Reyher (1964, 1965, 1966) indicate that some shading (and erasure) is an adaptive mechanism—an attempt to give the drawing a sense of three-dimensionality.

Distortions and Omissions

Gross distortion indicates poor reality contact or negative self-concept. Moderate distortions and omissions may indicate conflict/anxiety. The parts of the body that are omitted or distorted sometimes offer clues concerning the source of the problem.

Transparency

Transparency can indicate poor reality ties, except, of course, in the drawings of young children, where they are typically normal. The presence of a transparency in a drawing suggests poor judgment; anxiety/conflict; sexual disturbance; or regressive, psychotic conditions.

Sex of First Drawn Figure

Most normals draw the same sex drawing first (estimates range from 85 percent to 95 percent). Some studies indicate that homosexuals frequently draw the opposite sex first, but there are other interpretations of this finding, such as confused sexual identification; strong attachment or dependence on a person of the opposite sex (e.g., spouse, mother, lover); ambivalence or conflict regarding one's sexual identification; poor self-concept; or greater interest and/or awareness of the opposite sex compared with the same sex. Differentiation among these and other possibilities can often be made by reference to other available data, either test-related data or history data. Younger children (below age eight) often make a drawing that is of the same sex as the clinician.

MALE-FEMALE DRAWING COMPARISONS

Levy (1950) presents the following drawings (Figure 5–10) done by a male. Note that the female drawing is much larger than the male drawing. The woman's stance, her posture, and her arm position sug-

Figure 5–10 Are the drawings of a man and a woman, done by a male.

gest an active approach to life. The male's posture and the position of his arms suggest a passive, introverted, and somewhat dependent approach. The male figure looks like a retiring, gentle person, while the female looks like a firm, take-charge person. The patient appears to be a spectator rather than a "man of action." He appears to need nurturance and support from a more adequate and dynamic mother figure.

INTERPRETATIONS CONCERNING BODY PARTS

Head

The head is a symbol of intellectual and fantasy activity and a symbol of impulse and emotional control. The head is also the site of socialization and communication. Therefore, normal subjects give a great deal of attention to the head. Unusually large heads indicate aggressive and expansive tendencies; an inflated ego; over-evaluation of the intellectual; high achievement; fantasy as a primary source of satisfaction; regression; inhibition and dependency; possible anxiety. An unusually small head can indicate feelings of inadequacy; sexual impotence; a feeling of intellectual inadequacy; or weak ego conditions. When the head is drawn by an adult of average or better intelligence in a child-like fashion, (e.g., as a circle rather than an oval; with dots or circles for eyes; ears stuck on like jug handles; mouth a single line) the clinician may infer that the patient is grossly immature; that the patient is regressed; or that he or she is experiencing a good deal of anxiety/conflict. An over-emphasis of hair on the head and hair emphasis on the chest or face may indicate virility strivings; sexual preoccupation; compensation for feelings of sexual inadequacy or impotence; possible aggressive, assaultive tendencies; narcissism; possible anger and aggressive tendencies; and possible anxiety or conflict. When hair is absent, the possible interpretations include feelings of sexual inadequacy; castration fears; a possible schizophrenic condition; and low physical vigor.

Facial Features

When facial features are omitted, the possible interpretations include psychosis; evasiveness; superficiality in interpersonal relationships, inadequate environmental interest; or possible withdrawing tendencies. On the other hand, over-emphasis of facial features has been said to indicate over-concern with outward appearances; or feelings of inadequacy and weakness that are compensated for by aggressive and socially-dominant behavior.

Eyes

Unusually large or strongly reinforced eyes indicate suspiciousness and other paranoid characteristics; hypersensitivity to social opinion; or socially outgoing tendencies. Unusually small or closed eyes have been said to indicate introversive tendencies, self-absorption, or contemplative, introspective tendencies. Eyes drawn with the pupils omitted (empty eyes) can indicate "... an introversive, self-absorbed tendency in withdrawing persons who are not interested in perceiving their environment, or who perceive it and themselves only vaguely, a condition seen in neuroses and schizoid personalities which may be due to an inability to cope or a communications difficulty" (Odgon, 1979, p. 76).

Nose

The nose is sometimes said to be a phallic symbol or a symbol of a power motive. Thus, a large nose or one that is otherwise emphasized may indicate sexual difficulties, including psychosexual immaturity and/or castration fears; sexual impotency; or aggressive tendencies. When the nose is omitted, interpretations include a shy, withdrawn, or depressive personality style; or feelings of castration. A nose that is drawn as a button or a triangle suggests immaturity; a regressive response to conflict; or anxiety in older children, adolescents, or adults. A sharply-pointed nose strongly suggests acting-out tendencies. A shaded, dim, or truncated nose may indicate castration fear.

Mouth

Mouth emphasis indicates regressive defenses; oral emphasis in the personality; possible verbal aggressiveness associated with a dependent, immature personality; possible sexual difficulties, verbal sadism; or depressive or primitive tendencies. When the mouth is omitted the interpretations include oral aggressive tendencies; depressive conditions; difficulty or reluctance to communicate; rejection of the need for affection; in children, possible obsessions and anxiety; or a shy, withdrawn, depressed syndrome.

A cupid bow mouth in females figures has typically been associated with exhibitionistically inclined, sexually precocious adolescent females, while a single line, unsmiling mouth suggests depression. A slash line mouth suggests verbal aggression; anger; hypercritical, or possibly sadistic tendencies. A tiny mouth suggests denial of oral dependent needs, while a mouth with a large grin in an adult suggests either forced congeniality or inappropriate affect. If an adult drawing has teeth showing this suggests infantile, aggressive, or sadistic tendencies.

Ears

Large ears may indicate hypersensitivity to criticism, ideas of reference, paranoid tendencies, or possible auditory hallucinations. Ears are often omitted in drawings by normal subjects.

Chin

An over-emphasized chin suggests aggressive, dominance tendencies; possible strong drive levels; possible compensation for feelings of weakness; or possible feelings of social inadequacy. A weak chin may indicate feelings of weakness or inadequacy, especially in social situations; or feelings of either psychological or physiological impotence.

Neck

The neck is typically regarded as the link between intellectual life (symbolized by the head) and affect (basic body impulses) symbolized by the body. The neck represents the link between ego control (head) and id impulse (body). Thus, neck emphasis typically indicates concern regarding the need to control threatening impulses. Odgon (1979) states, "Labile affect, fear of labile affect, concern regarding acting-out tendencies, and the need to separate one's cognitive activity from one's affect life may be represented in the treatment of the neck" (p. 78).

An unusually short, thick neck indicates tendencies to be gruff, stubborn, and rigid; impulsivity; or a desire to keep impulses from hindering intellect. An unusually long neck suggests an attempt to separate intellectual ideas from emotions; or a cultured, socially stiff, or even formally rigid and overly moral approach to life. An exceptionally long, thin neck can indicate schizoid or psychotic problems. When the neck is omitted, impulsivity is suggested (if the patient is over ten years of age).

Shoulders

Well-drawn and neatly rounded shoulders have typically been said to be normal, indicating adequate, well-balanced control of impulses and behavior. Broad shoulders in a drawing typically indicate a need for physical power. Absence of shoulders suggests the presence of a thought disorder. Pointed shoulders indicate acting-out tendencies, while tiny shoulders suggest inferiority feelings. Large or broad shoulders indicate possible aggressive, acting-out tendencies; excessive defensiveness; or in females, possible sex-role confusion or masculine protest.

Breasts

Unusually large breasts drawn by male patients may indicate emotional immaturity; maternal over-dependence; unresolved Oedipal problems; psychosexual immaturity; or strong oral and dependency needs. Unusually large breasts drawn by females may indicate an identification with a dominant mother, exhibitionism, or narcissistic problems.

Waistline

Ogdon (1979) notes the following concerning the waistline:

> In males, the waistline separates the area of physical strength from the area of sexual functioning; in females, the upper part of the body is also related to nutritional factors and secondary activity while the lower part bears more directly on sexual and reproductive activity. (p. 80).

In adults, a heavy line separating the lower body from the rest of the body can suggest acute sexual conflict. An unusually high or low waistline is said to suggest blocking and conflict regarding sexual tendencies. An excessively tight waistline (corseted appearance) may indicate precarious emotional control of body impulses, perhaps expressed by temperamental outbursts. An elaborate belt possibly indicates sexual preoccupation; control of body impulses via rationalization or sublimation; phobic or neurotic behavior.

Trunk

The body typically symbolizes basic drives and therefore, attitudes related to the development and integration of these drives in the personality indicated by the manner in which the trunk is drawn. If the body is drawn in fragmented fashion, the clinician should consider this an indication of serious personality disorganization. Children typically draw the trunk as a simple oval or rectangle. If the body is represented in this manner by an adult of average or better intelligence, this could indicate a regressed state, an extremely immature personality, or the presence of severe anxiety/conflict. A large trunk may symbolize unsatisfied drives, whereas a long, narrow trunk may indicate possible schizoid tendencies. Rounded trunks are said to suggest a passive, feminine, or perhaps an infantile, regressive, personality. If the trunk is omitted by an adult, it is possible the patient is severely disturbed. A small trunk suggests a denial of drives, feelings of inferiority, or both.

Genitalia

Genitalia are rarely drawn, but when they are, they indicate severe psychopathology; overt aggression (in children); sexual preoccupation and curiosity (adolescents). It is important to note that normal art students and persons in psychoanalysis often produce nude drawings which may include genitalia, as do patients in sex therapy.

Arms, Hands, Fingers

The arms reflect the type and quality of the patient's contact with the environment and interpersonal relations. Arms drawn as relaxed and flexible are considered normal. Arms drawn akimbo suggest narcissistic or bossy tendencies, whereas arms behind the back possibly suggest reluctance to meet people halfway; need to control aggressive, hostile feelings or behavior; or guilt feelings. Folded arms may indicate suspicious, hostile attitudes; possible rigid attempts to maintain control of violent impulses; a passive, non-assertive orientation; or unwillingness to interact socially. Frail, thin, small, or shrunken arms suggest feelings of inadequacy or a general feeling of ineffectiveness. Long, strong arms suggest acquisitive and compensatory ambition; a need for achievement or physical strength; or active, aggressive contact with the environment. Omission of arms is said to indicate guilt feelings; depression; feelings of inadequacy and ineffectiveness; dissatisfaction with the environment; strong withdrawal tendencies; or passivity. Outstretched hands suggest a desire for environmental or interpersonal contact, or a desire for help or affection. Short arms indicate a lack of ambition; feelings of inadequacy; passivity; or possible castration fears.

Hands

Hands placed behind the back indicate an evasive interpersonal approach; guilt feelings concerning other people; guilt feelings concerning masturbation; or merely a feeling of insecurity concerning the ability to draw hands adequately. Large hands can suggest compensation for inadequacy feelings, while small hands may indicate feelings of insecurity and helplessness. Hands drawn as mittens suggest repressed or supressed aggressive tendencies with the aggression expressed indirectly. Clenched fingers suggest aggression and rebelliousness, or conscious attempts to control anger. Fingers without hands, or large fingers in adult drawings indicate regression; or infantile aggressive assaultive tendencies. Long fingers have been found in drawings of patients with regressive tendencies, whereas omission of the fingers indicates a feeling of difficulty in interpersonal relationships, or masturbatory guilt. Talon-like fingers or spiked fingers may indicate infantile, primitive, aggressive, and hostile acting-out tendencies, sometimes associated with paranoid or psychosomatic features.

Legs

Legs or feet are typically symbolic of security feelings and/or feelings concerning mobility. Crossed legs indicate defensiveness against sexual approaches, while long legs may suggest a strong need or striving for autonomy, and short legs could indicate feelings of immobility and constriction.

Feet

Elongated or large feet have been associated with strong security needs; possible sexual factors (e.g., a need to demonstrate virility, castration fears). Emphasis on feet has typically been said to indicate feelings of sexual inadequacy, or possible aggressive, assaultive tendencies. Omission of feet suggests a feeling of constriction, with a lack of independence; loss of autonomy; feelings of helplessness; or in children, shyness, aggressiveness, or emotional disturbance. Small feet have been said to indicate insecurity, constriction, or dependence.

Profile View

A profile may indicate evasiveness, a reluctance to face and communicate with others, reserved interpersonal style, serious withdrawal or oppositional tendencies, or paranoid tendencies.

CASE EXAMPLES

The following illustrations, taken from Schildkrout et al. (1972), illustrate some of the structural and content variables described above. Note the brief interpretations by the authors. Figure 5–11 was drawn by a fourteen-year-old boy who was referred for disruptive classroom behavior and academic failure. The next illustration (Figure 5–12) was done by a thirteen-year-old boy who was referred by Children's Court after he was charged with assaulting a teacher. The next drawing (Figure 5–13) was done by a fifteen-year-old boy who jumped off a train, because he was afraid the police would arrest him for riding on the roof.

Figure 5–11 Is a drawing by a fourteen-year-old boy who was referred for disruptive classroom behavior and academic failure.

Figure 5–12 Is a drawing by a thirteen-year-old boy who assaulted a teacher.

EXPLORING THE LITERATURE

Handler and Reyher (1965) reviewed and summarized fifty-one studies concerning anxiety/conflict. Large size, small size, heavy line, light line, omission, lack of detail, distortion, head simplification, and body simplification were found to be excellent anxiety/conflict indices. For shading, hair shading, erasure, and reinforcement, the number of studies in agreement with traditional clinical interpretation (present more frequently when anxiety is present) is balanced by an equal or greater number of findings in the opposite direction (present less frequently when anxiety is present, where increased frequency was expected), and an equal or greater number of non-significant findings. While this is not quite the case for placement in the upper left-hand

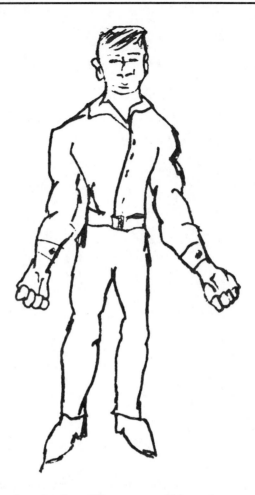

Figure 5–13 Is a drawing by a fifteen-year-old boy who was arrested for riding on the roof of a train.

corner, more than half of the findings for this index did not agree with the traditional clinical interpretation. Some studies found significantly less shading, hair shading, erasure, reinforcement, placement in the upper left-hand corner, and less emphasis line in situations where more was predicted. While the data suggest that these traditional measures may be poor indices of conflict/anxiety, Handler and Reyher (1964) suggest an alternative interpretation: These findings indicate that the anxiety-producing characteristics of the task and/or situation may create a desire to finish the figures with a minimum of effort and to leave the situation as quickly as possible (flight). This motivation would also seem to characterize the clinical testing situation.

Accordingly, there is a problem in interpreting the significance of presence (or absence) of shading, hair shading, erasure, reinforcement, and emphasis line in human figure drawings. Handler and Reyher's findings show that these indices are less likely to be associated with concurrent external and internal sources of stress. However, traditional clinical interpretation stresses the importance of these variables as being key indicators in internal conflict or stress. To further complicate the significance of these indices, Handler and Reyher found that they sometimes seemed to indicate an adaptive response to the task, in an appropriate attempt to make the figures as true to life as possible, and to give them substance. They seemed to denote adaptiveness, flexibility, and an appropriate reaction to a reality situation.

Since the figure-drawing test itself is stressful (i.e., the diagnostic testing situation), a flight reaction may be rather frequent, thereby producing a reduction of shading, reinforcement, etc. Thus, the presence, rather than absence of reinforcement, erasure, and shading may at times indicate a coping approach to anxiety and might be indicative of good ego strength. Handler and Reyher (1966) found that shading, erasure, reinforcement, and emphasis line correlated significantly and negatively with GSR, thereby indicating that these indices are probably more sensitive to external stress (albeit in the opposite direction) than to intrapsychic stress. Thus, the presence of shading, hair shading, erasure, and reinforcement or their conspicuous absence may indicate either the presence or absence of anxiety. The rather puzzling, conflicting findings for these variables and for emphasis line may mirror differential reactions to stress. In situations where patients are under moderate or severe anxiety, a withdrawal response might be expected. With patients whose anxiety is milder, a coping defense (and thus the presence of these indices) might be expected.

Fortunately, the proper interpretation of these indices can often be determined by comparing the figure drawings with the automobile drawings. For example, those subjects who show impoverishment on all three drawings are characterized by avoidant defenses to an anxiety-producing situation. When the patients show erasure, reinforcement, etc., in the human figure drawings, but not in the automobile drawing, the source of anxiety stems from internal sources of conflict. Since these patients use erasure, reinforcement, etc., they seem to cope with rather than avoid threatening material, i.e., they deal directly and actively with sources of threat represented by the human figure. When the automobile is characterized by erasure, reinforcement, etc., and the figures are not, the interpretation of an internal source of conflict still seems proper, but the defensive style is avoidant rather than coping. If the anxiety indices are present in both the figures and the automobile, the anxiety is probably due to external stress. Another useful clue in differentiating internal from external stress is the quality of the line. The data suggest that both light- and heavy-line quality may indicate anxiety, but that different processes underlie their presence. Heavy line probably reflects feelings of external stress, or pressure from without, while light line may represent a feeling of stress from within.

The degree of change in figure drawings under stress might indicate something about the quality of the patient's defenses. Those patients whose drawings changed drastically in response to stress would probably be more unstable than those whose drawings changed only moderately, in appropriate response to external threat. This suggests a modification of the DAP administration procedure: A series of drawings might be obtained as soon as the patient enters the testing room, and another series might be obtained after the patient and the clinician have had a chance to become acquainted with each other and rapport is established.

When the stress and non-stress drawings for each subject were inspected, two drawing patterns emerged under stress conditions—constriction and expansion. The constricted drawings were more often characterized by: heavier lines, mechanical breaks in the line, reduced line sketchiness, detached, or semidetached body parts, and decrease in size. This pattern seems to reflect increased rigidity and constriction in response to stress. Expansion was marked by: increased diffusion of body boundaries, increased vagueness of body parts, extremely sketchy lines, light lines, and increased size.

As part of a larger study with cancer patients and college students Trestman (1981) did an analysis of the Handler conflict/anxiety indices. He isolated two factors for the cancer patients: one which dealt with external stress and one which seemed to reflect intrapsychic stress. In general, his findings indicated that omission, distortion, head and body simplification, and delineation line absence reflect intrapsychic stress. Trestman found that those patients who viewed the cancer as most powerful had the highest DAP anxiety levels.

THE RESEARCH FINDINGS: VALIDITY

A number of reviewers (e.g., Roback, 1968; Swensen, 1958, 1968) have indicated that research literature does not support a number of clinical conclusions concerning the validity of the DAP. However, the quality of the various studies has typically not been taken into account by those who cite the negative literature. Handler believes that a careful review of the literature would reveal that a number of DAP studies seem quite poorly conceived; from their methodology it seems quite clear that there is little chance that positive results would be obtained. Hammer's (1958) comment on a study by Holzberg and Wexler (1950) is an excellent case in point. These authors found no significant difference between normals and schizophrenics drawing naked feet with toes delineated, with toenails indicated, or in the frequency of drawing internal organs—all signs of schizophrenia. Hammer correctly points out that such signs occur infrequently in drawings, but when they do, they almost invariably indicate schizophrenia. To test the validity of the signs, only instances in which the signs occurred should be included. Instead, the researchers compared a normal group with a schizophrenic group. They found low frequencies of occurrence in both groups and concluded that there was no significant difference between the groups for these variables. A better approach, Hammer emphasizes, would be to accumulate twenty such drawings and then determine the incidence of schizophrenia in the patients who made the drawings.

Another problem in research with the DAP is that in group comparison studies the extremes in each group tend to cancel each other out, and therefore no significant differences are found. For example, Handler and Reyher (1964) found that under stress conditions there were no significant size changes. However, when the data were analyzed on an individual basis, it became clear that the drawings of some individuals increased greatly in size in the stress condition, while the drawings of other individuals decreased greatly in size in the stress condition. When a mean was obtained, there was a cancellation effect, and the actual effect of stress on size was obscured.

Unfortunately, there are also problems encountered in the observations of practicing clinicians who have attempted to make public their idiosyncratic approach to DAP interpretation. For one reason or another a particular drawing sign has become associated with a particular interpretation, and sometimes the clinician clings rigidly to such an interpretation despite the fact that other possible interpretations are conceivable for such a sign. Sometimes, context and other possible meanings are ignored. Note that such an approach does not always have to be an interpretive error. For example, in the previous illustration concerning schizophrenic signs, if one or more studies had concluded that this sign occured exclusively with schizophrenics, then it would not be unreasonable to use this sign in clinical work. However, even in this example, context is important, and there are other possibilities. For example, the writer has obtained (infrequently) drawings from college males who attempt to inject humor into a DAP by drawing large naked feet with toes delineated. These subjects were almost invariably not schizophrenic.

THE DAP AND SCHIZOPHRENIA

Weiner (1966) argues that fragmented drawings with broken contours reflect impaired reality sense and indefinite ego boundaries, providing that the patient has labored conscientiously on the drawing, attempting to produce his best effort, and expresses satisfaction with the quality of the drawing. The same may be said for the second index of impaired reality sense, distorted image, provided that the distortions are relatively independent of artistic ability. Weiner emphasizes the importance of undifferentiated sexuality and physical omission, as DAP indices of schizophrenia. He offets additional clarity concerning eye and ear emphasis as indications of paranoid symptomatology. Although these signs cannot discriminate accurately the paranoid schizophrenics from other personality problems, if it is first determined that the patient is schizophrenic, then the presence of eye and ear emphasis is said to indicate the presence of paranoid symptomatology.

The drawing below (Figure 5–14), from a case study by Weiner (1966), was done by a twenty-three-year-old female, single, school teacher whose diagnostic status was unclear before testing. Weiner indicates that she became increasingly disturbed in the weeks following testing and was later hospitalized with an overt schizophrenic reaction. Note the gaps between the lines of the trunk, arms, and legs; she fails to close the ends of the arms and legs (body contour breaks). Weiner notes: "Such clear breaks in the body contour reflect indefinite, poorly delineated ego boundaries and suggest that this young woman is having marked difficulty maintaining a sense of her own reality as a single, unique and integral person" (p. 37). In addition, the patient omits body parts (hands, feet, facial features). Since her drawing is relatively well-proportioned, clinicians should not interpret these omissions merely as an indication of poor artistic ability, but rather as an indication of her distorted view of her body.

THE DAP AND OTHER TESTS

How does the DAP compare with and relate to other tests? As mentioned previously, the DAP is more sensitive to pathology than are the other tests, even the Rorschach. Thus, for example, if the drawings are pathological and the Rorschach is relatively free of pathology, then a possible interpretation would be a negative prognosis—a future increase in psychopathology.

Concerning the concurrence of themes in the DAP and the TAT, one study (Gallese & Spoerl, 1954) found between 33 percent and 100 percent agreement between the two tests concerning the projection of

Figure 5–14 Is a drawing by a twenty-three-year-old school teacher who was later hospitalized with a schizophrenic reaction.

From I. Weiner, *Psychodiagnostics in Schizophrenia,* 1966. Reproduced with permission of John Wiley and Sons, 605 Third Avenue, New York, NY 10058.

needs and conflicts (the mean percentage of agreement was 72 percent). However, Gallese and Spoerl note that the two tests illustrate the conflicts and needs quite differently. They state, "Most of the material from the Machover (DAP) was inserted on an unconscious level, and represents the more or less unadulterated basic needs" (p. 75). On the other hand, the TAT data illustrated these needs and conflicts in the total personality expression and the resulting stories were tinged and altered by the familiar techniques of defense. Thus, for example, while the DAP might contain data which suggested direct hostile feelings toward the father or the mother, the TAT stories would instead deal with indirect expression of these impulses, such as a story about "rebellion against society and its institutions, school teachers, and other dominating or superior groups or persons" (p. 76).

Shneidman (1958) cites a study by Katz who compared adult homicide or assault offenders with non-assaultive controls in the DAP and the TAT (as well as on other tests). Katz states:

> In the Thematic Apperception Test the results indicate that ability for establishing sound interpersonal relationships is severely impaired for virtually all of the assaultive subjects. . . . The drawings show indication for inconsistent motor control, a hostile view of the environment, basic inadequacy, and strong immature aggressive tensions directly expressed. . . . The essential differences in the drawing characteristics are reflected in those bodily features which are most directly related to and essential for the discharge of assaultive tensions (p. 622–623).

SUMMARY

In a recent issue of the *New York Review of Books* (August 18, 1983), Rosemary Dinnage reviewed a book by Jonathan Miller, entitled *States of Mind*. Dinnage comments that one primary theme in Miller's book is that the traditional picture of the mind as a mere mirror of nature has given way to a model which describes the mind as an active assimilator of various forces and experiences in all aspects of our functioning, including artistic creativity. The second major theme concerns the reawakening of interest in an unconscious that stresses innate skills and strategies which human beings typically utilize in daily functioning, without being aware that they are doing so. The clinical use of the Draw-A-Person Test (DAP) is quite consistent with these views, as well as with the more traditional conceptualization of unconscious representation through symbolism. By observing the artist producing the drawing, by listening to the artist's comments as he draws, and by analyzing the artist's productions, clinicians may be able to catch a kaleidoscopic glimpse of that person in various degrees of human splendor and complexity.

Drawings of a person are mental images, typically of one's self, displayed graphically. Therefore, they could contain all of the richness and complexity which is themselves, given that they can effectively conceptualize themselves in this medium as a life experience. The manner in which they experience themselves, the style in which they present this experience of themselves, and feelings about such public and private representation are all reflected in their drawings. Some people are quite adept at projecting these conscious, unconscious, stylistic, and phenomenological messages.

Attitudes about the past, the present, and the future may all be involved in the drawing. The clinician can choose to focus his or her attention on any one of these aspects, but a picture of the self-in-the-world emerges only when clinicians understand how the stylistic and symbolic representations in the drawing tell them about a person's past, how that person feels about himself or herself in the present, and his or her feelings about what the future holds.

Although DAP research has not been as encouraging as the research-oriented psychologist would like, there are enough positive studies to encourage a researcher to seek more innovative ways of demonstrating the utility of drawings in the process of understanding people in their complexity. In fact, Handler believes that many studies are poorly conceived, because they do not parallel the ways in which the drawings are used in the clinical situation. For example, they are typically investigated alone, taken out of context, and individual variables and signs are analyzed rather than allowing for contextual interpretation. A research design that parallels the clinical diagnostic situation, that focuses on the clinician doing the DAP interpretation (the interpretive process) rather than on the drawing elements themselves, might be a more fruitful approach, especially since the data seem to indicate that some clinicians are quite talented in this process, while others do quite poorly. Rather than test the clinical utility of the DAP with clinicians who have training and/or experience, focus should instead be on good interpreters, who demonstrate outstanding ability to interpret the DAP. Finally, it should be noted that Burley and Handler (1970) found that empathy was necessary but not sufficient for good DAP interpretation. It is not enough to be interested, involved, and well-intentioned. Cognitive flexibility and creativity are necessary in addition. Efforts on the clinician's part to facilitate the development of these skills should result in substantially better skill in the clinical interpretation of figure drawings.

REFERENCES

Attkisson, C., Waidler, V., Jeffery, P., & Lambert, W. (1974). Interrater reliability of the Handler Draw-A-Person scoring. *Perceptual and Motor Skills, 38,* 567–573.

Buck, J. (1948). The H-T-P technique: A qualitative and quantitative scoring manual. *Journal of Clinical Psychology, 4,* 317–396.

Burley, T. & Handler, L. (1970). Creativity, empathy and intuition in DAP interpretation. Unpublished manuscript.

Calden, G. (1954). Psychosurgery in a set of schizophrenic identical twins— A psychological study. *Journal of Projective Techniques, 18,* 316–325.

Crenshaw, D., Bohn, S., Hoffman, M., Matheus, J., & Offenbach, S. (1968). The use of projective methods in research: 1947–1965. *Journal of Projective Techniques and Personality Assessment, 32,* 3–9.

Dinnage, R. (1983). Review of "States of Mind." *New York Review of Books,* August 18, 36–37.

Fox, R. (1952). Psychotherapeutics of alcoholism. In G. Bychowski & J. Despert (Eds.), *Specialized Techniques in Psychotherapy*. New York: Basic Books Inc., Publishers.

Gallese, A. & Spoerl, D. (1954). A comparison of Machover and TAT interpretations. *Journal of Social Psychology, 43*, 73–77.

Gilbert, J. & Hall, M. (1962). Changes with age in human figure drawings. *Journal of Gerontology, 17*, 397–404.

Goodenough, F. (1926). *Measurement of intelligence by drawings*. New York: World Book Company.

Hammer, E. (1968). Projective drawings. In A. Rabin (Ed.), *Projective Techniques in Personality Assessment*. New York: Springer Publishing Company, Inc.

Hammer, E. (Ed.). (1958). *The clinical application of projective drawings*. Springfield, IL: Charles C Thomas, Publisher.

Hammer, E. (1954). A comparison of H-T-Ps of rapists and pedophiles. *Journal of Projective Techniques, 18*, 346–354.

Handler, L. (1967). Anxiety indexes in projective drawings: A scoring manual. *Journal of Projective Techniques and Personality Assessment, 31*, 46–57.

Handler, L. & Reyher, J. (1966). Relationship between GSR and anxiety indexes in projective drawings. *Journal of Consulting and Clinical Psychology, 30*, 605–607.

Handler, L. & Reyher, J. (1965). Figure drawing anxiety indexes: A review of the literature. *Journal of Personality Assessment, 29*, 305–313.

Handler, L. & Reyher, J. (1964). The effects of stress on the Draw-A-Person Test. *Journal of Consulting Psychology, 28*, 259–264.

Harrower, M. (1965). *Psychodiagnostic testing: An empirical approach*. Springfield, IL: Charles C Thomas, Publisher.

Hartman, W. & Fithian, M. (1972). *Treatment of sexual dysfunction*. Long Beach: Center for Marital and Sexual Studies.

Holzberg, J. & Wexler, M. (1950). The validity of human form drawings as a measure of personality deviation. *Journal of Projective Techniques, 14*, 343–361.

Jacobson, J. & Handler, L. (1967). Extroversion-introversion and the effects of stress on the Draw-A-Person Test. *Journal of Consulting Psychology, 31*, 433.

Jaffé, A. (1964). Symbolism in the visual arts. In C. Jung (Ed.), *Man and His Symbols*. New York: Doubleday & Company, Inc.

Jones, L. & Thomas, C. (1964). Studies on figure drawings: Structural and graphic characteristics. *Psychiatric Quarterly Supplement, 38*, 76–110.

Kissen, M. (1981). Inferring object relations from human figure drawings. *Bulletin of the Menninger Clinic, 45*, 43–54.

Koppitz, E. (1968). *Psychological evaluation of children's human figure drawings*. New York: Grune & Stratton, Inc.

Kris, E. (1962). *Psychoanalytic explorations in art*. New York: International Universities Press.

Levy, S. (1950). Figure drawing as a projective test. In E. Abt & L. Ballak (Eds.), *Projective Psychology*. New York: Alfred A. Knopf, Inc.

Levy, S., Lomax, J., & Minsky, R. (1963). An underlying variable in the clinical evaluation of drawings of human figures. *Journal of Consulting Psychology, 27*, 308–312.

Lewinshon, P. & May, J. (1963). A technique for the judgment of emotion from figure drawings. *Journal of Projective Techniques, 27*, 79–85.

Lubin, B., Wallis, R., & Paine, C. (1971). Patterns of psychological test usage in the United States: 1935–1969. *Professional Psychology, 2,* 70–74.

Machover, K. (1960). Sex differences in the developmental pattern of children as seen in human figure drawings. In A. Rabin & M. Haworth (Eds.), *Projective Techniques with Children.* New York: Grune & Stratton, Inc.

Machover, K. (1951). Drawing of the human figure: A method of personality investigation. In H. Anderson & G. Anderson (Eds.), *An Introduction to Projective Techniques.* New York: Prentice-Hall, Inc.

Machover, K. (1949). *Personality projection in the drawing of the human figure.* Springfield, IL: Charles C Thomas, Publisher.

Nichols, R. & Strumpfer, D. (1962). A factor analysis of Draw-A-Person test scores. *Journal of Consulting Psychology, 26,* 156–161.

Nordquist, V. & Handler, L. (1969, April). The relationship between heart rate and figure drawing anxiety indexes. Paper presented at the Southeastern Psychological Association Convention, New Orleans, LA.

Ogdon, D. (1979). *Psychodiagnostics and personality assessment: A handbook,* (2nd Ed.). Los Angeles: Western Psychological Services.

Roback, H. (1968). Human figure drawings: Their utility in the clinical psychologist's armamentarium for personality assessment. *Psychological Bulletin, 70,* 1–19.

Saarni, C. & Azara, V. (1977). Developmental analysis of human figure drawings in adolescence, young adulthood, and middle age. *Journal of Personality Assessment, 41,* 31–38.

Sarrel, P., Sarrel, L., & Berman, S. (1981). Using the Draw-A-Person (DAP) Test in sex therapy. *Journal of Sex & Marital Therapy, 7,* 163–183.

Sarrel, P. & Sarrel, L. (1979). *Sexual unfolding.* Boston: Little, Brown & Company.

Schildkrout, M., Shenker, I., & Sonnenblick, M. (1972). *Human figure drawings in adolescence.* New York: Brunner/ Mazel, Inc.

Schmidt, L. & McGowan, J. (1959). The differentiation of human figure drawings. *Journal of Consulting Psychology, 23,* 129–133.

Sherman, L. (1958). The influence of artistic ability on judgments of patient and nonpatient status from human figure drawings. *Journal of Projective Techniques, 22,* 318–340.

Shneidman, E. (1958). Some relationships between thematic and drawing materials. In E. Hammer (Ed.), *The Clinical Application of Projective Drawings.* Springfield, IL: Charles C Thomas, Publisher.

Strumpfer, D. & Nichols, R. (1962). A study of some communicable measures for the evaluation of human figure drawings. *Journal of Projective Techniques, 26,* 342–353.

Sundberg, N. (1961). The practice of psychological testing in clinical services in the United States. *American Psychologist, 16,* 79–83.

Swensen, C. (1957). Empirical evaluations of human figure drawings. *Psychological Bulletin, 54,* 431–466.

Swensen, C. (1968). Empirical evaluations of human figure drawings: 1957–1966. *Psychological Bulletin, 70,* 20–44.

Thomas, C. (1966). *An atlas of figure drawing variables.* Baltimore: The Johns Hopkins Press.

Trestman, R. (1981). Imagery, coping and psychological variables in adult cancer patients. (Doctoral Dissertation, University of Tennessee).

Urban, W. (1963). *The Draw-A-Person catalogue for interpretive analysis.* Los Angeles: Western Psychological Services.

Wagner, M. & Schubert, H. (1955). *DAP quality scale for late adolescents and young adults.* Kenmore, New York: Delaware Letter Shop.

Weiner, I. (1966). *Psychodiagnosis in schizophrenia.* New York: John Wiley & Sons, Inc.

Whitmyre, Jr. (1953). The significance of artistic excellence in the judgment of adjustment inferred from human figure drawings. *Journal of Consulting Psychology, 17,* 421–424.

Zucker, L. (1948). A case of obesity: Projective techniques before and after treatments. *Journal of Projective Techniques, 12,* 202–215.

6

The Bender-Gestalt Test

Arthur Canter, Ph.D.

Introduction The Bender-Gestalt Test (BGT), also referred to as the Bender Visual-Motor Gestalt Test or more simply as the Bender Test, has been one of the most widely used psychological tests since its development (Lubin, Wallis & Paine, 1971). Brown and McQuire (1976) noted that the Bender-Gestalt is among the ten most popular means of personality appraisal and among the ten most popular intelligence tests across all age groups in a survey of test practice preferences by clinical psychologists. Similar findings were reported in a survey of commonly used projective techniques for the period 1947–1965 by Crenshaw et al. (1969). Until recent years, one could hardly read a case report of an adult or child who had undergone psychological test examination without some reference to the findings of the Bender-Gestalt Test. The BGT ubiquitously shows up in psychological research reports of test appraisals of various psychopathological groups, test interrelationships, diagnostic signs, cortical dysfunction, behavioral changes as a result of treatment or an experimental condition, etc. For extensive reviews of studies of the BGT the reader is referred to Tolor and Schulberg (1963) and more recently Tolor and Brannigan (1980).

In practice, for many psychologists, the BGT becomes a clinical tool for sampling visual motor behavior. The clinician can make observations of the patient's behavior as well as study the performance of the patient. Based on clinical experience or the experience of other clinicians as reported in the literature on case studies of clinical research, the clinician makes inferences and hypotheses about some aspect or condition of the patient. If, in fact, the BGT does give reliable data on both personality characteristics and cognitive integrity as claimed in much of the literature, it is no wonder that it is so popular. However, there also has long been a disenchantment with the claims made for the BGT. This has led to research, in particular, the development of techniques in varying test administration and evaluating test performance such as objective scoring schemes (Tolor and Brannigan, 1980). New voices have appeared suggesting that severe limitations be placed upon the use of the BGT (Sola, 1983) even to the point of outright banning the test's use as a single neuropsychological technique (Bigler and Ehrfurth, 1981).

CONSTRUCTION

The original Bender-Gestalt Test was developed by Lauretta Bender for her studies of the so-called Gestalt experience of children and adults that were carried out in the early 1930s, culminating in her monograph published in 1938 (Bender, 1938). She used nine figures that she adapted for her purposes from Wertheimer's patterns that were published in his 1923 paper on the theory of Gestalt Psychology (see Bender, 1938). Bender's modifications of the Wertheimer figures consisted of accentuating or simplifying some features of the patterns. Her research goals were to examine the Gestalt experience of children at different stages of maturation and adults suffering from various psychopathological or intellectual defects. What was meant by the Gestalt experience was the response to a patterned visual stimulus as an integrated or whole perceptual experience. Whereas Wertheimer's data were based on the verbal reports of the subject's experience in viewing the Gestalten, Bender had her subjects copy them with pencil and paper giving rise to her calling the technique a visual motor Gestalt test. The nine test figures she used were published later in a separate series, and she provided a simple instruction pamphlet in response to the demand for her test. It is this set of cards and instructions that constitute the standard Bender-Gestalt Test.

Bender's monograph made quite an impact on the psychological world, coming at a time when there would shortly thereafter be a tremendous upsurge in the demand for and training of clinical psychologists. It must be remembered that in the period of the 1940s and early 1950s clinical psychology had few accepted standard tools for its role in psychodiagnosis. These were the Wechsler Scales, the Binet tests, the MMPI, the Rorschach, and the TAT. These tests and the BGT became the core instruments in the instruction of clinical appraisal techniques and were readily accepted by clinical psychologists. It mattered little that the original rationale for use of the BGT and its original purpose, centered about concepts of Gestalt psychology, were being displaced by other movements in psychology. Based on the studies being carried out at the time, the BGT seemed useful as a technique for appraising organic brain damage and personality. The use of the BGT as a projective personality test owes itself to the heightened interest of psychologists in all projective techniques during the same period. An analogous phenomenon had already taken place with the Rorschach test that in its original development by Rorschach was based on concepts that had gone out of favor and had been replaced by newer ones that were propounded by the projective test psychologist. At the same time, psychological sophistication demanded that the instruments used for diagnostic appraisal show evidence of reliability and validity using modern statistical and experiemental design techniques. The projective test psychologist in particular felt vulnerable to the criticism that was mounting. It was natural then that the BGT also began to receive research attention to develop objective criteria for the evaluative statements made in its clinical use and quantification of performance characteristics, neither of which was provided in Bender's original publication. Numerous methods for scoring BGT protocols, both for children and adults, were developed for various purposes. The major methods will be considered in detail in subsequent sections. Similarly, research studies of alterations in administration procedures, the use of the BGT figures as a visual memory test, multiple-choice matching test, sorting tasks, etc., appeared in literature and were more or less adopted by practicing clinicians (see Tolor and Brannigan, 1980).

It is interesting to note that Bender herself, in the foreword to Tolor's and Schulberg's first comprehensive review of the BGT (1963), rather decried some of the developments that had taken place "some 30 years and 300 research papers" after her own work. As she pointed out, the test arose from her clinical experience and not from controlled experiments. The major concern she expressed was that the "original meaning and values of the Gestalt test has been lost sight of by many of these investigators and their followers" (p. x, Bender, 1963). This is in reference to the application of principles of Gestalt psychology as particularly developed by Wertheimer, which she claimed, were of basic importance in understanding the test. To Bender, the subjective global evaluation of the patient's responses and reproductions of the test figures would be "more reliable and meaningful than any scoring method." The fate of the Bender test, as with Rorschach's original test and the Thematic Apperception Test, has been that it changed as it became employed by psychologists in an era when there were different approaches to examining psychological phenomena and evaluating human behavior than were true at the time the test was proposed. Whether the original theoretical basis for the BGT can be supported or not, or is even valid, is not a necessary condition for its continued use. This is an empirical matter and depends upon what kinds of inferences one wishes to make on the basis of the data and the operations defined to obtain the data. If the BGT works, it is justifiable even if those who make it work use different criteria than did the originator of the test. It is not unusual for clinical practice to outstrip its theory with changes in the former often causing changes in the latter rather than vice versa.

Reliability and Validity

Until objective scoring schemes and rating procedures for the BGT came into being, there was no evidence provided for test reliability. Establishing reliability in a clinical instrument has its problems even when the instrument yields an objective index of some kind. Clinicians are concerned with the capacity of the instrument to yield approximately the same values for equivalent states of the individual under identical conditions. Clinicians expect that as the individual's state varies, the index will vary. To the extent it is possible to reproduce this state, clinicians should be able to reproduce the index, if a reliable instrument existed. Test-retest methods for determining reliability thus may not be appropriate, depending upon what state is being measured, its variability over time, and its interaction with more stable properties of the person (e.g., the state-trait distinction). In clinical practice there is a tendency to be less concerned about apparent low statistical reliability of a test as long as there is some reason to believe that the test is a valid measure of the state. Translated to BGT terms, if a BGT sign or combination of signs is interpreted to indicate the presence of psychosis or an organic brain disorder, the evidence that such signs are highly predictive of the disorder is more convincing than being able to demonstrate that the individual will give the same signs on another testing at another time. The important issue is that the sign not mean one thing at one time and another thing at another time. Yet this is exactly what seems to take place in sign interpretation in projective tests and in global interpretations, and which increasingly complicates the task of determining the validity of the instrument. In the history of clinical assessment techniques used by psychologists, validity procedures have varied from case history matchings with test interpretation and correlation techniques to sophisticated statistical experimental design techniques. Their purpose is to demonstrate that singular or combinations of test characteristics will correctly identify characteristics of individuals or groups of persons bearing the same characteristic. The bulk of the BGT validation is based on studies of the test efficacy in detecting organic brain disorder and not personality appraisal (Tolor & Brannigan, 1980).

Bender Test Materials

The BGT that is currently available through various psychological test suppliers bears the copyright 1945 by Lauretta Bender and the American Orthopsychiatric Association, Inc. The test consists of nine cards, each 15.2 cm by 10.1 cm (4 × 6 inches). Each card has a design or pattern on its face side and a number from one to eight on the opposite side, and in the case of one card the letter "A" instead of a number. The designs may be noted in Figure 6–1. The pattern in design A, the circle and diamond-shaped figure, covers a span of approximately 5 cm across. Design 1 has dots spaced approximately 1.2 cm apart with each dot being a little over a millimeter in diameter. Design 2 contains rows of loops arranged in eleven columns of three as shown in Figure 6–1. The loops are elliptical in shape, approximately 2 × 3 mm in diameter, and the array covers a horizontal span of approximately 14 cm. Design 3 contains dots in a figure that fans out left to right. The horizontal span of the figure is approximately 4.5 cm and the vertical span at its extreme height is approximately 2.7 cm. Design 4 has a rectangular figure approximately 1.8 cm for each side. The combined figures occupy an area approximately 4.5 × 4.5 cm. Design 5 has an array of dots that form a little more than half of the top of a circle with a tail running out at a slant. The figure is approximately 2.7 cm in diameter. Design 6 has two intersecting sinusoidal curves. The horizontal one extends about 12.2 cm, and the vertically-oriented curve, which is slightly smaller, extends approximately 7.3 cm. Design 7 consists of overlapping hexagonal figures each about 4.2 cm in length and 1.3 to 1.4 cm in width. Design 8 is a horizontally-oriented hexagonal figure 7.6 × 1.4 cm.

There have been a number of variations in the test figures developed for use with special populations (see Tolor & Schulberg, 1963). In the Hutt adaptation of the BGT (Hutt, 1977) the test figures have been redrawn to enhance their vividness.

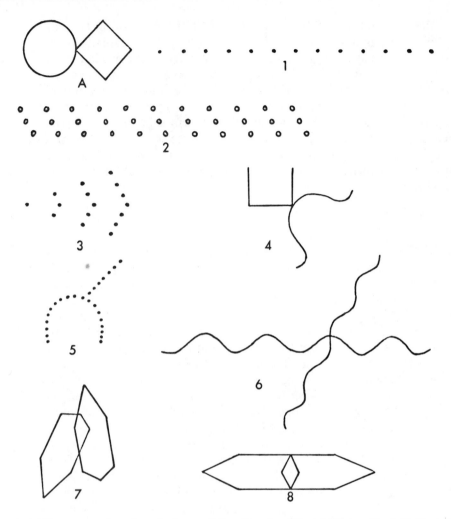

Figure 6–1 Illustrates the nine designs of the Bender Visual Motor Gestalt Test (BGT) figures.

The Bender Visual Motor Gestalt Test Figures, published by the American Orthopsychiatric Association, 1938. (Reproduced with permission.)

ADMINISTRATION OF THE TEST

There is no single standard procedure for administering the BGT. In Bender's own use of the test, Design A served as an introductory figure with the designs on cards one through eight given in a sequence. In a number of current techniques Design A, while leading off the test, is included as an integral part of the test for both scoring and interpretation. The procedures of administration that conform closely to Bender's instructions (Bender, 1946) will be referred to subsequently as traditional administration. The subject is given a sheet of plain white unlined paper $8\frac{1}{2} \times 11$ inches on which to copy all nine figures, but additional sheets are provided when needed, as may be the case for intellectually defective or confused subjects. A pencil with an eraser is provided. No other aids (e.g., rulers, coins for tracing circles, etc.) are provided.

The cards are presented one at a time correctly oriented before the subject (i.e., each card has an up position as identified by the location of the letter or numbers and names on the back of the card). The card is placed above the sheet of paper on the work surface. The subject is told simply to copy each design freehand. Variations in the wording are used, but in essence the subject is advised to copy the designs the way they appear. Card turning is discouraged. Any attempt to turn the cards during copying, despite instructions not to, is finally permitted, but note is made of the fact by the clinician who also notes when the paper is rotated, erasures are made, reworking of designs takes place, etc. In the traditional procedure, the subject is free to do much but is not encouraged to do any more than simply copy the designs. Questions by the subject as to how to proceed (e.g., if dots should be counted, etc.) are answered by "It is not necessary but do as you like." The traditional procedures do not make use of time limits, but some clinicians do record times taken by the subject to copy each design and/or the latency from the design presentation to the initiation of drawing. Notes are made of anything unusual that may aid the clinician in scoring the protocol or in the interpretation of the performance.

Variations in Administration

It is necessary for the clinician to be clear as to the purpose for which the BGT is to be used. What scoring scheme and interpretative system are to be employed? These matters will determine the mode of administering the test, the types of observations made, and what records of performance are kept. It should always be noted somewhere on the test protocols or accompanying data whether the traditional administration had been used or a variation, and if so, its general nature. For example, if a time limit was set for the subject, this should be indicated. If the subject was instructed to "copy the designs exactly as they are," such should be noted. Any restrictions placed upon the subject that depart from the rather unstructured traditional approach may alter the interpretations of test products, especially those based on projective test concepts. Where scoring schemes are used that measure degrees of departure from the actual design models, methods of administration that loosely guard against paper and/or test card positions may be affected. For many objective scoring methods the scoring and/or interpretation of the test need not be done by the same person who administers the test as long as the administration method is known. A review of various methods of BGT administration may be found in Chapter 2 of Tolor and Brannigan's book (1980). The test cards lend themselves to experimentation in adminstrative techniques apart from any scoring system. The cards or the paper may be oriented in different positions during presentation. Group administration is possible using slide projections of the design cards (Freed, 1964) or multiple individual sets of cards (Adams & Canter, 1969). Canter's (1966) variation in the BGT included the use of a specially prepared sheet of paper on which to copy the designs. Where the BGT is used as a memory-for-designs test, the technique of administration may vary accordingly, as is the case when the test is used as a recognition task with or without tachistiscopic presentation. A number of research studies have been carried out to determine what if any effects variations in administrative procedure would have on the subjects' responsiveness (see Tolor & Brannigan, 1980).

SCORING METHODS

As noted earlier, the traditional BGT was not scored in the sense of being subjected to a specific set of criteria for measuring or rating the various parameters of the subject's reproductions of the test figures. However, in the period since the publication of the original test, many scoring methods have been developed to objectify measures or rate BGT performances. Some of these involved minor adaptations of the test figures and/or techniques of administration. The various scores proposed were developed as indices of developmental stages in visual-motor ability, or as measures of specific and/or global manifestations of visual-motor disturbances that would be more reliable than the usual subjective scrutinizing methods employed by clinical psychologists. Also, the objective scores lend themselves to validation studies of the predictive and/or diagnostic power of the BGT (Tolor & Schulberg, 1963; Tolor & Brannigan, 1980). Controversy has always accompanied the development of new scoring methods whether on the basis of the inadequacy of the validation studies, the failure of the methods to yield accurate individual diagnoses, or on the scheme's apparent violation of basic Gestalt precepts. In any event, there is no widely accepted standard method for scoring BGT protocols although several methods have achieved a fair degree of popularity. Which method should one choose? This depends upon the applicability of the scores to the goals of the clinician, the suitability of the normative data for the types of subjects tested, the adequacy of the validation criteria supporting the particular scoring methods used, and the ease with which the method can be reliably used. Another factor that seems to play a role in whether a scoring method will be used with the BGT is the amount of effort required by the clinician to yield the interpretation he or she is inclined to use. The more cumbersome or apparently cumbersome the method seems to be, the more likely the clinician is inclined not to use it. Some scoring methods are easily carried out by a test technician with little clinical experience. Other rating or scoring procedures require considerable clinical experience. In the following, only a few methods of scoring the BGT will be described. These have been chosen for their current availability, their degree of acceptance, and their promise for future research and clinical use. For complete descriptions of the scoring of the BGT by any one of these methods, clinicians are required to secure a copy of the particular manual or detailed publication of the method.

The Pascal-Suttell Method (subjects fifteen years and older)

Pascal, in his early work with the BGT in the 1940s, noted that BGT productions could be graded in terms of neatness and accuracy of reproduction to the extent that a clinician could distinguish between psychiatric patients and nonpatients. His experience led to a series of studies that culminated in the publication of a method (Pascal & Suttell, 1951) of quantifying BGT productions that has stood the test of time and has proven to be valuable in a variety of research studies with the test. Pascal and Suttell proposed that the subject's performance in copying the BGT figures be regarded as a work sample which involves not only the capacity to perceive the designs and to reproduce them, but also a factor considered by them as a sort of attitude. If the task is regarded as a bit of reality with which the subject has to cope, the greater the attitude toward reality is disturbed, the greater the deviations in perception, reproduction, or both in response to the test stimuli. Thus, the scoring system they developed provides a continuum of scores ranging from accuracy in production (low scores) to extremely deviant reproductions (high scores) which is said to be correlated with a progression from low to extreme psychological disturbance. In turn, the progression in scores is "correlated with decreasing ability to respond adequately to stimuli in the environment" (p. 9, Pascal & Suttell, 1951). The method of scoring was empirically derived with tryouts on different types of patients using different types of drawing deviations until Pascal and Suttell could achieve the best discrimination between patient and non-patient. Slight alterations in test administration are required by the method: the subject is told there are nine designs to copy and the subject is told not to sketch the design, but to make single line drawings. In other respects the instructions follow traditional lines. No time limits are used nor is time recorded as part of the scoring. Design A as in the traditional approach is not scored. For Designs one through eight, the scoreable deviations are defined with examples for each. Each deviation carries a weighted score ranging from 1 to 8. The types of deviations determined by Pascal and Suttell to be the more serious as pathognomic indicators were given higher weights. For example, on Design 1, deviation #1 is called wavy line of dots, which refers to an obvious departure from the straight line of dots presented on the design card. If a subject's reproduction meets the criteria for the deviation, a score of 2 points is given. On the other hand, deviation #6, which is called double row, requires that, if the subject reproduces the design on two lines as described in the criteria, a score of 8 points be given. The scoreable deviations for the eight designs include such errors in reproduction as the drawing of circles or loops instead of dots and vice versa, dashes for dots or circles, overworking elements of lines, dots, or loops, distortions, rotations, parts of designs missing, use of guidelines, failure to join lines where appropriate, second attempts, extra angles, asymmetries, etc. Design 1 has ten scoreable deviations, Designs 2, 3, 4, 5, and 6 each have thirteen scoreable deviations, Design 7 has eleven, and Design 8 has twelve scoreable deviations. There are seven other scoreable deviations for what Pascal and Suttell call configuration. These include different weighted scores for:

1. placement of Design A,
2. overlapping of the designs,
3. compression (using only half the sheet of paper for all designs),
4. lines drawn to separate the designs,
5. order (mild departure from a logical order in placement of designs),
6. no order (haphazard or confused design placements), and
7. relative size of reproductions.

The manual provides illustrations as examples of each type of deviation and a large sample of scored records for instruction and practice in scoring. A summary score sheet is provided for noting and recording the scoreable deviations. The raw scores, i.e., the total of weighted deviation scores, may be converted to a standard score (Z-score) based on the Pascal and Suttell's normative population. Their tables provide cumulative frequencies and ogives plotted from these frequencies for the Z-scores of patients and non-patients. The patients are divided into psychoneurotic and psychotic. Pascal and Suttell (1951) proposed a range of cut-off points in the scores to screen individuals "in need of psychiatric help."

Scorer reliability was tested by blind scorings of 120 records by both authors independently. They reported a correlation coefficient of .90. Other studies support their findings that high scorer reliability may be obtained with practice. That is to say, it is important for any scorer to achieve a high level of accuracy and proficiency in the scoring as a necessary condition before obtaining higher reliability. Information regarding test-retest reliability as well as the influence of various demographic variables on the Pascal-Suttell scores can be found elsewhere (Pascal & Suttell, 1951; Tolor & Brannigan, 1980).

Hain Scoring Method (subjects fifteen years and older)

Hain's method, developed in 1963–1964 (Hain, 1964), is an example of a simple system of scoring the BGT reproductions that approaches the test performance as a whole in contrast to the Pascal-Suttell card-by-card method. By the time of its appearance, several studies using the Pascal-Suttell scoring system failed to demonstrate clinically useful diagnostic precision, although significant discrimination can be made between groups of organic and non-organic patients. Hain proposed his method in the hope of achieving greater diagnostic precision. He noted which types of errors seem to be frequently made by brain-damaged patients, non-brain-damaged psychiatric patients, and normal subjects. He carried out studies, including cross-validation groups, of the discriminating power of thirty-one signs or errors he noted to be frequently made by patients. The final scoring system contains fifteen signs or errors that appeared to discriminate between organic and non-organic patients. Each sign was weighted in relation to the degree that it discriminated between the patient groups. Any single instance of an error was scored for the category, and no category was scored more than once. The signs and their weights are as follows: Perseveration, Rotation, Reversal, or Concretism are given 4 points each; Added Angles, Separation of Lines, Overlap, Distortion are given 3 points each; Embellishments, Partial Rotation are given 2 points each; Ommission, Abbreviation of Designs 1 or 2, Separation, Absence of an Erasure, Closure, Point of Contact on Figure A are given 1 point each. The range of scores is from zero for no scoreable errors to 34 when every type of error is made at least once. In practice, scoring can proceed more rapidly with the Hain than the Pascal-Suttell method. Once an error category is noted, the scorer need not look for any more instances of it. Hain has a manual available for defining the categories and their application (see footnote in Hain, 1964). In a sense, Hain's method is more in keeping with Bender's notion of treating the test performance as a whole, although her objections to quantifying alterations in the Gestalten still applies. Cutoff scores for discriminating organic from non-organic patients are offered. Subsequent studies have yielded mixed results that suggest there are weaknesses in the scoring method in that it produces a relatively high number of false negatives, i.e., failure to reflect presence of brain damage, despite relatively few false positives (Tolor & Brannigan, 1980; Pardue, 1975).

The Koppitz Developmental Bender Test Scoring System

The Koppitz scoring method (1963) is probably the most widely used system for evaluating childrens' records and comes close to being a standard method in this area. The Pascal-Suttell, Hain, and other systems were developed primarily for adults, but have been applied to children's records with less than satisfactory results. The Koppitz system has been subjected to much research to evaluate its efficacy. Even more so, it has been the major means by which children's BGT productions have been evaluated in studies of the properties of the BGT performance that correlate with or differentiate among other parameters of children's performances, status, and capacities. For a review of these studies see Koppitz (1975) and Tolor and Brannigan (1982). The Koppitz system was designed to assess typical stages of visual-motor integration as manifested by copying the BGT figures in children from ages five to ten years. It is noted by Koppitz that by age ten most normal children can copy the figures accurately. The system has been standardized for ages 5.0 to 10.11 at six-month intervals. Beyond age ten the test is no longer regarded as a development test for normal children and any use of the system for normal teenagers is actually decried by Koppitz. She does accept the possible use of this system for children older than ten who show marked immaturity or malfunction in visual-motor perception.

The Koppitz system contains thirty scoring items defined with a variety of examples in the 1963 manual. Her recent monograph (1975) contains a revised scoring manual that includes the same thirty items of the original manual. The criteria for scoring have not been changed, but rather clarified and sharpened to reduce confusion and error in scoring. The original admonition for scoring is retained: "Only clear cut deviations are scored. In case of doubt an item is not scored" (Koppitz, 1975, p. 172). The use of a protractor and a ruler facilitate scoring of some items as it does in the Pascal-Suttell method.

The Koppitz method of administration of the BGT to children follows the traditional lines closely. The child is advised that there are nine cards from which he or she is to copy the figures on a blank sheet of paper. Extra paper is available if needed and a pencil with an eraser provided without specific instructions beforehand that erasures are permitted. The types of deviations scored include: rotations of designs from a central axis, integration, usually referring to omission of parts or marked deviations in spacing of elements, distortion, usually referring to converting dots to circles or alterations in configurations, perseveration (i.e., the repeating of rows or columns of elements beyond certain limits), and some other deviations unique to particular designs. The scored items are applied design-by-design and each receives a weight of one point making a maximum possible Developmental Score of 30. Each deviation is identified by its index number and summarized by this index number when scored, allowing the results of groups to be compared not only by total scores but also by distribution of types of items. For example, one child has a Developmental Score of 8 formed by deviation items 1a, 4, 10, 14, 18a, 21b, 22, 23. Another child with the same Developmental Score of 8 may have deviations noted on items 1a, 3, 8, 12a, 13, 17a, 17b, 24. The two records, while developmentally equivalent by total score, are qualitatively dissimilar. One child may be noted also to have different emotional indicators than another. In addition to the deviation item, the protocols are scored for the presence of up to twelve Emotional Indicators (EI). The original ten items from the 1963 manual were augmented by two more (Koppitz, 1975). The Emotional Indicators are identified on the summary of scores by a Roman numeral and they include the following: I, confused order (comparable to Pascal-Suttell's notion); II, wavy line in figures 1 and 2; III, dashes substituted for circles in figure 2; IV, increasing size of figures 1, 2, or 3; V, large size (compared to stimulus card); VI, small size; VII, fine line; VIII, careless overwork or heavily reinforced lines; IX, second attempt; X, expansion; XI, box around design; XII, spontaneous elaboration or addition to design. Each of the forementioned is said to be associated with some emotional factor, e.g., withdrawal, anxiety, acting-out behavior, impulsivity, low frustration tolerance, etc. Brief summaries of research studies in support of the interpretations given to the emotional indicators are provided in the more recent Koppitz manual (1975, Chapter 10). She also provides a large number of plates of children's records scored for the Developmental Score and the Emotional Indicators to help the scorer learn and become more proficient in the method. There is an extensive listing of normative data by grade level (Koppitz, 1975, pp. 39–41).

The Hutt Adaptation of the Bender Gestalt (HABGT)
(subjects fifteen years and older)

Max Hutt's approach to the BGT is probably the best-known example of the use of the test as a projective technique in a systematic and organized manner. At the time of this writing, Hutt's method is in its third edition (Hutt, 1977). The historical development of the HABGT is presented in this edition and is of interest in its coverage, not only of Hutt's own work, but also of the projective and non-projective uses of the BGT as a means to study what he calls "perceptual-motoric behavior." The Hutt adaptation refers not only to the method of evaluation and interpretation of a subject's copying of the test figures but also to the subtle differences in the test designs themselves. The same nine Wertheimer figures are used, but the line quality and spacing characteristics of elements in the designs have been altered to give smooth lines and more sharply delineated features that reproduce more evenly than the original BGT figures. The test cards for the HABGT are available from the publisher of the manual (Grune & Stratton, Inc., New York).

The HABGT is usually administered in three phases: copy, elaboration, and association. For the copy phase, the subject is not told how many cards there are and is given access to a stack of paper. The instructions explain that the cards will be shown one at a time, each will have a simple drawing on it, and the task is to copy the drawing as well as the subject can. "Work in any way that is best for you." It is pointed out that it is not a test of artistic ability, but the subject is to try to copy the designs as accurately as possible, working as fast or as slowly as desired (Hutt, 1977). Questions by the subject are answered by paraphrasing the instructions or by a non-commital phrase, "Do it anyway you think it best" or "That's entirely up to you." The clinician then takes a single sheet of paper from the stack, presents it vertically to the subject and places the first card A facing up with the instruction repeated, "Copy this as well as you can." The availability of the paper allows the subject choice of using a single sheet or more for the test without advice. Thus, if the subject chooses to use one sheet for each design, he or she is allowed to do so. The stack of design cards is visible for the subject to plan, if the subject wishes, how to proceed with the size. If the subject asks how many cards there are, the response is, "Just this stack of cards." Rotation of the paper is permitted, but note is made of this fact. Initial attempts to rotate the test cards are interrupted by the clinician who then states, "You are supposed to copy it this way." However if the subject insists on shifting the cards, it is permitted and notation is made of the act. As with the traditional method, the cards are presented in a sequence A through eight. Spontaneous remarks and all relevant test behaviors are noted for later study. With the HABGT, it is important to observe and make notes about the subject's method of work, apparent planning, impulsive actions, frequent erasures, direction and order in which the subject attacks each design (e.g., from bottom up), use of sketching movements, apparent blocking on any figures, etc. Extreme variation in time is also noted. After the copy phase is completed, the subject's drawings are removed from sight, the elaboration phase is undertaken, followed by the association phase. Both of these procedures exemplify the projective use of the test. For the elaboration phase the subject is instructed to modify or change the figures on the cards in any manner desired. The emphasis is placed on making the changes more pleasing to the subject and any wording appropriate to this intent may be used, e.g., more aesthetic, better looking, etc. The cards are presented again in sequence and the subject recopies the designs in keeping with these new instructions. If time considerations require reducing the total testing time, Hutt suggests the clinician use only cards A, 2, 4, 6, 7, and 8 as an abbreviated elaboration procedure.

The association phase follows closely upon the elaboration phase and makes use of the subject's drawings resulting from it. The subject is asked to look at the design card and the modification made of it during the elaboration procedure and to verbalize associations to each: "What could they be?" "What do they look like?" In this respect, the association phase is much like the free association technique used in inkblot tests and other ambiguous stimulus tests. Various other projective test procedures have been employed by clinical psychologists using the BGT. The clinician may have the subject sort the cards according to preference. A test-of-limits procedure may be used when certain responses or associations are suggested by the clinician and the degree of acceptance or rejection of them by the subject is evaluated. Where peculiar or abnormal responses are noted during the copy or association phases, the clinician may carry out a type of inquiry or, as Hutt refers to it, "an interview analysis" (Hutt, 1977, p. 72).

A global measure of the degree of psychopathology manifested on the copy phase of the test is provided by the Psychopathology Scale (PS). The PS consists of seventeen factors, each defined objectively (Hutt, 1977, Chapter Five). Scoring is facilitated by the use of a scoring template provided with each package of the HAGBT revised record forms. Sixteen on the PS factors are scored on a scale from one to ten. These include: Sequence, Use of Space I, Collision, Shift of Paper, Closure Difficulty, Crossing Difficulty, Curvature Difficulty, Change in Angulation, Perceptual Rotation, Retrogression, Simplification, Fragmentation, Overlapping Difficulty, Elaboration, Perseveration, and Re-Drawing of Total Figure. The one other factor scale, scored from 1 to 3.25, is the Position of First Drawing. Scores may range from a minimum of 17.0 to a maximum of 163.25. The sum of the scale values constitutes the Psychopathology Scale score. Hutt also provides an Adience-Abience Scale as an attempt to measure a personality characteristic said to be related to the subject's perceptual openness or closedness. This is thought of as a perceptual personality style related to the openness of the individual to new learning experiences or the tendency to block out such experiences. The Adience-Abience Scale includes factors relating to: space and size, organization, change in form of Gestalt, and distortion. (Hutt, 1977, pp. 159–162).

Canter's Background Interference Procedure
for the Bender Test

The Background Interference Procedure (BIP) proposed by Canter (1963, 1966, 1968) is an innovation that makes use of a two-phase administration of the BGT. In the first phase, the subject copies the usual BGT figures on blank paper, but in the second, or background interference procedure phase, the test is carried out on specially prepared interference paper. This sheet is printed with a randomly placed array of intersecting curved black lines which the subject must ignore in copying the test figures. The BIP sheet, as it is called, may have carbon paper as an interleaf between it and a blank sheet of paper.

The BIP Bender is administered with some modifications of the traditional method to accommodate the BIP sheet itself and to permit precision in the scoring of deviations from the stimulus figures on the design cards. For the standard phase administration of the BGT the usual blank sheet of paper, pencil with eraser, and stack of design cards are presented to the subject. The subject is advised that there are nine designs to be copied and all are to be placed on one side of a single sheet of paper. The instructions convey the idea of drawing the figures freehand without sketching and to make the figures about the same size as they appear on the cards. To reduce the opportunity for casual or deliberate paper rotations, Canter recommends use of a test board which clamps the paper in a fixed position relative to the stimulus card. If the board is rotated, the cards are rotated with it. When the board is rotated severely, the clinician interrupts the action and states, "You are to work on the paper held this way," returning the test board and paper to its proper orientation to the subject. Erasures are permitted as are restarts, but notations are made of both. The design cards are exposed in the usual sequence A through eight. Questions regarding counting and so forth are answered in the usual fashion, "Make your copy as much like the one on the card as you can." If the subject asks for more paper because he or she is running out of room (e.g., overly large designs) extra paper is provided, however, if there is sufficient space left on the sheet the clinician suggests it be used. When the standard sheet phase of the test is completed, the copies of the design cards and the board are removed from sight and some other type of task is given to the subject. This may be a brief test or subtest, when a battery of tests is being used, or a rest period of at least ten minutes. Then the BIP phase is introduced with the design cards, pencil, and test board all brought back into view and a

BIP sheet clamped in position on the test board instead of a blank sheet of paper. The instructions given to the subject indicate that the same figures are to be copied and that they are to be done exactly as they were before, "Only this time the drawing is to be done on this special paper." The subject is encouraged to attempt the task even if it seems difficult or impossible. If the initial drawing of Card A results in a small reproduction, representing an obvious attempt to fit an empty space on the BIP sheet, the subject is stopped, the paper withdrawn and a fresh BIP sheet is provided. The instruction is given to draw the figures the same size as was done before even if the subject has to go over the printed lines. If the subject appears to ignore the clinician's instructions, he or she is permitted to continue with the test and notation is made of the fact.

The purpose of the BIP sheet is to produce an interference effect, and the scoring measures the differences in deviations in copying the test figures to both standard and BIP presentations. It was reasoned that a repeat copy procedure would provide a means for correcting drawing defects due to lack of skill, mental defect, autism, etc. It was felt that idiosyncratic errors would be repeated thus having a cancelling effect. New errors appearing only on the BIP sheet could be more safely attributable to the effects of the distraction lines. The major hypothesis was that interference-induced errors were more likely to occur in patients with organic brain disorder than in non-organic psychiatric patients. The research findings in support of the hypothesis are summarized in Canter's manual (1983). The procedure requires that both phases of the test be scored by the same method. Canter's modification of the Pascal-Suttell scoring method (Canter, 1968 and 1983) was chosen as the preferred method. The modification includes redefinition of a number of the Pascal-Suttell deviations, omission of others, altered weights for some, and the use of a maximum deviation score for each design. The latter is applicable to copies too distorted to be recognizable or containing an overly large number of errors in various combinations. If the subject is unable to carry out the task even after an attempt is made or the standard phase is successfully copied, the maximum deviation score may be used for each design. The scores derived in the Canter method include: (1) a Total Error Score for standard procedure copy, (2) a Total Error Score for the BIP copy, (3) a Difference Score (D-score), the algebraic difference between the standard and BIP total error scores, and (4) Number Positive, the total number of designs in which the error score for BIP exceeded that for the standard on that design by two points. From the size of the Total Error Score for standard phase administration the Base Level of performance is indexed, ranging progressively from a Level I to Level VII, using cut-off points provided in the test manual. Base Level I indicates an error range from zero to fifteen. Base Level

II, represents a range from sixteen through twenty-nine, and successively each Base Level has a range of twenty error points until Base Level VII. This is used to represent Total Error scores on the standard performance of one hundred points or more. The maximum Total Error score for either standard or BIP performance is 180. A matrix using the Base Level, the D-Score and the NP value is provided in the manual for classifying the BIP performance as: A, no organic brain disorder; B, borderline or equivocal; and C, organic brain disorder. There is a score for the presence of Design Overlap (as in Pascal-Suttell and Collision in other systems), but this is not entered into the matrix classification. The matrix to classify BIP Bender records was determined by a cross-validation study carried out by Canter as part of the development of the technique (Canter, 1968). The matrix is applicable only to ages fifteen and older, although the scoring system (i.e., the adapted Pascal-Suttell method) appears suitable for children as young as age eight. However, as has been determined in a study by Adams and Canter (1969), there is a maturational development in the capacity to cope with the BIP analogous to the development in perceptual-motor ability to copy the BGT figures themselves. By age twelve to thirteen normal children are able to deal with the BIP effect as effectively as do adults. While Canter's scoring method was used in the development of the indices used to classify organic brain disorder among psychiatric patients, the BIP itself does not preclude the use of any other scoring scheme applicable to BGT performance. Hain's method has been used with the BIP (Pardue, 1975) as has the Koppitz (Hayden et al., 1970) and, more recently, Schlange's method, as used in a German study comparing it to the Koppitz and Canter scoring methods for children (Wallasch and Moebus, 1977). For any objective scoring scheme, it is possible to use a D-score to indicate the difference in deviation scores on the standard and BIP phases of the test as a measure of BIP effect. The D-Score concept permits examination of three possible effects attributable to the BIP:

1. the positive BIP effect indicative of impaired function,
2. a zero BIP effect indicative of no change due to the interference procedure, and
3. a negative BIP effect, indicative of actual improvement under interference conditions.

While the focus of attention has been on the positive BIP effect and its efficacy in detecting brain damage, it is conceivable that the study of negative BIP effects in known cases of organic brain damage may be useful in evaluating the capacity of a brain-damaged person to adapt to stress and/or arousal.

INTERPRETATION

General Considerations

The interpretation of BGT results is complicated not only by the availability of different scoring systems, but also by the use of the test for different purposes based on varied concepts of personality formation and psychopathological functioning. Much of what is interpretable on the BGT stems from three sources: reports of clinical case studies and observation of patient records; validation studies supporting a particular scoring system; and correlational studies, generally of BGT scores, BGT item characteristics, and extra-test parameters such as IQ, educational achievement, learning disability, cultural status, psychiatric diagnosis, maturational status, and scores on other psychological tests. As Tolor and Brannigan (1980) have indicated, the bulk of BGT interpretations has been directed toward the diagnosis of organic brain pathology whether by score cut-off points or signs (i.e., specific type of deviations in design copies). The validation of personality diagnosis and types of psychopathologies by the BGT has received little controlled research. Yet the clinical use of the BGT is heavily saturated with interpretation based on unvalidated or poorly validated psychodynamic and projective test concepts. As long as this state of affairs exists, BGT interpretation will be more art than science and will require apprenticeship training under the supervision of an experienced clinician for one to learn the art. In actual practice, the BGT is most likely to be only one of a number of other tests used to evaluate a patient or a school child. Under such circumstances, the additional data from the other tests may not only temporize over-inclusive interpretations, but may contribute to the analysis of the BGT results themselves. Even when the BGT is used primarily as a screening test, it is ordinarily not good practice to use it as the sole examination technique.

Interpretation of Bender Scores

If BGT scores are used, it is important to keep in mind the purpose of the scoring system as set forth by its developer and the criteria for their interpretation. Thus, for example, if a high score said to be representative of pathology, as is usually the case, the question to ask is, what kind of pathology. The normative data supplied for different score ranges may indicate only a high probability of psychopathology without differentiating between cortical damage, functional psychoses, emotional instability, low intelligence, or even drawing ineptitude. It is necessary to look beyond the size of the score and into correlative data that will support or deny one or more of the possibilities: age, educational status or background, cultural/ethnic factors, occupational factors, intelligence, and perhaps features of the test performance and the test behaviors themselves (for example, apparent inattentiveness, clumsiness in handling materials, content of spontaneous speech, obvious hand tremors, observable visual acuity problems, etc.). Are there any features in the subject's known background, scores on other tests (e.g., IQ), and behavioral manifestations that would lead the clinician to have certain expectations? Are the results in keeping with these expectations? A person with an educational history, occupational status, and pre-morbid estimate of intelligence all consistent with above-average intelligence is expected to produce a fairly low error score on the BGT. If it is high, the implication is that there is a pathological process in evidence. One proceeds to delineate the possibilities or, lacking the data to do so, to indicate which possibilities are the most likely and which the least likely. If the particular scoring method provides rather circumscribed indices supported by validation studies (e.g., a score or index representing organic brain damage) the task for the clinician may be to find evidence in support of cognitive defect from other tests used in the battery and known case history data. Thus an adult patient who complains of memory problems, episodes of confusion, deterioration in behavior without obvious symptoms of psychosis, and who scores in the organic range of the BGT, may be presumed to be correctly identified by the test. Additional test data may be used in this case to help delineate the extent of cognitive impairment. If, on the other hand, this same patient scored in the non-organic range on the BGT, the clinician may conclude that the apparent cognitive impairment is functional or that the BGT result is a false negative, depending on the strength of other data and results of specialized neurological examinations (e.g., computerized axial tomography). One may then use the BGT score as a means of detecting pathology or disorder and the other test data to give greater specificity to the nature of the disorder. For adults, the use of the BGT is most likely to be for the detection of organic brain disorder. For children the BGT not only may be used as a screen for organic brain disorder, but following Koppitz's scheme, may be used to define a feature of developmental retardation that is correlated with learning disability. According to Koppitz's system, it may also be used to detect emotional disturbances that interfere with school adjustment (Koppitz, 1975, for case examples).

Interpreting Features of Bender Test Protocols

In this section, consideration will be given to commonly occurring deviations in copying BGT figures that are considered to be signs of pathology specific to certain personality/psychodynamic characteristics. The approach is basic to the use of the test as a projective technique. For a more detailed representation, the reader is directed to Hutt's work (Hutt & Briskin, 1960; Hutt, 1977) and to the examples found in DeCato and Wicks (1976).

The way the reproductions on the sheet of paper are organized indicates something about the patient's planning and organizational attitudes. Thus, sequence in the placement of drawings on the sheet of paper is noted as to its regularity or orderliness, ranging from a rigid, overly methodical sequence to an apparently confused or haphazard one. An overly methodical sequence is considered to be indicative of rigid impulse control, while irregular sequence is indicative of poor impulse control. Noting the point in the record when a shift in sequence has taken place, may be used to call attention to the particular design and its potential symbolic value. If the sequence is orderly, but the patient appears to have run out of room, and has to fit in subsequent designs, it may be considered evidence of poor planning. The compression or expansion of the drawn figures relative to the test stimuli is considered to reflect modes of expressive behavior. Constricted use of space (e.g., small figures cramped together) is said to be indicative of fearfulness, withdrawal, or avoidant behavior, while expansive use of space is related to assertiveness, boldness, and manic mood.

On adult protocols the actual overlapping of one design by another, referred to as collision in several scoring systems, indicates a marked disturbance in ego function. It reflects poor anticipatory planning, difficulty with figure-ground relationships, and extreme impulsivity (Hutt, 1977). As such, it is found frequently in cases of organic brain-damaged patients who often display a loss in ego control. The phenomenon appears to be found frequently in normal, young children (under eight years of age), but in older children and adolescents it is taken to indicate ego control problems.

Difficulty in joining parts of the designs or in having the parts touch each other (e.g., in designs A, 2, 4, 7, and 8), referred to by Hutt as closure difficulty, is a problem commonly noted in pathological level records, but is considered a normal developmental problem in children. Closure difficulty in the adolescent and adult is related to fearfulness and interpersonal relationship but generally indicative of some form of emotional maladjustment.

The rotation of the copied designs when the stimulus card and the test paper are in the normal position is another obvious drawing deviation that appears to be correlated with pathology. The degree and frequency of such rotation must be considered. The more severe the rotation of any design the more likely it is considered to be a pathological indicator. Originally thought to be pathognomic of psychosis, rotation has not been demonstrated by research studies to have differential diagnostic value. However, rotations occur more frequently in varied disorders including organic brain damage, schizophrenia, neuroses, reading disabilities, and mental retardation (Tolor & Brannigan, 1976). It has been suggested that the direction of the rotation, i.e., clockwise versus counterclockwise, may be indicative of behavioral tendencies: counterclockwise—oppositional behavior, clockwise—depressive mood.

The counting and recounting of elements of the designs containing dots or loops (i.e., designs 1, 2, 3, and 5), as noted in the clinician's observation of the copied performance, are taken to indicate perfectionism. Work-over, which refers to going over drawn lines and thickening them somewhat extensively, is taken to reflect anxiety or lack of self-confidence. Irregularities in curve reproduction (e.g., designs 4, 6) reflect changes in emotional expression with the increase in curvature associated with emotional lability and acting-out behavior, while decreased or flattened curvature is reflective of decreased or inhibited emotionality as found in depressive patients.

Distortions in the reproduction of designs where there is a substitution with more primitive Gestalt forms (e.g., dashes for dots, open loops for circles) are taken to reflect regression. Here the mature patient produced a result comparable to that obtained from the immature. Gross configural distortion, where the essential character of the design figure is destroyed, is representative of more severe disturbances in perceptual-motor functioning. Alteration of designs or parts of designs relative to the stimulus card representation may provide inferences about psychodynamic issues. For example, design 4 with its open square and a touching curve is often taken as a symbol of potential male-female relationships. In this view, decreasing the axis of the square, while flattening the curve, may reflect problems in heterosexual relationships. The tail of design 5 also may be regarded as a phallic symbol and problems in its reproduction or attachment reflective of problems in masculinity. Design 8 with its central diamond may be regarded as a symbol for female sexuality. The overlapping hexagonal figures of design 7 may be thought of as representing phallic symbols or interpersonal interactions (e.g., aggressiveness).

The symbolic interpretation of BGT protocols is more likely to come into play where the copies are not overly distorted or disrupted. Extreme disintegration of the Gestalt forms is more likely to indicate organic pathology, severe mental defect, or psychopathology. In a sense, there is too much "noise" in the system for differential interpretations.

It should become apparent that the projective test approach is based on conceiving the BGT as a microcosmic representation of the patient's real world of experience, motivational systems, attitudes, etc. There is a certain amount of dualism represented in the interpretative concepts. If the general quality of anxiety is in its vagueness or diffuseness, then any apparent expression of this vagueness (e.g., hesitancy in drawing, lightly drawn lines) may represent this quality. If the quality of impulsiveness is to be boundless, i.e., going beyond controls, then the failure to place controls during the drawing (e.g., running figures together or making them overly large) are the microcosmic representations of the quality of impulsiveness. This approach to the task on a projective test is widespread but rarely examined for its validity. There is sort of logic or psychologic to these notions that is taken to be almost self-evident. One has to assume that styles of behavior manifested on one level have their direct representations on another. Supporting these notions with research data is another matter and not easily done.

CASE EXAMPLE

The following case was chosen to illustrate the use of the BGT as part of a screening battery of tests to aid the diagnostic work-up of a patient seen in a psychiatric clinic. This case also illustrates the sensitivity of the BGT to changes in the mental status of the patient even when there is only minimal change in linguistic-cognitive function in the early progression of the neurological disorder finally accepted as the diagnosis: Alzheimer's disease.

The patient is a married white female in her early fifties (age fifty when first tested) who had been sent to the clinic because of complaints of depression, memory problems, and poor concentration dating back at least one year. She has a college degree in arts and drama and has been able to maintain active interest in her social, recreational, and family pursuits without difficulty until recently. Six months prior to the admission to this clinic, she had been treated for a depressive syndrome by a local psychiatrist. She showed improvement in mood, but then later complained of the return of her depression and continued memory problems. The psychiatric work-up revealed mild depressive symptoms, anxiety, and an apparent memory deficit on the mental status examination in an otherwise intellectually-intact woman. She was referred for psychological testing with the question of cortical dysfunction. A screening battery was chosen, consisting of the complete Wechsler Adult Intelligence Scale, the Wechsler Memory Scale, Form 1, and the Canter BIP-Bender test.

The patient was generally pleasant and cooperative, demonstrating a good sense of humor, even joking about her apparent deficiency. However, the clinician noted she was nervous and unsure of herself, constantly seeking reassurance about the correctness of her answers on the intelligence test. It was also noted that she tended to give up easily, become overtly upset when experiencing difficulty, and at one point, even becoming angry at her failure. During the testing she was noted to exhibit a hand tremor that increased under apparent stress (e.g., on timed tasks on the WAIS). The WAIS yielded a verbal IQ of 108, performance IQ of 106, and a full scale IQ of 108 with relative deficiencies noted on Block Design, Digit Symbol, and Picture Arrangement. The WMS yielded a Memory Quotient of 67, corrected for her age, with marked deficiencies noted in the Logical Memory subtest, Visual Reproduction and Associate Learning. The BGT was administered by Canter's two-phase method. The BIP phase was carried out after completion of the WAIS verbal tests. Canter's scoring method yielded an error score for the standard paper phase of the test of 32 (see Figure 6–2). This falls into Level III, or moderate degree of pathology noted to be frequently found in all types of psychiatric patients. If scored by the Pascal-Suttell method, the results are comparable: a raw score of 43, for an adult with college background, corresponds to a Z score of 83, which is above the cut-off for psychiatric disorder. At this point the BGT, judged solely by the objective scores, indicates undifferentiated psychopathology. Mental retardation was ruled out because of the history and the IQ test results. The differential diagnosis would be between non-organic psychotic disorder or one primarily attributable to cortical dysfunction. In trying to rule toward cortical dysfunction, the clinician looked for clues from the cognitive tests, the history and psychiatric examination, as well the BGT results themselves. Examining the results of the BIP copy phase (not illustrated) the clinician found that the patient made significantly more errors on designs A, 2, 3, and 7, yielding a BIP error score of 44. The difference in error scores (standard minus BIP), the D-score, is found to be +12 which according to Canter's norms is a significant BIP effect, which, for a Level III record with the NP of 4 (the 4 designs significantly worse), is taken to indicate a positive index for organic brain dysfunction. This finding supports the interpretation that cognitive deficits noted on the WAIS and the WMS were due to brain disorder rather than a severe anxiety disorder, mood disorder, or thought disorder. A qualitative analysis of the standard BGT copy results along the lines set forth by Hutt were also carried out. Hutt's complete system was not applicable because of the more restrictive method of administration and the lack of an elaboration and inquiry phase as described earlier.

The sequence of the design placement is mildly irregular with two shifts noted, one from the vertical downward placement to a horizontal ordering, and the second, shifting back to the vertical in an apparent effort to fit Design 8 on the sheet (see Figure 6–2). It may be conjectured that had Hutt's directions been followed, the patient may have used a second sheet of paper for Design 8 or may have

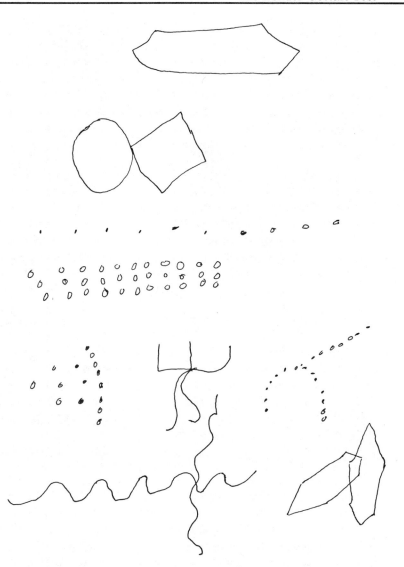

Figure 6–2 Illustrates the completed Bender Visual Motor Gestalt Test as completed by a married white female in her early fifties who was referred for testing because of complaints of depression.

followed the downward placement altogether. However, it does indicate failure to plan adequately for the space limitations set by the clinician's instructions. The fact is that Design 8, being out of order, is also the only design to contain a gross disruption (fragmentation or distortion) of its gestalt by the omission of the inner diamond. The possibility this raises is that under the intensification of stress or emotional disturbance, there is a primary breakdown of perceptuo-motor function. The patient becomes forgetful and even lacks awareness of this. The clinician knows the patient tends to overreact to stress by her behavior on the WAIS. On the BIP phase, she drew the inner diamond but showed a haphazard sequence, i.e., a greater disruption of planning and judgment. The tendency for increased compressed use of space going from Design 1 onward is suggestive of tension, anxiety, and even withdrawal tendencies. There is also a decrease in the size of the designs at the same point which not only suggests withdrawal but also an inhibiting or lowering of mood. It is as if she first approached the test with enthusiasm and expansiveness but quickly retreated and began to experience a constriction of mood as might be the case for a depressed patient. The irregularity in curvature noted on Designs 4 and 6 and the angulation problems apparent from the start (the square on Design A) and reappearing on Designs 7 and 8, are suggestive of disturbances in emotional behavior and/or perceptual processes independent of emotional reactivity. What Hutt calls retrogressive signs are evidenced by the substitution of loops and dashes for dots in Designs 1 and 3. The fact that the patient is able to reproduce the desired dots indicates she retains the capacity to do so, but lacks the control to keep from resorting to the more primitive response. Considering the maturity of the patient, her intelligence and educational background (including art training), this type of error is unexpected and signals a true disruption in perceptuo-motor functioning. On the BIP copy phase not shown here, the added stress of the interference lines disrupted perceptual-motor functioning to a more marked degree. Angulation errors increased as did the primitivization of loops formed for dots. Closure difficulty that was not evident on the standard sheet copy is present on the BIP copy. Ordinarily this deviation is interpreted in the Hutt system to indicate emotional maladjustment, but considering the nature of the BIP sheet in this instance, the error is more likely to reflect a mild breakdown of visual tracking.

In summary, the evidence of the Bender BIP combination is strongly indicative of cortical dysfunction due to organic brain disease. In view of the other tests results, in particular the marked memory deficiencies, visual constructional and visual tracking speed defects, the relative intactness of other cognitive-intellectual functions (abstract reasoning, language functions, general judgment), and the age of the patient (fifty), the most likely diagnosis is early Alzheimer's disease or some other diffuse cortical disease.

In response to the psychological test findings a CAT (computerized axial tomography) Scan and EEG examinations were ordered. The CAT Scan revealed dilated ventricular structures and prominent cortical sulci consistent with mild cortical atrophy. The EEG indicated bilateral slow activity over both temporal areas with no evidence of focal lesion or stroke and was considered consistent with diffuse organic brain disease. The standard neurological examination was negative except for the defective mental status. Serological, blood chemistry, thyroid studies, etc., were all negative. The tentative diagnosis offered by both neurology and psychiatry was early Alzheimer's disease. It must be pointed out that Alzheimer's disease is a diagnosis by exclusion. The depression/anxiety symptoms were considered by the psychiatrist to be secondary phenomena.

Follow-up studies were carried out over the next four years during the course of which it was possible to repeat cognitive tests and the BIP Bender. Figure 6–3 illustrates the obvious deterioration in perceptual-motor functions on the standard copy phase two years after the original testing. The Canter method yielded scores on the standard copy of 71 for the total error score (Level V, extreme pathology) and a D-score of +31 (with six of nine designs showing significant deterioration on BIP over standard). Thus, as poorly done as the standard BGT is, the BIP copy is even worse. In other tests there are only minor changes in intellectual functioning, chiefly in abstract reasoning. Memory impairment remained prominently defective. Testing carried out two years later than the second series, or four years after the initial testing, revealed relative stability of the verbal IQ (104), but a marked deterioration in the patient's ability to do the BGT. While she was barely able to complete the standard copy with some semblance of recognition of designs, she was totally unable to carry out the BIP, exhibiting a catastrophic reaction when confronted with the BIP sheet. Similar reactions have been noted by Canter to occur on the BIP in cases of senile dementia and in some cases of multiple sclerosis where diffuse cortical dysfunction is in evidence. As the patient was confronted more and more in her daily living with her memory impairment and perceptual motor difficulty, she became increasingly depressed as might be expected. Throughout the follow-up period of four years, the standard neurological examinations were essentially negative except for a defective mental status. However, both the CAT Scan and EEG were repeated with the results consistently indicative of diffuse brain damage. The patient was treated several times for acute depression, each time resulting in improved mood, but without ameliorating effect on her memory deficiencies or on behavior dependent upon visual perceptual orientation. For example, she had to give up driving her car around her hometown because she would frequently get lost. The patient and her family refused to accept the initial diagnosis. This led to diagnostic work-ups in another major medical center where the diagnosis of early Alzheimer's disease was confirmed.

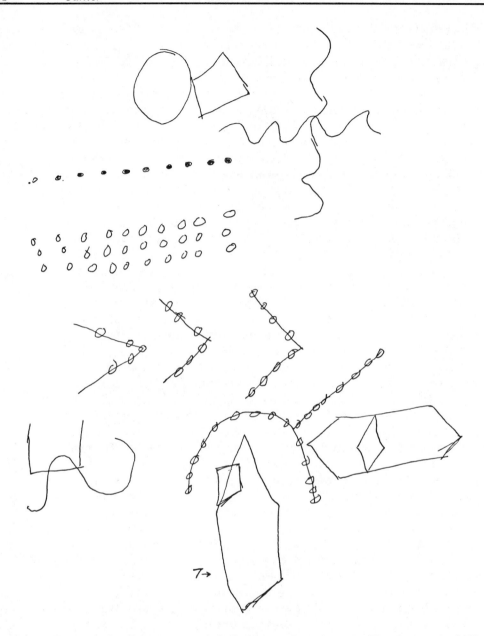

Figure 6–3 Was completed two years after the original testing (see Figure 6–2) and illustrates the obvious deterioration in perceptual motor skills. She was diagnosed as having Alzheimer's Disease.

ASSETS AND LIABILITIES

Assets

The BGT is relatively inexpensive in so far as formal psychological tests go. It is also highly portable when used in the traditional manner: a stack of design cards, sheets of blank $8\frac{1}{2} \times$ 11-inch paper, and #2 pencils with erasers.

It is a fairly simple, straight-forward test requiring little skill and training to administer as a copy test even when augmented with a memory phase. The addition of elaboration and inquiry phases as in Hutt's adaptation is another matter requiring an appropriate professional background and training. However, ordinarily, the BGT is a relatively brief test, taking only ten minutes for most subjects.

It is applicable to a wide range of subjects, children, adults, the aged, the mentally retarded, the psychiatric or neurologically impaired, and the hearing impaired.

In the hands of a trained and experienced clinician, depending upon technique used, the BGT can serve as a broad-band test providing measures of perceptual-motor, cognitive, and personality functioning.

It is a fairly innocuous-appearing test and is rarely perceived as a threat to self-esteem or as a challenge of one's personal integrity. As such, it is facilitative of rapport and often serves well as the initial test of a battery containing more exacting or detailed procedures. It also serves well as a vehicle for observing work habits, effort, and cooperativeness under untimed and benign conditions, but can be used to judge the effect of performance under pressure conditions by use of appropriate instructions and/or timing procedures.

When objective scoring schemes are used, the test does not require a background of professional training in clinical psychology and clinical experience to administer and score. This approach increases the cost effectiveness in the use of the test by freeing the clinician to spend more time and effort in more involved techniques.

The test appears to be highly sensitive to subtle impairments of perceptual-motor functions that might go undetected in more complex tasks.

Liabilities

There is no single accepted method of scoring BGT protocols that one can refer to as the standard method.

There is no alternate or parallel set of designs available to test subjects who are overly familiar with the original set.

Systematic research supporting the commonly held relationships between BGT performance and personality dynamics is lacking.

There is a significant positive correlation between error scores and IQ that have to be taken into account. The BIP D-score method overcomes this problem with its lack of correlation with IQ (Yulis, 1969).

The test cannot be used with the blind and its valid use with persons having severe visual acuity problems not correctible with lenses is most doubtful. Similarly the motor handicapped, not having use of the preferred hand, cannot complete the traditional test. Such cases require multiple-choice or recognition methods.

The role that drawing skill plays in the production of scoreable deviations or elaborations is not known. Yet, psychological interpretations are made of copy production characteristics that may be merely a function of drawing ineptitude as well as personality dynamics. Tolor and Brannigan (1980) correctly point out that this problem is a pivotal one for research in understanding BGT productions and their bases.

SUMMARY

The Bender Gestalt Test is a fairly straightforward-appearing examination procedure that, in its simplest use, merely requires the subject to make freehand copies of the nine figures chosen by Lauretta Bender from Wertheimer's study of visual perception and Gestalt psychology. As a specific test, the BGT has a long history of use as a tool to study the deviations in perceptual-motor functioning that reflect changes in childhood maturational development, intellectual status, cortical function, and psychological health. The problem of how to measure and evaluate the responses produced by the test procedure has been subjected to considerable research leading to the development of different objective scoring and rating methods. The typical scoring involves operational definitions of certain types of errors in the subject's reproduction of the test figures, as for example, overcrowding, overlapping, failing to join lines accurately, errors in reproducing angles and curves, etc. The greater the amount and degree of errors in reproduction, the more likely the record will be considered indicative of psychopathology or mental defect in the adult. Children's records are scrutinized with reference to the expected improvement in accuracy of reproduction of design features as a function of maturation. Other methods of evaluating responses to the BGT stimuli are based on concepts applicable to projective and/or expressive techniques for personality appraisal. Such approaches to the BGT are often used in combination with an objective scoring method. However, there is relatively little research support for the validity of the projective use of the BGT. There is an increasing amount of criticism directed toward the use of the BGT as a single examination procedure for the comprehensive personality appraisal or for its simple use as a screening test for cortical dysfunction. As with any other singular examination procedure, good clinical practice demands that the BGT be considered in context of other formal examinations, history, and clinical examination data. This is true of the individual tests that make up the typical neuropsychological test battery, the EEG, the CAT Scan, and other single laboratory examinations, as it is for the BGT. Further research may help establish ways of adapting different procedures to the original BGT to further analyze the responses to the test stimuli to increase its usefulness for differential diagnosis.

REFERENCES

Adams, J. & Canter, A. (1969). Performance characteristics of school children on the BIP-Bender Test. *Journal of Consulting and Clinical Psychology, 33,* 508.

Bender, L. (1938). *A visual motor gestalt test and its clinical use.* American Orthopsychiatric Association Research Monograph, No. 3. New York: American Orthopsychiatric Association.

Bender, L. (1946). *Instructions for the use of the visual motor gestalt test.* New York: American Orthopsychiatric Association.

Bender, L. (1963). Foreword. In A. Tolor & H. Schulberg, *An evaluation of the Bender-Gestalt Test.* Springfield: Charles C Thomas, Publisher.

Bigler, E. D. & Ehrfurth, J. W. (1981). The continued inappropriate singular use of the Bender Visual Motor Gestalt Test. *Professional Psychology, 12,* 562–569.

Brown, W. R. & McGuire, J. M. (1976). Current assessment practices. *Professional Psychology, 1,* 475–484.

Canter, A. (1963). A background interference procedure for graphomotor tests in the study of deficit. *Perceptual and Motor Skills, 16,* 914.

Canter, A. (1966). A background interference procedure to increase sensitivity of the Bender-Gestalt Test to organic brain disorder. *Journal of Consulting and Clinical Psychology, 30,* 91–97.

Canter, A. (1968). The BIP-Bender Test for the detection of organic brain disorder: Modified scoring method and replication. *Journal of Consulting and Clinical Psychology, 32,* 522–526.

Canter, A. (1983). *The Canter background interference procedure for the Bender-Gestalt Test.* Los Angeles: Western Psychological Services.

Crenshaw, D., Bohn, S., Hoffman, M. M., Matthews, J., & Offenbach, S. (1969). Projective methods in research: 1947–1965. *Journal of Projective Techniques and Personality Assessment, 32,* 3–9.

DeCatto, C. M. & Wicks, R. J. (1976). *Case studies of the clinical interpretation of the Bender-Gestalt Test.* Springfield: Charles C Thomas, Publisher.

Freed, E. X. (1964). Frequencies of rotations on group and individual administrations of the Bender-Gestalt Test. *Journal of Clinical Psychology, 20,* 120–121.

Hain, J. D. (1964). The Bender-Gestalt Test: A scoring method for identifying brain damage. *Journal of Consulting Psychology, 28,* 34–40.

Hayden, B. S., Talmadge, M., Hall, M., & Schiff, D. (1970). Diagnosing minimal brain damage in children: A comparison of two Bender scoring systems. *Merril-Palmer Quarterly of Behavior and Development, 16,* 278–285.

Hutt, M. L. & Briskin, G. J. (1960). *The Hutt adaptation of the Bender-Gestalt Test.* New York: Grune & Stratton, Inc.

Hutt, M. L. (1977). *The Hutt adaptation of the Bender-Gestalt Test* (3rd edition). New York: Grune & Stratton.

Koppitz, E. M. (1963). *The Bender-Gestalt Test for young children.* New York, Grune & Stratton, Inc.

Koppitz, E.M. (1975). *The Bender-Gestalt Test for young children.* Volume II. *Research and Application* 1963–1973. New York: Grune & Stratton, Inc.

Lubin, B., Wallis, R. R., & Paine, C. (1971). Patterns of psychological test usage in the United States: 1935–1969. *Professional Psychology, 2,* 70–74.

Pardue, A. M. (1975). Bender-Gestalt test and background interference procedure in discernment of organic brain damage. *Perceptual and Motor Skills, 40,* 103–109.

Pascal, G. R. & Suttell, B. J. (1951). *The Bender-Gestalt Test. Quantification and validity for adults.* New York: Grune & Stratton, Inc.

Sola, S. A. (1983). On "testing for organic brain damage": A critique of traditional methods. *Clinical Neuropsychology, 5,* 47 (abstract).

Tolor, A. & Schulberg, H. C. (1963). *An evaluation of the Bender-Gestalt Test.* Springfield: Charles C Thomas,

Tolor, A. & Brannigan, G. G. (1980). *Research and clinical applications of the Bender-Gestalt Test.* Springfield: Charles C Thomas, Publisher.

Wallasch, R. & Moebus, C. (1977). Validierung und Kreuzvalidierung des Goettinger Formreproduktionstests von Schlange et al. (1972) und der Background Interference Procedure von Canter (1970) zur Erfassung von Hirnschaedigungen bei Kindern zusammen mit zwei auderen Auswertungssystemen fur den Bender-Gestalt test sowie weiteren Verfahren. *Diagnostica, 2,* 156–172.

Yulis, S. (1969). The relationship between the Canter Background Interference Procedure and intelligence. *Journal of Clinical Psychology, 25,* 405–406.

7

The Kaufman
Assessment Battery
for Children (K-ABC)

Alan S. Kaufman
Randy W. Kamphaus
Nadeen L. Kaufman

Introduction When this chapter was written, the Kaufman
Assessment Battery for Children (K-ABC; Kaufman & Kaufman,
1983a,b) had been in use for about five months. While it is difficult
to predict the eventual popularity of the instrument, it has attracted
much attention thus far, and interest has been great in this new
approach to intellectual assessment and educational intervention.

The K-ABC is a new, individually administered measure of intelligence and achievement for ages 2–6 through 12–6. By now, most
psychologists are familiar with the characteristics of the K-ABC that
differentiate it from its predecessors. These include its theoretical
base, the 1980 Census-based standardization sample; high interest
level to young children; availability of sociocultural norms; intelligence and achievement norms on the same sample; much smaller
differences between scores obtained by whites and minority group
members; and so forth. Perhaps most important of all these aspects

is the K-ABC's theory of intelligence that is based on the distinction between sequential and simultaneous mental processes. It is this theory that dictates many of the unique aspects of the K-ABC, such as the placement of problem solving and acquired knowledge measures in separate scales.

The selection of the sequential-simultaneous dichotomy as the basis for constructing the mental processing (i.e., intelligence) scales was the result of an extensive review of the literature in the fields of neuropsychology, cognitive psychology, and psychobiology. From these diverse areas of research, a common thread was noted: Several researchers each identified two types of information processing—serial versus parallel (Neisser, 1967), successive versus simultaneous (Das, Kirby & Jarman, 1979; Luria, 1966); analytic/sequential versus gestalt/holistic (Levy, 1972), to name but a few.

After reviewing these and other authors' definitions of their dichotomous theories of information processing remarkable consistencies were apparent. There were many similarities in the definitions of serial, successive, and analytic/sequential processing, including the experimental tasks used to assess these processes. The same was the case for what has been termed parallel, simultaneous, or gestalt/holistic processing. It was the convergence of theories and research that argued for the construction of an intelligence test based on what, in the K-ABC, has been termed sequential and simultaneous mental processing.

Sequential processing refers to the child's ability to solve problems by mentally arranging input in sequential or serial order. Time is an important aspect of this type of processing, since the stimuli are typically not all available at the same time. What is important is the sequential processing of the stimuli regardless of the type of item content, method of presentation, or mode of response. Simultaneous processing, on the other hand, refers to the child's ability to synthesize information (from mental wholes) in order to solve the problem. Again, the content is not as important as the process. The item content, for instance, may be meaningful as on the Gestalt Closure task or abstract designs like those on the Triangles subtest.

Sequential processing may be related to learning grammatical relationships and rules, understanding the chronology of events, and making associations between sounds and letters. Simultaneous processing is probably involved in learning the shapes of letters, deriving meaning from pictorial stimuli (like maps), and, at more advanced levels, determining the main idea from a paragraph of text. While either sequential or simultaneous processing may appear to be more important for acquiring a particular school skill, most academic skills are complex; whereas one process is primary, the other process tends to be secondary yet necessary for achieving curriculum objectives. So, for instance, while simultaneous processing is important in comprehending the overall configuration of a map, sequential processing is necessary to execute the task of taking the correct turns in sequence to go from point A to point B.

The Mental Processing Composite (MPC) is the combination of the sequential and simultaneous processing scales, that essentially represents the integration of the two processing styles. Since academic achievement appears to require an integration of both processing styles, the MPC is an important global estimate of mental processing ability or intelligence.

The Achievement scale is the combination of all K-ABC subtests that measure acquired facts or applied skills and offers an overall estimate of the child's level of previous learning. This scale is a combination of tasks assessing school learning (Arithmetic, Reading/Decoding, Reading/Understanding), general information (Faces & Places), early language development (Expressive Vocabulary), and language concepts (Riddles). The K-ABC Achievement scale is an equal partner to the intelligence scales and should be administered to every child. The Achievement scale is necessary to get the whole picture of the child allowing examiners to assess the contribution to the child's learning of non-intellective factors such as primary language spoken in the home, educational opportunities, motivation, and early learning environment. Perhaps the most essential purpose of the Achievement scale is to allow examiners to see how effectively the child's processing abilities have been applied to learning situations, i.e., to determine how well the child has been able to apply his or her intelligence within a meaningful, real-life context.

In addition to the aforementioned scales, the K-ABC offers a special Non-verbal scale, a global scale designed to assess the intelligence of hearing impaired and limited English proficient children. It is administered to children ages 4 through 12–6 and consists of mental processing scale subtests that can be administered in pantomime and responded to motorically. This special short form of the K-ABC includes the Face Recognition, Hand Movements, Triangles, Matrix Analogies, Spatial Memory, and Photo Series subtests, although all subtests are not given at all age levels.

The remainder of this chapter is devoted to presenting an overview of the K-ABC for those learning to use the battery and those generally interested in finding out more about the instrument. Although the K-ABC manuals are probably the most complete manuals ever released concurrently with an intelligence test, this chapter also incorporates some new information that has been learned since the K-ABC's release based on recent research and clinical experience. The chapter concludes with an illustrative case report based on an actual clinical evaluation conducted by Nadeen L. Kaufman.

CONSTRUCTION AND TECHNICAL PROPERTIES

The K-ABC was constructed in three major phases: item and subtest development, national tryout, and national standardization. In 1978 and 1979, over fifty mental processing and achievement subtests were developed. The tasks were administered to about six hundred children in several pilot studies in Georgia, Illinois, Nebraska, Arizona, and South Carolina. Item analyses and factor analyses were conducted in order to select subtests and items for the national tryout held in Spring 1980.

The national tryout edition of the K-ABC consisted of twenty subtests containing over eight hundred items. The sample was comprised of 794 children spanning the K-ABC age range of 2–6 to 12–6 years. Testing sites were in Minnesota, New York, North Carolina, Louisiana, New Mexico, and Arizona.

The data obtained in the national tryout were subjected to several types of analysis including classical item analysis techniques, item analysis by the Rasch-Wright one parameter latent trait model, item bias analysis, internal consistency reliability studies, and factor analysis (Kaufman & Kaufman, 1983b, *K-ABC Interpretive Manual,* for a detailed discussion of the statistical studies).

In addition to the statistical studies, informal evaluations of the K-ABC items and subtests were made by independent reviewers and tryout examiners. Four educators, two Black and two Hispanic, were asked to identify K-ABC items or subtests that might assess content not within the everyday experience of minority group children. A remarkably small number of items were identified and subsequently modified or eliminated from the K-ABC.

National tryout examiners were asked to complete comprehensive questionnaires on the K-ABC asking them to rate each subtest in several categories (e.g., design of materials) and give any other opinions they may have on the K-ABC. This feedback was invaluable, contributing to several changes in the K-ABC. These evaluations probably contributed most to making the eventual K-ABC relatively easy to administer and score, and the tasks interesting to children.

The statistical data and informal feedback were used to develop the standardization edition of the K-ABC. The standardization sample consisted of two thousand children tested in twenty-four states during Spring and Summer 1981. The sample was stratified by geographic region, sex, race, or ethnic group (White, Black, Hispanic, other), socioeconomic status (highest educational attainment of parents or adults in the household), community size, and educational placement of the child (regular or special classes) based on the 1980 Census data. An overview of the representation of the sample by sex, race, socioeconomic status, and geographic region is shown in Table 7–1. The K-ABC sample reflects rather well the 1980 Census statistics.

Table 7-1 Representation of the K-ABC Standardization Sample by Geographic Region, Race or Ethnic Group, Parental Education and Community Size Ages 2.6 through 12.6

Region	K-ABC Sample		U.S. Population	Race or Ethnic Group	K-ABC Sample		U.S. Population
	N	%	%		N	%	%
East	401	20.0	20.3	White	1,450	72.5	73.1
North Central	565	28.2	26.5	Total			
South	628	31.4	34.0	Minorities	550	27.5	26.8
West	406	20.3	19.2	Black	311	15.6	14.5
				Hispanic	157	7.8	9.1
				Native American, Asian, or Pacific Islander	82	4.1	3.2
TOTAL		2,000					

Parental Education	K-ABC Sample		U.S. Population	Community Size	K-ABC Sample		U.S. Population
	N	%	%		N	%	%
Less than high school education	384	19.2	21.1	Central city	579	28.9	27.8
High school education	813	40.6	41.1	Suburb or small town	876	43.8	43.8
Some college	413	20.6	19.8	Rural area	545	27.2	28.3
College degree	390	19.5	18.0				

Inspection of this table reveals that the composition of the K-ABC norming sample is quite different from the norming samples of intelligence tests based on 1970 Census data, particularly with regard to ethnicity. The proportion of minority group children in the K-ABC norm group is almost double (27% versus 15%) that which was included in the WISC-R norming sample (Wechsler, 1974).

Educational placement is frequently not used as a stratification variable in sample norms for existing intelligence tests. In fact, exceptional children are systematically excluded from most samples. With the K-ABC, however, an effort was made to include exceptional children in the standardization sample in proportion to their representation in the population as shown by statistics obtained from the U.S. Office of Civil Rights 1978 survey of elementary and secondary schools. For details on the representation of exceptional children in the K-ABC standardization sample and detailed breakdowns by age for all the stratification variables, the reader is referred to Chapter 3 of the *K-ABC Interpretive Manual* (Kaufman & Kaufman, 1983b).

In addition to the regular standardization program, a supplementary sample program involving 119 white and 496 black children was undertaken to provide an adequate sample to base the sociocultural norms. The total sociocultural norm sample was comprised of 807 black and 1,569 white children representing a combination of cases from both the regular and supplementary norm programs.

Standardization sample data provided the basis for numerous reliability studies. Internal consistency reliability of the subtests was assessed by the split-half method. Mean values ranged from .72 for Magic Window to .88 for Number Recall for the preschool ages. The school-age ranges' mean values ranged from .71 for Gestalt Closure to .85 for Matrix Analogies. Achievement subtest reliability coefficients were generally higher with mean value ranging from .77 for Faces & Places at the preschool level to .92 for Reading/Decoding for the school-age level. Across all subtests, intelligence and achievement, the median split-half coefficient was .83 for preschool children, and .84 for ages 5 through 12–6.

Global scale composite score reliability coefficients, based on subtest split-half coefficients, showed a high level of internal consistency. Mean values for the MPC were .91 and .94 for the preschool and school ages respectively. Mean coefficients for the Achievement global scale were .93 for the preschool ages and .97 for the school-age range.

Test-retest reliability coefficients, reported in Chapter 4 of the *Interpretive Manual,* were generally similar to the internal consistency coefficients. The test-retest study, with a mean of eighteen days between first and second testings, showed a consistent pattern of gain scores for the K-ABC global scales. The Achievement scale was minimally affected by practice effects showing gains of only about two standard score points between testings. The MPC, on the other hand, showed a gain of about five points between testings. Of the two processing scales, the Simultaneous scale showed the greatest practice effects with gains of six to seven points. Whereas, the Sequential processing scale showed minimal gains of one to two standard score points.

The foremost question to be addressed regarding the construct validity of the K-ABC was whether or not factors conforming to the sequential and simultaneous dimensions emerged when all the mental processing subtests were factor analyzed. Factors corresponding to these dimensions had emerged in factor analyses of previous editions of the K-ABC (Naglieri, Kaufman, Kaufman & Kamphaus, 1981; Kaufman, Kaufman, Kamphaus & Naglieri, 1982). Readily identifiable sequential and simultaneous factors appeared at every age group for the standardization sample. Selected factor solutions from this analysis are shown in Chapter 4 of the *Interpretive Manual* (Kaufman & Kaufman, 1983b). The entire two-factor solution for all eleven age groups is shown in Tables 7–2 and 7–3.

Results of the factor analysis of all K-ABC subtests, confirmatory factor analysis, internal consistency, developmental changes, conver-

Table 7–2 Varimax Rotated Loadings on K-ABC SEQUENTIAL Factors in Analyses of Mental Processing Subtests

Subtest	Age in Years											
	2½	3	4	5	6	7	8	9	10	11	12½	Mean
Sequential Processing Scale												
3. Hand Movements	60	57	62	26	47	39	35	34	37	41	35	43
5. Number Recall	59	74	58	62	78	83	77	95	92	74	54	73
7. Word Order			69	89	79	75	78	53	69	63	96	75
Simultaneous Processing Scale												
1. Magic Window	17	17	30									21
2. Face Recognition	36	23	24									28
4. Gestalt Closure	36	20	14	22	12	07	03	07	04	07	04	12
6. Triangles			36	21	17	22	13	17	18	25	26	22
8. Matrix Analogies				32	30	25	23	28	23	41	36	30
9. Spatial Memory				30	27	26	22	16	27	36	09	24
10. Photo Series					25	36	26	20	22	17	36	26
Percent of Reliable Variance	26	25	27	26	27	28	23	23	26	24	27	

Note: Decimal points are omitted from factor loadings. Loadings of .35 and above are italicized. Percent of reliable variance was computed by dividing the rotated eigenvalue by the sum of the split-half reliability coefficients (Kaufman & Kaufman, 1983b, Table 4–1).

Table 7–3 Varimax Rotated Loadings on K-ABC SIMULTANEOUS Factors in Analyses of Mental Processing Subtests

Subtest	Age in Years											
	2½	3	4	5	6	7	8	9	10	11	12½	Mean
Sequential Processing Scale												
3. Hand Movements	12	19	25	51	33	32	44	47	43	38	56	36
5. Number Recall	38	31	16	24	15	13	12	07	13	09	27	19
7. Word Order			32	34	24	36	25	29	24	26	10	27
Simultaneous Processing Scale												
1. Magic Window	80	62	47									63
2. Face Recognition	34	37	50									40
4. Gestalt Closure	48	50	79	63	55	53	48	57	52	50	44	54
6. Triangles			47	74	75	71	67	78	69	73	70	69
8. Matrix Analogies				54	45	42	67	59	62	58	70	57
9. Spatial Memory				68	63	54	52	71	54	56	58	60
10. Photo Series					76	67	66	67	75	66	63	69
Percent of Reliable Variance	30	23	27	36	34	32	32	39	35	33	37	

Note: Decimal points are omitted from factor loadings. Loadings of .35 and above are italicized. Percent of reliable variance was computed by dividing the rotated eigenvalue by the sum of the split-half reliability coefficients (Kaufman & Kaufman, 1983b, Table 4–1).

gent and discriminant validation, and correlations with other tests as indices of construct validity are presented and discussed in Chapter 4 of the *K-ABC Interpretive Manual* (Kaufman & Kaufman, 1983b).

The results of over forty validity studies with the K-ABC are also given in Chapter 4, including studies comparing the K-ABC to numerous individually and group administered tests with samples of normal and exceptional children. Most notable are the correlations of the K-ABC with both the WISC-R and Stanford-Binet. For a sample of 182 children from regular classrooms the MPC correlated .70 with WISC-R Full Scale IQ. The mean MPC for the sample was 113.6 and for the Full Scale IQ 116.7 with the K-ABC being about three points tougher than the WISC-R for this sample. For a sample of 121 children the MPC correlated .61 with Stanford-Binet IQ. The mean MPC for this group was 114.5 and the mean Stanford-Binet IQ was 116.5. In this case, the K-ABC was about two points tougher than the Binet. Apparently, the 1980 K-ABC standardization sample showed an increase in ability compared to the decade-old WISC-R and Stanford-Binet standardization samples, thereby producing a somewhat steeper set of norms for the K-ABC.

Whereas the K-ABC norms yield slightly lower scores than the WISC-R or Binet for children in general, this finding does not seem generalizable to certain minority groups. Native American children earned higher intelligence scores on the K-ABC than the WISC-R in separate studies of Navajos (7-point difference) and Sioux (4 points). Furthermore, Black children across the 2–6 to 12–6 year range averaged 95 on the MPC, and Hispanic youngsters averaged 99. These mean values are considerably higher than the average IQs reported in the literature for Blacks and Hispanics on conventional intelligence tests such as the WISC-R.

ADMINISTRATION

Administration of the K-ABC has been greatly simplified by the application of administration and scoring rules that are consistent across subtests. This simplification allows less conscious decision making during administration, permitting examiners to focus more appropriately on the child's behavior during testing.

The easel format of the K-ABC makes it different from traditional intelligence tests such as the Wechsler series of scales and the Binet. Because of the easel format, the K-ABC is administered more successfully across the corner of a table rather than across the width of a table. This is a change for Wechsler and Binet users, but when examiners become aware of the other properties of the easel format (e.g., the self-contained nature of the subtests), they will most likely become comfortable testing across the corner of the table. Besides, as examiners of young, particularly preschool, children know, it is often necessary to be near the child during testing in order to better control the situation.

In addition to meeting examiners' needs for convenient administration, the K-ABC attempts to meet the developmental characteristics of children in numerous ways. For example, younger children are exposed to generous amounts of full color artwork and photographs to help maintain their interests.

The K-ABC employs a developmentally focused administration by designating different numbers of subtests for different ages. So, the first decision made when administering the K-ABC is to determine the appropriate subtests to administer given the child's chronological age. Generally, there are two starting points: ages 2–6 through 4 begin with Test 1, Magic Window; and ages 5 through 12–6 begin with Test 3, Hand Movements. One then moves forward in the easels, administering tests in turn until messages on the easels and the Individual Test Record indicate when it is necessary to skip ahead to the next test appropriate for the child's age. For example, for 2–6 and three-year-old children taking subtest 5, Number Recall, a message appears on the test record after item nine (the designated stopping point for these ages) which says "Go to 11. Expressive Vocabulary." The examiner then stops testing at item 9, proceeds to easel 3, skipping easel 2, and begins administering subtest 11, Expressive Vocabulary.

Following these procedures, K-ABC administration is developmentally tailored in that the number of subtests administered increases with age. The number of subtests administered to each age are seven subtests for age 2–6, nine subtests for ages 7 through 12–6. Administration time likewise increases with age. The entire K-ABC averages thirty-five minutes for 2–6 year olds, fifty to sixty minutes for 5 year olds, and seventy-five to eighty-five minutes for children ages 7 to 12–6.

The developmental tailoring of the K-ABC extends beyong quantitative differences (number of subtests, length of administration) and has important qualitative differences as well. Several subtests are geared to take advantage of the cognitive strategies that predominate among preschool children, and others are especially useful for assessing structures that emerge for the first time at the school-age level. For example, Face Recognition and Magic Window are administered only at ages 2–6 to 4–11, both of these subtests measure the types of perceptual skills that are quite challenging to preschool children, and call upon well-developed simultaneous processing. For school-age children, however, Face Recognition and, to a lesser extent, Magic Window demand sequential processing (Kaufman, Kaufman, Kamphaus & Naglieri, 1982). Consequently, these subtests are replaced for school-age children by tasks like Matrix Analogies and Photo Series that are excellent measures of simultaneous processing and that tape the type of abstract thinking processes that characterize the concrete operational child.

The basal and ceiling rules for the K-ABC are consistent across subtests and are designed to assist examiners in determining the critical range of items for each child. These rules are explained in the *K-ABC Administration and Scoring Manual* (Kaufman & Kaufman, 1983a). However, because they are so crucial to proper administration, they warrant further discussion.

The first line of attack with the K-ABC is to administer each subtest by starting and stopping where the Individual Test Record indicates. Thus, for a mental processing subtest, the examiner gives the sample item first since every child gets the sample item, regardless of chronological age, then proceeds to the first item designated for the child's age and stops testing after the last item designated for the child's age is administered. This rule is quite adequate for the majority of children, at a given age, since the specified item sets represent a full range of difficulty; item "p values" in a set for each age typically range from about 10 percent to 95 percent. It is only when children are at the extremes of the ability spectrum that examiners are instructed to take advantage of exceptions to the starting and stopping points in order to find a more appropriate range of items for a bright or slow child.

The first exception to the starting and stopping points' rules occurs when the child fails (obtains a score of zero) on all of the items in the first unit of items designated for the child's age. (Units of items are those items between the black horizontal lines on the protocol for each subtest; Kaufman & Kaufman, 1983a, *Administration and Scoring Manual,* p. 26.) When the entire first or easiest unit is completely failed, it is clear that the designated set of items lacks enough "floor" for this particular child. In this situation the examiner always goes back to item 1 and administers the test until the child discontinues or reaches the original starting item.

The second exception to the rules occurs with the precocious child, one for whom there is inadequate "top" in the designated item set. For the child who obtains scores of 1 (correct responses) on all the items in the last unit designated for the child's age, the examiner continues testing until the child gets one item wrong.

Although a finite set of items is generally administered to children of a given age, a discontinue rule (consistent from subtest to subtest) is also invoked when necessary. This discontinue rule instructs examiners to stop testing when a child fails an entire unit of items prior to reaching the designated stopping point. This procedure allows examiners to stop administering items when the probability that the child will pass more items is virtually nil, therefore avoiding unnecessary frustration.

The K-ABC is further sensitive to the developmental needs of children, especially preschool children, by offering sample and teaching items on the mental processing subtests. By giving examiners the flexibility to communicate the tasks' demands to the child using whatever means deemed appropriate, the burden of ensuring that the child understands just what is expected of him or her on each subtest rests with the examiners. By contrast, with many existing intelligence tests where examiners are not allowed to deviate from the oral instructions, the burden is on the child to understand how to respond.

The procedures for the sample and teaching items are essentially the same. For each item the examiner administers the item according to the standardized instructions given in the easel. If the child fails the item, the examiner demonstrates or explains the nature of the correct response using whatever verbal or gestural cues seem most likely to communicate best to the particular child, and gives the child a second trial; languages other than English are wholly permissible for giving verbal instructions during the teaching times. If the child fails the second trial, then the examiner attempts once more to communicate the nature of the task to the child before proceeding to the next item. In many cases, however, the second trial is passed because the child merely imitates the examiner's modeling of the correct response. All three items (sample and two teachings) are handled similarly with the exception that the sample item is never scored. Only the first trial of the teaching items is scored. The child's response to the second trial of a teaching item never affects the scoring of the item, and teaching is not permitted after the three items are completed (there are no teaching items on the Achievement scale).

The inclusion of the flexibility to alter the formal instructions in order to communicate the task demands does not adversely affect the reliability of the K-ABC subtests or scales (Kaufman, 1983). Generally, K-ABC subtest reliability coefficients are comparable to reliability coefficients obtained on other individually administered measures of intelligence (Kaufman & Kaufman, 1983b).

Specific instructions for administering the individual tasks are given in the K-ABC easels as opposed to a separate manual. The instructions pertaining to each task are listed on what is known as the Remember page which follows the tabbed page of each subtest. Although national tryout examiners' comments were utilized to improve markedly the accuracy and clarity of these instructions, there are still some administration pitfalls which have been noted when training examiners to administer the K-ABC. These pitfalls and hints for facilitating administration will now be addressed for each mental processing subtest.

Magic Window

Measures the child's ability to identify and name an object whose picture is rotated behind a narrow slit so that the picture is only partially exposed at any point in time (ages 2–6 through 4–11). The instructions for this task are generally readily understood. Many prospective clinicians, however, have noted that it is frequently difficult to see the timing guide and item numbers when administering the task because of the two discs being placed back to back in a mini-easel. One suggestion, for easing administration, is to make sure that both discs are in the correct starting position prior to placing the discs before the child. If this procedure is followed, and if the examiner is well practiced with the five-second exposure at each item, the items can ɔe administered without looking at the back of the discs. The examiner can determine which item is administered next by placing a score for each item on the Individual Test Record after it is administered.

Face Recognition

Measures the child's ability to attend closely to one or two faces whose photographs are exposed briefly, then selects the correct face(s), shown in group photograph (ages 2–6 through 4–11). During this task examiners must be alert in order to begin timing the five-second interval as soon as the stimulus page is exposed to the child. Hence, as the instructions on the easel say, examiners begin timing the five-second interval before giving the verbal clue.

Hand Movements

Measures the child's ability to copy the precise sequence of taps on the table with the fist, palm, or side of the hand as performed by the examiner (ages 2–6 through 12–5). Several points need to be made regarding this subtest. First, in order to tap the table at the rate of one movement per second, it is only feasible to raise the hand four to eight inches above the table between movements. Second, examiners are advised to begin forming their hand to assume the position of the next movement in the sequence when they begin raising their hand from the table just after tapping the table for the previous movement. Finally, the longer Hand Movements items have proven difficult to score for some clinicans. For these examiners, it may be helpful to encode verbally the child's response and record it using the symbols: F = fist, S = side, and P = palm.

Gestalt Closure

Measures the child's ability to mentally fill in the gaps in a partially completed inkblot drawing, and requires naming or describing that drawing (ages 2–6 through 12–5). The questions that typically arise about the administration of this subtest have more to do with scoring than administration. Many examiners ask whether or not it is permissible to question responses in Appendix A of the *Administration and Scoring Manual* (Kaufman & Kaufman, 1983a). Generally, examiners should use their experience with the Wechsler or Binet scales in guiding their probing of verbal responses. This principle is explained on page thirty-three of the *Administration and Scoring Manual* (Kaufman & Kaufman, 1983a), where examiners are advised to use neutral statements such as "tell me more about it" or "explain what you mean" to probe verbal responses that are incomplete or ambiguous; for Gestalt Closure, this certainly includes responses that may not be delineated in the scoring appendix.

Number Recall

Measures the child's ability to repeat—in sequence—a series of numbers spoken by the examiner (ages 2–6 through 12–5). The nuance required in this subtest is for examiners not to drop their voice after saying the last digit in the sequence. A hint for examiners in this regard is to imagine that there is an added digit at the end of the sequence and think of the digit as part of the sequence, but not vocalize it when administering the item.

Triangles

Measure the child's ability to assemble several identical rubber triangles (blue on one side, yellow on the other) to match a picture of an abstract design (ages 4–0 through 12–5). One of the frequent questions regarding administration of this task is how to recognize when a response is a drastic rotation and is, therefore, scored 1 (since rotations are not penalized), or when the response is a mirror image that should be scored 0. A simple test for telling the difference between these two responses is to try to rotate the child's production to make the correct response. If the examiner is unable to rotate the design to match the model exactly, then the response is incorrect and is scored 0.

Word Order

Measures the child's ability (both with and without an interference task) to point to silhouettes of common objects in the same order as these objects were named by the examiner (ages 4–0 through 12–5). The most cumbersome aspect of this subtest is the color interference task. This task, however, can be administered more elegantly when the child practices rapidly naming the rows of colors several times (three or four times) before beginning item 14. Essentially, the examiner's aim is to get the child under verbal stimulus control, so that the child is less likely to block when asked to name the colors quickly.

Matrix Analogies

Measures the child's ability to select the picture or design that best completes a 2×2-inch visual analogy (ages 5–0 through 12–5). Two questions that occur frequently regarding this subtest are: "When is a response considered a rotation?" and "Can children at age five pick up the flexible vinyl chips?" Most rotations are clearly identifiable 90-degree rotations that occur when the child selects the correct chip, rotates it, and places it squarely on the correct part of the matrix. More questionable responses are those when the child selects the correct chip and does not place it squarely on the page, but rather places the chip at an angle on the page. This angle should be less than 30 degrees from the correct orientation to be scored as correct. Of course, the first time a rotation occurs, the examiner should show the child the correct response.

With regard to the second question, there is considerable evidence based on practical experience, that even preschoolers at ages three and four can manipulate the vinyl chips. One need only to recall the experiences of special educators who for years used the old level P of the *Peabody Language Development Kits* and its manikin. Even developmentally delayed three- and four-year-olds were able to pick up the little flexible vinyl shoes and place them appropriately on the manikin's feet. Preschoolers are also adept at manipulating the flexible vinyl clothing in colorform kits based on Superman and other characters. Early experience of examiners using the K-ABC has confirmed these observations.

Spatial Memory

Measures the child's ability to recall the locations of pictures arranged randomly on a page (ages 5–0 through 12–5). A hint for scoring this subtest is given on page 39 of the *Administration and*

Scoring Manual (Kaufman & Kaufman, 1983a). This suggestion involves recording the child's response by placing marks in a miniature grid as the child points to each location. Another possible scoring stragegy may be taken from page 49 of the *Interpretive Manual* (Kaufman & Kaufman, 1983b). The correct response shown for the illustrative item on that page conforms to an upside down letter "L". For the sequentially-oriented examiner, this verbal encoding of the response may be a valuable adjunct for determining the correctness of a child's response.

Photo Series

Measures a child's ability to organize a randomly arranged array of photographs illustrating an event and then order them in their proper time sequence (ages 6–0 through 12–5). Probably the most frequently asked question about this task is "Why is the child not allowed to arrange the cards on the table prior to responding?" This aspect of administration was initiated to focus on the necessity of mental manipulation of the stimuli to achieve correct solution to an item, rather than on actual physical manipulation of the cards that leads to an unwanted stress on visual-motor feedback. The organizational skill required to handle a great many stimuli without moving them depends heavily on simultaneous processing, despite the sequential aspects of the ordering; indeed, Photo Series emerged as the best measure of simultaneous processing for school-age children (Kaufman & Kaufman, 1983b). Hence, it is important for examiners to follow the standardized procedures for administering this subtest since altering the directions might alter the processing demands of the task.

There are other topics on K-ABC administration covered in the *Administration and Scoring Manual* (Kaufman & Kaufman, 1983a) that are of interest to K-ABC examiners, ranging from establishing rapport to using a language other than English to teach a task. Generally, if one is well versed in the procedures pertaining to start and stop rules, sample and teaching items, and the specific rules for administering the K-ABC subtests, the K-ABC is straightforward to administer. The next section will illustrate that the K-ABC is also relatively easily scored.

SCORING

First and foremost, every item on the K-ABC is scored dichotomously; correct responses are scored 1 and incorrect responses are scored 0. Thus, there are no bonus points for quick performance (only

Triangles require timing the child's responses), and there is no partial credit. Even if a child gets only part of a two-part item correct (e.g., Arithmetic item 11), no partial credit is given.

It is important for examiners to be aware of the different scoring criteria for verbal responses on mental processing versus achievement subtests as explained on page 37 of the *Administration and Scoring Manual* (Kaufman & Kaufman, 1983a). To reiterate briefly, verbal responses on the Magic Window and Gestalt Closure subtests are considered correct if the child communicates understanding of the concept depicted in the item. On these subtests, the rationale is that one is trying to assess the child's simultaneous processing ability, not the child's eloquence in communicating the concept. On the achievement scale, one is trying to assess knowledge and the effectiveness with which the child communicates that knowledge. Thus, as is evident from the scoring guide given in Appendix A of the *Administration and Scoring Manual,* verbal responses are scored more leniently on the mental processing scales. For example, for item 5 (scissors) on Magic Window the response "for cutting" is considered correct, whereas for item 6 (scissors) on Expressive Vocabulary the response "cutter thing" is scored as incorrect.

Item scores are used to compute subtest raw scores by adding the number of items scored 1 (including giving credit for early items that were not administered because the child started at an advanced starting point). On the K-ABC, subtest raw scores are converted to standard scores on the interior pages of the Individual Test Record using Table 1 in Appendix C of the *Administration and Scoring Manual* (Kaufman & Kaufman, 1983a).

Appendix C contains not only the subtest standard score norms in Table 1, but also separate tables for global scale standard scores (Table 2); bands of error (Table 3); national percentile ranks (Table 4); sociocultural percentile ranks (Table 5); age equivalents (Table 6); grade equivalents for Arithmetic, Reading/Decoding, and Reading/Understanding (Table 7); out-of-level norms (Table 8); prorating (Table 9); global scale comparisons (Table 10); and subtest strengths and weaknesses (Table 11). Mental processing subtest scaled scores have a mean of 10 and standard deviation of 3 making them readily comprehensible to Wechsler users. The achievement subtest standard scores and global scale standard scores are set at the familiar metric of a mean of 100 and standard deviation of 15. The other derived scores contained in Appendix C are described in detail in Chapter 5 of the *Interpretive Manual* (Kaufman & Kaufman, 1983b).

Two of the tables given in Appendix C deserve special mention because tables of their nature have traditionally not been included in intelligence test manuals. Tables 10 and 11 of Appendix C form the empirical bases for K-ABC interpretation to be discussed in the next section. The global scale comparison tables are used to test whether differences among the child's standard scores on the global scales are large enough to be statistically significant at the .05 and .01 levels. Space is provided for making these comparisons on the front of the Individual Test Record. Like Table 10, Table 11 forms the basis for ipsative interpretation of the K-ABC profile. Values are given for comparing the child's scaled score on each individual mental processing subtest to his or her mean mental processing scaled score, and for comparing each achievement subtest standard score to the child's mean achievement standard score. These tables are for determining if standard score differences are stable and not due to chance fluctuations that have been offered in supplementary interpretive texts for the WISC-R (Kaufman, 1979) and McCarthy scales (Kaufman & Kaufman, 1977).

INTERPRETATION

The *K-ABC Interpretive Manual* (Kaufman & Kaufman, 1983b) devotes three chapters (Chapters 5, 6, and 7) to interpretation and educational translation of K-ABC test scores. Chapter 5 describes in detail the procedures for empirically evaluating the child's performance, from filling out the Individual Test Record with the appropriate derived scores to determining significant strengths and weaknesses in the child's profile. The five empirical steps reprinted from Chapter 5 are as follows:

Step 1. Obtain the derived scores and describe them with bands of error, descriptive categories, national and sociocultural percentile ranks, age equivalents, and grade equivalents.
Step 2. Compare standard scores on the Sequential Processing and Simultaneous Processing Scales.
Step 3. Compare standard scores on the Mental Processing and Achievement Scales.
Step 4. Determine strengths and weaknesses among the Mental Processing subtests.
Step 5. Determine strengths and weaknesses among the Achievement subtests.

A few points about the five empirical steps warrant elaboration. Before computing the derived scores described in Step 1, examiners should determine which scores are relevant to the particular case. For example, when testing a white child whose parents have a high school education, the sociocultural norms will likely not differ from the national norms. Similarly, age equivalents and grade equivalents are de-emphasized on the K-ABC because of the widely known flaws of these particular scales. Therefore, the clinician may not want to expand the effort to compute grade equivalents unless there is a good reason for doing so, e.g., to communicate test results to someone (like a parent) who may be unfamiliar with standard score or percentile rank score scales. In this instance, grade equivalents may be the most convenient vehicle for explaining a child's performance in reading or arithmetic.

When applying steps 2 and 3 to the interpretation of a profile it is necessary to be aware of Table 5.12 on page 193 of the *Interpretive Manual* (Kaufman & Kaufman, 1983b). In fact, clinicians should probably tab this page when they are tabbing the pages for the norm tables. This table gives data on interscale scatter, the relative unusualness of standard score differences between global scales. It is important to be aware of these data; although a stable (i.e., real, repeatable) difference may be found between global scales at the .05 or .01 level, that same size difference may occur fairly frequently within the normal population. For example, for many at the school-age level a difference of 12 points between the Sequential and Simultaneous Processing Scales is significant at the .05 level. For the total standardization sample, however, close to half the children in the sample showed a discrepancy between the two types of processing of about 12 points. Hence, although a 12-point discrepancy is statistically significant it is not abnormal. Values are given in Table 5.12 which were obtained by 16 percent, 10 percent, 5 percent, 2 percent, and 1 percent of the standardization sample. A child with an unusual amount of scatter may have more than a mere preference for a particular processing style. For example, if a child shows unusually large discrepancies among pairs of global scores, along with some soft neurological signs, a referral to a neurologist may be indicated.

Chapter 6 of the *Interpretive Manual* (Kaufman & Kaufman, 1983b) provides another series of steps that enables the clinician to generate hypotheses explaining the significant profile fluctuations identified by the application of the five empirical steps summarized earlier. A condensed version of the steps to hypothesis generation are as follows:

> *Step 1*. Try to interpret the significant strengths and weaknesses from the vantage point of the sequential-simultaneous model.
> *Step 2*. Select a significant strength or weakness. Write down all shared abilities and influences affecting performance on this subtest.
> *Step 3*. One by one, evaluate the merits of each ability and influence that was written down.
> *Step 4*. Repeat steps 2 and 3 for every other significant strength and weakness, taking each in turn.

Step 5. Identify the most appropriate hypotheses about strengths and weaknesses by integrating K-ABC data with background information, test behaviors, and scores on other tests.

Chapter 6 also gives tables of shared abilities and influences that affect performance on individual subtests. The tables are initial guides for developing hypotheses. It cannot be emphasized enough that K-ABC users must apply their theoretical, research-based, and experiential knowledge to the K-ABC to add new shared hypotheses to these tables. An example of the use of the K-ABC method of hypothesis generation is given in the illustrative case report at the end of this chapter.

The method of hypothesis generation described in Chapter 6 is consistent with approaches to interpreting the WISC-R (Kaufman, 1979) and McCarthy Scales (Kaufman & Kaufman, 1977). This method also accords well with the philosophy of intelligence testing—that intelligence testers are flexible, fitting the interpretation to the child rather than vice versa. Hence, it is necessary for clinicans to develop alternative hypotheses to explain the profile of a child if the sequential-simultaneous model does not adequately account for the observed fluctuations.

Once hypotheses are tested and conclusions are drawn, then K-ABC clinicians can use Chapter 7 of the *Interpretive Manual* (Kaufman & Kaufman, 1983b) to recommend teaching approaches based on the sequential-simultaneous model. Chapter 7 is most relevant when the best explanation for the child's scores is the sequential-simultaneous model; however, it is also useful in those cases offering other theories explaining the child's profile because of the framework it provides for educational intervention. Chapter 7 presents a logical approach for making recommendations that is derived from a review of research on approaches to educational remediation. Essentially, the K-ABC method emphasizes utilizing a child's processing strengths to teach curricular areas. Hence, the teaching of processes or modality training are not advised.

The *Interpretive Manual* offers more than a conceptual framework for educational intervention. It also offers precise suggestions for teaching certain specific reading, mathematics, and spelling skills using a simultaneous, sequential, or combined simultaneous-sequential approach. Some of these approaches were developed for use in the remediation pilot studies conducted by Dr. Judy Gunnison and her colleagues and cited in Chapter 7. These pilot studies did show promising results for the K-ABC approach to educational intervention, particularly regarding the improvement of the reading comprehension of disabled readers.

ASSETS AND LIABILITIES

The K-ABC provides many assets for psychologists evaluating children, including:

1. A strong theoretical foundation (supported by considerable evidence of construct validity) on which to base measurement of children's intelligence.

2. Intelligence and achievement scales with completely separate (non-overlapping) content, normed on the same sample of children, thereby relieving concerns about making intelligence-achievement comparisons with other instruments.

3. Sample and teaching items that allow for fairer, more accurate, assessment of preschoolers, minority children, and exceptional (e.g., retarded) populations.

4. Limited oral instructions on the subtests and limited verbal responding, again encourage a more accurate assessment of the skills of preschoolers, minority children, and other groups as well.

5. Colorful items enhance rapport and valid assessment of young children in particular.

6. A 1980, census-based standardization sample which reflects a vast growth in the minority group population since 1970.

7. A Non-verbal Scale for use with children who cannot be administered many existing intelligence tests, such as hearing impaired or youngsters who do not speak or understand English.

8. Sociocultural norms for generating hypotheses about cultural influences on a black or white child's performance.

9. A complete interpretive system offered in the test manuals.

10. A framework as well as examples of materials for use in designing educational intervention programs.

11. Administration and scoring rules that are straightforward, allowing clinicians to spend more time observing the child and enhancing the accuracy for the scoring process.

12. Empirical documentation of smaller black-white, Hispanic-white, and native American–white differences on the K-ABC than on IQ tests.

13. Results of over forty validity studies included right in the test manual.

Liabilities associated with the K-ABC, the first of which is shared by existing intelligence tests, include:

1. Limits on what the K-ABC assesses. The K-ABC does not assess some of the skills assessed on existing intelligence tests and does not include some tasks that have traditionally been a part of a psychologist's test battery, such as measures of design copying, dictation spelling, or measures of verbal expression that require more than a one-word response.

2. A Sequential Processing Scale—in terms of reliability and information yield—is less robust than the Simultaneous Processing Scale. The Sequential Processing Scale appears to measure sequential processing (as opposed to simple short-term memory), but would have benefitted from a sequential task that did not require memory.

3. A heavy dependence on visual stimuli, making the K-ABC unsuitable for visually-impaired children.

4. Failure, perhaps, to reward adequately those bright children who are extremely adept at spontaneously expressing their thoughts in words, and who excel at verbal reasoning.

5. Too few manipulative tasks for preschool children.

6. An insufficient number of easy items on several tasks preventing adequate discrimination among 2–6-year-olds who are below average in intelligence or achievement.

ILLUSTRATIVE CASE REPORT

Name: Jeremy B.
Date of Birth: 2/20/74
Chronological Age: 9 years 2 months

Dates of Evaluation: 4/12/83, 4/25/83
Observation at School: 4/21/83
Grade Level: 3.8

K-ABC Profile

Global Scale Standard Scores

Sequential Processing	115 ± 9	Simultaneous Achievement (p ≤ .05)
Simultaneous Processing	108 ± 6	
Mental Processing Composite	112 ± 6	
Achievement	119 ± 4	

Achievement Standard
  Scores
  Faces & Places   99 ± 9   Weakness
  Arithmetic   133 ± 9   Strength
  Riddles   106 ± 9
  Reading/Decoding   118 ± 7
  Reading/Understanding   123 ± 7

Mental Processing Scaled Scores

Sequential Processing
  Hand Movements   16   Strength
  Number Recall   11
  Word Order   10

Simultaneous Processing
  Gestalt Closure   8   Weakness
  Triangles   10
  Matrix Analogies   16   Strength
  Spatial Memory   13
  Photo Series   9   Weakness

Background and Referral Information

Jeremy was referred for a complete psychoeducational diagnostic evaluation by Dr. M who has been the therapist for the B family. Jeremy has experienced some difficulty in his present school setting and information was sought to determine the possible cause and extent of his academic problems. Jeremy is reported to have poor writing skills and he also has trouble with mathematics. His parents see him as somewhat distractible with better verbal and social skills. The school has considered the possibility of holding Jeremy back next year in his current third grade placement. Besides his school life, Jeremy is cared for by a neighbor after school since both parents work full-time. He has piano lessons, Cub Scouts, and Little League to keep him busy. Jeremy is the only child at home because his two considerably older brothers live on their own.

Jeremy attends a combined third/fourth grade class at a public school. All classes are dual graded in this school, where the teacher instructs one group of children while the other works independently, and vice versa. The school is right near an airport and noise level tends to be high. A visit to Jeremy's class revealed a bustling classroom environment filled with numerous sources of extraneous noise and movement. Control of this large group of children appeared inconsistent and Jeremy was a willing victim of each passing source of stimulation. Jeremy was observed intermittently laying his head down on his desk with eyes closed, yawning, stretching, sitting with hands clasped over his head, and rummaging through the inside of his desk. He also engaged in much "looking on" behavior, following the activities and conversations of other more rowdy children. In spite of these behaviors, Jeremy also spent much time working quietly at his desk. He tends to be impulsive about things that don't hold intrinsic interest for him. Throughout his work Jeremy started and stopped as myriad interruptions (self-imposed) occurred. The general pattern was one of passivity or daydreaming while the teacher was talking, and one of selective distractibility when he was performing written work. Jeremy's teacher sees him as having the ability to do well, but considers him unwilling to work. When questioned about her ideal goals for him, she responded, "For him to have all his classwork done and ready to be handed in on time for one week."

Appearance and Behavioral Characteristics

Jeremy is a handsome, muscular boy who is a bit on the small side for his nine years. He speaks with beautiful articulation and verbalizes his thoughts on a mature level of communication. For example, in describing his teacher, he commented, "I like her, I just don't like the things she does." On occasion, he attempted to manipulate the testing situation by using spontaneous conversation to interrupt some of the tasks. Jeremy was mildly distractible, looking around the bland testing room even for a second's duration in between test items. Discouraged easily, Jeremy needed much positive reinforcement to try his hardest and overcome his desire to give up easily. Despite this frustration, he took feedback well when encouraged to continue.

Jeremy was able to talk about his problem in school, and expressed his concerns in statements such as, "I can't take the double class grade." He mentioned that he gets into trouble for talking and not getting his work done. He described this vignette of his problems forgetting things: He tries to work fast to complete his work, but he needs to press hard on his pencil when writing. Soon he needs to stretch his fingers out. He forgets that he's in the middle of a work activity as he watches what's going on in the class. Suddenly he remembers that he was not finished, but by this time he doesn't want to go back because he has lost his train of thought.

Tests Administered

Kaufman Assessment Battery for Children (K-ABC)
Woodcock-Johnson Psychoeducational Battery:
    Reading Aptitude Cluster

> Math Aptitude Cluster
> Reading Achievement Cluster
> Math Achievement Cluster
> Bender-Gestalt Visual-Motor Test
> Kinetic Family Drawing
> Informal assessment of written arithmetic skills

Test Results and Interpretation

Jeremy's performance on the K-ABC revealed even development in both cognitive approaches, as he earned a Sequential Processing standard score of 115 ± 9, which did not differ significantly from his Simultaneous Processing standard score of 108 ± 6. Thus, Jeremy's intellectual functioning is best summarized by his Mental Processing Composite of 112 ± 6, which classifies him as Above Average and ranks him at the 79th percentile when compared to other nine-year-olds. The chances are ninety out of a hundred that his true Mental Processing Composite is somewhere in the range from 106 to 118.

Jeremy's Achievement standard score of 119 ± 4 (115 to 123 with 90 percent confidence) also falls into the Above Average range. Although his obtained Achievement score ranks him at the 90th percentile, his performance in this domain does not differ significantly from his overall intelligence score of 112. Jeremy did earn an Achievement score that is significantly higher than his Simultaneous Processing score of 108 ($p \leq .05$). This finding is inconsequential, however, because his Sequential and Simultaneous scores differed minimally from each other; and, as stated, the best estimate of his general mental ability was commensurate with his overall Achievement level.

Within the Achievement domain, Jeremy exhibited considerable scatter as his standard scores ranged from 99 (identification of famous faces and places) to 133 (oral arithmetic). This large range of scores is unusual in that only 8 percent of the children in the representative standardization sample had ranges of 34 or more points. Overall, he performed much better in applied school-related skills (average percentile rank of 94 on arithmetic, reading decoding, and reading comprehension tasks), than in his fund of factual information, whether responding to pictorial or verbal stimuli (56th percentile overall). Jeremy's truly superior performance on the Arithmetic subtest (99th percentile) was surprising in view of referral information, and clearly underscores the fact that his difficulties with arithmetic in the classroom do not mean that he does not understand mathematical concepts and their applications. Despite his outstanding success in responding to oral arithmetic questions (which are accompanied by pictorial stimuli), it was apparent that Jeremy has not yet learned his multiplication tables.

Jeremy displayed an average or typical amount of variability on the separate Mental Processing subtests (scaled score range of 8 to 16), but he nevertheless revealed some significant strengths and weaknesses in his profile. He demonstrated an excellent visual short-term memory (as contrasted to his relatively weak visual long-term memory on the Faces & Places subtest), ranking in the 98th percentile in his ability to copy the examiner's sequential hand movements, and performing well on a spatial memory test requiring recall of the location of pictured objects. Jeremy also excelled (98th percentile) in an abstract visual analogy task, suggesting highly developed analogic thinking skills.

These exceptional abilities were offset by significant weaknesses (31st percentile) in identifying partially completed inkblot drawings and in ordering photographs of an event in proper chronological sequence. Taken together, these weaknesses suggest a relative deficiency in Jeremy's ability to synthesize stimuli and understand part-whole relationships. This hypothesis is supported by performance below his own average in assembling triangles to match an abstract design. Indeed, problems with part-whole relationships may account for his below-average score in the verbal achievement test of factual information which requires the synthesis of separate attributes to infer a concept (e.g., "What lives in a hive, has a stinger, and makes honey?").

The two drawing tests that were administered provided consistent indicators that Jeremy has a visual-motor problem interfering with successful written work. His BGT copying of abstract designs was at about a seven-year-old's level of ability. The meager stick figures he drew for the Kinetic Family Drawing were poorly spaced on the paper as were both his handwriting and his arrangement of numerical computations on a page. These test results and observations are consistent with the previous discussion of Jeremy's more generalized problems with relationships between parts of a whole. Further diagnostic testing to explore the specific academic areas of reading and math was done with the Woodcock-Johnson Psychoeducational Battery.

Reading aptitude tasks measuring the cognitive skills most associated with successful performance in reading earned Jeremy an expected grade score of 4.5 (83rd percentile). A different group of subtests which directly measure a variety of specific reading achievement skills revealed his actual achievement level to be grade 5.0 on the Woodcock-Johnson, and about grade 6.5 on the K-ABC reading subtests.

A corresponding aptitude-achievement comparison was made for Jeremy's mathematical skills. Here his aptitude for performing math tasks was assessed by a set of different cognitive tests and registered an expected grade score of 4.1 (70th percentile). The one task he had problems with required him to rapidly circle the matching pairs in a row of numbers. He functioned in the range of grade 2.0 to 3.0 in this task. Jeremy's actual math achievement cluster score was grade 4.6. It is interesting to note the discrepancy between his math skills when use of a pencil is required (grade 3.5 to 4.5) and when he solves problems orally (grade 5.0 to 7.0). On the K-ABC, Jeremy's excellent performance on the oral arithmetic subtest also yielded a high grade equivalent of about 7.0.

Discussion and Recommendations

Jeremy has acquired above-average skills in both reading and math despite reports from his teacher that he is doing poorly in his schoolwork. Because his threshold for distracting stimuli is low, Jeremy is particularly susceptible to the variety of noises and activities going on daily in his classroom. He is less well developed in his visual-motor skills, and in his understanding of part-whole relationships. These difficulties also promote errors for Jeremy when he is writing math computations. His organization of work and materials is sometimes a problem. Also Jeremy may not be reading enough for pleasure to enhance his general information acquisition. Aware of his school problems, Jeremy does not appear to be involved in classwork or class social activity.

The following specific recommendations are offered at this time:

1. Jeremy will work best with programmed text type of workbooks. For written work exercises, both the immediate feedback and a multiple-choice or short answer response style will promote success.

2. To help the spacing problem in written material, try folding the paper into many boxes and encourage whole problems to be kept within these quadrants.

3. Keep to routines and structure to help basic organizational skills develop.

4. Introduce typewriter skills to help communicate longer written material more efficiently.

5. Encourage interest in reading books that are on an appropriate level of difficulty. This might begin by a regular brief session when a parent reads such a piece out loud to him. Jeremy has not yet developed the need to read on his own for pleasure, and may soon discover how valuable this activity can be. Since he expressed interest in science, two books he might enjoy are *Bet You can* by Vicki Cobb and Kathy Darling

(1983), Avon/Camelot paperback) which is a fifth-grade-level text, and *Bet You Can't* (same authors, 1980) which would need parental help since it is seventh-grade reading level.

6. Jeremy needs a more productive classroom environment. Investigating options that will reduce the effects of combined grade classrooms and provide more individual attention to his learning needs may enhance both his academic and his emotional development.

Dr. Nadeen L. Kaufman, Examiner

REFERENCES

Das, J. P., Kirby, J. R., & Jarman, R. F. (1979). *Simultaneous and successive cognitive processes*. New York: Academic Press.

Kaufman, A. S. (1979). *Intelligence testing with the WISC-R*. New York: John Wiley & Sons, Inc.

Kaufman, A. S. (1983). Some questions and answers about the K-ABC. *Journal of Psychoeducational Assessment, 1*, 205–218.

Kaufman, A. S., & Kaufman, N. L. (1977). *Clinical evaluation of young children with the McCarthy Scales*. New York: Grune & Stratton, Inc.

Kaufman, A. S., & Kaufman, N. L. (1983). *K-ABC administration and scoring manual*. (a). Circle Pines, MN: American Guidance Service.

Kaufman, A. S., & Kaufman, N. L. (1983). *K-ABC interpretative manual*. (b). Circle Pines, MN: American Guidance Service.

Kaufman, A. S., & Kaufman, N. L., Kamphaus, R. W., & Naglieri, J. A. (1982). Sequential and simultaneous factors at ages 3–12 ½: Developmental changes in neuropsychological dimensions. *Clinical Neuropsychology, 4*, 74–81.

Luria, A. R. (1966). *Higher cortical functions in man*. New York: Basic Books Inc., Publishers.

Naglieri, J. A., Kaufman, A. S., Kaufman, N. L., & Kamphaus, R. W. (1981). Cross-validation of Das' simultaneous and successive processes with novel tasks. *Alberta Journal of Educational Research, 27*, 264–271.

Neisser, U. (1967). *Cognitive psychology*. New York: Appleton-Century-Crofts.

8

The Wechsler Intelligence Scale for Children-Revised

Annette M. LaGreca
Sharon A. Stringer

Introduction Assessment represents an important initial step in all clinical work with children and families. Through the assessment process, problems of concern are identified and treatment strategies developed. Beyond initial problem identification, assessment remains a continuing area of importance in order to effectively tailor treatment plans to children's needs and to evaluate the impact of interventions.

Several important distinctions have been made between the assessment process for children versus adults (Evans & Nelson, 1977; LaGreca, 1983). Most notably, with children care needs to be taken to utilize multiple sources of input (e.g., parents, teachers, and the child) as well as multiple methods of assessment (e.g., interviews, observations, testing) in order to gain full understanding of the child and family.

Within this broad-based assessment context, individualized tests of intelligence play an important role. Many childhood problems are, at least in part, related to the child's cognitive functioning (e.g., learning disabilities, hyperactivity, etc.). Information regarding the child's skills and capabilities can determine whether a child's inappropriate classroom behavior is a result of boredom or a sign of learning difficulties. The important role of individualized intelligence tests are highlighted during the early to middle elementary school years when children meet their first serious academic challenge and when many child behavior problems are reported to be school related. Even in cases where the referral problem bears no obvious relationship to a school setting, such as the parents' physical abuse of a six-year-old child, the child's cognitive skills or deficits may potentially contribute to family functioning (Burgess, 1979) and have implications for how treatment should proceed.

Despite their clinical utility, intelligence tests are not without their limitations. Legitimate concerns have been raised regarding racial and cultural bias (Hilliard, 1975; Mercer, 1974, 1977; Williams, 1972), as well as the misuse and abuse of these measures in educational placement decisions (Hobbs, 1975). Certainly existing intelligence tests are limited in that they sample only a selected subset of skills that contribute to an individual's intelligence. The breadth of human intellectual functioning is not truly captured by current measures. Moreover, test performance depends not only on capability, but also on the child's previous learning experiences and on the child's ability to display appropriate task-oriented behavior. As such, these measures reflect an interaction of learning, behavior, and skills and, therefore, must be interpreted within the context of a thorough understanding of the child's learning history and current behavior style.

Although these limitations have been the subject of much controversy, individualized intelligence tests do have considerable merit when used in a knowledgeable manner. They are good predictors of school achievement (DeHorn & Klinge, 1978; Stedman, Lawlis, Cortner, & Achterberg, 1978; Thorndike & Hagen, 1977), and consequently they play a critical role in determining appropriate educational placements. Furthermore, the individualized nature of the tests permits the skilled examiner to go beyond determining the child's overall level of functioning and identify specific areas of strength and weakness that may be essential for providing appropriate academic instruction.

In order to use intelligence tests "intelligently," Kaufman (1979a) has outlined three general considerations to guide the clinician. First, the clinician should assume that the test measures what the individual has learned. Thus, the child's previous learning experiences and cultural background are viewed as contributing to his or her current scores; the scores are not to be interpreted as indications of innate, fixed ability. As such, children who perform poorly may be directed toward remedial educational experiences that improve their learning base, and potentially affect their future level of functioning.

Second, the clinician should recognize that the test provides a sample of behavior rather than an exhaustive assessment of the child's skills. Thus, one must exercise caution in generalizing the test results to other situations or different circumstances. For example, a child who performs well during the one-to-one testing situation may not necessarily display a comparable degree of attention and concentration when placed in an open classroom or a group instruction setting. Additional testing and observations of the child's behavior in academic situations are desirable supplements to the information provided by intelligence tests.

Third, the clinician must acknowledge that the test assesses cognitive functioning under restrictive procedures. Although the standardized administration and scoring procedures provide objective means of evaluating children's skills and making normative comparisons, they do not capture fully the process and complexity of children's cognitive skills. Standardized administration procedures may, in some cases, produce an underestimate of what the child can do (Hardy, Welcher, Mellits & Kagan, 1976). For instance, a low score on a particular subtest may reflect one child's inability to complete the task, yet reflect another child's misunderstanding of standard instructions. In the latter case, alternate wording of the test questions may yield different results and affect the interpretation of the child's performance. Due to the necessary limitations of the standardized testing procedures, it is the examiner's responsibility to be a keen observer of the child's behavior during the test and to employ testing-the-limits procedures (see Kaufman, 1979a; Sattler, 1982) when needed so that an accurate understanding and interpretation of the test results can be obtained.

With these cautions in mind, the following will examine more closely the Wechsler Intelligence Scale for Children-Revised (WISC-R). In the following chapter sections, an overview is provided of the WISC-R, with particular attention devoted to issues of administration, scoring, interpretation, and special uses. In-depth discussion of the issues presented here can be found in Kaufman (1979a) and Sattler (1982), as well as in the WISC-R manual (Wechsler, 1974).

OVERVIEW OF THE WISC-R

Description of the Test

The WISC-R is perhaps the most widely used measure of children's intellectual functioning. It has been normed for use with children between the ages of 6–0 and 16–11 years, although some problems may arise when using the test near the lower and upper age limits, as will be discussed later in this section. The WISC-R, published in

1974 (Wechsler, 1974), updated and replaced the original WISC (Wechsler, 1949). (The reader is referred to Sattler, 1982, and Swerdlik, 1977, for detailed comparisons of the two versions of this test.)

The Wechsler series of intelligence tests, with the WISC-R as one component, covers the age range from 4–0 years through adulthood. The series includes the Wechsler Preschool and Primary Scale of Intelligence (WPPSI; Wechsler, 1967) for children between the ages of 4–0 and 6–6 years, and the Wechsler Adult Intelligence Scale-Revised (WAIS-R; Wechsler, 1981) for individuals aged 16–0 years and older. (See Sattler, 1982, for a detailed description of the WPPSI and Zimmerman, this volume, for a detailed description of the WAIS-R.)

The WISC-R's composition is similar to other tests in the Wechsler series. As with these other instruments, the WISC-R is comprised of Verbal and Performance Scales, that yield separate IQ scores (Verbal IQ, Performance IQ), distinct from the test's overall or Full Scale IQ. Each IQ score has a mean of 100 and a standard deviation of 15, based on the deviation method of deriving IQ scores (see Sattler, 1982, and Wechsler, 1974, for a more detailed discussion).

Each major scale consists of five required subtests and one supplementary subtest (see Table 8–1). The ten required subtests are

Table 8–1 Description of WISC-R Subtests and the Unique Abilities They Measure[a]

VERBAL SCALE

Information: Thirty questions that sample general factual information. Measures fund of general knowledge. Scores influenced by educational and cultural opportunities; outside interests.

Similarities: Seventeen word pairs of increasing difficulty are presented and the child must explain their similarity. Measures logical, abstract thinking; ability to form verbal concepts. Influenced by cultural opportunities; outside interests.

Arithmetic[b]: Eighteen oral arithmetic problems that require mental computation (no pencils or paper). Measures computational skills; numerical reasoning. Influenced by anxiety; ability to concentrate; distractibility; schooling experiences.

Vocabulary: Thirty-two words arranged by increasing difficulty and abstractness; the child is asked to explain their meaning. Measures general word knowledge; language development. Influenced by educational background; cultural experiences; outside reading and interests.

Comprehension: Seventeen questions regarding problem situations that cover social norms, interpersonal relations and practical concerns. Measures practical common sense; awareness of social rules and mores; ability to use past experiences. Influenced by cultural opportunities; moral development.

Digit Span[c]: Contains two parts. The child is asked (a) to repeat series of digits (three to nine digits in length), and (b) to repeat series of digits backwards (two to eight digits in length). Measures short-term auditory memory. Influenced by attention span; anxiety; distractibility.

PERFORMANCE SCALE

Picture Completion[b]: Twenty-six drawings of everyday objects that have an important part missing; child points to (or names) the missing part. Measures long-term visual memory; visual alertness; ability to differentiate between essential and nonessential details. Influenced by concentration; visual acuity; cognitive style.

Picture Arrangement[b]: Twelve series of comic-strip type pictures are presented in mixed-up order; the child rearranges the pictures to tell a story. Measures temporal visual sequencing; social awareness; nonverbal reasoning and planning ability. Influenced by cultural background; exposure to comics; visual acuity.

Block Design[b]: Child is asked to assemble red and white blocks (either four or nine blocks) to match two-dimensional pictures of abstract designs; eleven designs in all. Measures nonverbal concept formation; ability to analyze a whole into components; visual-spatial organization. Influenced by cognitive style; visual-motor speed.

Object Assembly[b]: Four jigsaw puzzles are presented; child assembles pieces to form an object (girl, car, horse, face). Measures anticipation of part-whole relationships; ability to use sensory-motor feedback; visual-motor speed and coordination. Influenced by cognitive style; experience with puzzles.

Coding[b]: Copying symbols that are paired with numbers (or geometric shapes) in a fast and accurate manner. Measures visual-motor speed and accuracy; short-term visual memory; ability to follow directions. Influenced by distractibility; anxiety; visual acuity.

Mazes[c,b]: Nine mazes of increasing difficulty; child must draw a route out. Measures visual planning; ability to follow a visual pattern; visual-motor coordination; foresight. Influenced by experiences with solving mazes.

---

[a]Adapted from Sattler (1982) and Kaufman (1979).

[b]Denotes tests that are timed. Performance on these subtests may also be influenced by the child's reaction to working under a time pressure.

[c]Denotes the supplementary subtests

used to compute the IQ scores. For children under eight years of age, it is recommended that the Mazes subtest be substituted for Coding when computing Performance and Full Scale IQs (see Kaufman, 1979a; Wechsler, 1974). However, a decision to do this should be made prior to test administration and not be based on the child's poor performance on Coding. Based on the child's chronological age at the time of testing, the raw scores obtained on these subtests are converted to standard scores (called scaled scores) which have a mean of 10 and a standard deviation of 3. This standard score format facilitates intratest comparisons, and enables the clinician to identify areas of relative strength and weakness for a particular child.

All tests on the Verbal Scale are administered orally, and require a verbal response from the child. These tests, designed to assess *verbal comprehension* skills, specifically tap the child's ability to understand, reason, and express himself or herself through language. By contrast, all the Performance subtests provide visually-oriented materials (e.g., puzzle pieces, blocks) that require a motor response from the child (e.g., pointing, copying, puzzle assembly) and minimal verbal expression. The subtests on the Performance Scale assess non-verbal or *perceptual organization* skills, that include the child's ability to perceive, organize, and reason with visual/spatial stimuli. Some degree of visual-motor coordination is also tapped by these subtests.

Comparison with Other Instruments

Although several individualized intelligence tests overlap the age range covered by the WISC-R (see Figure 8–1), the WISC-R has clearly been the test of choice for assessing school-age children.* Relative to the Stanford-Binet, which covers a comparable age range, the WISC-R has several advantages. For one, it provides a more balanced assessment of a child's cognitive skills by tapping both verbal and perceptual skills. In contrast, the Binet has been criticized for its heavy focus on verbal abilities, especially at the test's older age levels (Sattler, 1982). Moreover, unlike the twelve standard subtests found on the WISC-R, the Binet tasks change across age levels, making it difficult to adequately compare the performance of children who differ in chronological age or to compare the same child's performance at

---

*The Kaufman Assessment Battery for Children (K-ABC; Kaufman & Kaufman, 1983) is a newly designed instrument for assessing the cognitive abilities of children between 2–6 and 12–5 years of age. Kaufman has discussed the utility of this instrument for assessing school-aged children and its relationship to the WISC-R (Kaufman, this volume; Kaufman & Kaufman, 1983).

The McCarthy Scales of Children's Abilities (McCarthy, 1972) also can be used with children in the early elementary grades. However, it is most often employed with preschoolers due to its relatively low ceiling age at 8–6 years (Kaufman & Kaufman, 1977).

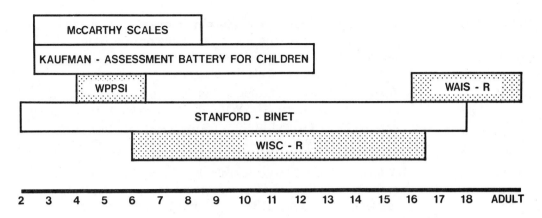

AGE IN YEARS

Figure 8–1 Illustrates in graph form several individualized intelligence tests as related to the age of a child.

two different points in time. Finally, the WISC-R appears to be a better instrument for determining an individual's relative strengths and weaknesses and was designed, in part, for this purpose. Due to a different theoretical perspective guiding the test construction, the Binet does not appear to have a consistent factor structure and is less satisfactory for identifying individuals' strengths and weaknesses (Sattler, 1982).

Although, as a general rule, the WISC-R is preferred to the Binet for assessing school-aged children, there are several notable exceptions that primarily arise when testing at the lower or upper age limits of the test. These are as follows:

1. The Stanford-Binet may be preferable for assessing children between the ages of six and eight years who are referred for developmental delays or who are suspected of functioning within the Mentally Retarded range. In such cases, the WISC-R will sample skills that are beyond the child's capabilities and, therefore, reveal more about what the child cannot rather than what the child can do. A more comprehensive sampling of the child's skills will be obtained with the Binet (or by a combined Binet/McCarthy assessment) since the lower age limits of the Binet are at the two-year-old level.

2. For children, adolescents, and adults who are functioning within the profound to moderate ranges of retardation,

the Binet may be the preferred instrument. As in the previous example, the lower test ages on the Binet will permit a broader sampling of such individuals' skills and provide a more accurate IQ estimate.

3. Although a less common situation, the assessment of gifted adolescents on the WISC-R also presents problems. The WISC-R will not provide an adequate ceiling nor will it fully sample gifted adolescents' areas of strength. In such cases, the Stanford-Binet or the WAIS-R (for a 16–0 year old) would be preferable. In addition, Sattler (1982) recommends the use of achievement tests as supplementary measures since gifted individuals may have variable areas of strength.

4. Children with severe visual or motor handicaps (e.g., cerebral palsy) will not be able to complete the Performance sections of the WISC-R. Their skills may be assessed more adequately with the Stanford-Binet which is more verbally oriented.

PSYCHOMETRIC PROPERTIES OF THE WISC-R

This section will briefly review the psychometric properties of the WISC-R. Detailed discussion of these issues can be found in the test manual (Wechsler, 1974) as well as in Kaufman (1979a) and Sattler (1982).

Standardization Sample

The WISC-R was standardized on a sample of 2200 children between the ages of 6–6 and 16–6 years (Wechsler, 1974). Two hundred children (100 males and 100 females) were sampled at each of eleven age groups. The 1970 Census Bureau data were used to select a sample of children representative of the U.S. population. The standardization sample included Blacks, American Indians, Orientals, Puerto Ricans, and Mexican-Americans. In addition, four geographic regions, urban and rural residents, and a wide range of socioeconomic classes were represented (Wechsler, 1974).

Reliability

The reliability of the WISC-R is excellent. Reviews of the psychometric properties of the WISC-R (Kaufman, 1979a; Sattler, 1982; Wechsler, 1974) report high internal consistency for the scales. Split-half reliability coefficients were found to be .90 for the Performance IQ, .94 for the Verbal IQ, and .96 for the Full Scale IQ. Average reliability coefficients for the individual subtests are adequate, ranging from .70 (Object Assembly) to .86 (Vocabulary). The literature reports somewhat higher reliability for the Verbal subtests than for Performance subtests. However, Block Design, a Performance subtest, has one of the highest reliability coefficients.

The test-retest reliability of the WISC-R, assessed by retesting 303 children from the standardization sample after a one-month interval (Wechsler, 1974), also suggests that the IQ scores obtained are stable. Test-retest correlations were .93 (Verbal IQ), .90 (Performance IQ), and .95 (Full Scale IQ). It is important to note that, on the average, Full Scale IQ scores were about 7 points higher for the retest, and this difference primarily was due to a practice effect for the Performance subtests. The average Performance IQ score improved by 8 to 10 points at retest compared to a 3 to 4 point improvement for the Verbal IQ score (Wechsler, 1974).

Standard Error of Measurement

The standard error of measurement (SEM) indicates the band of error around a particular test score, and enables the examiner to estimate with some degree of confidence the range within which an individual's true score lies. A band of ±1 SEM around a particular score determines a 68 percent confidence interval; ±2 SEM determines a 95 percent confidence interval. The standard errors of measurement for the WISC-R IQ scores are: 3.19 (Full Scale), 3.60 (Verbal), and 4.66 (Performance).

As an illustration of the clinical use of SEMs, consider a child who obtains a Full Scale IQ = 100. The examiner can say with 68 percent confidence that this child's true score falls between 97 and 103 (e.g., 100 ± 3.19), or the examiner can say with 95 percent confidence that the true score falls between 94 and 106 (100 ± 6.38). By using the SEM in this manner, the examiner shifts attention away from a fixed score and instead stresses the range of scores within which the individual's abilities are likely to lie.

Validity

The validity of a test indicates the degree that a test measures what it's supposed to measure (Sattler, 1982). The criterion validity of the WISC-R has been assessed by examining its correlation with other intelligence tests such as the 1949 WISC, the Stanford-Binet, the WPPSI, the McCarthy Scales of Children's Abilities, and the Peabody Picture Vocabulary Test. Correlations between these tests vary from the upper .30s to the low .80s (Sattler, 1982; Wechsler, 1974), indicating satisfactory concurrent validity. Studies also report that, on the average, the WISC-R yields lower IQ scores than the WISC, the Slosson Intelligence Test, the WAIS, the WPPSI, and the Peabody Picture Vocabulary Test (Sattler, 1982; Wechsler, 1974). The average difference in scores between the WISC-R and these other tests ranges from one or two points (WISC-R and the WPPSI) to five points (WISC-R and the Slosson Intelligence Test). Although these findings suggest that the mean scores obtained from different instruments may be comparable, in practice, an individual child's scores may differ markedly when using two different tests. For example, one set of investigators (Rasbury, McCoy & Perry, 1977) found that WISC-R scores differed from WPPSI scores by more than 10 points, in about 10 percent of the cases. These individual differences are indicative of errors in measurement and should not be interpreted as changes in the child's ability. Considerable caution is needed when comparing the performance of an individual child on two instruments.

The construct validity of the WISC-R has been investigated largely through factor analysis. Kaufman (1975) and Silverstein and Legutki (1982), using the standardization sample, found that the factor structure of the 1949 WISC and the WISC-R were similar. Kaufman's (1975) factor analysis of the total standardization sample for the WISC-R yielded three main factors: Verbal Comprehension, Perceptual Organization, and Freedom from Distractibility (see Table 8–2 for the grouping of the subtests).

The Verbal Comprehension factor closely parallels the Verbal Scale (with the exception of the Arithmetic subtest), and the Perceptual Organization factor parallels the Performance Scale (with the exception of the Coding subtest). These data suggest that the two main scales of the WISC-R largely assess abilities they were designed to measure. The third factor, Freedom from Distractibility, includes subtests from both the Verbal and Performance scales. This factor appears to assess the individual's ability to concentrate and tune out distracting influences.

Other studies have reported that a similar WISC-R factor structure is evident in samples of Black children, Mexican children, mentally retarded children, adolescent psychiatric populations, and learning-disabled children (DeHorn & Klinge, 1978; Reynolds & Gutkin, 1980; Sattler, 1982; Schooler, Beebe & Koepke, 1978). Recent studies (Hale, 1983; Hale, Raymond & Gajar, 1982) examining the construct validity of the WISC-R, found similar factor structures of the WISC-R across different socioeconomic status groups as well.

As a check on the predictive validity of the WISC-R, a number of studies have examined the relationship between WISC-R factor scores and achievement tests such as the Peabody Individual Achieve-

Table 8–2 Factor Structure of the WISC-R and Factor Loadings of Individual Subtests[a]

	MEDIAN FACTOR LOADING
Verbal Comprehension	
Information	.63
Similarities	.64
Vocabulary	.72
Comprehension	.64
Perceptual Organization	
Picture Completion	.57
Picture Arrangement	.41
Block Design	.66
Object Assembly	.65
Mazes[b]	.47
Freedom from Distractibility	
Arithmetic	.58
Coding	.42
Digit Span[b]	.56

[a]Adapted from Sattler, 1982. Only median factor loadings of .40 or greater are included.

[b]Indicates a supplementary subtest

ment Test and the Wide Range Achievement Test (Brock, 1982; Grossman & Johnson, 1982; Hale, 1978; Sattler, 1982; Stedmen et al., 1978; Wright & Dappen, 1982). In general, the studies indicate that both WISC-R IQ scores and factor scores are good predictors of school achievement (Grossman & Johnson, 1982; Stedman et al., 1978). (See Sattler, 1982, for a further discussion of validity issues.)

Short Forms of the WISC-R

The WISC-R takes approximately sixty to ninety minutes to administer, depending on the individual child. If possible, it is advisable to administer the test in one session (Wechsler, 1974). Both Kaufman (1979a) and Sattler (1974, 1982) recommend that all twelve subtests be administered when time permits. Short forms of the WISC-R, however, may be used for practical reasons. For example, if a particular child cannot endure a lengthy test session, a short form of the WISC-R may be administered as a screening device. Although several short forms of the WISC-R are reported to have high validity (Sattler, 1982), methodological problems often arise related to sampling of skills, averaging of scores, and reliability of measurement. Short forms are not recommended for diagnosis of special populations (King & King, 1982;

Kramer, Shanks, Markley & Ryabik, 1983). Kaufman (1979a) provides specific guidelines for the administration and scoring of short forms of the WISC-R.

CLINICAL USE OF THE WISC-R

Administration

The WISC-R manual contains detailed instructions on test administration and establishing rapport (Wechsler, 1974). In addition, Sattler (1982) provides excellent suggestions for establishing rapport, organizing the test situation, and avoiding common administrative errors, such as the examiner's failure to record responses, errors in timing subtests, and providing too much help to the child. This section offers practical suggestions to aid in the administration of the WISC-R that supplement these other sources. It is assumed that the reader has thoroughly reviewed the administration procedures described in the WISC-R manual.

In general, it is helpful to extend the child's active examinee role to administration procedures. For example, the clinician may allow the child to return blocks and puzzle pieces to the boxes at the completion of the Block Design and Object Assembly subtests. Participation in such administrative tasks may help the child become less anxious about test performance. Such sharing procedures enable the examiner and child to approach the WISC-R as an interactive process. Also, informal conversation between subtests may relax a child and allows the examiner to obtain supplementary information regarding school, interests, and family background. With these general recommendations in mind, specific suggestions for administering individual WISC-R subtests follow.

Verbal Subtests

Several subtests on the Verbal Scale (Information, Similarities, Vocabulary, Comprehension) permit the examiner to probe vague or unclear responses. As indicated in the test manual, it is permissible to probe by saying "Tell me more about it," or "Explain what you mean." Most importantly, it is advisable to avoid using a probe, in question format, such as "Can you tell me what you mean?" This format discourages guessing and may well meet with a response of "no" from the child, whereas the more directive probes are likely to elicit further response elaboration.

Another consideration, often arising when testing children with learning or emotional problems, is that the child may be acutely aware of and concerned about poor performance. All verbal subtests require several consecutive failures before testing is discontinued, and children may miss several earlier items before the consecutive criterion is reached. Missed items may exacerbate the child's feelings of failure and undermine further effort and motivation. Since the examiner wishes to maintain good rapport and facilitate optimal performance, several tactics may be useful. For one, after the failure criterion is reached, the examiner might make up an easy item for the child to complete. For example, after the child reaches five consecutive failures on the Vocabulary subtest, the examiner may ask the child to define an easy word such as "shoe." In this way, the child will end the task on a successful note, rather than on one of failure.

A second strategy involves preparing the child for the test and then providing encouragement throughout the assessment. Before the test begins the examiner should inform the child that some items will be difficult, but to try his or her best. For instance, the examiner might say, "Some of the things we will be working on today are easy and others are hard. That's because some are for children your age, and others are for older children. All kids your age find some of these items to be hard. It's really okay to guess if you're not sure of an answer. What is most important is that you try your very best." Once testing begins, the examiner should make a point of praising the child's effort, not the performance. Statements such as, "I really like the way you're working," or "You're doing such a good job of trying," or "You're working really nicely," can encourage a child during frustrating subtests. (Encouragement should be provided throughout the test and not just during the verbal portions.)

Several additional suggestions pertaining to specific verbal subtests follow.

Information   During this subtest, it may help rapport to begin testing with one or two items that fall below the child's normal entry point. For example, an eight-to-ten-year-old child starts with item 5, yet the examiner may present items 1 and 2 before going on to item 5. Beginning the test with an obviously easy item may relax a child who is worried about his or her performance. This is often the case with children experiencing learning or emotional problems.

For this subtest, it is permissible to repeat an item if asked, but the item should be repeated verbatim.

Similarities   It is important to follow the instructions for providing help. For instance, a child who gives one-point responses should be given an example of a two-point response only for items 5 and 6. If a child does poorly on this task, it will be important to test-the-limits* (see Sattler, 1982) after the WISC-R administration is completed. Often, children falling near the test's younger age limit may not understand the idea of the task (e.g., the child describes differences instead of similarities). In such cases, it will be important to know whether or not the child is capable of providing satisfactory answers if the wording of the instructions is altered or if several examples are provided.

Arithmetic   This task is relatively easy to administer. However, the examiner must be careful to begin timing immediately after the item is read for the first time. Items can be repeated verbatim once at the child's request, or if he or she appears not to have understood the item.

If a child cannot complete any item beyond the first counting task, a testing-the-limits procedure may be appropriate to see if the child has any basic numerical skills. For instance, the examiner may ask some simple computations ("What is 1 + 1?" "What is 2 + 3?"). Or, the examiner can ask a child to show a certain number of fingers ("Show me three fingers."). (See Sattler, 1982, for more detailed suggestions.)

Vocabulary and Comprehension   The main consideration for administering these subtests is to know the scoring criteria thoroughly. Particularly when assessing children with learning problems or language difficulties, it will be critical for the examiner to know: when to probe a vague response; when the response is a marginal 0- or 1-point response that needs further elaboration to determine an accurate score; and when to discontinue testing. Unnecessary probing and overtesting can create a difficult and trying experience for the child, and is likely to sacrifice the examiner's rapport. Successful administration of these subtests requires an excellent mastery of the scoring criteria.

One additional caution for the Comprehension subtest is that items must be repeated verbatim, rather than in phrases or altered wording.

---

*Testing-the-limits refers to the process of readministering individual subtests or subtest items with altered instructions or procedures, after the standard WISC-R administration has been completed. When testing limits, the examiner modifies test instructions or subtest items in such a way as to better understand the nature of a child's difficulty with a particular task. For example, if a child appears to miss several Block Design items due to extreme concern about being timed, the examiner may later readminister the missed items without time limits. If the child's scores then improve, it is likely that time pressures interfered with the child's performance. If scores do not improve under these altered conditions, then one might more readily conclude that poor performance was a function of the child's inability to complete the task rather than a function of time pressures.

Digit Span   Although Digit Span is a supplementary test, its inclusion is recommended in a WISC-R administration. It provides the information needed to interpret the Freedom from Distractibility factor, and it is the only task that directly assesses auditory short-term memory. Although Digit Span is generally easy to administer, examiners should carefully watch the pacing of digits (one per second). It's also essential to ensure that the child is attending to the task before reciting the digit series, as the sequence cannot be repeated. If a child is spinning around in a chair or looking out the window, it will be impossible to determine whether poor performance is due to task difficulty or unnecessary distractions. (If the child begins the task by attending and becomes distracted mid-item, however, this behavior may suggest anxiety, poor memory skills, or concentration difficulties.) Digit Span is often the last subtest to be administered and the examiner may add an easy item at the end of the subtest, to finish the testing session on a positive note.

Performance Subtests

The performance subtests of the WISC-R generally are more difficult to administer than the verbal items, and require more practice and planning on the examiner's part for valid administration. Examiners should be thoroughly familiar with the test instructions and materials prior to administration, and should have the testing kit well organized in advance so that minimal time is spent readying materials and maximum time is devoted to observing the child. The performance subtests afford excellent opportunities to observe a child's work strategies and problem-solving skills; this cannot be accomplished if the examiner is looking for the next subtest item.

Several general considerations apply to these subtests. Since timing is important for all the subtests, the examiner should have a stopwatch readily accessible but not necessarily highlighting its presence. The recommended preference is for a silent stopwatch (e.g., a digital one). Often children will request to look at the stopwatch, and this can be used to reinforce their task orientation (e.g., "As soon as we finish this test you can take a look at it"). In many cases, however, it may be best to politely and firmly refuse the request; this prevents unfortunate accidents (e.g., a dropped and broken stopwatch).

The examiner's probing techniques are also important during timed subtests. Questions such as "Are you finished?" may provide hints about the correctness or incorrectness of the child's answers. The examiner avoids offering cues, however, by reminding the child before beginning subtests to state when he or she is finished. Accurate timing is always important, but it will be especially critical for older children as speed has a large effect on their task performance (Kaufman, 1979a).

Another consideration is that the child be seated comfortably and in a position to easily reach and manipulate test items. The examiner must be careful to place subtest pieces in front of the child in their proper orientation. Examiners have been known to place subtest pieces too far from the child, out of the child's line of vision, or even at a marked angle to the proper orientation (this appears to happen most often when the examiner is not seated directly across from the child). Certainly, these administration errors will limit the child's performance and should be avoided.

Many children wish to complete an item even after the time limit has elapsed. This may be permissible in order to maintain rapport with the child. However, the child should be encouraged to move on to the next item (or next subtest), particularly if the item is a frustrating one that is not likely to be solved.

As a last general caution, the examiner should check whether or not the child wears glasses for reading or working. If so, they certainly should be worn during the test administration. A child who cannot see the test items properly will not perform at his or her best.

Specific suggestions for administering the performance subtests follow.

Picture Completion   Although this task is generally easy to administer, the examiner should be careful of timing and also make sure the cards are placed directly in front of the child. The examiner may need to handle the materials firmly to prevent the child from looking ahead to other test items. Common administration errors for this task involve the examiner neglecting to give needed cautions (e.g., "Yes, but what's missing?"), or repeating the cautions more than once. Sattler (1982) notes that children should be aware of being timed on this subtest.

Picture Arrangement   Organized test materials are a must for this subtest. The cards in the twelve picture series should be prearranged in the kit according to their order of presentation, so the examiner can lay out the pieces rapidly and attend to the child's behavior. As each item is completed, the examiner can check the child's responses quickly by picking up the cards in sequence from the child's left to right, glancing at the letter sequence on the back of the cards as they are gathered up. This will facilitate rapid recording of responses and a smooth subtest administration.

The examiner should carefully note the different task instructions for children of different ages, and the various procedures for second trials on missed items (Wechsler, 1974). For children exhibiting problems with this task, a good testing-the-limits procedure is to ask the child to tell a story to go along with the pictures. (See Sattler, 1982, for additional suggestions.)

Block Design   As with Picture Arrangement, the instructions for this task are difficult, and require varying procedures for children of different ages. It is advisable to check the manual carefully.

In order to involve the child in the task, it often helps to have the child mix up the blocks after an item is completed while the examiner is recording the response and readying the next design card. However, before starting a new item, the examiner should check that no more than one block (out of four) or three blocks (out of nine) have a mixed red-and-white side facing up.

Occasionally, a child will try to match the top and sides to the examiner's model. This kind of problem can be avoided by making sure the model is placed in a position requiring the child to look down on it (Wechsler, 1974). However, the examiner should be alert to the possibility of the child attending to the sides of the blocks and specifically direct the child to only match the top of the design.

Object Assembly   As with Block Design, organization is a big factor for this subtest. The examiner may find it helpful to number the backs of the puzzle pieces (in sequence from the examiner's left to right, top to bottom) so they can be placed rapidly before the child in the proper orientation. In between subtest items, it may be helpful to have the child firmly close his or her eyes, hold up the screen for the examiner, and involve the child in conversation. This can be accomplished in a friendly and playful manner. It is not a good idea to have the child hold up the screen without keeping eyes shut because the temptation to peek at the examiner, turn the screen over, or try to see the puzzle designs through the screen, may invalidate the subtest administration.

Coding   Although this subtest is fairly easy to administer, there are several cautions. The child should be given a red pencil without an eraser (Wechsler, 1974). The examiner should always have an extra coding form on hand, in case the child being tested is left-handed and blocks the Key as he or she fills in the sample items. In such cases, an extra Key should be placed above or to the right of the child's coding form during the task (Wechsler, 1974). This subtest typically is not given when a child has visual or motor defects (Kaufman, 1979a; Sattler, 1982).

Mazes   Again, red pencils without erasers are required. This subtest has fairly complicated instructions that vary according to the child's age. In addition, there are a series of several cautions that should be given, if necessary (e.g., "You're not allowed to go through a wall"), but that may be stated only once (see Wechsler, 1974, pp. 104–105).

Scoring Issues

The WISC-R manual provides considerable detail regarding the scoring criteria applicable to each subtest (Wechsler, 1974). It is imperative that examiners become thoroughly familiar with the scoring rules prior to administering the test. This section will review some basic aspects of scoring the WISC-R.

Verbal Subtests   All responses to Verbal items should be recorded verbatim along with any probes the examiner uses (usually marked by a Q on the protocol). The items of several Verbal subtests (Information, Arithmetic, Digit Span) are scored on a pass/fail basis, with one point given for each correct response. In addition, half points are sometimes given for two of the Arithmetic items (see Wechsler, 1974, p. 81). The items for these subtests are fairly easy to score. For the remaining Verbal subtests (Similarities, Vocabulary, and Comprehension), the scoring is more complex, as there are two levels of correct responses (worth 1 or 2 raw score points) for most or all of the items. Generally speaking, abstract or conceptual types of responses are given 2 points, whereas concrete responses are credited with 1 point. Difficulties in assigning scores arise because children may offer a variety of explanations that do not fit the examples in the manual. This may be especially true for children from different cultural backgrounds (e.g., minority or bilingual children). One major improvement of the WISC-R over the WISC, however, is that more detailed scoring criteria are supplied for sample responses (Sattler, 1982). The WISC-R scoring supplement by Massey and colleagues (Massey, Sattler & Andres, 1978) is also useful in this regard. Finally, considerable practice with feedback from an experienced examiner is desirable for developing accurate and reliable scoring skills for the verbal subtests.

Performance Subtests   Relative to verbal portions of the WISC-R, the individual items of the performance subtests can be scored more objectively. However, the overall scoring strategies vary considerably from one subtest to the next which adds to the complexity of obtaining accurate test scores. One subtest is scored on a pass/fail basis (Picture Completion). Other subtests (Picture Arrangement, Block Design, and Object Assembly) have items that are scored on a pass/fail basis, but the child may earn additional points depending on whether the item was completed on the first of two trials or within specified time limits.

Object Assembly additionally provides some credit for partially correct responses. Coding scores are obtained based on the number of items completed correctly within the time limits of the test with bonus points for early completion. On the other hand, no bonus points are given for the Mazes subtest; scores are based on the number of errors made by the child within the specified time limits for the items. The details of scoring each of the performance subtests are covered in the WISC-R manual (Wechsler, 1974) and the examiner should have mas-· tered the scoring procedures before administering the test.

INTERPRETATION OF TEST RESULTS

There are two critical aspects of test interpretation that apply to most individualized intelligence tests and especially to the WISC-R. They are: an inter-individual or normative analysis and an intra-individual analysis of the child's relative strengths and weaknesses. The normative comparison involves understanding the child's cognitive skills in relation to other children of the same age. This kind of analysis involves using the three IQ scores (mean is 100, standard deviation is 15) and the subtest scaled scores (mean is 10, standard deviation is 3) to gauge where the individual child's abilities lie relative to others. Such information is used to determine appropriate educational placements (e.g., Does the child qualify for gifted education? or for special education services?). In addition, this information can be used to evaluate a child's strengths and weaknesses relative to others the same age and provide clues as to why a child is experiencing difficulty in a given educational setting. For example, a child who obtains a Verbal IQ score of 85 might display considerable difficulty in a private learning academy where other children more typically display verbal skills in the above-average range.

The second main aspect of test interpretation has to do with identifying the child's specific areas of strength and weakness, relative to his or her own ability level. The interpretation of relative strengths and weaknesses is dependent on the presence of significant differences between Verbal and Performance IQs or between subtest scores (Sattler, 1983). This kind of analysis is important for planning specific educational strategies for an individual child. For instance, a child who is functioning in the mildly retarded range (e.g., Full Scale IQ of 60) may have a relative strength in visual memory skills and this could be utilized in a classroom situation to teach the child new information. With the WISC-R, the intra-individual analysis involves comparing the child's Verbal versus Performance IQs and closley examining the patterning of subtest scores.

In the subsections that follow, several steps are outlined for the analysis of WISC-R protocols. The comments here are necessarily more general than detailed, given the limitations of space. It is recommended use is made of the procedures specifically described by Kaufman (1979a) for profile attack and test interpretation, and the discussion will be based on an overview of this method. (LaGreca and Stringer have found Kaufman (1979a) to be an invaluable resource for WISC-R interpretation and strongly recommend this source to interested readers.)

Before embarking on a description of test interpretation, it must be re-emphasized that the scores obtained for an individual child are never interpreted in isolation. Careful and detailed observations of the child's behavior during the test situation and in the classroom, supplementary tests, and information about the child's cultural background, interests, and learning history, must be considered in order to fully evaluate and make sense of an individual's performance. In particular, observations of the child's behavior during the test situation provide essential clues for interpreting the child's test scores. Yet, the integration of behavioral observations with test performance appears to be an area of considerable difficulty especially for beginning examiners.

Before one can begin to interpret WISC-R scores, it is important to determine whether or not the test appears to be reasonably accurate or valid. A child who refuses to complete several test items, or who displays a significant language barrier (e.g., a bilingual child), will not perform optimally on the WISC-R, and considerable caution must be used in reporting such test results. Although these kinds of testing problems may suggest that similar difficulties will interfere with the child's school functioning, the examiner must be extremely careful to avoid any suggestion that the test represents a reasonable estimate of the child's abilities.

Interpreting IQ Scores

Generally, the first step in WISC-R interpretation is to examine the three main IQ scores in order to obtain a global estimate of the child's ability level, and to provide a framework for understanding areas of relative strength and weakness. Although it represents a beginning point of departure for test interpretation, in many cases, the Full Scale IQ score will provide a summary of the child's ability level. The exceptions to this are when the Verbal and Performance IQs are discrepant, or when there is considerable scatter among the subtest scores. In such situations, the Full Scale IQ may not adequately represent the child's overall ability level. (As mentioned in the introductory section of this chapter, in this context, ability level refers only to those abilities that are tapped by the WISC-R subtests, and not to intellectual functioning in the broad sense of the term.)

Full Scale IQ To interpret the Full Scale (FS) IQ score as a summary index of ability, the examiner must first consider the standard error of measurement (SEM) around the FSIQ or, in practical terms, the confidence level. The FSIQ ± 6 (i.e., FSIQ ± 2 SEM) represents approximately a 95 percent confidence interval; however, an 85 to 90 percent confidence interval (FSIQ ± 5) is advocated for most testing situations (Kaufman, 1979a). The confidence interval determines the range of scores within which the individual's true score is likely to lie. This data can then be used to estimate the child's ability classification and percentile rank as compared with others the same age (standardization sample). (See Wechsler, 1974, pp. 25–26.) Some of this information is presented in Table 8–3.

As an example, suppose a child obtains a FSIQ of 128. The examiner can say with 90 percent confidence that the child's true score falls between 123 and 133, representing a level of functioning within the Superior to Very Superior range. This child performed at a level that exceeded approximately 97 percent of the standardization sample.

Verbal and Performance IQs The next step in the analysis involves closely examining the Verbal (V) and Performance (P) IQ scores. In particular, the examiner looks to see whether or not these scores are significantly different and the extent to which the IQ scores represent adequate summaries of their respective subtests. When the V and P IQs differ markedly, the FSIQ will not adequately reflect the child's performance level. Moreover, when there is significant subtest scatter, all three IQ scores (V, P, and FS) may be misleading as summary indices.

In order to determine whether or not the V and P IQs are meaningfully different, the issues of statistical and clinical significance must be considered, as well as demographic factors that influence these IQ scores. In terms of statistically significant differences be-

Table 8–3 Ability Classification and Percentile Ranks Associated with IQ Scores

IQ Score	Classification	Percentile Rank
130 and above	Very Superior	98–99+
120–129	Superior	91–98
110–119	High Average	75–90
90–109	Average	25–73
80–89	Low Average	9–23
70–79	Borderline	2–8
69 and below	Significantly Below Average	2 or less

tween V and P IQs, Kaufman's (1976a) analysis of the standardization sample data demonstrated that a 9-point difference was significant at the p less than .15 level, a 12-point difference at the p less than .05 level, and a 15-point difference at the p less than .01 level. As a rule of thumb, a 12-point V-P difference is recommended as an acceptable level of statistical significance for the purposes of interpretation and planning appropriate remediation (Kaufman, 1979a).

Beyond statistical significance, the clinical or practical significance of a V-P discrepancy also is important. One way of judging this issue is to examine the frequency of a given V-P discrepancy; the less frequent or more unusual the discrepancy, the greater the clinical significance. Children in the standardization sample displayed an average V-P difference of 9 to 10 points (mean difference of 9.7; standard deviation of 7.6) (Kaufman, 1976a). This finding is comparable to that previously obtained for the WISC (Seashore, 1951). It is also important to note that a 9-point V-P difference or greater was obtained by almost 50 percent of the WISC-R standardization sample; a 12-point difference or greater approximately 34 percent of the sample, and a 15-point difference or greater by about 25 percent of the sample. (See Kaufman, 1976a or 1979a, for detailed information on the frequency of various V-P discrepancies.) These data indicate that V-P differences that are statistically significant are also fairly common occurrences! So although a 12-point V-P discrepancy is considered statistically significant and meriting interpretation, it is not rare or unusual to find a difference of this magnitude. Consequently, Kaufman (1976a, 1979a) cautions against diagnosing the presence of an abnormal condition (such as a learning disability) on the basis of such a commonly occurring V-P split. Other pertinent data certainly would be needed to substantiate such diagnoses.

It is important to note that the magnitude of V-P differences were found to be roughly comparable across children of different ages, race and sex; however, parental occupation and FSIQ level are modifying factors (Kaufman, 1976a). Children from higher socioeconomic (SES) backgrounds or who obtained higher FSIQs (average and above average) generally displayed V-P discrepancies of greater magnitude than those from low SES backgrounds or who obtained low FSIQs (below average).

The data on V-P differences presented thus far does not take into account the direction of the V-P split (e.g., V greater than P or P greater than V). When considering age, race, sex, or FSIQ level, approximately equal percentages of children in the standardization sample demonstrated V greater than P and P greater than V discrepancies. For example, one-third of the sample displayed a V-P split of 12 points or greater, and about half this group had VIQ greater than PIQ while the other half had PIQ greater than VIQ. (Kaufman,

1976a reports the percentage of cases with V greater than P and P greater than V for 9-, 12-, and 15-point discrepancies.) Thus, the frequency of a particular discrepancy (V greater than P or P greater than V) is more unusual than a discrepancy.

One important demographic factor, socioeconomic class as indexed by parental occupation, modifies this data on directionality. Children of professional parents tend to obtain VIQs greater than PIQs, whereas the reverse pattern is found among children of unskilled workers (Kaufman, 1976a). This suggests that a P greater than V discrepancy is particularly noteworthy for a child from a professional family and, similarly, a V greater than P difference is unusual for a child from a low SES background. The skilled clinician may modify the interpretation of a V-P discrepancy based on the background information obtained for a given child.

After considering statistical and clinical significance, the clinician is in a position to interpret the meaning of a V-P difference. Although it may be tempting to assume that a significant V-P discrepancy reflects the child's differential abilities in verbal comprehension versus perceptual organization skills, this need not be the case. Further investigative work is needed prior to arriving at such a conclusion.

Several situations could arise for which V-P differences may not be meaningful, such as: the presence of considerable subtest scatter; a recent retesting; a child who compensates verbally for poor performance skills; or IQ scores that do not correspond to factor scores. (See Kaufman, 1979a, for detailed discussion of these issues.) With regard to the last situation, as mentioned previously, the VIQ is intended to reflect verbal comprehension skills and the PIQ to reflect perceptual organizational skills. However, the factor structure of the WISC-R does not conform exactly to this dichotomy (see Table 8–2). When a child's Arithmetic score differs from (much lower or higher) other Verbal subtests, or when Coding differs from other Performance subtests, the VIQ or PIQ may not accurately estimate the abilities they were designed to measure. In such cases, the clinician may wish to pro-rate the VIQ (without Arithmetic) or the PIQ (without Coding) to obtain better estimates of the child's verbal comprehension and perceptual organization abilities. Note that this pro-rating is performed for the clinician's benefit, to facilitate interpretation, and such scores are not included in the reporting of test results. (See Kaufman, 1979a, for a detailed discussion and guidelines on this issue.)

Significant V-P differences can reflect several meaningful factors, other than (or in addition to) differential abilities in verbal versus non-verbal intelligence. These factors include: typical work style (reflective versus impulsive); degree of anxiety about testing; ability to work well under time pressure; degree of coordination difficulties; and language background (for a minority or bilingual child). The clinician must integrate observations of the child's behavior with the test results to determine which explanations represent the most reasonable interpretation of the test findings.

Children with slow, deliberate, reflective work styles or compulsive work habits may be penalized on Performance subtests that place a premium on speed of performance (e.g., Picture Arrangement, Block Design, Object Assembly). On the other hand, these work styles may inflate verbal subtest scores if extra points are earned due to elaborate verbal responses. (See Kaufman, 1979a, for a detailed discussion of this issue.) A V greater than P pattern in a child with a reflective or compulsive work style may be more indicative of the child's approach to tasks than a sign of differential verbal versus nonverbal abilities. (Certainly P greater than V splits would be particularly noteworthy in such children.) Detailed behavioral observations of the child's work habits (e.g., aligning puzzle pieces slowly and meticulously) and response style (e.g., detailed, lengthy responses to verbal items) would be necessary to support such an interpretation.

An impulsive working style can also depress scores on Performance subtests (Kaufman, 1979a). In such cases, the child's overly quick response style may preclude careful examination of the task stimuli and lead to errors.

Children who are unable to work effectively within time limits due to immaturity, performance anxiety, or other factors also may do poorly on many of the Performance subtests. This could result in a depressed Performance IQ, relative to the child's actual ability level. Behavioral observations are essential for evaluating this hypothesis. (For example, did the child freeze at the sight of the stopwatch or ask repeatedly about the amount of time remaining? Was the child so oblivious to time constraints that subtest items were completed well after designated time limits?) A useful testing-the-limits procedure for such cases would involve readministering timed items (after test completion) to determine whether the child can complete them when time restrictions are removed.

Most of the Performance subtests involve some degree of visual-motor coordination, and children with motor coordination difficulties may perform poorly on several of these subtests. As a rule of thumb, the Performance subtests are administered in approximate order of increasing visual-motor involvement (Picture Completion, Picture Arrangement, Block Design, Object Assembly, and Coding). Picture Arrangement requires little or no coordination effort whereas Coding scores are heavily dependent on psychomotor speed. Observations of coordination difficulties (e.g., awkward pencil grip, awkward and slow motor movements) coupled with a pattern of Performance scores that decline in direct relation to the increased motor demands of the subtests, provides evidence for coordination difficulties. In such cases, PIQs are likely to be depressed relative to the child's actual ability level and may contribute to a V greater than P pattern.

Children from different language backgrounds, such as bilingual children or those who speak black dialect, may perform poorly on Verbal subtest items (Kaufman, 1979a); in these cases the WISC-R may underestimate the child's verbal comprehension abilities and contribute to a P greater than V pattern. In fact, Kaufman (1979a) advocates using the PIQ as an estimate of overall ability level in cases where the child's Verbal IQ may be underestimated due to language barriers. Due to depressed VIQs, the FSIQ may not accurately represent the child's overall ability level. In support of this point, some evidence suggests that PIQ scores (versus VIQ or FSIQ scores) may be better predictors of school achievement for Spanish-speaking youngsters during the early elementary school years (Mishra & Hurt, 1970; Mishra & Lord, 1982; Phillipus, 1967).

In summary, the V and P IQs can be compared to identify relative areas of strength or weakness for a given child. However, the clinician also must be mindful of the normative level of V and P IQs. As an example, consider a child who obtains a VIQ of 135 and a PIQ of 120. Although the 15-point V greater than P discrepancy may reflect relatively better functioning in verbal versus non-verbal areas, the clinician must be careful not to describe the child's non-verbal skills as weak; they may be weak relative to verbal skills, but they are certainly well above average, in fact in the Superior range. In general, caution should prevail when describing weaknesses in children with above-average ability levels, and strengths in children with below-average ability levels. A bright child's relative weaknesses may still be well above average, and a slow child's relative strengths may be much below average. Statements concerning strengths and weaknesses must be carefully worded so as not to be misleading. As Sattler (1983) notes, the examiner should clearly distinguish between strengths or weaknesses relative to the child's own ability level (intra-individual analysis) and strengths or weaknesses that are relative to others the same age (normative comparison). The skilled clinician is always mindful of the child's relative abilities as well as normative level of performance.

Interpreting Subtest Scatter

Beyond evaluating the three main IQ scores, a detailed examination of the patterning of subtest scores is an important part of WISC-R interpretation. The presence of significant differences between subtest scaled scores helps the clinician identify an individual's areas of strength and weakness. As with the analyses of V-P discrepancies, the issues of statistical significance and frequency or unusualness must be considered.

Determining Unusual Subtest Scatter   One index of the degree of subtest scatter is the difference between a child's highest and lowest scaled scores, usually referred to as the *scaled score range*. Based on WISC-R profiles from the standardization sample, Kaufman (1976b) found that the average scaled score range was 7 points (standard deviation of 2.1). This means that about two-thirds of the children in the standardization sample had scaled score ranges between 5 and 9 points, suggesting that a fair amount of subtest scatter is normal. The average scaled score range was found to be comparable across children grouped by age, sex, race, parental occupation, or IQ level (Kaufman, 1976b).

If the clinician accepts a scaled score range occurring in 15 percent or fewer cases as a cut-off for unusual, then the following criteria indicate minimum ranges: 7 points for the Verbal Scale; 9 points for the Performance Scale; and 10 points for the Full Scale (Kaufman, 1976b). Thus, a child whose Verbal subtest scores ranged from 7 to 14 points would be considered to have an unusual spread of verbal scores.

A second index of subtest scatter is the number of subtests deviating from the mean scale scores. To determine this, mean subtest scores on the Verbal Scale, Performance Scale, and Full Scale are computed, and then the number of subtests that deviate by 3 points or more from their respective scale means are noted. (Verbal subtests are compared to the Verbal Scale Mean, Performance subtests to the Performance Scale Mean, and all subtests to the Full Scale Mean.) The criteria of ± 3 provides for statistical significance at the p less than .05 level (Kaufman, 1979a). (See Kaufman, 1976b and 1979a, for detailed discussion of this method and rationale.)

On the average, children display one subtest score that deviates significantly from the Verbal or Performance Mean, and two that deviate from the Full Scale Mean (Kaufman, 1976b). These figures are similar for 10 and 12 subtest WISC-Rs, and generally are comparable across children of different ages, sex, race, parental occupation, and IQ level (Kaufman, 1976b). Using the 15 percent criteria, the following requirements would be needed to determine unusual scatter: two subtests deviating from the Verbal Mean, three from the Performance Mean, and four from the Full Scale Mean.

The above guidelines should aid the clinician in establishing whether or not a child displays significant subtest scatter. Evidence of significant scatter (e.g., a scaled score range of 10, and four subtests that deviate from the overall test mean) can have implications for both academic remediation and diagnosis. Moreover, evidence of significant subtest scatter should caution the clinician against using the Scale IQs as indices of unitary abilities. If a child displays significant scatter within the Verbal or Performance Scale, the respective IQ scores may not estimate the child's verbal comprehension or perceptual organization abilities. In such cases, a more detailed analysis of patterns of subtest scores will be necessary to identify areas of strength and weakness.

Identifying Strengths and Weaknesses   Even though a child may not display unusual subtest scatter according to the criteria noted above, it is common to find individual subtests that deviate significantly from the overall scale means. Subtests that deviate by three or more points from their scale mean may represent areas of relative strength or weakness, and are examined closely to better understand the individual's unique pattern of functioning.

The following steps are recommended for identifying areas of strength and weakness from subtest scores (Kaufman, 1979a):

1. Calculate the Verbal and Performance Scale Means by averaging the appropriate (five or six) subtest scores. All means should be rounded off to the nearest whole number.

2. Check the individual subtests against their respective scale means. Any subtests that are three points or more above the mean are identified as strengths (S), and those 3 points or more below the mean are identified as weaknesses (W). Differences of less than three points are treated as chance fluctuations.

3. Subtests that represent areas of strength are examined for any commonalities. To the extent possible, the examiner looks for shared abilities among the subtests that may represent more global areas of strength. Other subtests that fall at or above the scale mean can be grouped with the subtests representing strengths to determine shared abilities. The examiner should exhaust all reasonable possibilities for determining shared abilities before interpreting a subtest score as representing a unique ability (i.e., an ability that is tapped by that particular subtest, but no others). A similar procedure is followed for examining weaknesses.

4. If a subtest cannot reasonably be grouped with other scores to interpret shared abilities representing an area

of strength (or weakness) the examiner should consider interpreting the subtest score as an indication of a unique ability (or unique weakness).

5. Interpretations of strengths and weaknesses must be integrated with observations of the child's behavior during the test situation, information on the child's background, and other pertinent test scores. The examiner should examine these additional sources of information in order to corroborate hypotheses regarding the child's cognitive abilities.

Individual profile analysis, or the identification of strengths and weaknesses from individual subtest scores, represents a challenging and difficult task for the examiner. A thorough understanding of the WISC-R subtests, their shared and unique abilities, and the kind of background and behavioral factors influencing these scores, are essential to the interpretation of subtest patterns. Although a comprehensive summary of common subtest patterns is beyond the scope of this chapter, the reader is referred to several excellent sources of information on profile analysis (Banas & Wills, 1977, 1978; Kaufman, 1979a; Sattler, 1982).

The reader should also be aware that several alternative methods for grouping subtests have been proposed. Most notably, Bannatyne (1971, 1974) recommended reorganizing the WISC subtests into the following categories: *verbal conceptual ability* (Similarities, Vocabulary, Comprehension); *spatial ability* (Picture Completion, Block Design, Object Assembly); *sequencing ability* (Arithmetic, Digit Span, Coding); and *acquired knowledge* (Information, Arithmetic, Vocabulary). These categories may facilitate interpretation of shared abilities (or weaknesses) among WISC-R subtests.

Example As an example of this approach to profile analysis, consider the case of a ten-year-old child who obtains the following WISC-R scores:

VERBAL SCALE		PERFORMANCE SCALE	
Information	12	Picture Completion	12–S
Similarities	11	Picture Arrangement	9
Arithmetic	8–W	Block Design	8
Vocabulary	11	Object Assembly	7
Comprehension	11	Coding	6
(Digit Span)	10		
Verbal Scale Mean = 11		Performance Scale Mean = 8	
VERBAL IQ =	103	PERFORMANCE IQ =	88

FULL SCALE IQ = 96 ± 5

The FSIQ ± 5 (91–101) indicates that this child is functioning in the Average range. However, this IQ score is somewhat misleading as there is a 15-point difference between the VIQ and PIQ, which merits closer examination and interpretation. This child's profile does not display a significant amount of subtest scatter, according to the criteria outlined above. However, one subtest score (Arithmetic) deviates from the child's Verbal Scale Mean, and one (Picture Completion) deviates from the Performance Scale Mean. Thus, the clinician's task in a case like this would be to determine: (a) a likely explanation for the V greater than P discrepancy, (b) the meaning of a significant weakness in Arithmetic and a significant strength in Picture Completion.

With respect to the V-P discrepancy, note that the VIQ is likely to be an underestimate of this child's verbal comprehension skills, since the Arithmetic subtest score is low and pulls down the overall VIQ. (The Arithmetic subtest does not load on the Verbal Comprehension (VC) factor of the WISC-R.) If the examiner prorated the child's VIQ, without Arithmetic, to obtain an estimate of the VC factor, the VIQ would be 107. This V greater than P pattern would be unusual if the child is from a low SES background or is bilingual; it is less unusual for a child from a professional family.

The examiner would need much more information about the child before making sense of these test scores. For example, there are several hypotheses as to why the VIQ is greater than the PIQ. It is possible that this child was anxious about being timed; note that performance is relatively lower on tasks that involve timing. This child could also be a slow worker or was immature and unconcerned about working within time limits; this would also depress scores on timed tasks. As another possibility, this child could be experiencing motor coordination problems. Note that the Performance subtest scores declined as greater motor coordination was involved. In order to rule out or rule in some of these hypotheses, the examiner would have to consider the child's behavior during the test (e.g., any signs of anxiety, immaturity, motor difficulties?). The examiner would also need to consider the child's cultural background and school experiences (e.g., is the child bilingual?). Supplementary measures may be useful as well. For instance, the Visual Motor Integration Test (MVI; Beery, 1967) would provide an assessment of the child's visual-motor skills without the time limits imposed by many of the Performance subtests. A poor score on the VMI would support the hypothesis of visual-motor difficulties. A good VMI score would negate this hypothesis, but might indicate that the child performs better without time limits.

The examiner would also need to closely examine the meaning of the significant weakness in Arithmetic and strength in Picture Completion. Again, several possibilities arise that would need to be verified via behavioral observations and other information about the child. For instance, the significant weakness in Arithmetic might reflect difficulty with timed items, poor number concepts, or distractibility, among other possibilities. Support for the hypothesis of poor number concepts might be gleaned from math achievement tests, teacher reports of academic difficulties in math, and behavioral evidence of the child attending well to the subtest, but still giving incorrect responses. Evidence for distractibility might include observations of the child fidgeting and asking for items to be repeated during the subtest; relatively low scores on other subtests that are influenced by distractibility, such as Digit Span and Coding; and parent and teacher reports of inattention at home and in school.

A similarly detailed examination of hypotheses for the strength on the Picture Completion (PC) task would be important. Note that the score obtained on Picture Arrangement (PA) is above the Performance Scale Mean, and together with the significant score on PC, may suggest a common area of strength. It is possible that this child is relying on good verbal skills to compensate for performance deficits (Kaufman, 1979a). Both the PA and PC subtest scores can be influenced by strong verbal skills. Behavioral observations are needed to support this hypothesis, such as evidence of the child verbalizing problem-solving strategies during Performance tasks. One should further note that if the child is verbally compensating for performance difficulties, the PIQ may be an overestimate of perceptual organization abilities; thus the V greater than P discrepancy may be even greater than the current IQ scores indicate.

As another possible interpretation, the strength in PC coupled with an above-average score on PA can suggest a relative strength in visual organization without essential motor activity (Kaufman, 1979a). As discussed previously, observations of motor coordination difficulties would be needed to substantiate such a hypothesis.

Additional Issues

There are several additional issues of interest germane to the interpretation of WISC-R profiles. They include: when to interpret the third factor; speed of performance; and qualitative analyses of test responses. The following will briefly discuss these issues. More detailed information can be obtained in Kaufman (1979a) and Sattler (1982, 1983).

Freedom from Distractibility As mentioned earlier, factor analytic studies of the WISC-R yielded three factors: Verbal Comprehension, Perceptual Organization, and Freedom From Distractibility (Kaufman, 1975). The subtests that load on the third factor include

Arithmetic, Digit Span, and Coding. Although the factor has been labeled Freedom From Distractibility, a child's performance on these subtests can also be influenced by his or her ability to work with number concepts and/or symbols, anxiety, sequencing ability, and short-term memory skills.

Kaufman (1979a) advocates that the following criteria be used to guide the interpretation of the third factor.

1. At least one of the three component subtests should represent a significant strength or weakness.

2. If one is satisfied, the examiner should check the scores on the other subtests that load on this factor. The third factor should be considered if the other subtest scores are in the same direction as the significant score(s). For example, if one of the three subtest scores represents a significant strength, then the other two subtest scores should be at or above the relevant scale means in order to interpret the third factor as representing a unitary strength. If the three subtest scores are not in the same direction (above the mean or below the mean), then it is likely that there is too much subtest scatter to interpret the third factor as representing a unitary strength or weakness.

In the above case example of a ten-year-old child, Arithmetic was a significant weakness. In addition, the Digit Span score (10) was below the Verbal scale mean (11), and the Coding score (6) was below the Performance scale mean (8). Thus, the third factor should be explored as a possible explanation for a unitary area of weakness for this child.

If there is reason to suspect that the third factor represents a unitary area of strength or weakness, further detective work is needed to determine the meaning of this factor. The child's testing behavior and responses to the subtests' items must be carefully evaluated.

For instance, low scores on the third factor can represent distractibility, anxiety, poor numerical skills, difficulties with sequencing, and poor short-term memory skills, among other possibilities (Kaufman 1979a). In order to interpret the third factor, behavioral observations are needed to support such hypotheses. A child who is distractible might fidget, look around the room, or lose task concentration if there is even a slight noise. A child who is test anxious might display a stiff or rigid posture and frequently ask about his or her performance. Difficulties with numerical skills might be demonstrated by a child trying to count on his or her fingers, or tracing math problems in the air or on the desk; supplementary math achievement measures might help to confirm such a hypothesis. Considerable skill is needed for an examiner to interpret the meaning of third factor scores.

There are two additional cautions for the examiner. Kaufman (1979a) notes that, if a weakness on the third factor is attributed to distractibility or anxiety, one cannot say that the child additionally displays deficiencies in numerical problem solving (Arithmetic), short-term memory (Digit Span), or psychomotor speed (Coding). Even though such deficits may exist, the child's behavioral difficulties have depressed the child's scores on these subtests. In the face of considerable distractibility or anxiety, it is difficult or impossible to ascertain exactly what the child's skills are in these areas.

By the same token, the examiner can presume that the WISC-R is underestimating the child's abilities when extreme distractibility or anxiety are present (Kaufman 1979a). These non-intellectual factors are likely to have a negative effect on other WISC-R subtest scores in addition to those comprising the third factor.

Speed of Performance   Another interpretive issue concerns the child's speed of performance on certain timed subtests. Scaled scores on three performance subtests (Picture Arrangement, Block Design, and Object Assembly) are increasingly affected by speed of performance as children get older. For these subtests, bonus points are rarely earned among children under eight years of age, but are commonplace for adolescents (Kaufman, 1979b). In fact, bonus points are essential for obtaining an above-average score among adolescents. Those fourteen-and-a-half years of age or older may solve every item correctly on Picture Arrangement, Block Design, and Object Assembly, yet not obtain scaled scores above 10 on any of these subtests (Kaufman, 1979b). Thus, speed accounts for a large part of an older child's performance on these subtests, and consequently, on their Performance and Full Scale IQs as well.

This may raise an interpretive issue for older children. If an older child performs poorly, the examiner must determine whether this is due to cognitive factors (i.e., inability to do the task quickly) or because of the child's typical response style or other non-intellectual factors, such as anxiety or poor motor coordination. For instance, an adolescent with an extreme reflective response style may be severely penalized, due to a slow and careful approach to the tasks. This response style would be less debilitating for a reflective seven year old. (See Kaufman, 1979a, for a detailed discussion of this issue.)

Qualitative Analyses of Test Responses   Until now, the discussion has stressed the process of examining and interpreting various WISC-R scores. However, the quality of the child's responses to individual subtest items also provide important information for the examiner. This kind of analysis is essential for supporting the interpretation of test scores and obtaining an understanding of the child's behavioral style and thinking processes.

The examiner can evaluate the richness of a child's language concepts by examining the quality of responses to verbal subtest items. Some children give Vocabulary responses that are brief and to the point. Others provide detailed and elaborate answers. Still others give vague responses at first, only to receive full credit after further probes from the examiner. Just knowing that a Vocabulary response is credited with 2 points is not sufficient to appreciate the quality of a child's expressive language skills.

Qualitative analyses are important for Performance subtests as well. For example, when examining a child's poor performance on Coding, the examiner should determine whether problems resulted from errors in copying the symbols or from an accurate, but slow performance.

Responses to various subtest items may also reveal information about the child's level of maturity, family background, or behavioral difficulties. The Comprehension subtest may be especially useful in this regard. Dependency responses to Comprehension items can suggest that the child comes from an overprotected family situation (e.g., "Ask my mother what to do" in response to the question about being sent to buy a loaf of bread and the grocer didn't have any more). Aggressive responses might be evident in a child who displays difficulty with behavioral control (e.g., "Hit him back" in response to the question about a smaller child starting a fight). Although the examiner must be careful not to interpret such responses in the absence of corroborating evidence from the child's background, the examiner might further explore the meaning of such responses. (The reader is referred to Glasser and Zimmerman, 1967, and Sattler, 1982, for a detailed discussion of these issues.)

CASE REPORT

The following case report illustrates several issues on test interpretation that have been discussed throughout the chapter. The report is not intended to represent a comprehensive assessment battery, but rather an initial screening of a school-related problem.

Identifying Information

Name: John R *Age:* 9 years, 7 months *Grade:* Third

Referral and Background Information

John R was referred for evaluation by Mrs. M his teacher. John repeated the second grade last year and continues to display poor academic progress in his third grade placement. His teacher reported problems with school absences, as well as articulation and expressive language difficulties. Although individual achievement tests have not been administered, Mrs. M estimates that John's reading and math skills are at the first grade level.

John and his two-year-old sister, Sara, live with their parents in a large suburban area. Mr. R is an insurance salesman and Mrs. R is employed part-time as a salesclerk. John's parents reported that he has experienced learning problems since entering school; they were additionally concerned about his nervousness in academic situations and speech difficulties. According to both teacher and parental reports, John relates well to peers and has several friends. His main interests are bike riding, watching television, fishing, and caring for his pet hamster.

Tests Administered

Wechsler Intelligence Scale for Children-Revised (WISC-R)
Visual Motor Integration Test (VMI)

Observations

John is an attractive child with blond hair and blue eyes who looks younger than his age. He came willingly to the examination room, and was extremely attentive, cooperative, and hard working throughout the evaluation. Although aware of wrong responses, John accepted failures calmly and matter of factly, simply stating "I can't do this" if he could not solve a problem after several minutes. John appeared to be mildly anxious during the testing session; he smiled infrequently and rarely responded to the examiner's questions with more than a brief statement.

During the verbal tasks, John's articulation difficulties were apparent. Although his speech was understandable, he pronounced many words incorrectly, such as "pitures" for "pictures" and "fumb" instead of "thumb." As the session progressed and John appeared to fatigue, his speech became more difficult to comprehend and he began to run his words together. Despite these articulation problems, the quantity of John's responses on several verbal tasks were often succinct, accurate, and indicative of age-appropriate conceptual thought.

On the timed visual items, John's work style was careful, persistent, and slow, thus earning him few bonus points for fast completion. His problem-solving strategies were generally efficient on most tasks with the exception of one that involved assembling block designs. On this task, John had difficulty reproducing some of the angles in the designs and mainly relied on a trial-and-error work strategy. His general approach was to spin the blocks until they resembled part of the model he was trying to reproduce.

John experienced considerable difficulty with the design copying tasks. This did not appear to be the result of fine-motor coordination problems, as his pencil grip was comfortable and his motor movements were well controlled. However, on one copying task (VMI), John repeatedly rotated the answer sheet, so that he was mainly drawing horizontal lines. Visual-motor difficulties were especially apparent when multiple items were to be copied quickly (Coding). On this task, John appeared disoriented and had trouble finding his place several times as he moved back and forth between the sample key and the answer sheet. Several symbol reversals were also noted on this task.

Test Results

WISC-R

Verbal Scale	Score	Performance Scale	Score
Information	4–W	Picture Completion	11–S
Similarities	11–S	Picture Arrangement	10
Arithmetic	6	Block Design	6
Vocabulary	7	Object Assembly	11–S
Comprehension	11–S	Coding	3–W
(Digit Span)	(7)		
VERBAL IQ = 86		PERFORMANCE IQ = 87	

FULL SCALE IQ = 85 ± 5

VMI = 7 years, 10 months (age equivalent)

Test Interpretation

On the WISC-R, John obtained a Verbal IQ of 86, a Performance IQ of 87, and a Full Scale IQ of 85. This latter score places him in the Low Average range of functioning, and ranks him at the 16th percentile compared to children his age. There is a 90 percent chance that his true Full Scale IQ falls between 80 and 90. However, in light of the significant scatter among the subtest scores, the Verbal, Performance, and Full Scale IQs must be viewed cautiously as they may not represent meaningful summaries of John's cognitive abilities. His scaled scores ranged from 4 (Information) to 11 (Similarities, Comprehension) on the Verbal Scale and from 3 (Coding) to 11 (Picture

Completion, Object Assembly) on the Performance Scale. Thus, in some areas he scored below the second percentile yet in others he was above the 60th percentile when compared to others his age.

The pattern of scores on the Verbal Scale suggests that John does well with verbal reasoning tasks that either require a minimum of expression or focus on specific real-life situations (Similarities, Comprehension). On such tasks, his skills are within the average range (63rd percentile). In sharp contrast to his good conceptual skills, John has difficulty with verbal tasks that depend heavily on acquired knowledge, rote memory, and school-related experiences (Information, Arithmetic, Vocabulary, Digit Span). His performance on these tasks was well below average (ninth percentile) and is consistent with school reports of frequent absences and poor academic progress.

An examination of John's Performance test scores also reveals definite areas of strength and weakness. When presented with non-verbal tasks that involve concrete and meaningful stimuli, such as pictures of objects and cartoons of social situations (Picture Completion, Picture Arrangement, Object Assembly), John's problem-solving skills were in the average range (about the 60th percentile). With abstract and symbolic stimuli, however, John displayed marked visual-perceptual difficulties and problems with directionality. This was apparent from his poor performance on tasks that involved reproducing abstract designs and symbols (Block Design, Coding, VMI), observations of his confusion during such tasks, and the presence of reversals. John performed well below average on these abstract, non-verbal tasks (second percentile).

Taken together, the test results suggest that John may perform best when provided with a meaningful context for academic tasks. His verbal and non-verbal reasoning skills are within the average range. However, perhaps due in part to excessive absences, his current achievement is much below par. Moreover, significant problems with visual perception of abstract stimuli and directional confusion are present, and likely contribute to his poor reading and academic skills.

Conclusions and Recommendations

John's average reasoning abilities, coupled with problems in visual-perception, directionality, and acquired knowledge, are consistent with the presence of a learning disability. Further testing is indicated, however, before such a diagnosis can be reached. In general, John's articulation problem did not appear to interfere measurably with his performance on the WISC-R, although it does warrant remedial attention.

Based on current test findings it is recommended that:

1. John should receive further educational testing (e.g., Woodcock Johnson Psychoeducational Battery; Woodcock Reading Mastery Test) to obtain an assessment of his current level of academic skills in reading and math. Supplementary tests, such as the Detroit Test of Learning Aptitude, may be useful for pinpointing specific cognitive processing difficulties. Based on the outcome of these test findings, John should be considered for placement in a special education program for children with learning disabilities.

2. John should be evaluated for the presence of vision or hearing problems. This will be important for excluding sensory handicaps as a factor contributing to his learning difficulties.

3. John should be evaluated by a speech therapist to determine the nature of his articulation disorder and to plan a remedial program.

4. As long as John continues in his current academic placement, his teacher, Mrs. R, may try to capitalize on his areas of strength and minimize his areas of weakness. This might be accomplished by providing concrete materials for him to work with and setting tasks within a meaningful context. For example, in presenting new material, John could be given an introduction to the task or it could be related to something he has already done correctly. John should be allowed to work at his own pace, and rote memory skills should be de-emphasized. In addition, instructions for new tasks should be presented both visually and verbally.

SPECIAL POPULATIONS

In describing the assessment of exceptional and handicapped children, several authors have drawn an analogy between the examiner who administers an individual intelligence test and the investigator who conducts an experiment using an N–of–1 research design (Brock, 1982; Sattler, 1982). This analogy is good because it highlights the point that assessment is an interactive process requiring individualized procedures, particularly with the exceptional child.

A casebook approach to assessing children of varying exceptionalities is not desirable, and thus, authors have advocated that individual examiners use their clinical judgment to select particular assessment instruments (Barnett, 1982; Kaufman, 1979a; Sattler, 1982;

Stetson, 1983). However, several considerations may guide the clinician in designing an individual assessment. As stressed throughout this chapter, a comprehensive assessment should cover multiple areas. In addition to sampling cognitive skills, the examiner might include assessments of affect, creativity, physical abilities, social skills, and current school functioning. Furthermore, information from multiple sources is needed. In this regard, obtaining parents' and teachers' reports of the child in a number of settings is emphasized. Finally, in order to make realistic and appropriate recommendations, the clinician should be familiar with community resources and special education facilities (Barnett, 1982).

This section will briefly discuss some special considerations for assessing children of varying exceptionalities. In most cases, the examiner will be interested in gaining an understanding of the child's strengths as well as problem areas. For this reason, testing-the-limits procedures will be important for children who display performance deficits. Several authors (Glasser & Zimmerman, 1967; Sattler, 1982) offer invaluable suggestions in this regard. Moreover, the inclusion of other measures to supplement the WISC-R is usually desirable with special populations. Table 8–4 lists a number of individualized assessment procedures that are often employed with exceptional children. Further details and recommendations are provided by Kaufman (1979a), Sattler (1982, 1983), and Stetson (1983).

Ethnic Minorities

One of the most valuable approaches to assessing minority children is one that focuses on identifying cognitive strengths (Sattler, 1982). In order to accomplish this, several considerations may be important. For one, the examiner will need to become familiar with the characteristics and values of the particular child's culture and take these values into account when interpreting the test results. The System of Multicultural Pluralistic Assessment (SOMPA; Jirsa, 1983; Mercer & Lewis, 1978), a sociocultural assessment battery, was designed for this purpose.

Secondly, every effort should be made to facilitate the child's interest and motivation (Sattler, 1982). Strategies that may be helpful include providing concrete incentives for participation in the testing, or beginning the session with a fun task that minimizes verbal demands (e.g., drawing a picture).

Finally, to counteract the cultural bias inherent in any one instrument, it is advisable to employ several assessment instruments. It is especially desirable to include a non-verbal measure of intellectual functioning, such as the Progressive Matrices Test or the Draw-A-Person Test.

When using the WISC-R to assess bilingual children, children who speak black dialect, or those whose native language is not English, the examiner should pay particular attention to the correct pronunciation of test instructions and test items. Moreover, the child's non-verbal functioning (i.e., Performance IQ on the WISC-R) should be stressed as a predictor of school achievement rather than verbally oriented measures (Kaufman, 1979a).

Children with Specific Learning Disabilities

Children with learning disabilities generally have average or higher intelligence, but display significant underachievement in areas such as reading, writing, spelling, or math. These academic problems are thought to result from specific cognitive processing difficulties. Children whose underachievement is primarily due to behavior problems, sensory handicaps, mental retardation, or environmental disadvantage are not considered to be learning disabled.

Assessments of children with learning disabilities are primarily directed toward diagnosing the problem, so that placement in appropriate educational programs can be initiated, and identifying specific areas of strength and weakness for program planning. The WISC-R is commonly used to determine the child's level of intellectual functioning and to eliminate the possibility of mental retardation. (See Kaufman, 1979a, and Sattler, 1982, for discussions of the WISC-R with learning-disabled children.) However, other tests are needed to supplement the information obtained from a WISC-R assessment. Individualized achievement tests (for screening and diagnosis of academic problems) and processing tests are commonly employed. (See Table 8–4.)

Table 8–4 Selected Assessment Instruments Employed with Exceptional Children

Instrument	Child Assessment Uses
Intelligence Tests (Non-Verbal)	
Columbia Mental Maturity Scale	Children with language and communication handicaps or hearing impairments; bilingual and minority children
Draw-A-Person Test (screening only)	
Leiter International Performance Scale	
Nebraska Test of Learning Aptitude	
Peabody Picture Vocabulary Test-Revised (screening only)	
Raven's Progressive Matrices	(continued)

Table 8–4 (continued)

Instrument	Child Assessment Uses
Intelligence Tests (Verbal) Stanford-Binet Intelligence Scale	Children with motor handicaps or suspected mental retardation; gifted adolescents
Auditory Processing Tests Wepman Auditory Discrimination Test Stetson Auditory Discrimination Test Detroit Tests of Learning Aptitude (selected subtests) Illinois Test of Psycholinguistic Abilities	Children with learning disabilities or with language handicaps
Visual Processing Tests Detroit Tests of Learning Aptitude (selected subtests) Motor-Free Visual Perception Test Illinois Test of Psycholinguistic Abilities	Children with learning disabilities, attention problems or suspected visual handicaps
Visual-Motor Tests Bender Visual Motor Gestalt Test Developmental Test of Visual Motor Integration	Children with learning disabilities or suspected motor handicaps
Achievement Tests (General Screening) Peabody Individual Achievement Test Wide Range Achievement Test Woodcock-Johnson Psychoeducational Battery	Children with learning disabilities, mental retardation; gifted children; minority and bilingual children
Achievement Tests (Diagnostic) Key Math Diagnostic Arithmetic Test Woodcock Reading Mastery Test	(Same as for achievement screening tests)
Adaptive Behavior Scales AAMD Adaptive Behavior Scale Vineland Adaptive Behavior Scales	Children suspected of mental retardation
Sociocultural Assessment System of Multipluralistic Assessment	Children from ethnic minorities

Adapted from Clarizio (1982), Sattler (1982), and Stetson (1983).

Mental Retardation

According to the American Association on Mental Deficiency, mental retardation refers to significantly sub-average intellectual functioning, in the presence of deficits in adaptive behavior that occur during the developmental period (birth through eighteen years). As with the learning disabled, assessments of children with mental retardation focus on both diagnosis and individual educational planning.

Although the WISC-R is commonly employed for diagnosis, children in the early elementary grades who are suspected of functioning in the mentally retarded range, may not be adequately assessed with this instrument (see the section on "Comparison with Other Instruments," this chapter, as well as Sattler, 1974, 1982.) In addition to the WISC-R, measures of adaptive behavior, such as the Vineland Adaptive Behavior Scales or the AAMD Adaptive Behavior Scale, are necessary for diagnosing this problem and establishing the child's eligibility for special education services. Beyond these measures, achievement tests can be valuable for identifying areas of skill and planning remediation.

Sensory Impairments

Assessing children with sensory impairments, such as visual, hearing, or motor handicaps, can present special challenges for the examiner. Several authors (Russ & Soboloff, 1958; Sattler, 1974) note the following problems. Some children may fatigue easily, as they are not accustomed to working for long periods of time. Attentional problems may arise due to physical discomfort and must be distinguished from those due to cognitive difficulties. In addition, rapport may be difficult to establish due the child's increased dependency. In most cases, only portions of the WISC-R may be used, and supplementary tests are needed. (See Sattler, 1982; Kaufman, 1979a, for further information.)

Children with visual handicaps, such as blindness or severe visual impairments, may be assessed with the Verbal Scale of the WISC-R. A special form of the Stanford-Binet, the Perkins-Binet, also has been developed for assessing children with visual handicaps (blindness, low vision). As another alternative, the Blind Learning Aptitude Test can be used. When testing children who are partially-sighted, the examiner should be sure that adequate lighting is provided, and that the child is wearing glasses (Margach & Kern, 1969).

With the hearing impaired, all verbally oriented tests should be avoided. The examiner may use the Performance section of the WISC-R, although, if the child cannot speech read, the instructions may need to be given in pantomime. Other non-verbal measures of intelligence that may be used include the Leiter International Performance Scale, Progressive Matrices, and the Hiskey-Nebraska Test of Learning Aptitude.

Children with hearing impairments are often attentive to visual cues. Consequently, the examiner must be especially careful to avoid giving the child clues about performance through facial expressions, head nods, or other body movements (Sattler, 1974).

Children with motor impairments, such as cerebral palsy, will experience considerable difficulty with the Performance sections of the WISC-R; generally only the Verbal Scale will be administered. Kaufman (1979a) advocates using the Performance Scale only with those children displaying mild motor handicaps, though the Coding subtest should not be administered. If speech or auditory difficulties coexist with motor deficits, it may be extremely difficult to obtain an adequate assessment of the child. A test that minimizes both verbal and motor demands, such as the Columbia Test of Mental Maturity, may be useful in such cases.

Gifted Children

Although definitions of giftedness vary, most often the term refers to children who display very superior cognitive abilities (e.g., a Verbal or Performance IQ of 130 or greater) or who demonstrate an exceptional area of talent (e.g., music, art). For elementary school-aged children, the WISC-R is commonly used to determine a child's eligibility for a gifted educational placement. With a gifted child, the Stanford-Binet may be preferable as an index of overall ability because it has a higher ceiling. However, neither intelligence test may be satisfactory for identifying specific areas of strength. Supplementary measures, such as achievement tests, tests of creativity, and work samples, may be useful in such cases to assess the child's special abilities.

SUMMARY

The goal of the present chapter has been to present a thorough overview of the WISC-R, a major instrument for assessing the cognitive abilities of school-aged children. Despite the limitations inherent in any standardized measure of intellectual functioning, the WISC-R represents a reliable and well-validated tool, that is part of the assessment armamentarium for all child-oriented clinicians. When used in a careful and thoughtful manner, it can provide invaluable information regarding a child's cognitive functioning and an important perspective on the child's school achievement. Although extensive research on the WISC-R already has accumulated, continued efforts to better understand its diagnostic utility with special child populations will be of continued interest and importance.

REFERENCES

Banas, N., & Wills, I. H. (1977). Prescriptions from WISC-R patterns. *Academic Therapy, 13,* 241–246.

Banas, N., & Wills, I. H. (1978). Prescriptions from WISC-R patterns. *Academic Therapy, 13,* 365–370.

Bannatyne, A. (1971). *Language, reading, and learning disabilities.* Springfield, IL: Charles C Thomas, Publisher.

Bannatyne, A. (1974). Diagnosis: A note on recategorization of the WISC scaled scores. *Journal of Learning Disabilities, 7,* 272–274.

Barnett, A. J. (1982). Designing an assessment of the child with cerebral palsy. *Psychology in the Schools, 19,* 160–165.

Beery, K. E. (1967). *Developmental test of visual-motor integration.* Chicago: Follett Publishing Co.

Brock, H. (1982). Factor structure of intellectual and achievement measures for learning-disabled children. *Psychology in the Schools, 19,* 297–304.

Burgess, R. L. (1979). Child abuse: A social interactional analysis. In B. B. Lahey & A. E. Kazdin (Eds.), *Advances in Clinical Child Psychology* (Vol. 2). New York: Plenum Publishing Corp.

Clarizio, H. F. (1982). Intellectual assessment of hispanic children. *Psychology in the Schools, 19,* 61–71.

DeHorn, A., & Klinge, V. (1978). Correlations and factor analysis of the WISC-R and the Peabody Picture Vocabulary Test for an adolescent psychiatric sample. *Journal of Consulting and Clinical Psychology, 46,* 1160–1161.

Evans, I. M., & Nelson, R. O. (1977). Assessment of child behavior problems. In A. R. Ciminero, K. S. Calhoun, & H. E. Adams (Eds.), *Handbook of Behavioral Assessment.* New York: John Wiley & Sons, Inc.

Glasser, A. J., & Zimmerman, I. L. (1967). *Clinical interpretation of the WISC.* New York: Grune & Stratton, Inc.

Grossman, F. M., & Johnson, K. M. (1982). WISC-R factor scores as predictors of WRAT performance: A multivariate analysis. *Psychology in the Schools, 19,* 465–468.

Hale, R. L. (1978). The WISC-R as a predictor of Wide Range Achievement Test performance. *Psychology in the Schools, 15,* 172–175.

Hale, R. L. (1983). An examination for construct bias in the WISC-R across socioeconomic status. *Journal of School Psychology, 21,* 153–156.

Hale, R. L., Raymond, M. R., & Gajar, A. H. (1982). Evaluating socioeconomic status bias in the WISC-R. *Journal of School Psychology, 2,* 145–149.

Hardy, J. B., Welcher, D. W., Mellits, E. D., & Kagan, J. (1976). Pitfalls in the measurement of intelligence: Are standard intelligence tests valid instruments for measuring the intellectual potential of urban children? *Journal of Psychology, 94,* 43–51.

Hilliard, A. G. (1975). The strengths and weaknesses of cognitive tests for young children. In J. D. Andrews (Ed.), *One Child Indivisible.* Washington, D. C.: National Association for the Education of Young Children, 17–33.

Hobbs, N. (Ed.). (1975). *Issues in the classification of children* (Vol. 2). San Francisco, CA: Jossey-Bass.

Jirsa, J. E. (1983). The SOMPA: A brief examination of technical considerations, philosphical rationale, and implications for practice. *Journal of School Psychology, 21,* 13–21.

Kaufman, A. S. (1975). Factor analysis of the WISC-R at 11 age levels between 6½ and 16½ years. *Journal of Consulting and Clinical Psychology, 43,* 135–147.

Kaufman, A. S. (1976). Verbal-Performance IQ discrepancies on the WISC-R, (a). *Journal of Consulting and Clinical Psychology, 44,* 739–744.

Kaufman, A. S. (1976). A new approach to the interpretation of test scatter on the WISC-R, (b). *Journal of Learning Disabilities, 9,* 160–168.

Kaufman, A. S. (1979). *Intelligent testing with the WISC-R,* (a). New York: John Wiley & Sons, Inc.

Kaufman, A. S. (1979). The role of speed on WISC-R performance across the age range, (a). *Journal of Consulting and Clinical Psychology, 47,* 595–597.

Kaufman, A. S., & Kaufman, N. L. (1977). *Clinical evaluation of young children with the McCarthy Scales.* New York: Grune & Stratton, Inc.

Kaufman, A. S., & Kaufman, N. L. (1983). *Manual for the Kaufman Assessment Battery for Children.* Circle Pines, MN: American Guidance Service, 1983.

King, L. A., & King, D. W. (1982). Weschler short forms: A brief status report. *Psychology in the Schools, 19,* 433–438.

Kramer, J. J., Shanks, K., Markley, R. P., & Ryabik, J. E. (1983). The seductive nature of WISC-R short forms: An analysis with gifted referrals. *Psychology in the Schools, 20,* 137–141.

LaGreca, A. M. (1983). Interviewing and behavioral observations. In C. E. Walker & M. C. Roberts, *Handbook of Clinical Child Psychology.* New York: John Wiley & Sons, Inc.

Margach, C., & Kern, K. C. (1969). Visual impairment, partial-sight and the school psychologist. *Journal of Learning Disabilities, 2,* 407–414.

Massey, J. O., Sattler, J. M., & Andres, J. R. (1978). *WISC-R scoring criteria.* Palo Alto, CA: Consulting Psychologists Press.

McCarthy, D. (1972). *Manual for the McCarthy Scales of Children's Abilities.* New York: Psychological Corporation.

Mercer, J. R. (1974). Latent functions of intelligence testing in the public schools. In L. P. Miller (Ed.), *The Testing of Black Students: A Symposium for the American Educational Research Association.* Englewood Cliffs, N.J.

Mercer, J. R. (1977). The struggle for children's rights: Critical juncture for school psychology. *School Psychology Digest, 6,* 4–19.

Mercer, J. R., & Lewis, J. F. (1978). *System of Multicultural Pluralistic Assessment* (SOMPA). New York: Psychological Corporation.

Mishra, S. P., & Hurt, M., Jr. (1970). The use of Metropolitan Readiness Tests with Mexican-American children. *California Journal of Eductional Research, 21,* 182–187.

Mishra, S. P., & Lord, J. (1982). Reliability and predictive validity of the WISC-R with native-American Navajos. *Journal of School Psychology, 20,* 150–154.

Phillipus, M. J. (1967). *Test prediction of school success of bilingual Hispano-American children.* Denver, CO: ERIC Document Reproduction Service No. ED 036 577.

Rasbury, W. C., McCoy, J. G., & Perry, N. W., Jr. (1977). Relations of scores on WPPSI and WISC-R at a one-year interval. *Perceptual and Motor Skills, 44,* 695–698.

Reynolds, C. R., & Gutkin, T. B. (1980). Stability of the WISC-R factor structure across sex at two age levels. *Journal of Clinical Psychology, 36,* 775–777.

Russ, J. D., & Soboloff, H. R. (1958). *A primer of cerebral palsy.* Springfield, IL: Charles C Thomas, Publisher.

Sattler, J. M. (1974). *Assessment of children's intelligence.* (Rev. Ed.). Philadelphia: W. B. Saunders Company.

Sattler, J. M. (1982). *Assessment of children's intelligence and special abilities* (2nd ed.). Boston: Allyn and Bacon, Inc.

Sattler, J. M. (1983). Assessment of children's intelligence. In C. E. Walker, & M. C. Roberts, *Handbook of Clinical Child Psychology.* New York: John Wiley.

Schooler, D. L., Beebe, M. C., & Koepke, T. (1978). Factor analysis of WISC-R scores for children identified as learning disabled, educable mentally impaired, and emotionally impaired. *Psychology in the Schools, 15,* 478–485.

Seashore, H. G. (1951). Differences between verbal and performance IQs on the WISC. *Journal of Consulting Psychology, 15,* 62–67.

Silverstein, A. B. & Legutki, G. (1982). Direct comparisons of the factor structures of the WISC and the WISC-R. *Psychology and the Schools, 19,* 5–7.

Stedman, J. M., Lawlis, G. F., Cortner, R. H., & Achterberg, G. (1978). Relationship between WISC-R factors, wide range achievement test scores, and visual-motor maturation in children referred for psychological evaluation. *Journal of Consulting and Clinical Psychology, 46,* 869–872.

Stetson, E. Educational assessment of the child. In C. E. Walker, & M. C. Roberts, (1983). *Handbook of Clinical Child Psychology.* New York: John Wiley & Sons, Inc.

Swerdlik, M. E. (1977). The question of the comparability of the WISC and WISC-R: Review of the research and implications for school psychologists. *Psychology in the Schools, 14,* 260–270.

Thorndike, R. L., & Hagen, E. (1977). *Measurement and evaluation in psychology and education* (4th Ed.). New York: John Wiley & Sons, Inc.

Wechsler, D. (1949). *Manual for the Wechsler Intelligence Scale for Children.* New York: Psychological Corporation.

Wechsler, D. (1967). *Manual for the Wechsler Preschool and Primary Scale of Intelligence.* New York: Psychological Corporation.

Wechsler, D. (1974). *Manual for the Wechsler Intelligence Scale for Children-Revised.* New York: Psychological Corporation.

Wechsler, D. (1981). *Manual for the Wechsler Adult Intelligence Scale-Revised.* New York: Psychological Corporation.

Williams, R. L. (1972). Abuses and misuses in testing black children. In R. L. Jones (Ed.), *Black Psychology.* New York: Harper & Row, Publishers, Inc.

Wright, D., & Dappen, L. (1982). Factor analysis of the WISC-R and the WRAT with a referral population. *Journal of School Psychology, 20,* 306–312.

9

Wechsler Adult Intelligence Scale-Revised

Alvin Enis House
Marjorie L. Lewis

"Intelligence, operationally defined, is the aggregate or global capacity of the individual to act purposefully, to think rationally and to deal effectively with his environment." (David Wechsler, 1958, p. 7.)

Introduction In 1981 David Wechsler issued, through the Psychological Corporation, the most recent edition of his grouping of tasks for the assessment of global intelligence in the adult individual—the Wechsler Adult Intelligence Scale-Revised (WAIS-R). This falls into a tradition of mental testing which began in 1939 with the Wechsler Bellevue Intelligence Scale, Form I (W–B). The W–B was revised and reissued in 1955 as the Wechsler Adult Intelligence Scale (WAIS). Aside from relatively minor revision, updating, and replacement of items, there was essential overlap between the W–B and the WAIS in form and nature of tasks. This same consistency is preserved in the present revision. Chapter 2 in the WAIS-R manual (Wechsler, 1981) details the most recent modifications. These are, overall, slight and somewhat cosmetic in nature—gender-free language has been substituted in some items and minority individuals introduced into the Information and Picture Completion subtests. There are some substantive changes in Comprehension and Similarities items. The Information scale appears to have received the greatest revision with twenty items retained from the WAIS and nine items replaced. This is not surprising given the temporal and cultural specificity of Information items. The basic structure of the Wechsler test remains the same—six verbal and five performance subtests. Wechsler (1981) briefly reports on experimentation with two new scales as possible additions to the WAIS-R but indicates that one was not adequately developed for inclusion and the other correlated so highly with Block Design as to add little additional information to the test. The two most novel changes both paralleled changes made in the Wechsler Intelligence Scale for Children-Revised (WISC-R): Both trials of Digit Span are scored and the Verbal and Performance subtests are alternated in administration. For the WAIS-trained examiner the transition to the WAIS-R is direct and relatively painless.

This consistency in form overlies a stability in Wechsler's basic views of the nature of human intelligence and the role of intelligence testing (Edwards, 1974; Wechsler, 1958, 1975). Wechsler rejected conceptions of intelligence that tied it to particular abilities or attributes of the individual such as abstract reasoning, learning acuteness, or adaptability: "Intelligence is multifaceted as well as multi-determined. What it always calls for is not a particular ability but an overall competency or global capacity, which in one way or another enables a sentient individual to comprehend the world and to deal effectively with its challenges. Intelligence is a function of the personality as a whole and is responsive to other factors besides those included under the concept of cognitive abilities." (Wechsler, 1981, p. 8.) Further, Wechsler believed that intelligence tests can yield an adequate assessment of this global capacity.

Hale (1983) has suggested that there seem to be two general approaches taken to discussions of intellectual assessment. One is clinical or test-oriented and presumes the reasonableness of measuring intelligence, and focuses on the practical business of how to do this as well as possible with available tools. The alternative approach is conceptual and experimental and presumes the inadequacy of simplistic attempts to deal with complex issues, and focuses on sophisticated issues of definition and analysis. As Hale noted, the two positions are often perceived in opposition and there have been few attempts to integrate the contributions of each (his own paper is a notable exception).

The present discussion focuses on the applied use of the WAIS-R in adult assessment, and falls more or less clearly within the test-oriented tradition. Nevertheless, House and Lewis do appreciate the importance of stepping back to survey the foundations the house is built upon. Psychological assessment and intellectual assessment, in particular, have become a controversial activity—fraught with the stress of professional skepticism, consumer advocacy, legislative mandate, and the threat of litigation. The present-day qualified psychological examiner is required by the exigencies of the times to be able to speak to the assumptions, criticisms, weaknesses, and strengths of the instruments he or she uses, and the conceptual and methodological models upon which these instruments are based. These issues go well beyond the scope and intent of the present chapter, and the reader is referred to the extensive literature on the nature of human intelligence and its measurement (cf., Carroll, 1979; Frank, 1976; French, 1979; Guilford, 1980; Horn & Cattell, 1966; Kelderman, Mellenbergh & Elshout, 1981; Pellegrino & Glaser, 1979; Sattler, 1982a; Snow, 1979; Sternberg, 1979), as well as the debates over the IQ controversy (Block & Dworkin, 1976; Blum, 1978; Eysenck & Kamin, 1981; Jensen, 1969).

ADMINISTRATION

Standard Administration

The basic reference for administration of the WAIS-R is, of course, the test manual (Wechsler, 1981). The Wechsler manuals enjoy the well-deserved reputation of being among the best written and most complete test guides in the psychological literature. The present manual continues this tradition. The test instructions are clearly written and well organized, the general conceptual issues underlying interpretative scoring are discussed with care, and the manual coordinates with both administration of the test stimuli and with the scoring Record Form. Given this admirable state of affairs it would seem reasonable to begin preparation to use the WAIS-R with a complete and thorough understanding of the manual. Unfortunately, the interaction with many examiners suggests that a detailed study of the test manual is often the belated action of the experienced psychologist rather than the starting point of the novice. For the WAIS-R such action is completely without excuse or justification—working familiarity with the test manual is a prerequisite for a competent administration of the WAIS-R. The basic instructions, scoring rules, examples, and decision rules (for initiation and termination points) should be available knowledge for the examiner. It is difficult to stress this point strongly enough—a poorly administered instrument yields useless information. The psychologist loses all the advantages of a standardized stimulus exposure which allows for clear, relatively unambiguous interpretations of significant variation as a function of individual differences. The purpose of psychological assessment is to allow for clear decision making. An improperly administered test reduces this process to subjective guessing under the deceitful disguise of pseudoscience.

The prerequisite necessity of familiarity with the administration manual is of overwhelming advantage to the examiner who has all standard administration instructions memorized. This is, admittedly, not a popular recommendation.

The greatest advantage of committing the instructions to memory is that it frees the examiner to observe the client. A well-trained examiner is able to supplement the standardized test data with valuable observations of the test and extratest behavior of the client. It is difficult to do this when reading the test manual—reading the instructions and keeping the place, so one knows what to do next. With the basic wording of instructions a part of working memory, attention is freed to concentrate on the really important source of information—the client.

A secondary consideration that the novice examiner may wish to consider is that with or without conscious effort to memorize a set of instructions—this is exactly what will happen within a remarkably few sets of administrations. A conservative estimate is that within the first fifty or so presentations of the WAIS-R, the wording of the instructions and prompts of any given examiner will become largely or completely routine—but not necessarily correct. If the examiner does not learn the standardized set of instructions verbatim, over time he or she will come to memorize his or her own variations of these. These variations may or may not be a source of systematic error in the results.

Overall experiences have convinced psychologists of the value of memorizing the standard instructions. For many psychologists this is easiest within the context of actual practice administrations, rather than as an isolated academic exercise. House and Lewis are convinced that the examiner will not regret the small amount of effort this requires. In fairness, however, it must be noted that this is not a universally accepted recommendation. Lezak (1983), for instance, believes that the possibility of systematic drift in the wording of instructions is greater if examiners attempt to memorize the commands; and she recommends continued reading of the instructions from the manual. This is a point of difference for which there is simply no data available for a rational decision. House and Lewis agree with Lezak in that the examiner should always have the test manual available during the testing. Without systematic observation of testing behavior, it is not possible to know whether these recommendations differ in degree (emphasis) or kind (actual operations).

Many examiners find that highlighting or underscoring portions of the instructions, administration rules, or scoring criteria in the manual is a useful exercise, especially during their initial experience with the instrument. Similarly, some examiners find the use of plastic index tabs for easy turning to certain subtests or to the expanded scoring criteria for Vocabulary, Comprehension, or Similarities personally helpful. These aids and systems can be helpful in learning to administer the test and in increasing confidence during that stressful early period in which examiners are painfully aware of inexperience with a new instrument. House and Lewis advise that novice WAIS-R examiners try at least a few practice administrations before undertaking such modification of their manuals, lest they end up as one zealous student with every word in the manual highlighted and every page marked with tab or paperclip.

It may prove useful at this point to briefly review the eleven subtests of the WAIS-R with respect to their basic content, form of administration, scoring, and interpretation. The WAIS-R is an omnibus type of intelligence test, tapping a wide variety of tasks. However, rather than shifting task requirements from item to item, such as on the Binet scale, the WAIS-R groups items into eleven subtests, each having roughly similar content and task requirements within the subtest. These eleven subtests have passed from the W-B to the WAIS to the present WAIS-R. Definitions and item content continue to be based on Wechsler's original conceptual analysis of intelligence. Six of the subtests are classified as Verbal: Information, Digit Span, Vocabulary, Arithmetic, Comprehension, and Similarities. Five subtests are classified as Performance (non-verbal): Picture Completion, Picture Arrangement, Block Design, Object Assembly, and Digit Symbol (called Coding on the WAIS-R). On the WAIS the Verbal subtests were administered first (Information, Comprehension, Arithmetic, Similarities, Digit Span, Vocabulary), followed by the Performance subtests (Digit Symbol, Picture Completion, Block Design, Picture Arrangement, and finally Object Assembly). One significant administrative change in the WAIS-R is the alternation between Verbal and Performance subtests throughout the testing period. This is intended to enhance and maintain an optimum level of interest and motivation on the part of the client. This change has been justified by the beneficial results obtained. This can be especially noticed in the test performance of individuals with systematic impairment with either verbal or spatial tasks. Alternating between easy and hard tasks (for clients) allows for the dissipation of frustration and embarrassment, helping to maintain both their dignity and their task commitment and motivation.

The present discussion will consider the subtest scales in the order they are presented to the client: Information, Picture Completion, Digit Span, Picture Arrangement, Vocabulary, Block Design, Arithmetic, Object Assembly, Comprehension, Digit Symbol, and Similarities. The reader is also referred to the excellent discussion of the WAIS-R subtests in Lezak (1983), and to previous analyses of the WAIS subtests (Golden, 1979, 1981; Matarazzo, 1972; Maloney & Ward, 1976; Zimmerman & Woo-Sam, 1973).

WAIS-R Subtests

Information   The WAIS-R Information subtest consists of twenty-nine factual inquiry questions sampling the client's general fund of knowledge. A kind of trivia test of American civilization, the item content was selected to represent the sort of background information that a developmental exposure to the U.S. culture would bring within the common knowledge of most citizens. The item difficulty ranges from the easy (seldom failed in an intact sample) to the difficult (seldom passed in an intact sample). Information is believed by most examiners to reflect acquired knowledge and to correlate with formal education. This is certainly one source of general cultural facts, and groups with a college education tend to score higher than groups with a high school education, who in turn, score higher than populations with only a grade school education. However, a pattern of generalized reading across diverse topics will also yield a high Information score regardless of formal education; and the examiners have met at least a few individuals who produced high Information scores despite limited education and reading. These few seemed, in informal analysis, to be simply bright individuals who, despite limited cultural training (books or school), had remained throughout their lives alert to knowledge as they encountered it. Doing well on the Information subtest requires not only information, but the ability to select the right information to report on. On occasion, individuals will demonstrate the inability to control their cognitive search and/or reporting—rambling on, adding unnecessary or unrelated details, and in extreme cases, perseverating in response from item to item.

Testing on Information begins with Item 5. Items 1 through 4 are passed by all but the most impaired, and these questions are given only if either Item 5 or Item 6 is failed. Testing continues until five items are consecutively failed. Scoring is relatively easy and objective—examiner judgment is required only in determining the adequacy of responses to Items 15 and 21. Some neutral probing may on occasion be necessary to elicit enough information to allow the proper scoring of the identity of the historical personalities the client is asked to identify. As with most of the subtests, it is desirable to record verbatim the client's responses. This both allows scoring to be checked, and provides a good sample of the client's speech patterns, natural vocabulary, and thought processes.

Information, along with Vocabulary, is usually seen as one of the best measures of general ability among the WAIS-R subtests. For eight of the nine age groups reported in the WAIS-R standardization data, Information has the second highest correlation with the Verbal IQ; for the average intercorrelation of the tests across all nine age samples, Information has the second highest correlation with Verbal IQ. For five of the nine age groups, Information has the second highest correlation with the Full Scale IQ; and Information has the second highest average correlation with Full Scale IQ across all nine age groups. It consistently loads highly on the first verbal factor identified in most common factor and principal components analyses carried out on the WAIS-R subtest intercorrelations (see below).

Picture Completion   Picture Completion presents the client with a series of twenty pictures from which "there is some important part missing." (Wechsler, 1981, p. 63). Testing begins with the first item, and for the first two items the correct response is identified if the client fails an item. The first time a client identifies an unessential missing part the examiner prompts: "Yes, but what is the most important thing missing?" (Wechsler, 1981, p. 63.) No further help is allowed. Testing continues until five items are failed. Clients are allowed a maximum exposure of twenty seconds for each stimulus card. For three of the items, the client must identify or point to the correct location as well as labeling the missing part. If he or she fails to do so the examiner must probe: "Show me where." (Wechsler, 1981, p. 64.) Scoring is relatively straightforward and objective. It is useful to record verbatim the client's responses on the record blank. The WAIS-R Record Form allows adequate space for this. This allows identification of alert and perceptive individuals who correctly identify the missing part but show an impoverished vocabulary in their poor verbal labeling. Recording the response also facilitates the identification of perseverative response patterns. Some authors have paid considerable attention to a content analysis of Picture Completion responses and errors common in psychiatric and non-psychiatric populations. Weiner (1966) gives common errors in both schizophrenic and non-schizophrenic groups on the WAIS Picture Completion subtest that overlaps considerably in item content with the WAIS-R subtest. It may also be useful to note extremely short or long latencies, especially if the delay costs the client credit for an otherwise correct response.

Digit Span   The Digit Span subtest actually consists of two different tasks—an immediate recall task calling for the repetition of increasing numbers of digits; and a concentration span task requiring the client to repeat backwards an increasing series of numbers immediately after hearing each series. Scoring is simple: the item is passed if repeated or reversed correctly. Two trials are given for each digit series. Digits Forward begins with a three-digit series and proceeds until both trials of a digit series are failed. Digits Backward begins with two practice items (the second only administered if the first is failed and corrected by the examiner), and then proceeds with a two-digit series and continues until both trials of a series are failed. Digits Forward proceeds to a maximum memory span of nine digits; Digits Backward proceeds to a maximum concentration span of eight digits in reverse order.

An entire chapter (book) could easily be written on the subtleties of measuring human memory. Wechsler (1945) and other investigators have produced memory tests, usually batteries made up of a number of types of memory tasks covering immediate and short-term recall (cf., Russell, 1981; Williams, 1978). The WAIS-R Digit Span gives a rapid screening of immediate auditory recall for digits and for the more complex cognitive task of holding a digit series, "operating" on it to reverse the order, and then reporting it aloud. Lezak has humorously compared the averaging of performance on these two tasks to an orthopedic physician averaging a broken arm and a broken leg to give a "mean orthopedic index."*

It seems advantageous, in addition to the standrad scoring of the Digit Span subtest, to note the client's highest pass on both Digits Forward and on Digits Backward separately. Lezak (1983) suggests that spans of 6 or better forward are clearly within normal limits, a span of 5 is marginal, a span of 4 is borderline, and a span of 3 is defective (p. 268). With respect to Digits Backward, Lezak suggests that raw scores of 4 or 5 are within normal limits, a span of 3 is borderline or defective depending upon the client's educational level, and a span of 2 is defective for individuals less than 60 years of age (Lezak, p. 269). Indication of memory or concentration difficulty should be followed with more intensive investigation.

Picture Arrangement   Picture Arrangement consists of ten sets of picture cards that are presented to the client in a standard order. The client is asked to rearrange the cards so that a sensible story is told from left to right. The picture series form wordless comic strips. The theme of the first series is explained to the client as they are

*Remarks made by Muriel Lezak during her presentation on Neuropsychological Assessment. Workshop presented by Muriel Lezak and Nils Varney, Chicago, Illinois, July 21–23, 1982.

presented. If the client has difficulty with the first series, the correct order is demonstrated and the client is given a second trial. No further help is given. Testing continues throughout the series or until four consecutive failures occur (beginning with the second item). Scoring is determined by producing the correct order within the allowed time limit. Two sets have two sequences that are given full credit; four sets have additional sequences that are given partial credit. Alphabetical and numerical coding on the back of the cards makes administration, recording, and scoring a relatively easy task for the examiner.

Picture Arrangement is grouped within the Performance subtests, but (as is clear or unclear from the intercorrelation patterns) this task is as closely related to the verbal tasks as it is to the non-verbal tasks. Its factor loadings are equally complex. Picture Arrangement has been conceived as reflecting perceptual vigilance, visual sequencing ability, and/or the ability to process social cues. For the W-B and the WAIS a pattern of low Picture Arrangement with relatively intact Block Design was specifically seen as indicative of right temporal lobe difficulty.* However, even if this pattern was reliable, the WAIS-R Picture Arrangement may be the most significantly altered of the WAIS subtests; and it is not at all clear that this hypothesized neuropsychological relationship could be expected to continue. This question will probably attract considerable attention within the neuropsychology field.

Vocabulary   The Vocabulary subtest presents the client with written and oral presentations of thirty-five stimulus words and asks for their meanings. Testing begins with the fourth word and continues until the series ends or five consecutive failures occur. The first three words are presented only if a failure (score of 0) is obtained on any one of the Items 4 through 8. The scoring is complex, calling for the awarding of 2, 1, or 0 points based on the adequacy of the verbal definition given. Both general criteria, specific criteria, and examples of 2, 1, and 0 point answers are given for the stimulus words. Vocabulary tends to be the WAIS-R subtest requiring the most administration time and tends to be the most difficult to score. Considering the complexity of the task and the general domain of knowledge being assessed, this is not wholly surprising. Vocabulary tests in all forms have long been recognized as the most accurate, stable, and general measures of mental ability or intelligence. Within the WAIS-R, Vocabulary has the highest correlation with the Verbal IQ across all age groups tested in the standardization sample; for eight of the nine age groups, it has the highest intercorrelation with the Full Scale IQ (for

---

*Remarks made by Ralph Reitan during his presentation on clinical interpretation of the Halstead-Reitan battery. Advanced workshop on Neuropsychological Assessment, Ralph Reitan, James C. Reed, and Jan Janesheski, Chicago, Illinois, July 25–29, 1983.

the fifty-five to sixty-four age group Comprehension correlates with the FSIQ .79 and Vocabulary correlates with FSIQ .78). This is one of the most robust subtests on the WAIS-R and is often used as an estimate of premorbid verbal and general mental ability in cases of known brain injury. Many brief forms of the WAIS-R make use of Vocabulary as one of the best single measures of intelligence. Paradoxically, when a near full battery is given, Vocabulary is often the subtest omitted because of the amount of time required for administration and scoring. House and Lewis believe it is difficult to envision a general psychological evaluation without some measure of general word use, and the WAIS-R Vocabulary subtest is an excellent measure of this verbal ability.

Block Design   The WAIS-R Block Design subtest is a modification of the Kohs' Block Design Test and is one of the best non-verbal measures of intelligence on the WAIS-R. In fact, the intercorrelation between Block Design and Verbal IQ is higher than the intercorrelation between Digit Span and the Verbal IQ across all age samples in the standardization sample. For two age groups the Block Design/Verbal IQ intercorrelation is as high as the Arithmetic/Verbal IQ intercorrelation. The Block Design subtest is a measure of general intelligence and is often included within short forms of the WAIS-R as the Performance subtest with the highest loading on a general intellectual factor. It usually requires a significant degree of visual-spatial ability and loads heavily on the second or spatial factor identified in most factor and principal components studies.

In this subtest, the client is presented with nine cards depicting geometric designs in white and red, and with a number of identical plastic cubes each having two red, two white, and two red and white sides split on the diagonal. The task is to reproduce the design on the card with the cubes. The client's performance is timed and, after the second item, additional points are awarded for rapid, errorless performance. Block Design is one of three subtests where rapid, errorless performance is rewarded (Block Design, Arithmetic, and Object Assembly), and one of five subtests where speed is an explicit factor in scoring (Block Design, Arithmetic, Object Assembly, Picture Completion, and Digit Symbol; Digit Span might be added to the list in the sense that delays are likely to be associated with failure). The instructions explicitly identify and demonstrate that the blocks are all alike. The first design is copied by the client from a model constructed by the examiner. The second design is copied from a stimulus figure after the examiner demonstrates the correct response. For both the first and second designs, a failure by the client is followed by a second demonstration and a second trial (for half credit). After Design 2 no further help is given; the client is instructed to work as quickly as possible. The first five designs are constructed with four blocks. When Design 6 is reached, the examiner gives the client five additional blocks and instructs him or her to make the remaining designs using nine blocks. Testing continues until the series is completed or until three consecutive designs are failed (both trials of Designs 1 and 2 must be failed to be counted a failure). The final design presents a figure that is rotated 45 degrees and the client should not be allowed to turn the stimulus card to give the figure a flat base. Constructions (on any design) rotated 30 degrees or more are considered failed. The first instance of such a rotation is corrected (but scored a failure).

Block Design is often presented as a more culture free task than subtests such as Information or Vocabulary (Maloney & Ward, 1976). Unfortunately, Block Design scores can be depressed by a variety of factors including visual or motor impairments, any kind of brain injury, and motivational influences (such as depression). A good score on Block Design tends to be more informative than a bad score unless some of the alternative explanations for a poor performance can be ruled out.

Arithmetic The Arithmetic subtest consists of fourteen mathematics problems presented orally to the client (the first item requires the client to count a row of blocks) to be worked without paper or pencil. Testing begins with Item 3; the first two items are administered only if both Items 3 and 4 are failed. Testing continues until the series is completed or four consecutive problems are failed. All problems must be answered within a time limit for credit to be awarded; beginning with Item 10, a bonus point is awarded for rapid, correct answering. Scoring is objective and presents no difficulty. House and Lewis find it useful to note the response time taken by the client for the first nine problems. This may reveal a tendency for rapid, impulsive responding that the client has difficulty controlling as the problems become more difficult. It is unfortunate that the correct answer for one item on the restandardization of the WAIS-R is the same speed as the current national speed limit. House noted a number of cases where, following failures on previous items the client responds impulsively to that item: "55 miles per hour," and upon later inquiry freely admits this was a guess based on the speed limit. The effect of this is to give the client a two-point score and necessitates the additional administration of the remainder of the arithmetic problems. The reduction in the number of arithmetic problems from the WAIS to the WAIS-R has restricted the raw score range rather severely and two raw score points will always raise the scaled score one point and often two points. Such considerations cannot be allowed to affect the computation of the IQs, but during test interpretation such possibilities may need to be considered, especially if Arithmetic turns out to be the highest Verbal subtest.

The mathematical requirements of the Arithmetic items, even at the top of the scale, are not excessively demanding. Comparable problems would be solved within a basic high school mathematics class. However, the necessity to work the problems in your head, the common "math anxiety" in much of the general population, and the timed nature of the test combine to make the Arithmetic test mildly stressful for many clients—especially for those aware of educational limitations or cognitive impairments. To complete the task effectively requires the ability to concentrate, analyze the nature of the problem to be solved, mentally perform the required operations (addition, subtraction, division, multiplication), remember the partial results until the problem is solved and the answer reported. In three factor solutions to a principal component or factor analysis of WAIS-R tests, Arithmetic is usually found to load the minor third factor along with Digit Span and sometimes Digit Symbol. This is usually interpreted as either a "memory" or a "freedom from distractibility" factor. The tasks loading on the factor seem to have in common a requirement for sustained attention and the suppression of scores by even low levels of free-floating anxiety.

Object Assembly   Object Assembly presents the client with four cardboard puzzles of common objects to be assembled as quickly as possible. All four items are presented to all clients. If the first item is not assembled correctly within the time limits, the correct solution is demonstrated. No further help is given. Bonus points are awarded for rapid perfect performances, and partial credit is given for correct assembly of portions of a figure. Scoring is relativley objective, but may require some time and study until the examiner becomes thoroughly familiar with the correct juxapositions for each figure.

As with the other construction tasks, Object Assembly is sensitive to the presence of perceptual or motor disturbances. Peripheral declines in perceptual acuity or motor speed are undoubtedly the major factor accounting for the decline in raw score performance noted with advancing age for Object Assembly. The presence of perceptual or motor control difficulties must be carefully considered in interpreting the results of the test. As with the other timed tasks, concentration and sustained attention is important in obtaining a maximum score. The examiner should be alert to the client's apparent task motivation during testing. Object Assembly usually loads on the second, spatial factor in analyses of WAIS-R subtest intercorrelations. Along with Block Design it provides an opportunity to observe how the client handles materials, deals with constructional problems, and uses perceptual cues. The comparison of Block Design with Object Assembly is sometimes viewed as an opportunity to observe how the client deals with abstract versus concrete spatial problems. Although there is an apparent face validity to this argument, the number of items is so restricted that practical comparisons are difficult. House and Lewis have noted, along with others, that the first two stimulus figures are recognized by most clients, whereas the third and fourth figures are either not recognized or not recognized with confidence by many impaired and/or retarded clients. It is useful to follow testing with an inquiry to identify the objects the client was attempting to assemble. Observations of problem-solving style, the client's handling of frustration, and any perseverative responses can be valuable for a qualitative interpretation.

Comprehension   Comprehension is a complex subtest consisting of sixteen questions requiring explanations (as opposed to simple factual answers). Part of the complexity of the scale is that the questions are not all the same. Three of the questions ask the client to explain what he or she would do in a certain hypothetical situation. The problem solving required for these problems requires judgment and what is euphemistically called common sense. Ten of the questions require a conceptual analysis of a situation and a report regarding the relevant variables pertaining to the question. These problems range from the simple and concrete to the difficult and abstract. They are different from the three judgment questions because a report of the explicit action required by the situation is not requested. This changes, in a fundamental sense, the nature of the problem to be solved. House has encountered a large number of high functioning, retarded citizens who could explain the proper action needed in almost any realistic situation but could not give an adequate conceptual analysis of a simple abstract situation. Conversely, there are others who can explain quite adequately the significance of journalistic watchdogging of a central authority, but who are completely incapable of suppressing their gleeful response of: "Shout FIRE!" to Item 7. The remaining three Comprehension items call for proverb interpretations, a highly abstract verbal task.

Probably in part due to this diversity and complexity of item content, Comprehension is a good general test of intellectual ability and correlates highly with both Verbal and Full Scale IQs. It is also a lengthy test to administer and most difficult to score. Because of the open-ended nature of the response format a variation in client responses is possible. It would be helpful if more space could be devoted in the test manual to multiple examples of answers of different point values. Like Vocabulary and Similarities, the client's responses are scored 2, 1, or 0 points. For two items (3 and 4) requiring two reasons for maximum credit, if the client responds with one reason the clinician should ask for a second idea. This prompting is in addition to any probing needed to clarify the appropriate point value of a client's response. Part of the difficulty in administering Comprehension is that extended neutral probing may be necessary to elicit sufficient detail to allow for accurate scoring of a response. The examiner must exercise care not to lead or prompt the client with the questioning, but must reach a full understanding of the ideas the client is expressing. Scoring, ultimately, requires more judgment on the part of the examiner than any other WAIS-R subtest.

Balanced against the time and trouble required to administer Comprehension is the richness and diversity of information it yields. More than anywhere else in the WAIS-R, Comprehension allows for the observation of the client's natural thought processes and cognitive problem-solving style. It is here and on Similarities, that emotional and behavioral disturbances will make themselves most evident. Poor social judgment, weak superego strength, and social insensitivity may be openly displayed in responses to IQ test questions that would not be revealed otherwise. The tendency of proverbs to elicit latent cognitive distortions and looseness of associations is well known and utilized in psychiatric evaluations.

Digit Symbol   The Digit Symbol subtest is a coding task requiring the client to draw in the symbol assigned to each digit from 1 to 9 in blank boxes beneath an extended series of random selected digits. Three responses are demonstrated by the examiner and four practice responses are made. The timed administration is then begun. The client's score is the number of boxes correctly filled in within the ninety-second time limit. High scoring requires sustained concentration, rapid responding, and good fine-motor control. Extreme high scoring requires that the client rapidly learn the symbols assigned to each number so that repeated looking up at the key can be eliminated and all available time is spent in filling in blanks. Scoring is facilitated by an overlay key, perfect reproduction of the geometric symbols is not required—any recognizable rendering of the symbol is scored as correct. The primary task of the examiner is to monitor the client's performance and halt any skipping of digits: "Credit is not given for items completed out of sequence" (Wechsler, 1981, p. 85). Occasionally, despite the instructions, a client will halt at the end of a line and must be prompted to continue. The primary difficulty encountered with administration is the necessity of careful timing. It is possible for the examiner to become so engrossed in the client's perceptual-motor performance that the time limit passes unnoticed.

In three factor solutions Digit Symbol tends to load most heavily on the minor third factor which is usually interpreted as memory or freedom from distractibility. As with the other timed and perceptual-motor tasks, a variety of influences will reduce a client's score including any brain injury. Digit Symbol is usually viewed as one of the most brain sensitive of the Wechsler tasks.

Similarities   The Similarities subtest asks the client to identify how fourteen successive pairs of nouns are alike. Testing begins with the first item for all clients and proceeds throughout the series or until four consecutive failures are obtained. The client's responses are scored 2, 1, or 0 points according to general criteria and examples given in the test manual. Examiner judgment is required, but scoring of Similarities responses is generally the easiest of the three Verbal subtests requiring multiple point scoring (Vocabulary, Comprehension, Similarities). If full credit (2 points) is not earned on the first item, the examiner demonstrates a two-point response. No further help is given. A large number of partial (1 point) responses and some failure (0 point) responses automatically call for an inquiry, and frequent review of the examples in the test manual is advised. A similar situation exists for Vocabulary and for Comprehension. A failure to question, when probing is indicated, is one of the most common administration mistakes in WAIS-R testing. Testing should always be carried out with the assistance of the test manual (even when the instructions have been memorized).

Similarities performance loads heavily on general intelligence and on the first verbal factor identified in most factor studies. It requires abstract verbal reasoning. Especially with the more difficult items, the test provides an opportunity to observe the client's thought processes in action. Emotional or behavioral disturbances of thought processes may also become evident on this test, for example, the client who responded to the stimulus pair of two directions with the response: "I haven't been around California to see if they have weather there, but Northern people have four seasons: spring, winter, autumn, summer." An informal observation is that the item order on the WAIS-R does not appear to represent evenly increasing difficulty for many groups of clients. Especially, Item 9 seems easier (more 2-point responses) for many mildly impaired clients than the four item pairs preceding it.

Order of Presentation of Subtests   The alternation of Verbal and Performance subtests on the WAIS-R is an attempt to maintain the client's interest during the testing session, as well as to avoid frustration and loss of task motivation if a general class of activity is especially difficult for a client (verbal abilities for instance). For the average client, alternating Verbal and Performance subtests in the standard order of administration will effectively mix up tests so the client finds interesting versus uninteresting and hard versus easy. The examiner may, however, want to modify the order of presentation if atypical circumstances seem to be present. The order of administration of tests from an ability battery does not appear to have significant effects on the client's performance (Carter & Bowles, 1948; Cassel, 1962; Quereshi, 1968), unless the length of testing is extended (Neuger, O'Leary, Fishburne, Barth, Berent, Giordani & Boll, 1981). An extremely anxious client, for instance, who is having obvious difficulty concentrating on the Information questions will probably do badly when Digit Span is presented as the third subtest. Delaying the administration of Digit Span until later in the session when the client has relaxed somewhat, will perhaps yield a more valid score.

The Positioning of WAIS-R Testing Within A Psychological Evaluation   The WAIS-R is but a single instrument that can be used within the context of a comprehensive examination of a client's intellectual or global functioning. It is rare to give only the WAIS-R for the examination of a client. This raises the question of where the WAIS-R might be optimally placed within a series of testing devices. Two considerations suggest that it be placed relatively early in the testing. First, the order of presenting ability measures has little effect on scores, until fatigue becomes a factor. This would indicate the wisdom of finishing the WAIS-R early within a session while the client is fresh. Second, in more comprehensive evaluations that include personality measures, there is the possibility that the client will find these personality tests either frustrating and irritating (long personality inventories for instance), or upsetting and provocative (inkblot tests for instance). These emotional reactions may affect the client's cooperativeness and task motivation adversely, and it is wise to have already completed tasks such as the WAIS-R which require sustained effort and cooperation.

At the other extreme, beginning an evaluation with the WAIS-R can be a rather intimidating and frightening experience for some clients. It is suggested that the examination begin (following initial interviewing) with a task that will probably be more familiar in nature to the client (such as an achievement test) or easier for the client (such as a drawing task) than an intelligence test. The particular choice depends on the examiner's knowledge of the client and the results of the initial inquiry and mental status testing.

Intercorrelations and Factor Structure of the WAIS-R

Examinations and discussions of the interrelationships between the eleven Wechsler tests range from the simple and affirmatory ("there are three, or two, or one, or fourteen factors") to the complex and cautious ("the world is a confusing place and answers often shift with the questioner"). To some degree these contradictions and controversies reflect the diversity of opinion on the proper use of empirical classification approaches in the behavioral sciences, especially with reference to human traits (Guilford, 1975; Kim & Mueller, 1978a, 1978b). The widespread availability of high-speed computing facilities and statistical packages with "default options," which permit the unthinking factor analysis of correlation matrixes without the necessity of even consciously realizing the theoretical and statistical assumptions that are being made by the investigator, has without question led to the generation of an interesting body of highly sophisticated and completely worthless psychological literature. Comrey and Lee (1979) have discussed some of these difficulties. Perhaps most disturbing is the common failure to distinguish between exploratory (descriptive) and confirmatory (theory testing) factor analysis. It is believed that investigators would be well advised to take notice of Lawley and Maxwell's cogent appraisal: "It should always be kept firmly in mind that, except in artificial sampling experiments, the basic factor model is, like other models, useful only as an approximation to reality, and it should not be taken too seriously" (1971, p. 38). The brief, two-volume series by Kim and Mueller (1978a, 1978b) is an excellent introduction to the topic of factor and principal component analysis for the mathematically non-sophisticated consumer of psychological research. Carroll (1979) offers a cogent discussion of the faulty analysis of intelligence data within a factor model.

The discussion by Matarazzo of the factor structure of the W-B and the WAIS is a good starting point in attempting to evaluate the available factor studies of the Wechsler scales. He points out some sensible cautions in pushing the interpretations of factor studies too far. Matarazzo reviews Cohen's work on the factor structure of the W-B and WAIS (Berger, Berstein, Klein, Cohen, & Lucas, 1964; Cohen, 1952a, 1952b, 1957a, 1957b). Cohen found evidence of a general factor, that he interpreted as a *g* or general intelligence influence, that could be factored into four oblique (correlated) factors. The first loaded most heavily for the normal subject sample on Vocabulary, Comprehension, Similarities, and Information and was labeled by Cohen and his associates Verbal Comprehension. The second loaded highest on Object Assembly, Block Design, and Picture Completion and was labeled Perceptual Organization. The third loaded highest on Digit Span and on Arithmetic and was labeled Memory and/or Freedom from Distractibility. The fourth factor had only a small loading on Arithmetic, accounted for little variance (factors are extracted in order of the proportion of variance accounted for—the first factor will account for the most, the second the next most, and so forth), and was left unlabeled (Berger et al., 1964). Similar results have been obtained for the WISC-R (Kaufman, 1979).

When one examines the intercorrelation tables for the WAIS-R standardization data, the most basic conclusion to be reached is the same noted by Matarazzo (1972): For each of the nine age groups (and of course, for the average intercorrelation table across ages) all fifty-five of the subtest-to-subtest correlation coefficients are positive and greater than zero. There appears clear evidence of a general factor relating performance on the various tasks. For the average intercorrelations of the tests for all nine age groups the correlations between Verbal subtests range from lows of .45 (Digit Span/Comprehension and Digit Span/Similarities) to a high of .81 (Information/Vocabulary). For the Performance subtests the range is from a low of .38 (Digit Symbol/Object Assembly) to a high of .63 (Block Design/Object Assembly). For the correlation between Verbal and Performance subtests the range is from a low of .33 (Digit Span/Object Assembly) to a high of .56 (Arithmetic/Block Design).

A number of factor analytic studies have now been carried out with the WAIS-R, most using the data from the standardization sample. Silverstein (1982a) used a principal-factor analysis for the nine WAIS-R age groups and for three age groups from the WAIS standardization data. Two criteria for determining the number of extracted factors were examined: Kaiser's (1960) roots one criterion and the Parallel-analysis criterion (Humphreys & Ilgen, 1969; Montanelli & Humphreys, 1976). A two-factor solution was adopted for all age groups, and an additional three-factor solution was computed for the three youngest age groups. The factor matrixes were rotated to a varimax (orthogonal) solution. Not surprisingly the first WAIS-R factor loaded highest on Vocabulary, Information, Comprehension, and Similarities. The second WAIS-R factor loaded highly on Block Design and on Object Assembly. Silverstein concluded that these were essentially the Verbal Comprehension and Perceptual Organization factors previously identified for the W-B and WAIS, and believed his finding justified interpretation of the Verbal and Performance IQs. The third factor, that could be justified for the three youngest age groups, showed inconsistency across the age groups. For the sixteen to seventeen and the twenty to twenty-four age groups it seemed to be the previously described Freedom from Distractibility (high loading on Digit Span, Arithmetic, and Digit Symbol); for the eighteen to nineteen age group, however, the highest loadings were on Picture Completion, Picture Arrangement, and Object Assembly. Silverstein also examined the specific and common variance components for the WAIS-R and concluded that Digit Span, Arithmetic, Picture Completion, Picture Arrangement, Block Design, and Digit Symbol possessed sufficient specific variance to justify specific interpretation. Alternatively, the general factor can be examined. Silverstein estimates found the *g* factor to account for 55 percent of the total variance and 94 percent of the common variance. He notes that the best measures of g are those subtests that do not possess sufficient specific variance to justify separate interpretation.

Parker (1983) also performed a principal-factor analysis of the standardization data followed by a varimax (orthogonal) rotation. For each age group he extracted two, three, and four factors. Although he makes a passing reference to the "variety of potential criteria for the selection of the number of factors to extract (Gorsuch, 1974)," (p. 303), his choice of the numbers of factors to extract is based on "the consistency and frequency of studies reporting three and more factors in Wechsler tests (Matarazzo, 1972)." (p. 303). The results were then subject to inspection and subjective analysis. Parker believes the two-factor solutions reflect the Verbal and Performance divisions. He believes that the three-factor solution produced, with the exception of the eighteen to nineteen and the forty-five to fifty-four age groups, the Verbal Comprehension, Perceptual Organization, and Freedom from Distractibility factors found by Cohen for the W-B and WAIS. He reports that the confusion of pattern in the two age groups noted above were "neatly disentangled" by the four-factor solution. Based on his analysis of subtest associations with general intelligence and the unrotated first factor, Parker argues that the Verbal Comprehension factor is largely redundant with the general intelligence, g factor. Parker also finds that Digit Symbol and Picture Arrangement have high test specificity and probably measure constructs outside the domain of the other subtests (as well as the g factor). Of particular interest, because of the role it has played in neuropsychological interpretation, is Parker's suggestion that the Picture Arrangement subtest has significantly changed from the WAIS to the WAIS-R.

Blaha and Wallbrown (1982) report another analysis of the standardization data using the Wherry and Wherry (1969) hierarchical factor solution (principal-factor analysis, Minres estimate of communalities, varimax rotation). The initial factorization was determined by specifying a minimum eigenvalue of 1.00; and the secondary factorization was controlled by specifying a minimum eigenvalue of .50. Three factors were identified: a general g factor, with the highest loadings on Vocabulary, Information, Similarities, and Comprehension; a major group factor labeled "verbal-educational" which loads highest on Vocabulary, Information, Comprehension, and Similarities; and a minor group factor labeled "spatial-perceptual" which loads highest on Block Design and Object Assembly. Blaha and Wallbrown believe their results support the construct validity of the WAIS-R as a test of general intelligence. They report that the general-intelligence factor accounts for approximately 47 percent of the total subtest variance for the nine age groups. The verbal-educational factor accounts for approximately 6 percent of the total variance, and the spatial-perceptual factor accounts for approximately 5 percent of the variance. Blaha and Wallbrown interpret these results as supporting Wechsler's maintenance of separation of the Verbal and Performance IQs. They estimate that approximately 18 percent of the total subtest variance can be attributed to error with the remaining 25 percent attributable to subtest specific variance. Blaha and Wallbrown's report was one of few to discuss limitations and cautions in the use and interpretation of factor analytic methods, as well as acknowledging the importance of not confusing test scores and psychological constructs. They believe their results support the cautious use of significant discrepancies between the Verbal and Performance IQs to generate clinical hypotheses; and the cautious use of specific subtest results for clinical hypotheses if the examiner remains cognizant of the limitations involved and treats the hypotheses as tentative. An important observation made by Blaha and Wallbrown is that the factor structure of clinical groups referred for assessment may be more complex than that of the normals in a standardization sample. They cite WISC and WISC-R data consistent with this possibility. Primary factors such as Freedom from Distractibility and quasi-specific may emerge in these populations as important components of variance.

In a rather ambitious study, Naglieri and Kaufman (1983) subjected the WAIS-R standardization data to three factor analytic procedures: principal components analysis (not a common factor model), principal factor analysis with iteration of communality estimates, and principal factor analysis without iteration. In each case, a varimax rotation was used to produce the final component or factor solution. For each analysis six objective methods were used to determine the number of factors to be extracted:

1. eigenvalues equal to or greater than 1.0,
2. 75 percent of the total variance accounted for,
3. Cattell's scree test (1966),
4. Montanelli and Humphreys' (1976) parallel analysis method,
5. Wrigley's* decision rules applied to successive numbers of extracted factors, and
6. Kiel's modification of Wrigley's decision rules.**

---

*Wrigley, C. A procedure for objective factor analysis. Paper presented at the first annual meeting of the Society of Multivariate Experimental Psychology, 1960. Cited in Naglieri and Kaufman (1983).

**Kaufman, A. S. Comparison of tests built from Piaget's and Gesell's tasks: An analysis of their psychometric properties and psychological meaning. Unpublished doctoral dissertation, Columbia University, 1970.

As can be imagined, a great deal of data was produced and it is unfortunate that Naglieri and Kaufman do not actually report more of the resulting factor matrixes in their paper. Their own conclusions are that the two- and three-factor solutions are the most defensible for the WAIS-R, with the factors being a Verbal Comprehension factor, a Perceptual Organization factor, and (sometimes) a Freedom from Distractibility factor. They believe that the third factor should be interpreted when one of the three subtests most often defining Freedom from Distractibility (A, DS, DSy) deviates significantly from its respective Scaled Score mean (Verbal for Arithmetic and Digit Span and Performance for Digit Symbol).

Naglieri and Kaufman should be congratulated for recognizing that there is more than one factor analytic method, and that there are a number of possible criteria for determining the number of factors to extract. Unfortunately, some of their choices added little to the potential pool of knowledge. The choice of a principal components analysis was probably inappropriate since they are clearly interested in generalizing beyond the population studies. Principal components analysis is a theoretical alternative (although essentially identical statistical procedure) that assumes the variance observed is the variance of interest. The distinction is comparable to the choice of an error term in analysis of variance—what population are you interested in generalizing to? Kaiser's (1970) "Little Jiffy" is a good initial step in exploratory research; in this case, however, there are already several generations of exploratory research. Essentially then, examiners are left with a principal factor analysis with or without iterations. It might have been interesting if an Alpha or Image analysis had been included in the study. Also, there are a number of defensible alternatives to varimax rotation (Quartermax or Equamax orthogonal solutions and the oblique solutions).

One of the key issues is, of course, the number of factors to extract. This remains one of the most troubling questions in doing factor analysis. Despite various objective criteria (see Crawford, 1975), there is no final way for the data to decide for the examiner how many factors should be extracted and rotated. The examiner must direct the machine (or choose the default option, usually eigenvalue equals one) and pretend that the machine has chosen for you. In one basic sense, Naglieri and Kaufman did what is the most justified and defensible procedure in exploratory (descriptive) factor analysis. They examined a variety of alternatives and chose the one they liked the best (i.e., the one which is most useful, makes the greatest psychological sense, and makes the most coherent description of the data). Factor analysis is not the scientific road to truth, it is a descriptive tool. It is quite naive to assume that there is a correct statistical method that identifies the right number of factors, the right factor algorithm, or the right rotation solution. Their recommendation that a third factor be interpreted when one of the components significantly deviates from the scaled score mean, however, is a little like saying only pay attention to something when it is important to pay attention to it.

The problem of the number of factors can be viewed from another perspective—all the studies reviewed have concerned themselves only with the WAIS-R subtests. The composition and number of factors obtained depend on the data analyzed. Factor studies, for instance, have been carried out on various neuropsychological test batteries such as the WAIS, WRAT, and Luria-Nebraska tests (Shelly & Goldstein, 1982) or WAIS, Shipley-Hartford, and Halstead-Reitan tasks (Swiercinsky & Howard, 1982). Such studies have found, in addition to the familiar verbal-conceptual and spatial factors, other ability factors which load heavily on sensory or motor tasks not well represented on the Wechsler tests. These new factors did not appear by magic; they appeared because data was introduced into the correlation matrix reflecting the variance of a sufficient number of different tasks that it became useful within the mathematical solution to take them into account.

The final available factor study of the WAIS-R is different in an important way from the ones reviewed above. O'Grady (1983) carried out a confirmatory, maximum likelihood factor analysis of the WAIS-R standardization data. He tested four models: orthogonal two-factor, oblique two-factor, orthogonal three-factor, and oblique three-factor. O'Grady concluded from his analysis that none of the models provide a good fit to the data and none of the models are superior to a one-factor solution.

O'Grady believes his results raise serious questions about the adequacy of the available factor analytic studies of the WAIS-R (and WAIS) since these are usually based on two- or three-factor, orthogonal solutions which are not supported by his analysis. Actually, the choice of a single-factor model is based only on parsimony since none of the models does a good job of accounting for the data and the single-factor model does this bad job with the simplest underlying structure. O'Grady further believes that his data suggest that efforts to interpret specific ability components (verbal-conceptual, spatial, Verbal IQ, Performance IQ, etc.) in addition to a general intellectual ability measure are not justified for the Wechsler scales. Acceptance of these conclusions obviously depends on acceptance of the appropriateness of using a confirmatory factor analysis model. This is a complex topic and beyond the scope of this chapter, but it would seem fair to say that considerable differences of opinion exist on this question.

What then should be concluded on the factor structure of the WAIS-R? This pondering returns to the continuum described in the first paragraph of this section. The bias of House and Lewis is that the world is a confusing place and answers do sometimes depend on who is asking the question and how they ask it. But, with caution and with restraint, certain relationships seem potentially useful— there is evidence of a general ability factor reflected in the positive and significantly greater than zero intercorrelation pattern among the Wechsler tests. Further, there seems reasonable evidence of the usefulness of recognizing a verbal factor, a spatial factor, and a concentration factor (probably especially in impaired populations). Finally, there is sufficient specific variance among the subtests that clinical hypotheses (not conclusions) can be meaningfully formulated, especially in specific subgroups of the population. Both the Matarazzo (1972) chapter and the Blaha and Wallbrown (1982) article deserve close study by the WAIS-R examiner.

Non-standard Supplemental Administration

House and Lewis have found it useful in their work to incorporate a number of additional questions and inquiries into the standard administration of the WAIS-R. None of these involve modification of the basic administration or scoring of WAIS-R subtests and items. These additions can be considered supplemental rather than modifications of the standard administration and are intended to increase the amount of useful information gained from the investment of time in WAIS-R testing.

In addition to the item responses and scores, the WAIS-R Record Form provides space for recording basic identifying information on clients, such as name, marital status, race, occupation, education, birth date, test date, and the place of testing. House found that completing this information provides a convenient and comfortable opportunity to carry out a mental status evaluation of the client. In a friendly and conversational manner, the clients are asked to provide the correct spelling of their names, their birth dates, the current full date, the day of the week, the time of day, their marital status and the length of this status, their occupations or last significant occupation and how long this lasted, how far they went in school, the year they left school, and their age when leaving school. This information is easily recorded in two to three minutes, and clients provide it comfortably and willingly. House obtained this type of biographical data, without client objection, from literally hundreds of clients who range from the brain injured to the barely controlled manic state. The gain in valuable information regarding the client is tremendous. Most of the life history information can easily be checked against other information available on the client with family members and other informants. Basic data is thus available on gross orientation and long-term memory. The day, date, and time allow the scoring of the Temporal Orientation Test (Benton, Hamsher, Varney & Spreen, 1983; Benton, Van Allen & Fogel, 1964). Any significant failure can be noted and followed with more complete investigation later. In this electronic age, with the ubiquitous presence of multifunction watches and calculators, it is usually necessary to deliberately cover the clients' wristwatches before asking any question regarding temporal orientation; even cooperative clients automatically glance at their watches and invalidate the item. This is best done with a manila folder, the Record Form, or the Object Assembly shield, rather than the examiner's hand. The use of an object for such a close body approach will be less disturbing for many clients and will not disrupt their performance with panic nor lead to embarrassment for the examiner.

Novice examiners often seem to be reluctant to systematically carry out a formal mental status examination especially with respect to orientation. For some reason, examiners are perfectly willing to ask grown adults to add two single-digit numbers and relay the sum, but are convinced that these same adults will be insulted if asked to tell the correct date or the name of the city they are in or their full names. This is more a matter of examiner anxiety than the clients'. Most clients come to a psychologist perfectly willing, even expecting, to be asked all manner of silly questions. They tend to take almost anything asked as a matter of course; they take offense at items subtly (and usually unintentionally) communicated to them that should be taken offense at; and really become upset when given evidence that examiners do not know what they are doing or are treating them in a condescending or demeaning fashion. Mental status questions are no more intrinsically upsetting than questions about arithmetic or sex or why you left your last job. If examiners believe this is valuable information that will be useful in order to best serve the client, then they will ask these silly questions in the same relaxed, respectful, and careful manner they ask other apparently silly questions. For the extremely rare individual who hesitates or indicates some question or confusion about these inquiries, a few simple, direct, and honest words of explanation will be sufficient. Examiners should not feel compulsively obliged to explain to every client why they ask the date. This is a needless waste of most clients' time. If clients find the request puzzling, they will communicate this in some manner, and it is the job of the examiner to be alert to this communication and respond appropriately. Most clients will simply answer in the same manner that they provide the sum of four dollars and five dollars, although they are probably asked this even less often in their daily lives than they are asked the date.

The WAIS-R would probably be administered most often as part of a battery or selection of instruments in order to obtain a more comprehensive psychological assessment. If this is not the case, or if the other instruments will not include written responses by the client, the blank space on the lower left area of the first page of the WAIS-R Record Form provides a good area in which clients can be asked to sign their names. In addition to a sample of handwriting, this provides the examiner with the opportunity to note the client's handedness, grip, and placement in the use of a pencil. This can then be compared with later pencil handling during the Digit Symbol subtest. Unusual or inconsistent grip or placement in handling a writing instrument should be noted and recorded by the examiner. The Digit Symbol performance can be influenced, among other factors, by familiarity and experience with writing instruments.

During administration of the Information subtest, House finds it useful to follow the presentation of Item 6 with an inquiry as to the name of the present president of the United States, then the president before this one, then the president before that one. Some clients who fail the standard open inquiry are able to respond correctly in the context of the additional structure provided by sequential questioning. Their ability to transfer this gain can then be explored by repeating Information Item 6 to see if they can now respond correctly (only the original standard administration is used in scoring). The client's general fund of knowledge can be further assessed by then asking for the name of the state governor, and (if the governor question is failed) the name of the state.

Lezak (1983) reports expanding the presentation of Information Item 28 by spelling the word for the client, commenting that this word is pronounced differently by many individuals. Lezak has made another valuable recommendation for administering Information, especially to clients with little formal education. When testing to five failures will carry the inquiry into the top third of the subtest the examiner comments that the client has done so well that he or she will be asked questions to which only a few highly-educated individuals would know the answers. This can help ease the discomfort of being presented with a whole series of questions to which the client may have to respond "I do not know." It has been noted that many brain injured and high functioning mentally retarded individuals incorrectly assume that normal individuals should be able to correctly answer all of the Information items. It is important to anticipate and correct this common misperception if clients are not to be unduly discouraged and their task motivation, perhaps, reduced.

House often finds it helpful to follow the administration of the Information subtest with a request that the client report on a recent prominent news report. This again expands the available sample of the client's general fund of knowledge and awareness of significant environmental events. If warranted by the client's performance, it can be helpful to give the client a copy of the local daily paper and request that he or she read a brief news story to the examiner and then answer a few basic questions about the events reported in the story. There can be a great number of applications of the daily newspaper during a comprehensive psychological assessment and one should be a standard part of the examiner's equipment.

On the Block Design subtest, it is revealing to observe and record the general approach used by the client in reproducing the stimulus designs. Most intact clients are able to form conceptual gestalts of the first few designs, and quickly and systematically reproduce these with the blocks. As the designs become more difficult, it is possible to observe their problem-solving strategies in the face of frustration. One point of particular interest is the introduction on Design 6 of the additional five blocks and the instruction: "Now make one like this, using nine blocks. Be sure to tell me when you have finished." (Wechsler, 1981, p. 74.) Some clients, despite the instructional cue, never grasp the concept of a three by three array. A second point of interest occurs when the client is having difficulty correctly orienting a block within a design. The instructions both inform and demonstrate to the client that all blocks are alike. One costly error noted among lower functioning and impaired individuals is the response to difficulty in orienting a block by searching for the correct block—trying block after block in hopes of finding one that correctly fits the design. If clients do complete the design correctly, it is revealing to note on subsequent trials if they recognize the interchangeability of the blocks or persist in trial and error replacement.

With the supposition of perceptual-motor difficulty, a supplemental elaboration of the Block Design subtest that can be used is to follow the standard administration by presenting clients with pencil and paper and request that they copy several of the failed designs. With any failure, it is important to inquire if the client believes the produced design does actually match the stimulus figure. Clients may give up any attempt to match the test figure; may recognize that one or more features do not exactly match, but be unable to correct these; or may perceive their constructions to, in fact, match the test figures.

On the Object Assembly subtest, it is informative to ask the client to identify, by name, the test object, after completion of an item. Some clients can complete the object correctly, but cannot identify it.

On the Digit Symbol subtest, House finds a modification recommended by Edith Kaplan (reported in Lezak, 1983) of value. She notes the square reached by the client at the close of the ninety-second test period, but allows the client to continue filling in squares until reaching the end of the third row. The client is then stopped, all of the page except the final row is covered (the OA shield is useful for this), and the client is asked to fill in as many symbols from memory as possible. Kaplan reports that a correct recall of seven of the nine symbols is at the low end of the average range. This modification gives a brief measure of residual learning after exposure to a standard number of trials (time is uncontrolled).

The overriding goal of the qualified examiner is to learn as much reliable and valid information about the client as possible in the time available. The WAIS-R typically requires forty-five to seventy-five minutes to administer completely. This is a substantial investment of time. The justification of this expense is to gain the greatest amount of information possible from the client's test performance and behavior. For selected clients one or more of the additions discussed above may increase the gain obtained from this effort.

Testing the Limits   One of the most common supplemental modifications of the WAIS-R subscales probably involves testing the limits—continuing to present test stimuli after a client has met the discontinuation criteria in order to obtain additional information about his or her capabilities and functioning. This can involve three general strategies alone or in combination: the continued presentation of additional items in standard manner after the subtest could be discontinued, the allowance of additional time for the client to reach a solution to a timed item, or the re-presentation of a previously failed item in altered form.

It needs to be stressed that the purpose of testing the limits is to obtain additional qualitative information from the test—it does not affect standard scores, computation of scaled scores, or IQ values. It may be valuable to know that a client can pass the tenth item on Information after failing Items 5, 6, 7, 8, and 9; it does not add an additional raw score point to the client's Information score.

The first modification simply involves continuing to present items within a subscale after the subtest could have been discontinued. The items may be presented in order until all items have been administered, until a more conservative discontinuation criterion has been met, or extended testing may involve the presentation of only select items. The standard discontinuation rules have been questioned for the elderly on the WAIS (Storandt, 1977) and for Canadians on the WAIS-R Information subtest (Bornstein, McLeod, McClung & Hutchison, 1983). Both suggest testing the limits by administering entire subscales regardless of the pass/fail pattern. An example of testing the limits on selected items would be always administering the judgment items on the Comprehension subtest even when a client had discontinued the test at an earlier point.

The second modification allows the client to continue to work on subtest items after the time criterion has been reached. This modification may be made for motivational purposes—giving the clients who are close to a solution on a Block Design item a few additional seconds to complete the pattern so as not to unduly discourage them and perhaps reduce their task motivation for further items—or the extra time may be allowed to see if clients are capable of solving the item, even though they require more time. This modification may be especially important with populations for whom psychomotor slowing is a concern: this includes the elderly, the depressed client, or the heavily medicated client. This modification may be especially useful in the comprehensive evaluation of the brain injured client where it is important to differentiate between the absolute loss of a mental capability and the relative loss of efficiency due to slowing of the mobilization of adaptive behavior.

The third modification involves re-presentation of a failed item, either for a second try (for instance with a client believed to be suffering from performance anxiety) or with alterations of the test stimulus to clarify the nature of the problem. For instance the Arithmetic problems can be re-presented with the client allowed to use paper and pencil for their solution. Or a client might be asked to copy the Block Design figures with paper and pencil to clarify apparent problems with visual-spatial construction. Lezak (1983) presents a number of valuable ideas for testing the limits of WAIS-R subscale tests.

Non-standard Modification of Administration

As noted above, time is the basic issue in psychological assessment. The testing session or sessions represent a limited sampling of client behavior. The special value of psychological testing is that this sampling takes place under special conditions which allows a maximum of meaningful interpretations to be made of the client's behavior. But the basic equation always remains—time is exchanged for information. More time spent on one task is less time available to obtain other sorts of samplings. It is rare indeed to have the luxury of being allowed to obtain the answers to all our questions regarding any particular client. The practical requirements of programming needs, financial limitations, and the competing requirement on the examiner's time usually combine to force a compromise in the comprehensive assessment of any individual client. Examiners do the best that is possible in the time available. This has led, naturally enough, to considerations of how the cost-effectiveness (efficiency) of WAIS-R testing can be enhanced by modifying standard administration to shorten testing time. Three general approaches have been taken to decrease testing time: 1) administering fewer subtests than the standard eleven, 2) altering the start and/or stop rules to reduce the number of items presented, or 3) adopting a general rule to reduce the number of items presented (giving only odd or even numbered items, for instance).

Eliminating Subtests One strategy for reducing the time investment required for WAIS-R testing is dropping the administration of one or more total subtests. This approach usually follows one of two general patterns. The first involves a minimal reduction in the number of subtests eliminated (eliminating one or two Verbal and one or two Performance subtests for a total administration of nine to seven subtests), leaving the bulk of the WAIS-R intact, and yielding what will be herein referred to as an *abbreviated* WAIS-R. Abbreviated WAIS-R testing has the advantage, among brief or short forms, of usually retaining the Verbal IQ/Performance IQ comparison. Depending on the selection of subtests administered, the strong contributors to the three factor scales usually identified for the Wechsler tests can be summed. Finally, specific comparisons can be made among the subtests included in the abbreviated test. The WAIS-R manual contains a table for the extrapolation of Verbal or Performance scaled score sums on the basis of five or four tests, respectively, that are intended for those occasions when a test is spoiled. The same tables can obviously be used when a test is deliberately omitted. It is worth noting, that the manual clearly calls for the identification of such extrapolated findings as prorated on the Record Form and presumably in any report of the findings. The same process of extrapolation can be used for any number of obtained subtest results—the scaled scores are summed, divided by the number of tests, and this product is multiplied by the standard number of subtests within the appropriate test group (Verbal or Performance).

The alternative approach is more severe and reduces the number of subtests administered to some absolute or near absolute minimum, usually two, three, or four subtests administered. Two popular *approximated* WAIS-R tests, as such radically reduced administrations will be herein referred to, are the Vocabulary-Block Design diad and the Information-Vocabulary-Block Design triad. The most common justification offered of approximated WAIS-R administrations is for a rapid screening of intellectual functioning in order to identify those individuals whose suspect performance justifies the investment of the time and effort to administer a full WAIS-R (or other comprehensive instrument). Sattler's (1982) student's manual contains a table of validity coefficients of various approximated WAIS-R combinations (p. 203).

Ryan (1983) reports on the use of a Vocabulary-Block Design combination to estimate a Full Scale IQ in thirty psychiatric patients. He reported a significant correlation between the short form and the Full Scale IQ ($r(28) = .87$, p less than .001) and a non-significant pairwise t test computed between the mean IQs for the short form and the standard administration. Ryan observes that these results meet two of the three criteria Resnick and Entin (1971) had proposed for the acceptability of short forms for the WISC-R, but notes that their third criterion—minimal change in an IQ classification—was not met. He reports that using Wechsler's seven-category system, the short form would lead to 50 percent of the classifications changing.

Ryan, Larsen, and Prifitera (1983) investigated the utility of two approximated WAIS-Rs in a sample of sixty psychiatric inpatients: A two-subtest short form (Vocabulary-Block Design) and a four-subtest short form (Vocabulary-Arithmetic-Block Design-Picture Arrangement). The results were similar to Ryan (1983): Both short forms correlated highly with the Full Scale IQ (.89 and .93 for the two- and four-subtest forms respectively). Pairwise t test comparisons between means did not significantly differ between the four-subtest form and the Full Scale IQ; but the Vocabulary-Block Design form did yield a significantly higher IQ ($t(59) = 3.15$, p less than .01). Again, the IQ classification agreement was the weakest comparison: An agreement tally between the two-subtest short form and the Full Scale IQ was 63 percent for Wechsler's seven-group classification; between the four-subtest form and the Full Scale IQ the agreement tally was 72 percent. House and Lewis caution against the use of short forms when "precise IQ measurements are required."

Haynes (1983) reported a correlation of .88 between the complete WAIS-R and a Vocabulary-Block Design short form in a sample of thirty 16-year-old, adjudicated male delinquents. He found that the agreement in intelligence category classification of the delinquents between the two forms was 77 percent; no subject showed a classification change of more than one category shift. Haynes also tested short forms of the WAIS and the WISC-R. The correlation between forms for the WAIS was .89, and the agreement in intelligence classification was 84 percent (based on fifty subjects). The differences again suggest that the WAIS-R not be viewed as equivalent to the WAIS.

Silverstein (1982b) published a table of IQ equivalents for sums of scaled scores on a four-subtest short form: Vocabulary, Arithmetic, Picture Arrangement, and Block Design for the WAIS-R. This particular combination of subtests for a short form was recommended for the WAIS by Doppelt (1956). For a two-subtest short form of the WAIS-R Silverstein recommends the Vocabulary-Block Design combination. He gives an undefined estimation of standard error for the two-subtest form as 6–7 IQ points, and for the four-subtest form as 5–6 IQ points.

Reynolds, Willson, and Clark (1983) advocate the use of a four-subtest short form of the WAIS-R for clinical screening. Their choices are somewhat more novel than most short forms—Information/Arithmetic/Picture Completion/Block Design—being based on the statistical relationships between the subtests, clinical relevance (tapping different skills), and administration issues (ease and brevity of presentation). Like others, they caution against the use of their short form for diagnosis or placement decisions, but believe that this short form allows, in twenty–thirty minutes of testing time, a good estimation of general intelligence.

Discussion of approximated WAIS-R administrations does raise some interesting issues. Silverstein (1982c) has argued for the WAIS-R (and other instruments) that estimates of the validity of short forms based on a random selection of subtest scales can be used as a basis for evaluating the adequacy of selected combinations of subtests. In a follow-up discussion (1983), he maintains that, as an example, the best four-subtest WAIS-R short forms "are about as good as the short forms with five subtests selected at random." (1983, p. 373.) Feingold (1982), discussing the WAIS, had maintained the combination of Information and Vocabulary subtests correlated so highly with the Full Scale WAIS IQ that the addition of additional subtests contributed little predictive validity.

Eliminating Items Within Subtests An alternative approach to reducing the time required to administer the WAIS-R deletes selected items within some or all of the subtests. Satz and Mogel (1962) and Mogel and Satz (1963) proposed such an approach to a short form of the WAIS in which every third item of Information, Vocabulary, and Picture Completion are administered; every other item (odd only) on Comprehension, Similarities, Arithmetic, Picture Arrangement, Block Design, and Object Assembly are administered; and every item on Digit Span and Digit Symbol are administered. Several studies reported high correlations between the standard and abbreviated forms (Goebel & Satz, 1975; Holmes, Armstrong, Johnson & Ries, 1966; Marsh, 1973; Meikle, 1968; Watkins & Kinsie, 1970). Many of these same reports have, however, questioned the adequacy of the Satz and Mogel abbreviated form for profile analysis due to the introduction of exaggerated subtest scatter. Zytowski and Hudson (1965) report relatively low (below .90) validity coefficients for split-half scores correlated with whole subtest scaled scores except for Vocabulary. While the issue of profile analysis is the subject of much debate in general for the Wechsler scales, Goebel and Satz (1975) have advanced data supporting the use of profile analysis with this abbreviated form. Marsh (1973), however, cautions against profile analysis of this abbreviated WAIS. A similar approach was suggested for the WISC by Yudin (1966). Sattler's (1982b) student's manual provides a table showing "Yudin's Abbreviated Procedure for the WAIS-R" (p. 204).

Silverstein (1982d) reports calculations, based on the standardization data, of correlations between a Satz-Mogel-Yudin short form of the WAIS-R and the standard form of .94 for the Verbal scale (standard error 5.1 IQ points), .89 for the Performance scale (standard error 6.8 IQ points), and .95 for the Full Scale IQ (standard error 4.7 IQ points).

Altering Start and Stop Rules   A final alternative for reducing the time required to administer the WAIS-R is altering the level at which a subtest is begun (granting full credit for unadministered items as long as an initial criterion of some number of full passes are obtained on the initial items administered) and/or discontinuing the subtest after a lesser number of items are failed than is specified in the manual. House and Lewis suspect that informal changes of this nature are probably among the most frequent temptations for the average examiner to deviate from standard procedure—especially when dealing with apparently gifted or retarded individuals where there is increasing evidence of the examiner's ability to effectively estimate their functional level.

Vincent (1979) suggested a formal method for this type of modification for the WAIS based on the client's Information subtest score. If the client passed all Information items through number 10, then the starting point on selected Verbal subtests was estimated. If the client failed the estimated starting point, the examiner administered items in reverse order until two consecutive passes were obtained, and then worked forwards again until the discontinuation criteria were met. Vincent reported a correlation of .99 between the standard WAIS Verbal IQ and his modified administration. Similar results were reported by Ehrfurth, Phelan, and Bigler (1981) with a sample of neurologically impaired patients. Himelstein (1983) suggested a further modification of Vincent's method which extends its application by eliminating the requirement for passing the first ten Information items. The Information subtest is still used as a criterion, but the scaled score of the Information subtest is used to estimate the starting point for the Comprehension, Vocabulary, Arithmetic, and Similarities subscales. Himelstein reported a correlation of .99 between his modification of Vincent's procedure and the standard WAIS Verbal IQ in a sample of thirty-four vocational rehabilitation clients. Vincent (1979) also discussed modifications in the administration of several Performance Scale subtests. It is undoubtedly only a question of time before this or similar approaches are extended to the WAIS-R.

Short Forms of the WAIS-R

So-called short forms of the WAIS and the WAIS-R have had and probably will continue to have their champions and their critics. Wechsler (1958) and L'Abate (1964) have argued persuasively against the use of brief forms on the basis of the valuable information lost even if one is able to effectively estimate a single numerical score such as the Full Scale IQ. It seems relatively clear that one of the great strengths of the Wechsler scales have been the extent (range of difficulty) and diversity (in the kinds of tasks required) of the items. Number of items and diversity of items are two of the variables most clearly associated with the validity of ability tests. The reason the Wechsler and the Binet scales became the standards of reference in intellectual assessment derive from the comprehensiveness of their measures. Much of this is lost with abbreviated and approximated forms.

One of the most revealing criticisms against the use of short forms was clearly stated by Zimmerman and Woo-Sam (1973) in their discussion of the WAIS—the results of a short form of the WAIS (and presumably WAIS-R) are usually reported "as a WAIS, rarely as a 'brief-WAIS' score" (p. 178). Why a screening test using the WAIS-R subtests? The answer is often to appropriate the well-established reliability and validity of the Wechsler scales—which is based on full scale administrations. In this matter, House and Lewis find themselves in agreement with the recommendations of Zimmerman and Woo-Sam (1973) who suggest two alternatives to brief forms of the WAIS for screening purposes: 1) The use of either the entire Verbal or the entire Performance scales as a brief test, since both correlate well with the Full Scale IQ. This advice was taken from Ross (1959) and allows a short form that can be clearly identified as such and does not alter standard administration except with respect to the order of administration of subtests for the WAIS-R. 2) If a screening test is what is indicated or necessary, then use one of the many available brief screening tests such as the Quick Test (Ammons & Ammons, 1962) or the Shipley Institute of Living Scale (Shipley, 1946). The problem, of course, is not whether abbreviated or approximated forms of the WAIS-R can be constructed that correlate well with the Full Scale IQ—they can be constructed. Five minutes of study of the intercorrelations among the subtests and the summary IQs should make this clear. The problem is what examiners will do with the results of these brief forms. If they are going to pretend the short forms are interchangeable with Full Scale WAIS-R IQs and the rich fund of information which this is based on, then examiners deceive either the consumer or, worse, themselves.

Realizing that less information is lost with few deletions than with many, when a decision is made to reduce the length of a WAIS-R testing, House and Lewis are more comfortable with abbreviated than approximated versions of the WAIS-R. Among the Verbal subtests Vocabulary is sometimes dropped because of the time required to administer and score this subtest (Lezak, 1983) as well as the possibility that this subtest may be redundant with other data in a test battery (Lezak, 1983). Comprehension may also be eliminated due to the time required to administer and score. Unfortunately, both subtests have among the highest correlations with Verbal IQ and with the verbal comprehension factor identified in most analytic studies; additionally both subtests contribute valuable samples of the client's verbal reasoning, speech patterns, judgment, and abstracting ability.

Among the Performance subtests, Object Assembly is probably a frequent choice for deletion due to the time required to administer and the multiple factors which may reduce a client's score on this subtest (and the attendant complications of interpretation). Unfortunately, this subtest loads heavily on the spatial perception factor and is one of only two opportunities on the WAIS-R to observe the client's manipulative and construction activities. There is no final answer to the question of short forms. House has, on any number of occasions, given fewer than eleven subtests when it appeared clear that little additional useful information would be forthcoming. This decision was made in full knowledge that it represented a clinical inference (guess) of suspect validity. House and Lewis would hope that the examiner would work to become and remain cognizant of the issues involved in such choices, and would report such choices both fully and honestly enough that it is clear what has been done in the assessment.

PSYCHOMETRIC PROPERTIES OF THE WAIS-R

Reliability and Validity

Consistent with the prior history of the Wechsler scales, the reliabilities reported in the standardization sample for the WAIS-R are quite adequate, generally superior for psychometric instruments and consistent with the reliabilities and standard errors reported for the WAIS. No independent validity data are reported in the WAIS-R manual, but references are made to the data supporting the validity of the Wechsler-Bellevue Intelligence Scale (W-B) and the Wechsler Adult Intelligence Scale (WAIS). Given the basic identity in form and significant overlap in item content between the W-B, WAIS, and WAIS-R, this appears to be a defensible position. There is no real reason to suspect that the WAIS-R will not be as valid an instrument as its two predecessors. Matarazzo (1972) gives a basic review of the validity data on the Wechsler scales and the WAIS-R manual makes reference to his conclusion that the overall correlation between tests of global intelligence, including the WAIS, and school performance is in the order of .50.

Ryan, Prifitera, and Larsen (1982) have reported one investigation of the split-half reliabilities and standard errors of measurement of nine of the eleven WAIS-R subtests in a heterogeneous sample of fifty Veterans Administration psychiatric patients. Digit Span and Digit Symbol were omitted from the study since the split-half method would be inappropriate (Wechsler, 1981). The estimates of internal consistency and standard errors of measurement were generally similar to those reported in the scoring manual for the standardization sample. Only the Arithmetic subtest reliability coefficient differed significantly from that reported in the scoring manual for the thirty-five to forty-four age group, with the patient sample obtaining a reliability figure of .74 (SE_M 1.24) compared to .87 (SE_M 1.19) for the standardization sample ($z = 2.41$, p less than .05). Ryan, Prifitera, and Larsen conclude that the WAIS-R is a reliable instrument for the evaluation of a mixed psychiatric sample.

Ryan and Rosenberg (1983) have reported a validity study of the WAIS-R using sixty Veterans Administration psychiatric patients and comparing the Wide Range Achievement Test (WRAT) (Jastak & Jastak, 1978) as a measure of concurrent validity. The WAIS-R subtest scaled scores, Verbal, Performance, and Full Scale IQs were correlated with the WRAT Reading, Spelling, and Arithmetic standard scores. Of the resulting forty-two correlation coefficients, all were positive and thirty-eight were statistically significant at the .05 level (all three correlations with Object Assembly were non-significant, and the correlation between Digit Symbol and WRAT Reading was non-significant). The Verbal IQ was correlated more highly with the achievement test scores (.68, .67, and .76 for WRAT Reading, Spelling, & Arithmetic respectively) than the Performance IQ (.41, .42, and .66). Correlations between the WAIS-R Full Scale IQ and the WRAT Reading, Spelling, and Arithmetic standard scores were .62, .60, and .76 respectively. House and Lewis note that these findings are consistent with previous results reported for the WRAT and WISC-R (Sattler & Ryan, 1981) and the WRAT and WAIS (Jastak & Jastak, 1978).

WAIS/WAIS-R Comparisons

Four studies, beyond the data reported in the manual, have been carried out to date on the relationship between scores obtained on the WAIS-R and on the WAIS. Urbina, Golden, and Ariel (1982) tested a heterogeneous group of sixty-eight individuals that included both psychiatric and non-psychiatric subjects on both forms of the test. The interval between tests is reported to range from less than one day to seven months; 72 percent of the subjects are reported to have taken the WAIS first. Correlations between the subtest scaled scores, Verbal, Performance, and Full Scale IQs between the two forms were all high (range .57 to .90 for the subtests, .86 to .95 for the IQs) and statistically significant at the .05 level. All WAIS-R scaled score means and IQ means were lower than matched WAIS means, and the difference was significant at the .05 level for all subtests except Digit Span and for all IQs. An order effect of administration was noted with subjects taking the WAIS after the WAIS-R doing relatively better than subjects taking the WAIS first.

Lippold and Claiborn (1983) report a comparison of the WAIS and the WAIS-R in a clinical sample of thirty adult male Veterans Administration patients referred for neuropsychological evaluation. A combined administration procedure involving presentation of common and unique items in two orders was used to eliminate practice effects. All correlations between the two forms were reported to be statistically significant at the .001 level; correlations between the Verbal, Performance, and Full Scale IQs were given as .96, .97, and .98 respectively. A significant form effect was reported with WAIS scores higher for all IQs and all subtest scores. No order effect was found, but it is difficult to evaluate this finding clearly in light of the unusual administration procedure reported.

The most methodologically sound comparison in a clinical sample has been reported by Prifitera and Ryan (1983). The subjects were thirty-four Veterans Administration psychiatric and vocational counseling clients (thirty-two males, two females). Subjects were given both forms with the test-retest interval ranging from four to thirty-two days. The WAIS-R was administered first to fifteen subjects; the WAIS was administered first to seventeen subjects. The overall results are consistent with the previous studies and the standardization data: the two forms are highly correlated (.96, .87, and .93 for the Verbal, Performance, and Full Scale IQs repsectively), the WAIS-R yields consistently lower scores on the IQs and subtest scaled scores (all WAIS-R means were lower and all comparisons except Digit Span and Picture Arrangement were significant at the .05 level), and there is an order effect of administration with subjects taking the WAIS-R first enjoying a greater practice effect than subjects taking the WAIS first. These results are interpreted as indicating caution in interpreting results if a WAIS is used to reevaluate an individual who has been previously examined on the WAIS-R. Prifitera and Ryan voice a justified caution against assuming the two forms of the Wechsler scales are identical and call for further investigation before automatically replacing the WAIS with the WAIS-R in standardized neuropsychological batteries.

An interesting contrast in findings is reported by Smith (1983) for a comparison using a college population sample. The WAIS and the WAIS-R were administered in counterbalanced order to seventy college students (twenty-two males, forty-eight females). The test-retest interval varied from one week to one month. Again the tests were highly correlated and the WAIS-R usually yielded lower scaled scores and IQs, but the order effect was different—the practice effect was more pronounced for those subjects who had taken the WAIS first. Smith concludes that the WAIS-R is not an equivalent form of the WAIS, and if reevaluation is necessary within a short interval, when a client had previously been tested on the WAIS, the clinician might be advised to use a readministration of the WAIS rather than a WAIS-R. It is not clear whether the contrasting results of Smith with other studies is due to his use of a generally brighter, non-clinical college sample. This is an area which needs further investigation.

By way of a conservative summary of findings with respect to WAIS-R/WAIS comparisons the following conclusions seem justified: The two forms are highly correlated and both are probably yielding comparable estimates of global intelligence. WAIS-R subtest scaled scores and IQs are usually lower than WAIS subtest scaled scores and IQs; this effect may be more pronounced for older samples. There appears to be a complex order effect of testing with the WAIS and WAIS-R which may interact with other client characteristics, possibly education, age, or global intelligence.

Confidence Intervals and Standard Error(s)

On the basis of the standardization sample, Naglieri calculated IQ confidence intervals for the three IQ scores for the 85 percent, 90 percent, 95 percent, and 99 percent level of confidence. Knight (1983) suggests, however, that both Naglieri and the WAIS-R manual present a misleading interpretation of the standrd error of measurement. Knight discusses three formulas for calculation of standard error and presents values for each age group for the two interpretations of standard error not calculated in the manual. Knight also gives a table of the percentile abnormality of Verbal-Performance IQ discrepancies for the WAIS-R. Dudek (1979) discusses errors in the interpretation of the standard error of measurement.

Bias and Examiner Error

Concern over possible sociocultural item bias in mental testing is a critical feature of the current debate over IQ testing (Bersoff, 1981; Jensen, 1980; Reschly, 1981), despite equivocal evidence of significant item bias in the Wechsler scales for American sociocultural groups (cf. Hale, 1983; Ross-Reynolds & Reschly, 1983). In a study of the WAIS-R Information subtest with 150 Canadian psychiatric patients Bornstein, McLeod, McClung, and Hutchison (1983) found little evidence of American cultural bias. Their results, in fact, led them to recommend against the routine a priori Canadianization of Information items 1, 6, 22, and 27 which had become an accepted Canadian modifictaion of the WAIS. Of the new WAIS-R Information items, only Items 8 and 14 showed evidence of content bias. Bornstein et al., however, did find indications that the WAIS-R order of item difficulty may not be applicable to a Canadian sample, and suggests it may be necessary to administer all Information items to Canadian clients. A recent dissertation by Armstrong (1983) questions the use of the WAIS-R with Chicano students. The area of sociocultural content bias will undoubtedly remain the subject of much controversy and some rational investigation.

Problems of examiner scoring error or scoring bias is another topic of concern to professional examiners. In a study of WAIS administration and scoring, Franklin, Stillman, Burpeau & Sabers (1982) found a disturbingly high frequency of errors being committed by practicing school psychologists and by graduate students in school psychology eligible for state certification as psychological examiners. The most common examiner errors involved failing to credit responses with accurate point assignments and premature discontinuance of subtests. In an analogous study using college undergraduates trained to administer four WAIS Verbal subtests, Donahue and Sattler (1971) reported that "examiners" who liked their clients and who found the client warm awarded more point credit in scoring than they did to clients who were less liked and rated as being less warm. This is a disturbing finding due to the possibility of systematic bias. It is not clear, however, to what degree these results should be generalized to well-trained examiners in real life assessment situations. Ryan, Prifitera, and Powers (1983) in a study of examiner scoring reliability on the WAIS-R found scoring errors to occur frequently despite the experience of the examiner in psychological testing (psychologist or psychology graduate student). Ryan et al. recommend that IQ values be reported in conjunction with a precision range based on the standard error of measurement of the test. Certainly the examiner needs to be aware of the high risk of administration and scoring error, needs to be vigilant for the occurrence of mechanical scoring errors and arithmetic errors, and needs to cross-check results sufficiently to avoid gross misinterpretation. Similar findings of frequent scoring errors have been previously found for the WISC (Miller & Chansky, 1970, 1972).

INTERPRETATION

The Place of the WAIS-R in Psychological Assessment

Psychological tests are in essence nothing more than collections of things: colored blocks, poorly reproduced pictures, reproductions of inkblots, lists of words to be defined, and multiple-choice questions of occupational preference. It is the use of these stimuli materials by trained and experienced examiners that determines their value and the reference data against which an individual's performance can be compared. It seems appropriate, then, before considering specifics of WAIS-R interpretation, to review briefly the major uses to which the WAIS-R may be applied. The principal application of the WAIS-R, of course, is as a measure of intelligence, and the specific role it can play in the assessment of mental retardation, the determination of intellectual disability, and vocational assessment and planning. Another important application of the WAIS-R is as a test of brain function and integrity. The field of neuropsychological assessment is emerging from a period of struggle and immaturity into a stage of professional and empirical credibility. Although the days when neuropsychological tests were equated with a WAIS and a Bender Gestalt are gone, the WAIS-R will continue to occupy an important role within the assessment of brain-behavior relationships. The third role the Wechsler tests have played is that of a test of personality: symptomatic difficulties, coping abilities, and personality structure have been inferred from the Wechsler scale pattern.

The WAIS-R as a Test of Intelligence   Foremost and always, the WAIS-R, like its predecessors, was designed for the comprehensive assessment of general intelligence. Intelligence is one of those concepts within psychology, like anxiety, which prove so vexing and troublesome in conceptualization and definition that they would undoubtedly have been discarded long ago had they not proved so perversely useful and necessary. For Wechsler, the concept of intelligence that guided his work remained clear and compelling across most of his professional life—intelligence is the ability of an organism to deal effectively with its world, and the purpose of intelligence tests is to measure this general ability.

> What we measure with tests is not what tests measure—not information, not spatial perception, not reasoning ability. These are only means to an end. What intelligence tests measure, what we hope they measure, is something much more important: the capacity of an individual to understand the world about him and his resourcefulness to cope with its challenges. (Wechsler, 1975, p. 139)

The measurement of intelligence has been the theoretical rationale of intelligence testing, but the practical impetus has usually come from the opposite direction. It is the assessment of limitations of intelligence, of failures to cope, of deficiencies in understanding and resourcefulness that have fueled the development and application of intelligence testing. The social revolutions of the nineteenth century, which led to the widespread introduction of public education in the Western world, led just as surely to the forced recognition of individual differences in academic success as profound and as limiting as the overturned class concepts. It was out of this cultural matrix the Binet scales were first developed. Although less profound or pervasive in social impact, it was the similar need for widespread detection of intellectual limitations in the inductees of World War I that led to the development of the Army Alpha and Beta tests and turned the attention of academic psychology again to a practical concern with intellectual assessment. An important application of intelligence testing in adults, and the Wechsler scales in particular, has been the identification and delineation of mental retardation.

Modern conceptions of mental retardation have become intimately wedded to the individually administered, comprehensive intelligence test and to the concept of statistical deviation from the general population in composite abilities. The Wechsler scales are, without doubt, the standard of reference for the determination of limited intellectual functioning in the adult population. There is widespread professional acceptance of the 3 percent criterion: Scores depressed more than two standard deviations from the general population mean constitute the retarded range. Despite recognition of the difficulties in defining mental retardation exclusively as a function of tested IQ and the provision of criteria regarding impairment of adaptive behavior which must also be met in diagnosing retardation, the simple truth is that for practical purposes mental retardation is scoring below 69 on a Wechsler scale or a comparable device. There are several reasons for this: Existing tools for assessing adaptive behavior are not as successful as intelligence tests. Often the precipitating events that led to referral for intellectual assessment are taken as *prima facie* evidence of social impairment. While an unsupported or uncollaborated subjective impression of an examiner that a client is retarded would be generally viewed as unacceptable by professional examiners, the same psychologist could probably judge and report a client to be showing significant impairment of adaptive behavior and encounter little challenge in peer consultation.

Against this background of conceptual and procedural confusion, the individually administered intelligence test appears as a reliable, objective, and empirical standard for the establishment of intellectual impairment. The examiner of adult individuals has largely escaped the controversy, litigation, and legislation which has surrounded the use of IQ scores in the evaluation, placement, and qualification of children for educational and social programs. In disability adjudication decisions for most states, the IQ score obtained by a comprehensive, individually administered test of general intelligence (generally the appropriate Wechsler scale or the Stanford-Binet) plays the principal role.

The WAIS-R in Vocational Assessment   Another important role for the WAIS-R is the contribution it makes to vocational assessment and planning. In the comprehensive vocational assessment, global ability measures add to the psychological picture obtained by occupational interest tests, personality inventories, and tests of specific skills and abilities. In addition to the global IQ scores obtained from the WAIS-R, the richness of hypotheses that can be obtained from the scaled scores and individual items of the WAIS-R can be invaluable in suggesting potentially profitable lines of inquiry for vocational counseling or for further specific follow-up testing. Some caution, however, must be advised in overinterpreting the WAIS-R in vocational counseling. The prediction of success at human endeavors is a risky business, and many factors beyond intelligence may differentiate the winners from the losers: especially factors such as motivation, commitment, and self-discipline. While it is easier for the highly intelligent individual to accomplish many given challenges than it is for the lesser endowed individual, this is not to say it is any more or less possible for either to do so. Once measured intelligence exceeds a certain minimal level, non-intellectual factors such as drive and persistence are often more important in whether an individual can succeed in a given occupational course. Clients may be capable of obtaining the training needed for a skilled position, if they are willing to devote their whole lives to this task. Clients may, after considering the choices, decide they are unwilling to make the total commitment of time, energy, and restricted activities necessary to succeed. To the examiner this may or may not seem the best choice, but it is the client's life and his or her choice. The possesser of specialized and somewhat secret knowledge must guard against the vanity of assumed omniscience—as psychological assessors, examiners should be careful about assuming of what a client is or is not capable. What they are capable of will depend on many things, only some of which will be measured by psychological instruments, and of all of these factors, their tested intelligence should be only one consideration.

The WAIS-R as a Test of Brain Integrity   The Wechsler scales are important in neuropsychological evaluations and have been incorporated as elements in many neuropsychological batteries such as the Halstead-Reitan battery. Extensive research has been carried out with the W-B and the WAIS, and the interested reader is referred to the relevant sections of Lezak (1983) and Matarazzo (1972) for valuable introductions to this area. No studies have yet comprehensively evaluated the WAIS-R's contribution to neuropsychological testing. Lezak

(1983) indicates a belief that the strong structural and item similarities will lead to little significant change in the results obtained with the WAIS. As noted above in the factorial studies, however, some questions have been raised about the interchangeability of the WAIS and the WAIS-R. Regardless of the apparent similarities between the two versions of the Wechsler scales, independent empirical verification of possible brain-behavior relationships will be a desirable contribution to the WAIS-R literature. Even for the WAIS, empirical investigations suggested the necessity of considerable caution in neuropsychological inferences (Black, 1980; Lehman, Chelune & Heaton, 1979; Leli & Filskov, 1981; Todd, Coolidge & Satz, 1977; Vogt & Heaton, 1977). Even the commonly accepted inferences of significance to differences between the WAIS Verbal IQ and the Performance IQ are called into question by the possibility that the factor structure of intelligence scales may differ in brain-injured populations (Zimmerman, Whitmyre & Fields, 1970). The Wechsler Verbal factor may show greater recovery after brain insult than the spatial factor (Lansdell & Smith, 1975), and the WAIS version of the W-B may have introduced systematic artifact into the VIQ/PIQ difference. Rather than be constantly surprised (and disappointed) by failures to establish simple brain-behavior relationships, perhaps examiners should ponder the possibility that understanding one of the most complex structures known, will probably be one of the most complex tasks ever undertaken.

The WAIS-R as a Test of Personality As discussed later in the section on psychosis, the literature on using the Wechsler scales as an instrument for personality assessment is largely negative. This is not to say that there are not well-established empirical relationships between various personality patterns and Wechsler performance. For instance, a finding of higher Performance IQ than Verbal IQ has been well documented in conduct disorder samples of adolescents (Gibbs, 1982; Matarazzo, 1972; Sacuzzo & Lewandowski, 1976). The problem is that the relationships are not unique to personality/Wechsler scale relationships. Many factors can yield a higher Performance than Verbal IQ and it is not safe to infer personality pattern from WAIS or WAIS-R subtest scaled score pattern. Baron (1982) has discussed the difficulties in interpreting the correlation of personality measures with intelligence.

Nevertheless, WAIS data have been included in some interesting and ingenious studies of personality using profile analysis. Gibbs (1982) reports finding three distinctive WAIS/WISC-R patterns in a study of forty-eight delinquent females that were important in a diagnostic differentiation of personality types. Amolsch and Henrichs have produced an intriguing series of studies detailing an actuarial personality description from WAIS profile patterns (Amolsch & Henrichs, 1975; Henrichs & Amolsch, 1978; Henrichs, Krauskopf & Amolsch, 1982). These studies provide an invaluable source of interpretative hypotheses to be considered in Wechsler scale results. The bulk of the available literature, however, raises severe doubts about the uncritical use of WAIS or WAIS-R profile analysis in personality or psychiatric diagnosis (Blatt & Allison, 1968; Frank, 1970, 1976; Holmes, 1968; Rabin, 1965; Schofield, 1952; Shimkunas, Grohamann & Zwibelman, 1971; Wentworth-Rohr & MacIntosh, 1972). Similar difficulties have been reported with the WAIS-R (Berk, 1983; Hale & Landino, 1981).

Client Characteristics Affecting Interpretation

A number of situational or state characteristics of clients may interact with the testing experience to affect their WAIS-R performance. Unfortunately, several of the potentially most significant variables have received little or no systematic investigation, and the examiner is forced to rely on clinical lore and conventional wisdom.

Anxiety Excessive tension and anxiety is believed by most examiners to adversely affect WAIS (and by extrapolation WAIS-R) performance on tasks such as Digit Span requiring concentration and attention. It does seem the case that state or situational anxiety interferes with subtests such as Arithmetic, Digit Span, and probably Digit Symbol. It is less clear whether high trait anxiety has such a clear suppressive effect. Mishra (1982) was unable to demonstrate a relationship between the Taylor Manifest Anxiety Scale score and WAIS Verbal score, but she analyzed her results by total Verbal score, not by subtest.

Medication House and Lewis were unable to discover any systematic research of drug effects due to prescription medication on WAIS or WAIS-R performance. This is a glaring deficiency in the data base given the known psychomotor effects of neuroleptics and the high chance that psychiatric or neuropsychological patients referred for intellectual assessment may be taking one or more psychotropic medications. For the present all that can be stated is that the examiner should take care to inquire if the client is taking any prescription medication and cautiously interpret the scores of subtests requiring fine motor control of patients taking neuroleptics. Patients receiving other medications such as antidepressants, anticonvulsants, or lithium should be queried carefully as to psychomotor effects they have noticed in manual or speech expression.

Psychosis   The use of the Wechsler scales to make inferences regarding the psychiatric status of the client has a long history. Gilliland (1941) was one of the first to discuss the use of scatter on the W-B as a pathologic indicator. The classic volume by Rapaport, Gill, and Schafer (1945) was undoubtedly influential in stimulating the attempted use of the W-B as a diagnostic instrument for behavioral disorders including schizophrenia. Weiner (1966) included the WAIS as an important source of information and inference in his cogent and scholarly *Psychodiagnosis in Schizophrenia*. This clinical utilization proceeded parallel to a growing body of literature documenting the failure of the Wechsler scales to allow the accurate diagnosis of psychiatric disorders or to effectively discriminate between schizophrenia and organic brain syndromes (Blatt & Allison, 1968; Frank, 1970, 1976; Holmes, 1968; Rabin, 1965; Schofield, 1952; Shimkunas, Grohmann & Zwibelman, 1971; Wentworth-Rohr & MacIntosh, 1972).

The issue is not whether the Wechsler scales are valuable sources of examples of the client's cognitive functioning, judgment, and reasoning; or whether the Wechsler scales provide a rich source of hypotheses regarding the client's adjustment, personality dynamics, and potential conflicts and liabilities—the answer to both questions is clearly affirmative. The WAIS was a wonderful source of hypotheses, as indeed almost any diversified experience lasting sixty to ninety minutes with a client would be. The issue is whether the WAIS (and now the WAIS-R) could do something that it was never intended to do: diagnose and classify personality structure, dynamics, and psychopathology. It cannot, and there is no reason to expect the WAIS-R will be able to better this performance.

Holmes (1968) has pointed out that much of the speculation on diagnostic and personality interpretations of the WAIS appeared to be based on two questionable assumptions: First, the presence of severe psychopathology is usually going to interfere with clients' utilization of their intellectual capacities and lead to suppression of test scores. Second, normal individuals would obtain nearly equal subtest scaled scores. Holmes' data, as well as other studies, raise serious doubts about the viability of these assumptions. Another questionable assumption in older psychological literature is the supposition that schizophrenia is a functional disorder which should be easily discriminated from so-called organic disorders. The current literature on psychosis, especially schizophrenia, and advances in neuropsychology cast considerable doubt on the wisdom of seeking to differentiate between functional and organic psychoses.

Age Effects on the WAIS-R   The method of standardization of the WAIS-R results in an equal raw score earning increasing scaled score points after thirty-five years of age. The shifting age norms differentially reward retention of Performance task abilities; reflecting the greater decrement noted in these subscales with advancing age. Sattler (1982c) has displayed the effects of age corrections on the raw score needed to obtain a scaled score of 10; and the minimum raw scores needed to obtain a raw score of 10 for these age groups. Given these considerations, it is often of interpretative value to examine the age-scaled scores for the subtests as well as the reference group scaled scores; this allows a comparison of the client's level of achievement with a similar age group as well as with the criterion age group.

Storandt (1977) in her study of age and administration methods on the WAIS concluded that the standard cutoff times for timed subtests were applicable for older clients—their elimination contributed to significantly increased scores only for Picture Completion. She did find that bonus points for rapid solutions operate differentially in favor of the young, and questioned their applicability in situations where speed of performance would not be of interest. Finally, she reported that the standard discontinuance criteria for Arithmetic and for Block Design yield a slight underestimation of the capability of the older client on these tasks. This would suggest that testing the limits on these two subtests and on Picture Completion might be especially valuable for the older client. It remains to be seen if these findings will also be demonstrated for the WAIS-R.

Lezak (1983) cites a finding by Savage (1973) that clients over the age of seventy tend to be sensitive to failures and suggests that following standard administration with respect to the discontinuance criteria may produce negative reactions in older clients. She recommends an early discontinuance to reduce the older client's discomfort. If it appears that the client might have been capable of achieving a higher level, this can be noted and the subtest returned to at a later time, after the client's performance concern has dissipated. Lezak's general orientation is to use the instrument to help learn what the client can do and to obtain this information in the most humane way possible.

Gifted Individuals A rather academic limitation of the WAIS-R is the relatively low ceiling on the IQ tables for the standardization sample, and one sometimes hears that the WAIS-R is not the best instrument for the assessment of the gifted. The question of what would be a suitable instrument for measuring the capability of an individual who is probably more intelligent and creative than the examiner is an interesting one, but seems to have limited practical merit. Truly gifted individuals usually have better things to do than worry about the accuracy of their IQs and there is little indication that conventional intellectual assessments are useful in their career or life planning as adults.

Sensory Limitations   The WAIS-R Verbal subtests can be used as part of the assessment of blind and visually handicapped individuals. It is often useful to supplement this information with data from instruments designed for the blind (Davis, 1980; Shurrager & Shurrager, 1964).

The WAIS-R Performance subtests can be administered relatively easily to deaf and hearing-impaired individuals. The Verbal subtests can be administered through signing, and the client's fluency and comprehension of American Sign Language and/or finger spelling are important data to obtain in the assessment of hearing-impaired individuals. It is strongly urged that the examiner who is not fluent with signing and finger spelling not attempt the assessment of a deaf individual without the services of a qualified translator. There are few situations that will lead to stupid conclusions more quickly than doing a psychological assessment of an individual with whom you cannot communicate.

Motor Limitations   Clients with limitations in motor control or strength can be administered the WAIS-R Verbal subtests without difficulty, and the Picture Completion subtest can also be administered validly. It is generally worthless and unnecessarily frustrating to the client to administer Block Design, Object Assembly, or Digit Symbol when clearly established motor limitation exists. The suitability of Picture Arrangement will depend on the scope and nature of the motor difficulty. Picture Arrangement can often be administered in modified form by having the client verbally indicate the order in which the pictures should be arranged. This modification is facilitated by the elimination of bonus points for rapid performance on Picture Arrangement on the WAIS-R.

Communication Limitations   The valid assessment of intellectual functioning in the client with significant impairment of verbal communication is one of the most challenging demands placed on the qualified examiner. The Performance subtests can usually be administered without alteration. The suitability of modified administration of the Verbal subtest scales (for instance, by replacing vocal with written communication) will obviously depend on the nature and scope of the communication impairment. It is usually desirable to supplement the WAIS-R with additional instruments such as the Peabody Picture Vocabulary Test-Revised (Dunn & Dunn, 1981).

Client Faking   Still another client factor which must be considered during interpretation is the possibility of deliberate dissimulation and underachievement—faking bad. Some intellectual assessment is carried out within the context of disability determination, and substantial financial consequences may follow the adjudication of disability. Clients may consciously wish to qualify for compensation or special services; or they may be responding to the subtle (or not so subtle) communication from their family that everyone would be better off if they "showed these people" how badly they need "help" (money/services/placement).

Distortion by the sophisticated and intelligent client may be difficult to detect or demonstrate with any degree of certainty, especially if the examination is limited to intellectual and academic achievement measures. Fortunately (for the examiner as an agent of society) those individuals most likely to attempt to fake a retarded score are often limited (if in nothing else) in their ability to effectively simulate a disability. The most common error among deliberate fakers is a gross underproduction of ability that is obviously inconsistent with their daily activities and achievements.

House once assessed an individual seeking disability compensation due to alleged mental retardation. A previous application had been rejected when the examiner concluded that the client was faking his poor Wechsler performance. The client had failed literally every item on the WAIS. But, as the previous examiner reported, the client had been able to locate the psychologist's office without difficulty, was able to read the bus schedule in his pocket, and was able to clearly express his hope the psychologist could quickly file his report because several potential plans of the client's depended on the anticipated disability award. The examiner simply pointed out that these and additional documented demonstrations of competency were inconsistent with the pattern of total item failure.

When the same client was reexamined by House, it was clear that the client had learned something from his previous failure. The client no longer failed every item on the WAIS-R, but passed every fourth item on most of the subtests. Unfortunately for the client, the fail, fail, fail, pass pattern was quite regular, which the examiner pointed out was an unusual occurrence. Also, it allowed the client to pass items much more difficult than the previously failed items. Both the regularity and the magnitude of the difference argued against this being a functional or organic scatter. The examiner again concluded that the client was faking the test, but did suggest that it appeared he was learning how to take the Wechsler scales and that a different instrument might be necessary for the next application. Few cases are this grossly obvious, but the examiner should be alert to unusual client performance and attempt to understand the meaning of atypical results. The vast majority of clients are cooperative and interested in doing as well as possible on the tasks versus those certain deviations that can be identified by the attentive examiner.

Analysis of WAIS-R Results

Interpretation of the WAIS-R usually will begin with the Full Scale IQ; proceed to the comparison of the Verbal IQ and the Performance IQ; and (depending on the training, beliefs, and preferences of the examiner) continue to the consideration of individual subtest scaled scores, comparison of subtest scaled scores, computation of age-scaled scores, averaged Verbal and Performance scaled scores, factor scores, confidence intervals, Deterioration Index, etc. (Edwards, 1972; Maloney & Ward, 1976; Matarazzo, 1972; Zimmerman & Woo-Sam, 1973). Given the current doubt, certainty, criticism, and defense surrounding intelligence testing in general, it might be fair to say the activity begins in controversy and degenerates from there. Certainly the most conservative use of the WAIS-R is the use that was always the primary intention of its author as a global measure of general intelligence. The Full Scale WAIS-R IQ represents one of the best available measures of the intelligence of a client in the most commonly understood usage of that word (Wechsler, 1958, 1975). For clinical, statistical, and administrative purposes IQs are usually translated into functional categories of intelligence (i.e., average, superior, profoundly retarded, etc.). The WAIS-R manual uses the same Intelligence Classifications presented in the WAIS and W-B manuals (Wechsler, 1944, 1955, 1981). One of the most widely used alternative classifications for adults would probably be the system in DSM III (American Psychiatric Association, 1980). It should be noted that not all agree with the use of the Full Scale IQ as the most conservative result of the WAIS-R (see Lezak, 1983, for a critique of the use of the averaged IQ).

Beyond the use of the Full Scale IQ as a global estimate of intellectual ability, the interested reader enters into a statistical and methodological battleground. The issues are usually cast not so much in terms of whether there is additional information contained in the WAIS-R results beyond the Full Scale IQ, but rather in how to best extract that information. Based on results of their factor analysis of items for nine of the WAIS subtests, Klinger and Saunders (1975) reported the subtests were not pure factors and that there was more information to be had on the WAIS than was conveyed in the subtests' scaled scores. Still, the most common approach to a molecular analysis of the WAIS-R will probably be in terms of a comparison of scaled scores (or their averages such as Verbal IQ) against other scaled scores or averages. Silverstein (1982e) advises a profile analysis of the Wechsler scales (including the WAIS-R) by comparison of each subtest scaled score against the mean Verbal or mean Performance subtest scaled score. As Silverstein points out, this is the approach recommended by Wechsler in 1941. Silverstein provides a useful table for making these comparisons for the WAIS, WAIS-R, WISC, and WISC-R.

House and Lewis believe that valuable hypotheses can be formed on the basis of the comparison of Verbal and Performance IQs; on the basis of comparison of subtest scaled scores; on the basis of profile analysis as recommended by Silverstein; and on the basis of factor scores for verbal comprehension, spatial ability, and memory/freedom from distractibility factors. It is important, however, to be ever cognizant of the fact that these will be only hypotheses needing confirmation or disconfirmation on the basis of additional data. In the absence of corrective feedback, it is all too easy for the examiner to fall into the pattern of over-interpretation of psychological test data. A further caution is the need for empirical studies of the validity, for the WAIS-R, of subscale relationships believed to hold for the WAIS.

The Deterioration Quotient   Wechsler's deterioration index (see Matarazzo, 1972; Zimmerman & Woo-Sam, 1973, for calculation formula) was based on his belief that certain tests withstood the effects of aging (and presumably brain insult in general) better and could be considered "Hold" tests (Information, Vocabulary, Picture Completion, and Object Assembly); whereas other tests declined more precipitously with advancing age (and presumably brain injury) and could be designated "Don't Hold" (Similarities, Digit Span, Block Design, and Digit Symbol). Although the deterioration quotient concept stimulated much valuable research, the results have been largely disappointing (see Lezak, 1983, and Matarazzo, 1972, for discussions of the DQ literature). It is extremely doubtful that research with the WAIS-R will be any more supportive of simple brain-behavior relationships (see discussion of the WAIS-R as a measure of brain integrity).

Presentation of WAIS-R Results

The final result of a psychological assessment is usually a written report or case note. A range of variation can be found regarding the best organization and content for a psychological report. In particular, the question of whether or not to include a client's IQs or scaled scores in the body of the report is often met with different answers by different authorities. Concerns range from the limited ability of psychologists to restrict the access to written documents to the potential misinterpretation of the IQ concept by the consumers of psychological testing. One alternative to reporting IQs is to report confidence intervals. House and Lewis, however, tend to agree with the concerns of Hale (1983) over this practice. He points out that examiners often use confidence bands that are technically incorrect, but more importantly raises the critical concern that: "The belief that typical readers can interpret scores written in a confidence interval format with less ambiguity than point scores is, as far as the author knows, unsupported by empirical evidence." (Hale, 1983, p. 371.) His own suggestion is that examiners report only what the test results mean in terms of functional level and exclude standard scores from the report. The difficulty here is that an increasing number of consumers (Disability Adjudication Boards, for instance) are requiring the inclusion of standard scores in a report so they can draw their own conclusions regarding functional level. It is House's practice to include IQs and scaled scores within the body of his reports. As an integral part of this practice he accepts the responsibility of educating the consumers of his assessments as to the proper interpretation of these standard scores and is prepared to discuss with clients both their scores and what these numbers mean.

SUMMARY

House and Lewis found the Wechsler scales to be valuable sources of quantative and qualitative information in their psychological evaluation of clients. Their experience to date with the WAIS-R is consistent with their prior experience with the WAIS. There are important differences between the two versions, however, and considerable empirical investigation remains to be done before definite conclusions can be drawn as to what inferences, based on WAIS-R data, are most valid and meaningful. The WAIS-R student is strongly encouraged to sample heavily the available research literature, especially the factorial analytic investigations of the WAIS-R, WAIS, and W-B. The reader is further encouraged to remain attentive to his or her client and stay open to valuable qualitative observations. There is great cost in losing the distinction between the WAIS-R as a test instrument and psychological assessment as a process of knowledgeable decision making. For House and Lewis, psychological assessment is ultimately not the measurement of concepts such as intelligence but rather the understanding of another individual. In this attempt the WAIS-R can play an important role.

REFERENCES

American Psychiatric Association. (1980). *Diagnostic and statistical manual of mental disorders,* (3rd Ed.). Washington, DC: American Psychiatric Association.
Ammons, R. B. & Ammons, C. H. (1962). The quick test (QT): Provisional manual. *Psychological Reports, 11,* 111–161.

Amolsch, T. J. & Henrichs, T. F. (1975). Behavioral correlates of WAIS profile patterns: An exploratory study. *Journal of Personality Assessment, 39,* 55–63.

Amstrong, E. J. (1983). The extent of bias for the WAIS-R for Chicano and White high school students. *Dissertation Abstracts International, 43*(09), 2971–A.

Berger, L., Bernstein, A., Klein, E., Cohen, J., & Lucas, G. (1964). Effects of aging and pathology on the factorial structure of intelligence. *Journal of Consulting Psychology, 28,* 199–207.

Berk, R. A. (1983). The value of WISC-R profile analysis for the differential diagnosis of learning disabled children. *Journal of Clinical Psychology, 39*(1), 133–136.

Baron, J. (1982). Personality and intelligence. In R. J. Sternberg (Ed.), *Handbook of Human Intelligence.* New York: Cambridge University Press, 308–351.

Benton, A. L., Hamsher, K. deS., Varney, N. R., & Spreen, O. (1983). *Contributions to neuropsychological assessment.* New York: Oxford University Press, Inc.

Benton, A. L., Van Allen, M. W, & Fogel, M. L. (1964). Temporal orientation in cerebral disease. *Journal of Nervous and Mental Disease, 139,* 110–119.

Bersoff, D. (1981). Testing and the law. *American Psychologist, 36,* 1047–1056.

Black, F. W. (1980). WAIS Verbal-Performance discrepancies as predictors of lateralization in patients with discrete brain lesions. *Perceptual and Motor Skills, 51,* 213–214.

Blaha, J. & Wallbrown, F. H. (1982). Hierarchical factor structure of the Wechsler Adult Intelligence Scale-Revised. *Journal of Consulting and Clinical Psychology, 50,* 652–660.

Blatt, S. J. & Allison, J. (1968). The intelligence test in personality assessment. In A. I. Rabin, *Projective Techniques in Personality Assessment.* New York: Springer Publishing Co., Inc. 421–460.

Block, N. J. & Dworkin, G. (Eds.). (1976). *The IQ controversy.* New York: Pantheon Books, Inc.

Blum, J. M. (1978). *Pseudoscience and mental ability.* New York: Monthly Review Press.

Bornstein, R. A., McLeod, J., McClung, E., & Hutchison, B. (1983). Item difficulty and content bias on the WAIS-R Information subtest. *Canadian Journal of Behavioral Science, 15*(1), 27–34.

Carroll, J. B. (1979). How shall we study individual differences in cognitive abilities?—methodological and theoretical perspectives. In R. J. Sternberg & D. K. Detterman (Eds.). *Human Intelligence: Perspectives on Its Theory and Measurement.* Norwood, New Jersey: Ablex Publishing Corporation, 3–31.

Carter, J. W., Jr. & Bowles, J. W. (1948). A manual on qualitative aspects of psychological examining. Clinical Psychology Monographs (No. 2). *Journal of Clinical Psychology, 4,* 110–150.

Cassel, R. H. (1962). The order of the tests in the battery. *Journal of Clinical Psychology, 18,* 464–465.

Cattell, R. B. (1966). The scree test for the number of factors. *Multivariate Behavioral Research, 1,* 245.

Cohen, J. (1952). Factors underlying Wechsler-Bellevue performance on three neuropsychiatric groups. (a). *Journal of Abnormal and Social Psychology, 47,* 359–365.

Cohen, J. (1952). A factor-analytically based rationale for the Wechsler-Bellevue. (b). *Journal of Consulting Psychology, 16,* 272–277.

Cohen, J. (1957). The factorial structure of the WAIS between early adulthood and old age. (a). *Journal of Consulting Psychology, 21,* 283–290.

Cohen, J. (1957). A factor-analytically based rationale for the Wechsler Adult Intelligence Scale. (b). *Journal of Consulting Psychology, 21,* 451–457.

Crawford, C. B. (1975). Determining the number of interpretable factors. *Psychological Bulletin, 82,* 226–237.

Davis, C. J. (1980). *Perkins-Binet Tests of Intelligence for the Blind.* Watertown, Massachusetts: Perkins School for the Blind.

Donahue, D. & Sattler, J. M. (1971). Personality variables affecting WAIS scores. *Journal of Consulting and Clinical Psychology, 36,* 441.

Doppelt, J. E. (1956). Estimating the Full Scale score on the Wechsler Adult Intelligence Scale from scores on four subtests. *Journal of Consulting Psychology, 20,* 63–66.

Dudek, F. J. (1979). The continuing misinterpretation of the standrad error of measurement. *Psychological Bulletin, 86,* 335–337.

Dunn, L. & Dunn, L. (1981). *Peabody Picture Vocabulary Test-Revised.* Circle Pines, Minnesota: American Guidance Service.

Edwards, A. J. (1972). *Individual mental testing. Part II measurement.* Scranton, Pennsylvania: Intext Educational Publishers.

Ehrfurth, J. W., Phelan, C., & Bigler, E. D. (1981). The utility of a short form, modified WAIS with a neurologic patient population. *Clinical Neuropsychology, 3,* 42–43.

Eysenck, H. J. & Kamin, L. (1981). *The intelligence controversy.* New York: Wiley-Interscience.

Feingold, A. (1982). The validity of the information and vocabulary subtests of the WAIS. *Journal of Clinical Psychology, 38,* 169–174.

Frank, G. H. (1970). The measurement of personality from the Wechsler tests. In B. Mahrer (Ed.). *Progress in Experimental Personality Research.* New York: Academic Press, Inc.

Frank, G. H. (1976). Measures of intelligence and conceptual thinking. In I. B. Weiner (Ed.). *Clinical Methods in Psychology.* New York: Wiley-Interscience, 123–186.

Franklin, M. R., Jr., Stillman, P. L., Burpeau, M. Y., & Sabers, D. L. (1982). Examiner error in intelligence testing: Are you a source? *Psychology in the Schools, 19,* 563–569.

French, J. L. (1979). Intelligence: Its measurement and its relevance for education. *Professional Psychology, 10,* 753–759.

Gibbs, J. T. (1982). Personality patterns of delinquent females: Ethnic and sociocultural variations. *Journal of Clinical Psychology, 38*(1), 198–206.

Gilliland, A. R. (1941). Differential functional loss in certan psychoses. *Psychological Bulletin, 38,* 715.

Goebel, R. A. & Satz, P. (1975). Profile analysis and the abbreviated Wechsler Adult Intelligence Scale: A multivariate approach. *Journal of Consulting and Clinical Psychology, 43,* 780–785.

Golden, C. J. (1979). *Clinical interpretation of objective psychological interpretation.* New York: Grune & Stratton, Inc.

Golden, C. J. (1981). *Diagnosis and rehabilitation in clinical neuropsychology* (2nd Ed.). Springfield, Illinois: Charles C Thomas, Publisher.

Gorsuch, R. L. (1974). *Factor analysis.* Philadelphia, Pennsylvania: Saunders.

Guilford, J. P. (1975). Factors and factors of personality. *Psychological Bulletin, 82,* 802–814.

Guilford, J. P. (1980). Fluid and crystallized intelligences: Two fanciful concepts. *Psychological Bulletin, 88,* 406–412.

Hale, R. L. (1983). Intellectual assessment. In Hersen, M., Kazdin, A. E., & Bellack, A. S. *The Clinical Psychology Handbook*. New York: Pergamon Press, Inc., 345–376.

Hale, R. L. & Landino, S. A. (1981). Utility of WISC-R subtest analysis in discriminating among groups of conduct problem, withdrawn, mixed, and nonproblem boys. *Journal of Consulting and Clinical Psychology, 49,* 91–95.

Haynes, J. P. (1983). Comparative validity of three Wechsler short forms for delinquents. *Journal of Clinical Psychology, 39,* 275–278.

Henrichs, T. F. & Amolsch, T. J. (1978). A note on the actuarial interpretation of WAIS profile patterns. *Journal of Personality Assessment, 42*(4), 418–420.

Henrichs, T. F., Krauskopf, C. J., & Amolsch, T. J. (1982). Personality description from the WAIS: A comparison of systems. *Journal of Personality Assessment, 46,* 544–549.

Himelstein, P. (1983). An additional modification for the rapid calculation of the WAIS Verbal IQ. *Journal of Clinical Psychology, 39,* 259–260.

Holmes, J. S. (1968). Acute psychiatric patient performance on the WAIS. *Journal of Clinical Psychology, 24*(1), 87–91.

Holmes, D. S., Armstrong, H. E., Jr., Johnson, M. H., & Ries, H. A. (1966). Validity and clinical utility of the Satz and Mogel abbreviated form of the WAIS. *Psychological Reports, 18,* 992–994.

Horn, J. L. & Cattell, R. B. (1966). Refinement and test of the theory of fluid and crystallized general intelligences. *Journal of Educational Psychology, 57,* 253–270.

Humphreys, L. G. & Ilgen, D. R. (1969). Note on a criterion for the number of factors. *Educational and Psychological Measurement, 29,* 571–578.

Jastak, J. F. & Jastak, S. R. (1978). *The Wide Range Achievement Test: Manual of instructions*. Wilmington, Delaware: Jastak Association.

Jensen, A. R. (1969). How much can we boost IQ and scholatic achievement? *Harvard Educational Review, 39,* 1–123.

Jensen, A. R. (1980). *Bias in mental testing*. New York: The Free Press.

Kaiser, H. F. (1960). The application of electronic computers to factor analysis. *Educational and Psychological Measurement, 20,* 141–151.

Kaiser, H. F. (1970). A second-generation Little Jiffy. *Psychometrika, 35,* 401–415.

Kaufman, A. S. (1979). *Intelligent testing with the WISC-R*. (a). New York: Wiley-Interscience.

Kaufman, A. S. (1979). WISC-R research: Implications for interpretation. (b). *School Psychology Digest, 8,* 5–27.

Kelderman, H., Mellenbergh, G. J., & Elshout, J. J. (1981). Guilford's facet theory of intelligence: An empirical comparison of models. *Multivariate Behavioral Research, 16,* 37–62.

Kim, J. & Mueller, C. W. (1978). *Factor analysis*. (a). Beverly Hills: Sage Publications, Inc.

Kim, J. & Mueller, C. W. (1978). *Introduction to factor analysis*. (b). Beverly Hills: Sage Publications, Inc.

Klingler, D. E. & Saunders, D. R. (1975). A factor analysis of the items for nine subtests of the WAIS. *Multivariate Behavioral Research, 10*(2), 131–154.

Knight, R. G. (1983). On interpreting the several standard errors of the WAIS-R: Some further tables. *Journal of Consulting and Clinical Psychology, 51*(5), 671–673.

L'Abate, L. (1964). *Principles of clinical psychology*. New York: Grune & Stratton, Inc.

Lansdell, H. & Smith, F. J. (1975). Asymmetrical cerebral function for two WAIS factors and their recovery after brain injury. *Journal of Consulting and Clinical Psychology, 43,* 923.

Lawley, D. N. & Maxwell, A. E. (1971). *Factor analysis as a statistical method.* London: Butterworths.

Lee, H. B. & Comrey, A. L. (1979). Distortions in a commonly used factor analytic procedure. *Multivariate Behavioral Research, 14,* 301–321.

Lehman, R. A. W., Chelune, G. J., & Heaton, R. K. (1979). Level and variability of performance on neuropsychological tests. *Journal of Clinical Psychology, 35*(2), 358–363.

Leli, D. A. & Filskov, S. B. (1981). Actuarial assessment of Wechsler Verbal-Performance scale differences as signs of lateralized cerebral impairment. *Perceptual and Motor Skills, 53,* 491–496.

Lezak, M. D. (1983). *Neuropsychological assessment,* (2nd Ed.). New York: Oxford University Press.

Lippold, S. & Claiborn, J. M. (1983). Comparison of the Wechsler Adult Intelligence Scale and the Wechsler Adult Intelligence Scale-Revised. *Journal of Consulting and Clinical Psychology, 51*(2), 315.

Lutey, C. (1977). *Individual intelligence testing: A manual and sourcebook.* Greeley, Colorado: Lutey.

Maloney, M. P. & Ward, M. P. (1976). *Psychological assessment: A conceptual approach.* New York: Oxford University Press.

Marsh, G. G. (1973). Satz-Mogel abbreviated WAIS and CNS-damaged patients. *Journal of Clinical Psychology, 29,* 451–455.

Matarazzo, J. D. (1972). *Wechsler's measurement and appraisal of adult intelligence.* (5th Ed.). Baltimore: Williams & Wilkins.

Meikle, S. (1968). The effect on subtest differences of abbreviating the WAIS. *Journal of Clinical Psychology, 24,* 196–197.

Miller, C. K. & Chansky, N. M. (1972). Psychologists, scoring of WISC protocols. *Psychology in the Schools, 9,* 144–152.

Miller, C. K., Chansky, N. M., & Gredler, G. R. (1970). Rater agreement on WISC protocols. *Psychology in the Schools, 7,* 190–193.

Mishra, S. P. (1982). Intelligence test performance as affected by anxiety and test administration procedures. *Journal of Clinical Psychology, 38*(4), 825–829.

Mogel, S. & Satz, P. (1963). Abbreviation of the WAIS for clinical use: An attempt at validation. *Journal of Clinical Psychology, 19,* 298–300.

Montanelli, R. G., Jr. & Humphreys, L. G. (1976). Latent roots of random data correlation matrices with squared multiple correlations on the diagonal: A Monte Carlo study. *Psychometrika, 41,* 341–348.

Naglieri, J. A. (1982). Two types of tables for use with the WAIS-R. *Journal of Consulting and Clinical Psychology, 50*(2), 319–321.

Naglieri, J. A. & Kaufman, A. S. (1983). How many factors underlie the WAIS-R? *Journal of Psychoeducational Assessment, 1,* 113–119.

Neuger, G. J., O'Leary, D. S., Fishburne, F. J., Barth, J. T., Berent, S., Giordani, B., & Boll, T. J. (1982). Order effects on the Halstead-Reitan neuropsychological test battery and allied procedures. *Journal of Consulting and Clinical Psychology, 49,* 722–730.

O'Grady, K. E. (1983). A confirmatory maximum likelihood factor analysis of the WAIS-R. *Journal of Consulting and Clinical Psychology, 51,* 826–831.

Parker, K. (1983). Factor analysis of the WAIS-R at nine age levels between 16 and 74 years. *Journal of Consulting and Clinical Psychology, 51,* 302–308.

Pellegrino, J. W. & Glaser, R. (1979). Cognitive correlates and components in the analysis of individual differences. In R. J. Sternberg & D. K. Detterman, (Eds.). *Human intelligence: Perspectives on its theory and measurement.* Norwood, New Jersey: Ablex Publishing Corportion, 61–88.

Pickering, J. W., Johnson, D. L., & Stary, J. E. (1977). Systematic VIQ/PIQ differences on the WAIS: An artifact of this instrument? *Journal of Clinical Psychology, 33*(4), 1060–1064.

Prifitera, A. & Ryan, J. J. (1983). WAIS-R/WAIS comparisons in a clinical sample. *Clinical Neuropsychology, 5,* 97–99.

Quereshi, M. Y. (1968). The comparability of WAIS and WISC subtest scores and IQ estimates. *Journal of Psychology, 68,* 73–82.

Rabin, A. I. (1965). Diagnostic use of intelligence tests. In B. Wolman (Ed.). *Handbook of Clinical Psychology.* New York: McGraw-Hill, Inc., 477–497.

Rapaport, D., Gill, M., & Schafer, R. (1945). *Diagnostic Psychological Testing* (Vol. I). Chicago: Year Book Medical Publishers, Inc.

Reschly, D. (1981). Psychological testing in educational classification and placement. *American Psychologist, 8,* 1094–1102.

Resnick, R. J. & Entin, A. D. (1971). Is an abbreviated form of the WISC valid for Afro-Americans? *Journal of Consulting and Clinical Psychology, 36,* 97–99.

Reynolds, C. R., Willson, V. L., & Clark, P. L. (1983). A fourt-test short form of the WAIS-R for clinical screening. *Clinical Neuropsychology, 5,* 111–116.

Ross-Reynolds, J. & Reschly, D. J. (1983). An investigation of item bias on the WISC-R with four sociocultural groups. *Journal of Consulting and Clinical Psychology, 51,* 144–146.

Russell, E. W. (1981). The pathology and clinical examination of memory. In S. B. Filskov & T. J. Boll (Eds.). *Handbook of Clinical Neuropsychology.* New York: Wiley-Interscience, 287–319.

Ryan, J. J. (1983). Clinical utility of a WAIS-R short form. *Journal of Clinical Psychology, 39,* 261–262.

Ryan, J. J., Larsen, J., & Prifitera, A. (1983). Validity of two- and four-subtest short forms of the WAIS-R in a psychiatric sample. *Journal of Consulting and Clinical Psychology, 51,* 460.

Ryan, J. J., Prifitera, A., & Larsen, J. (1982). Reliability of the WAIS-R with a mixed patient sample. *Perceptual and Motor Skills, 53,* 1277–1278.

Ryan, J. J., Prifitera, A., & Powers, L. (1983). Scoring reliability on the WAIS-R. *Journal of Consulting and Clinical Psychology, 51*(1), 149–150.

Ryan, J. J. & Rosenberg, S. J. (1983). Relationship between WAIS-R and Wide Range Achievement Test in a sample of mixed patients. *Perceptual and Motor Skills, 56,* 623–626.

Saccuzzo, D. P. & Lewandowski, D. G. (1976). The WISC as a diagnostic tool. *Journal of Clinical Psychology, 32,* 115–124.

Sattler, J. M. (1982). *Assessment of children's intelligence and special abilities.* (a). (2nd Ed.). Boston: Allyn and Bacon.

Sattler, J. M. (1982). *Student's manual to accompany assessment of children's intelligence and special abilities.* (b). (2nd Ed.). Boston: Allyn and Bacon.

Sattler, J. M. (1982). Age effects on Wechsler Adult Intelligence Scale-Revised tests. (c). *Journal of Consulting and Clinical Psychology, 50,* 785–786.

Sattler, J. M. & Ryan, J. J. (1981). Relationship between WISC-R and WRAT in children referred for learning disabilities. *Psychology in the Schools, 18,* 290–292.

Satz, P. & Mogel, S. (1962). An abbreviation of the WAIS for clinical use. *Journal of Clinical Psychology, 18*, 77–79.

Savage, R. D., Britton, P. G., Bolton, N., & Hall, E. H. (1973). *Intellectual functioning in the aged.* New York: Harper & Row, Publishers, Inc.

Schofield, W. (1952). Critique of scatter and profile analysis of psychometric data. *Journal of Clinical Psychology, 8*, 16–22.

Shelly, C. & Goldstein, G. (1982). Intelligence, achievement, and the Luria-Nebraska Battery in a neuropsychiatric population: A factor analytic study. *Clinical Neuropsychology, 4*, 164–169.

Shimkunas, A. M., Grohmann, M., & Zwibelman, B. (1971). Sources of intellectual inefficiency. *Psychological Reports, 29*, 747–754.

Shipley, W. C. (1946). *Institute of living scale.* Los Angeles: Western Psychological Services.

Shurrager, H. C. & Shurrager, P. S. (1964). *Manual for the Haptic Intelligence Scale for adult blind.* Chicago, Illinois: Psychology Research.

Silverstein, A. B. (1982). Factor structure of the Wechsler Adult Intelligence Scale-Revised. (a). *Journal of Consulting and Clinical Psychology, 50*, 661–664.

Silverstein, A. B. (1982). Two- and four-subtest short forms of the Wechsler Adult Intelligence Scale-Revised. (b). *Journal of Consulting and Clinical Psychology, 50*, 415–418.

Silverstein, A. B. (1982). Validity of random short forms. (c). *Perceptual and Motor Skills, 55*, 411–414.

Silverstein, A. B. (1982). Validity of Satz-Mogel-Yudin-type short forms. (d). *Journal of Consulting and Clinical Psychology, 50*, 20–21.

Silverstein, A. B. (1982). Pattern analysis as simultaneous statistical inference. (e). *Journal of Consulting and Clinical Psychology, 50*, 234–240.

Silverstein, A. B. (1983). Validity of random short forms: III. Wechsler's Intelligence Scales. *Perceptual and Motor Skills, 56*, 572–574.

Smith, R. S. (1983). A comparison study of the Wechsler Adult Intelligence Scale and the Wechsler Adult Intelligence Scale-Revised in a college population. *Journal of Consulting and Clinical Psychology, 51*, 414–419.

Snow, R. E. (1979). Theory and method for research on aptitude processes. In R. J. Sternberg & D. K. Detterman (Eds.). *Human Intellience: Perspectives on Its Theory and Measurement.* Norwood, New Jersey: Ablex Publishing Corporation, 139–164.

Sternberg, R. J. (1979). Intelligence research at the interface between differential and cognitive psychology: Prospects and proposals. In R. J. Sternberg & D. K. Detterman, (Eds.). *Human Intelligence: Perspectives on Its Theory and Measurement.* Norwood, New Jersey: Ablex Publishing Corporation, 33–60.

Storandt, M. (1977). Age, ability level, and method of scoring the WAIS. *Journal of Gerontology, 32*, 175–178.

Swiercinsky, D. P. & Howard, M. E. (1982). Programmatic series of factor analyses for evaluating the structure of neuropsychological test batteries. *Clinical Neuropsychology, 4*, 147–152.

Todd, J., Coolidge, F., & Satz, P. (1977). The Wechsler Adult Intelligence Scale discrepancy index: A neuropsychological evaluation. *Journal of Consulting and Clinical Psychology, 45*(3), 450–454.

Urbina, S. P., Golden, C. J., & Ariel, R. N. (1982). WAIS/WAIS-R: Initial comparisons. *Clinical Neuropsychology, 4*, 145–146.

Vincent, K. R. (1979). The modified WAIS: An alternative to short forms. *Journal of Clinical Psychology, 35*, 624–625.

Vogt, A. T. & Heaton, R. K. (1977). Comparison of Wechsler Adult Intelligence Scale indices of cerebral dysfunction. *Perceptual and Motor Skills, 45,* 607–615.

Watkins, J. F. & Kinsie, W. B. (1970). Exaggerated scatter and less reliable profiles produced by the Satz-Mogel abbreviation of the WAIS. *Journal of Clinical Psychology, 26,* 343–345.

Wechsler, D. (1941). The measurement of adult intelligence. (2nd Ed.). Baltimore: Williams & Wilkins.

Wechsler, D. (1944). *The measurement of adult intelligence.* (3rd Ed.). Baltimore: Williams & Wilkins.

Wechsler, D. (1945). A standardized memory scale for clinical use. *Journal of Psychology, 19,* 87–95.

Wechsler, D. (1955). *Manual for the Wechsler Adult Intelligence Scale.* New York: The Psychological Corporation.

Wechsler, D. (1958). *The measurement and appraisal of adult intelligence.* (4th Ed.). Baltimore: Williams & Wilkins.

Wechsler, D. (1975). Intelligence defined and undefined. *American Psychologist, 30,* 135–139.

Wechsler, D. (1981). *Manual for the Wechsler Adult Intelligence Scale-Revised.* New York: Psychological Corporation.

Weiner, I. B. (1966). *Psychodiagnosis in schizophrenia.* New York: John Wiley & Sons, Inc.

Wentworth-Rohr, I. & MacIntosh, R. (1972). Psychodiagnosis with WAIS intrasubtest scatter of scores. *Journal of Clinical Psychology, 28*(1), 68.

Wherry, R. J. & Wherry, R. J., Jr. (1969). WHEWH program. In R. J. Wherry (Ed.). *Psychology Department Computer Programs.* Columbus, Ohio: Department of Psychology, The Ohio State University.

Williams, M. (1978). Clinical assessment of memory. In P. McReynolds (Ed.). *Advances in Psychological Assessment, Volume IV.* San Francisco: Jossey-Bass, 426–461.

Wrigley, C. (1960). *A procedure for objective factor analysis.* Paper presented at the first annual meeting of the Society of Multivariate Experimental Psychology.

Yudin, L. W. (1966). An abbreviated form of the WISC for use with emotionally disturbed children. *Journal of Consulting Psychology, 30,* 272–275.

Zimmerman, I. L. & Woo-Sam, J. M. (1973). *Clinical interpretation of the Wechsler Adult Intelligence Scale.* New York: Grune & Stratton, Inc.

Zimmerman, S. F., Whitmyre, J. W., & Fields, F. R. J. (1970). Factor analytic structure of the Wechsler Adult Intelligence Scale in patients with diffuse and lateralized cerebral dysfunction. *Journal of Clinical Psychology, 26*(4), 462–465.

Zytowski, D. G. & Hudson, J. (1965). The validity of split-half abbreviations of the WAIS. *Journal of Clinical Psychology, 21,* 292–294.

10

The Halstead-Reitan Neuropsychological Test Battery*

Jeffrey T. Barth, Ph.D.
Stephen N. Macciocchi, Ph.D.

Introduction The assessment techniques discussed in this book have at least one thing in common, which is that the behaviors, personality dimensions, psychopathological processes, and cognitive strategies being measured are mediated by the brain. Until recently, this seemingly obvious relationship between brain and behavior appears to have been ignored in the clinical psychological literature, even though the foundations of modern psychology as developed by Watson and Freud were based on neuronal potential and interaction as well as firm neurological principles. Fortunately, renewed interest in this organ of behavior has enabled the behavioral sciences to keep pace with scientific colleagues who are making quantum leaps in the

*The authors wish to express their sincere thanks and appreciation to Ms. Teresa Vaughn and Ms. Dawn King for their valuable assistance in the preparation of this manuscript.

understanding of biochemical, physiological, and histological actions within the central nervous system.

Neuropsychology, or the study of brain-behavior relationships, is the interface between psychology and the neurosciences with a firmly established role in each field. Clinical neuropsychology is often considered a specialty of clinical psychology, which is intimately concerned with the discovery and diagnosis of neuropathological processes. This view, although partially accurate, is essentially misleading and suggests a singular purpose (neurodiagnosis) that can be considered in direct competition with several medical specialties such as neurology and neuroradiology. Although clinical neuropsychology has many of its roots in neurodiagnostic issues, it is far from being at odds with other neuroscientific disciplines, and in fact, creates a communication vehicle that bridges the gap between the neurologist and the behavioral scientist or clinical psychologist. For this reason, clinical neuropsychologists are considered best prepared if they have training both as clinical psychologists and in specialty areas such as neuroanatomy, neuropathology, or neurophysiology.

The purpose of clinical neuropsychological assessment is not neurodiagnosis even though the literature in this field is saturated with studies attempting to differentiate normal subjects from various types of brain-damaged patients. These scientific endeavours are relevant and quite important when validating neuropsychological assessment procedures to ensure that they are measuring behaviors which are directly related to cerebral dysfunction; however, such validation has become secondary to more practical issues. Determining whether a patient is brain-damaged is seldom a useful endeavour if the examiner does not ask how such a statement or diagnosis will affect treatment or outcome. This is especially true if there is evidence of a progressive neuropathological condition characterized by acute and rapid behavioral, cognitive, and/or physical decline. In such cases, a neuropsychological assessment should certainly be secondary to a full neurological examination to determine whether a life-threatening condition is involved and what medical intervention should be instituted. Advanced radiological techniques such as Computerized Axial Tomography (CAT scan), Nuclear Magnetic Resonance (NMR), and the experimental Positron Emission Tomography (PET scan) have been added to the neurologists' diagnostic arsenal and contribute to exceedingly high rates for determining the presence or absence of brain damage, as well as lesion location and etiology. As such procedures become available in most large community hospitals and medical centers, neuropsychological diagnosis is no longer necessary in most cases. Exceptions include some conditions such as dementia related to Alzheimer's disease, where definitive diagnosis is only possible with brain biopsy or autopsy. In such instances, multiple neuropsychological examinations spaced at six- or nine-month intervals would assist in formalizing a diagnosis by documenting cognitive, memory, and behavioral decline that is associated with this disease process.

The primary purpose of a neuropsychological assessment is to evaluate the neurologically impaired patient's cognitive, behavioral, and psychological strengths and weaknesses and to determine their relationship to cerebral functioning. Psychologists are specialists in the observation and analysis of behavior and cognitive function, and, as such, play a significant complementary role to the neurologist, neuroradiologist, and neurosurgeon in the evaluation of patients suspected of demonstrating brain damage. Even though neurodiagnosis is secondary to the assessment of these skills and abilities, the neuropsychologist must be able to relate cognitive and behavioral test results to neuropathological disorders in order to help confirm the diagnosis or establish the possibility of related conditions. Neuropsychologists must use their backgrounds and training in neuroanatomy and neuropathology, as well as knowledge of brain-behavior relationships to understand the course of the disorder, communicate with and understand other health care professionals, coordinate treatment planning, initiate rehabilitation, and stimulate development of coping behaviors (Barth & Boll, 1981; Boll, 1977). Neuropsychological assessment of brain-impaired patients is also vital for assessing level and rate of improvement for both clinical and research purposes. For example, if a patient has experienced a moderate to severe closed head injury, there is an expected eighteen-month recovery curve (after coma) in which approximately 85 percent of all cognitive/behavioral recovery takes place. If neuropsychological evaluations are initiated at regular (three- to six-month) intervals following trauma, recovery can be objectively charted and predictions made concerning absolute level and quality of improvement over time. Similar documentation can be provided by neuropsychological assessment regarding the efficacy of various neurosurgical, radiologic, and chemotherapeutic interventions.

Neuropsychological assessment has typically been practiced within teaching hospitals and medical settings, where patients with serious neuropathological conditions are evaluated by a variety of health care specialties, and where treatment may include neurosurgery, chemotherapy, radiation, and other highly invasive techniques and procedures. As stated earlier, neurodiagnosis is seldom necessary in such cases, with confirmation of pathological process and prognosis, documentation of improvement or decline, delineation of cognitive, behavioral, and psychological strengths and weaknesses, and recommendations for rehabilitation and other therapeutic interventions being the primary purpose of such an assessment. Neuropsychological evaluation within other settings, such as community mental health centers, inpatient psychiatric facilities, or school systems, although oriented to similar issues, may first be concerned with whether a particular patient or student demonstrates significant impairment to warrant a full neurological examination.

In most cases, the need for such a neurological workup will be quite obvious from acute physical deficits such as incoordination, visual, tactile and/or auditory problems, headaches, seizures, etc., which will be exceedingly evident upon simple observation and verbal inquiry. Such symptoms should be red flags that signal the need for primary medical (neurological) intervention rather than a neuropsychological examination. If any health care specialist suspects a central nervous system disorder, he or she should make an appropriate referral to the medical community.

There are some occasions where a neuropsychologist will be asked to determine whether such a referral is necessary, particularly when there are questionable data regarding physical or other symptomatology. A neuropsychological evaluation can be helpful in this regard; however, the primary purpose of this assessment remains a clear definition of cognitive, behavioral, and psychological strengths and weaknesses related to brain function and pathology. This information can then be utilized to plan further assessment, psychotherapeutic and behavioral intervention, chemotherapy programming, and educational placement and remediation, as well as to develop discharge planning, daily living needs, and vocational adjustment and rehabilitation.

Another typical and appropriate referral question is a request for information regarding how a particular past, static neuropathological condition, such as closed head injury or controlled hydrocephalus, has affected cognitive and behavioral strategies for a particular client. Here, the neuropsychological examination can be of great value, as well as in more vague cases where there are behavioral abnormalities or difficulties in learning with no known associated neuropathological conditions. The key here again is relating cerebral functioning (as defined by the test data) to the more salient issue of a comprehensive assessment of cognitive and behavioral skills and abilities, and applying these findings to intervention strategies and coping behaviors.

Barth and Boll (1981), Boll (1978, 1981), Golden (1978), Jarvis and Barth (in press), Lezak (1983), Ranseen, Macciocchi, and Barth (1983), Reitan and Davison (1974), and Swiercinsky (1978), among others, have suggested that the earlier emphasis on neurodiagnosis from neuropsychological assessment data, although an extremely useful and necessary step in the overall learning process, has been somewhat detrimental to the field of neuropsychology and the clinical evaluation process, since it has fueled the fire in the search for the single, quick test for brain damage. Until recently, many psychologists and physicians believed there were a number of independent tests, such as the Bender-Gestalt, that can determine whether a person suffered from organicity. Aside from the fact that the term organicity is extremely vague, the supposition that one test can assess all cerebral impairment suggests that brain damage is unitary or has similar effects. Health care professionals have known for decades that this simply is not true, for brain damage is caused by many processes, and has differing severity and locations, and must be considered multidimensional. Therefore, it is astounding that so much energy has been expended searching for the perfect, single test for brain damage.

The brain is an immensely complex organ that exhibits a limitless variation in strengths and weaknesses based on healthy functioning and a variety of pathological states, therefore, neuropsychological assessment of the associated brain-behavior relationships must, quite obviously, be based on a multiple test or battery approach, as opposed to a single evaluation procedure.

In order to evaluate a representative sample of brain-behavior relationships and delineate cognitive, behavioral, and psychological strengths and weaknesses associated with cerebral impairment, a battery of psychometric tests must be utilized that assess major abilities and skills and that complement each other to build a comprehensive picture of the level and quality of functional integrity. The Halstead-Reitan Neuropsychological Test Battery is traditionally considered to be the most well-validated set of test procedures that meet these criteria.

DEVELOPMENT OF THE HALSTEAD-REITAN NEUROPSYCHOLOGICAL TEST BATTERY

In 1935, Ward Halstead developed his neuropsychology laboratory at the University of Chicago, where he pursued interests in the psychometric aspects of adaptive human abilities, or "biological intelligence" (Halstead, 1947).

Although his four factor theory of biological intelligence received minimal empirical attention over the years, his development of tests to assess these abilities in normal subjects and brain-damaged (lobectomized) patients has become the foundation of present day human quantitative neuropsychological research. Using factor analytic methods, Halstead identified eight tests (and ten test scores) that he believed would measure biological intelligence and separate normal from brain-damaged subjects (Russell, Neuringer & Goldstein, 1974). These tests included: the Halstead Category Test, Seashore Rhythm Test, Speech-Sounds Perception Test, Tactual Performance Test (Total

Time, Memory, and Localization), Finger Oscillation Test, Critical Flicker Frequency, Critical Flicker Fusion, and the Time Sense Test.

Ralph Reitan, one of Halstead's students, further refined the test measures by applying them to a variety of neurologically impaired patients and analyzing individual test results for differentially diagnosing these patients from normal controls (see Reitan & Davison, 1974). Reitan found these tests to be extremely sensitive to the integrity of the cerebral hemispheres, with Critical Flicker Frequency, Critical Flicker Fusion, and the Time Sense Test demonstrating lower levels of significance and, consequently, being eventually dropped from the formal battery.

Since both Halstead and Reitan's research endeavours required the evaluation of cognitive and behavioral abilities associated with biological intelligence and cerebral functioning, a battery of tests was considered necessary to assess such a concept. The battery was eventually modified by Reitan and now includes five tests (and seven test scores) adapted from the original Halstead measures (plus the Halstead Impairment Index, which will be discussed later), as well as the Trail Making Test A & B, the Halstead-Wepman Aphasia Screening Test and the Sensory-Perceptual Examination, and two allied procedures: the Wechsler-Bellevue Scale (Wechsler Intelligence Scales) and the Minnesota Multiphasic Personality Inventory (MMPI). Other tests that are considered allied procedures are often added to this battery in order to assess additional areas of brain functioning. These include: the Strength of Grip Test (Hand Dynommeter), academic achievement testing (Wide Range Achievement Test, Peabody Individual Achievement Test or Woodcock-Johnson), memory evaluation (Wechsler Memory Scale with Russell Revisions, Benton Visual Retention Test, or Selective Reminding Task), and lateral dominance assessment. It is not difficult to see that this test battery is an excellent vehicle for assessing a wide range of cognitive, behavioral, and psychological adaptive abilities and the cerebral systems which mediate these functions.

Reitan's modification of Halstead's original work led to many highly successful efforts at validation and cross validation of these test procedures for the individual and group determination of the presence or absence of brain damage, lateralization of brain damage to the left or right hemisphere, and the diagnosis of pathological process (see Boll, 1978; Hervern, 1980; and Reitan & Davison, 1974, for reviews). A wide range of criterion measures have been utilized in these studies including neurologists' and neurosurgeons' reports, autopsies, physical neurological examinations, skull x-rays, EEGs, pneumoencephalograms (PEG), angiograms, brain scans, blood flow studies (BFS), and, more recently, CAT scans.

As Boll (1981) points out, such validational efforts were necessary in the early development of the neuropsychological assessment battery in order to demonstrate its clinical validity and "to determine whether the behavioral variations between patients reflected underlying neurological status rather than other variables such as illness, drugs, hospitalization, and so on" (p. 582). He goes on to state, though, that:

> . . . it is unfortunate, but understandable, that what one does first is often assumed to be the issue of greatest or even sole interest . . . It is understandable that (these) impressive validity demonstration(s) would be seized on by applied clinicians as the development of a neurodiagnostic procedure . . . (however) it remains a fact that the goal of neuropsychological assessment is not now, and never has been, diagnosis or the creation of bigger and better neurodiagnostic techniques (p. 582).

The original purpose, with some mild modifications, for the development of this battery of neuropsychological test procedures, was to study brain-behavior relationships by assessing a range of cognitive abilities and brain functions. This remains a major goal that has been expanded to include the application of these findings to treatment and rehabilitation issues as well as to theoretical considerations in brain research.

HALSTEAD-REITAN NEUROPSYCHOLOGICAL TEST PROCEDURES FOR ADULTS (AGE 15 AND ABOVE)

The Halstead-Reitan Neuropsychological Test Battery (HRB) is technically comprised of ten tests, two of which are considered allied procedures. The Category Test, Speech-Sounds Perception, Seashore Rhythm, Tactual Performance Test (TPT), Finger Oscillation, Trail Making A & B, Aphasia Screening, and Sensory Perceptual Examination constitute the main battery with the Wechsler Intelligence Scales (WAIS or the preferred WAIS-R) and MMPI also contributing to the comprehensive nature of the assessment. Since these last two procedures are reviewed in separate chapters of this book, they will not be described here.

The Halstead Category Test

The Halstead Category Test is composed of 208 color and black-and-white slides of geometric figures that are divided into seven subsets of eight to forty slides per set. Each slide is projected onto an opaque screen within a self-contained viewing apparatus that is placed directly in front of the patient. Beneath the screen is a box with four lights numbered 1 to 4, and four levers (or buttons) directly below the lights. The patient is instructed to watch the slides presented on the screen, determine which number between 1 and 4 is suggested by each slide, and pull the lever corresponding to that number. Patients hear a doorbell sound if they choose the correct number, and a buzzer if their choice is incorrect. Patients are allowed only one choice per slide. The examiner controls the rate of slide presentation with an instrument panel attached to a clip board, and patients are usually allowed as much time as necessary to make each individual choice. Patients are told that each set of slides represents only one principle. They are also informed, at the beginning of each subset, that another group of slides will be presented in which the idea or principle may remain the same or be different from the set before it. It is then the patients' tasks to decide what that principle is so that it can be used to obtain the correct responses. It is imperative that patients never be told the principle being used in any of the subsets, since retesting (using the same slides) may be necessary to document decline or improvement in cognitive condition.

The first subset of slides requires the patient to identify Roman numerals and pull the lever corresponding to the correct number. There are eight of these relatively easy items that are designed to help the patient understand the task and experience success. The next subset begins with a slide of a four-sided figure similar to that shown in Figure 10–1. Obvious responses include a 4 (for a four-sided object) or a 1 (for one object). If the fourth lever is pulled, the patient will hear the buzzer, signifying an incorrect response. Since only one response per slide is allowed, the next slide is presented (see Figure 10–2). This one shows three similar four-sided figures which usually stimulates the patient to choose lever 3 (for three objects). This is a correct response generating a bell sound. All of the slides in that subset require the patient to respond to the number of items shown on the screen. In the third subset, the patient is required to identify the position of the different item on each slide. Identification of the quadrant in which an item is missing, or the quadrant itself which is missing, is the principle to be discovered in subset four. Subsets five and six involve the same principle, which is the proportion of the figure which is composed of solid lines. The last subset is made up of slides from the previous subsets, and the patient is instructed to make his or her choice based on experience with the previous principles.

Difficulties during testing generally arise from problems motivating the patient to perform at his or her best which is essential to data gathering for all of the HRB measures. Description of the test procedures to alleviate undue fear and a friendly, yet firm and profes-

HALSTEAD CATEGORY TEST: SLIDE 1, SUBSET 2

HALSTEAD CATEORY TEST: SLIDE 2, SUBSET 2

Figures 10–1 and 10–2 are representative slides from Subset Two of the Halstead Category Test requiring the client being tested to respond to the number of items shown.

sional attitude, are always necessary. Since subset three is much more demanding than the first two subsets, it is important for the examiner to offer any necessary reassurance and to encourage the patient to expend maximum effort at that point. Prompting the patient to look at the slides and how they change is useful throughout the testing as long as the principle is never divulged. It is also quite common for patients to attempt to choose more than one response per slide. Since this is not permitted, such behavior must be anticipated and discouraged (if necessary, by reminding the patient before each slide that only one choice is allowed). Finally, even though this test is not timed, the patient should not be allowed to spend too much time on each item. Fifteen to twenty seconds should be quite sufficient.

Scoring is quite simple for this test and requires only a record of the total number of errors (range = 0 − 208). Profile analysis may one day prove useful in determining specific learning impairment; however, to date, no empirical evidence is available to establish such relationships.

The Halstead Category Test is a learning task requiring a high level of new problem-solving skills. Individuals who demonstrate impairment on this assessment measure often exhibit deficits in abstract learning, concept formation, and judgement, as well as mental inflexibility and mental inefficiency.

Speech-Sounds Perception Test

The Speech-Sounds Perception Test involves a taped presentation of sixty nonsense words, all of which contain the "ee" sound. The patient listens to each word and is then required to identify that word from a printed list of four similar words on the answer sheet. For each of the sixty nonsense words on the tape recording, there are four choices on the answer sheet, only one of which is correctly matched with the stimulus word. The first taped stimulus word is "theets," and that word must be identified from the first four words on the answer sheet which are "theeks," "zeeks," "theets," and "zeets." The next word is "weej," and the choices are "weech," "yeech," "weej," and "yeej."

The scoring for this test is simply the total number of errors (range = 0 − 60).

This is a relatively slow-paced task requiring a significant level of attention and concentration as well as verbal/auditory perception and language processing.

The Seashore Rhythm Test

This test, which was adapted from the Seashore Test of Musical Talent, requires the patient to listen to a taped presentation of thirty pairs of rhythmic beats with similar tone and volume and determine whether the second set of beats is the same or different from the first set. This is recorded as an "S" or "D" on the answer sheet. The following are two written examples of what might be heard on the tape:

1st example pair
(line 1)   bop—bop, bop—bop—bop
(line 2)   bop—bop, bop—bop—bop

2nd example pair

(line 3)   bop, bop, bop—bop—bop, bop

(line 4)   bop—bop, bop—bop, bop—bop

In the first example, the answer would be "S," or same, since the second set of beats (line 2) is identical to the first (line 1). Different, or "D," would be the appropriate response to the second example since the second set of beats (line 4) is different from the first (line 3).

Scoring is based on the number of correct responses (range = 0 − 30), which is traditionally converted to a ranked score using Table 10–1.

In contrast to the Speech-Sounds Perception Test, this task is quickly paced and requires focused and sustained attention and concentration, since it is quite easy for the patient to lose his or her place when marking the answer sheet.

The Tactual Performance Test

The Tactual Performance Test (TPT) uses a wooden board with spaces for ten geometrically shaped blocks (a variation of the Seguin-Goddard Form Board). This board is mounted on a support stand and placed on a table in front of the seated patient, who is blindfolded throughout the test and is never allowed to see the board or blocks. The blocks (square, circle, triangle, star, cross, rectangle, etc.) are placed on the table between the patient and the form board. The examiner runs the patient's dominant hand over the blocks and the

Table 10–1 Seashore Rhythm Scoring Conversion Table*

Raw Score *#Correct*	Ranked Score *Conversion*
29–30	1
28	2
27	3
26	5
25	6
24	8
23	9
15–22	10

*Reitan, R. M. *Manual for Administration of Neuropsychological Test Batteries for Adults and Children,* Seattle, Washington, privately published, 1959.

corresponding spaces in the board to briefly acquaint the patient with the location and dimensions of each task, which is to place the blocks in their proper spots on the board as quickly as possible while remaining blindfolded and using only the dominant hand. The task is timed and at the end of the first trial, the blocks are removed from the board and replaced on the table. The patient is then instructed to go through this procedure again, this time using only the non-dominant hand. Once this trial is timed and completed, a third trial is performed using both hands. The board, blocks, and stand are removed from the patient's view after the third trial, at which time the blindfold can be removed. The last step in this assessment procedure is to ask the patient to draw a picture of the board on a plain white sheet of paper, including replications of all blocks remembered, and their location on the board. If the patient can remember the shape of a block but not its location, it should still be drawn on the paper wherever desired.

This test is one of the two most difficult procedures in the battery to administer and requires significant observational and practice experience to avoid the many pitfalls. The first problem the examiner may encounter is an inadequate blindfold. If a patient is able to see through or underneath the blindfold, data collection and interpretation become meaningless. Therefore, most neuropsychology laboratories suggest the use of sterile eye patches held in place by a standard black "sleep mask" type of blindfold. Although using such a procedure should be quite successful, testing the adequacy of the blindfold by making quick hand movements toward the patient's face will help to guarantee total visual blackout. Patients often attempt to use both hands to place the blocks on the board during the first two trials, so the examiner must be attentive throughout the testing and stop this rather natural behavior. Having the patient place the hand that is not being used under the table can be helpful. Certain patients will lose their orientation to the top of the form board and only place blocks on the bottom two-thirds. It may be that they have forgotten about the top of the board, and, under these circumstances, it is permissible to remind them to feel the entire board. Elderly patients in particular will become tired during the trials and will need to take a break. In these cases, stop the clock (stop watch), tell them to keep the blindfold on, and take a short break. If the blindfold must be removed for any reason, throw a blanket or sheet over the form board or remove it from sight. Patients who are completely unable to utilize one of their upper extremities may still be tested by using the intact arm for all three trials to determine whether learning and memory have been affected.

The scoring for this test is also more complicated than for most of the others, and there are essentially six pertinent scores. Timed scores include those for dominant hand (up to fifteen mins.), non-dominant hand (up to fifteen mins.), both hands (up to fifteen mins.), and total time for all three trials. Since some patients will be unable to complete this task within a reasonable time period, there is a fifteen-minute time limit for each trial (unless the patient is on the verge of completing the task at that cut-off time, at which point, a little more time may be given). The patient must be given the same opportunity and time to complete each trial so that the performance of both upper extremities may be compared on an equal basis. That is to say, if the patient is given over fifteen minutes to complete trial one (dominant hand) because he or she was close to completion at fifteen minutes, the same amount of time must be allowed for the non-dominant and both hands. Number of blocks placed in their correct location on the board is also recorded for each trial. In addition to the four timed scores, number of memories and localizations are recorded based on information provided by the drawing of the board. The memory score is calculated by counting the number of figures the patient draws that accurately represent form board blocks. Since not all patients have a flair for the arts, and those that do may reflect a surrealistic quality, when in doubt as to what shape has been drawn, ask the patient to name the design. If the block is accurately named or described, it may be considered an acceptable memory (range = 0 − 10). Localization is determined by the placement of the block drawing and if they are in correct juxtaposition. The blocks should be drawn in their approximate position on the board and in appropriate relation to other correctly placed blocks. Localization is then calculated as the number of blocks correctly placed (drawn) on the sheet of paper (range = 0 − 10).

The TPT is a measure of right-left differences in tactile, kinesthetic, and motor abilities in the absence of visual cues. It is a new problem-solving task requiring intact spatial analytic ability and incidental memory.

The Finger Oscillation Test

The Finger Oscillation Test requires the patient to use the index finger to quickly tap a lever connected to a mechanical counter. Five consecutive 10-second trials are attempted, first with the dominant hand, then with the non-dominant hand. If the scores for each hand are all within a five-point range of each other, no further finger oscillation testing is necessary; however, for the inconsistent patient, as many as ten trials with one or both hands may be necessary to obtain this range of a five or less tap variation for five consecutive trials within each hand. If five consecutive scores within a five-tap range are not obtained within a maximum of ten trials, most laboratories suggest dropping the highest and lowest scores and averaging the remaining eight.

The most typical problem in the administration of this test is patient hand fatigue. This can usually be remedied by allowing for short breaks after several trials; however, some neuropsychology laboratories have begun to alternate trials between dominant and non-dominant hands which should eliminate the fatigue factor. This does, however, change the administration of the test and, as such, may affect interpretation. Scoring is simply the average number of taps per ten seconds for dominant and non-dominant hands (range = 0 – 75 per hand).

The Finger Oscillation Test is a measure of right-left differences in motor speed and gross motor manipulation skills in the upper extremities.

The Trail Making Test

The Trail Making Test is a two-part assessment procedure that requires the patient to draw lines to connect circles that are printed on an 8½ by 11-inch piece of white paper. On Part A, there are twenty-five circles, each with a number in it from 1 to 25. The patient is requested to use a pencil to consecutively and quickly connect the circles, starting at 1 and ending with 25. A short practice run is completed and then the patient is timed while performing the main task. If the patient makes a mistake by connecting any circles out of order, he or she is stopped, asked to correct the mistake, and then allowed to continue. The clock continues to run during such corrections. Part B is quite similar; however, these circles have either numbers (1 to 13) or letters (A to L) in them. The task is to consecutively connect the circles beginning with 1 and alternating between number and letter in a sequence which begins 1 to A, A to 2, 2 to B, B to 3, and so on to the end. This is also timed and there is a practice session prior to this trial. Part B is considerably more difficult than Part A, so the patient must be urged to concentrate on the task.

Scores consist of the time needed to complete Parts A and B (up to three hundred seconds for each) and the number of errors on each trial (range = 0 – 25 for each).

Trial Making A & B is a measure of ability to sustain attention to two aspects of a problem-solving task simultaneously. It requires visual scanning and verbal and numeric processing, as well as sequencing skills.

The Halstead-Wepman Aphasia Screening Test

In this task, the patient is asked to follow thirty-two relatively simple commands requiring receptive and expressive language functions as well as visuo-constructional abilities and simple mental manipulation skills. Items include: drawing (copying) simple geometric designs such as a square, triangle, Greek cross, and a skeleton key; naming designs and objects such as line drawings of a fork and a baby; spelling simple words; writing words and phrases; writing the names for objects in pictures; reading letters, words, and sentences; articulating complex word groupings such as "Methodist Episcopal"; describing the meaning of phrases; carrying out simple mathematical computations; and demonstrating the use of a key and following commands associated with sequential movement of body parts.

This test is not typically scored, but rather evaluated from a qualitative standpoint to delineate gross communication deficits and language processing impairment.

The Sensory-Perceptual Examination (Reitan-Klove)

This set of tests is quite similar to the sensory evaluation that is a standard part of the traditional physical neurological examination. This is an extremely difficult test to administer, since it requires a high level of motor coordination and attention to the patient's threshold for tactile, auditory, and visual stimulation. A significant amount of practice is always required in learning to administer this test.

The original Sensory-Perceptual Examination included eight subtests of tactile, auditory, and visual processing; however, most laboratories no longer administer one of the tests for astereognosis (tactile recognition of a penny, nickle, and dime) or the complete visual field evaluation. The tactile subtest involves lightly (just above tactile threshold) touching the back of the patient's hand and asking the patient to identify which hand is being touched, while keeping his or her eyes closed. First, unilateral stimulation (touching one hand at a time) is attempted with bilateral simultaneous stimulation (touching both hands at once) being interspersed among unilateral ones shortly after baseline tactile thresholds are established. Four unilateral right, four unilateral left, and four bilateral simultaneous stimulation trials are attempted. The score consists of the number of errors on the right and left sides with special note being made of suppression errors (where only one side is reported as being touched during bilateral simultaneous stimulation). This unilateral and bilateral stimulation procedure is also carried out for hand-face stimulation (right hand and left cheek, or left hand and right cheek). The patient is never told (in this subtest or others) that both sides may be stimulated together (bilateral simultaneous stimulation).

The auditory subtest is quite similar to the above procedure. The examiner stands behind the seated patient and makes a slight noise (just above auditory threshold) next to the patient's ear by rubbing the thumb and index finger together lightly. Unilateral and bilateral simultaneous stimulation are also required and the patient is asked to indicate which ear is being stimulated. Scoring is identical to the tactile subtest.

The visual subtest involves the same stimulation format; however, the examiner with arms extended approximately three feet in front of the patient out to the sides and equidistant between him or her and the patient. The patient is asked to focus on the examiner's nose and report whether the examiner's right or left fingers move in the patient's peripheral vision. Unilateral and bilateral simultaneous stimulation are initiated and this procedure is performed at three different levels of peripheral vision (high, middle, and low).

The subtest of finger agnosia requires the patient to identify which finger is being (lightly) touched on each hand, while keeping eyes closed. Fingers are usually numbered (1 to 5) so that responses are defined and the order of stimulation is random. The score reflects the number of misidentifications per hand out of twenty trials.

Fingertip number writing perception follows naturally from the finger agnosia subtest and asks the patient to identify numbers that are written on their fingertips with a stylus or empty ball-point pen, while keeping eyes closed. They are told that the numbers will be 3, 4, 5, and 6, and each of these is written on the patient's palm at the beginning of the test to familiarize him or her with the particular number formation. There is a pre-arranged order of presentation so that each number is written once on each finger of each hand. Scoring is based on the number of errors for each hand out of twenty trials.

The last subtest is tactual form recognition involving the identification of plastic geometric shapes (circle, square, triangle, and cross) placed in the patient's hand after it is inserted through an opening in a board, so that no visual feedback will be available. The patient's responses are designed to be non-verbal and are made by pointing with the free hand to identical plastic shapes attached to the top of the board facing the patient. Each of the plastic shapes is presented twice to each hand with the scores being the time required to identify each shape and the number of errors per hand out of eight presentations.

Comprehensive neuropsychological assessment utilizing the Halstead-Reitan Battery requires a high level of technical expertise, objective data collection, and a dedication to obtaining the best possible performance that the patient can offer. Instructions are typically memorized so that the examiner may focus full attention to patient observations and appropriate motivational techniques. During the 1940s, Halstead was one of the first to recognize that such testing requirements were ideally suited to administration and scoring by highly trained technicians (Boll, 1981), and although these assessment procedures are sometimes given by doctoral level professionals, it is more typical to find neuropsychological laboratories and assessment centers employing technicians in this important duty. Well-trained technicians can accurately and reliably administer and score this test battery, which frees the clinician to interview the patient, interpret test results, and write reports that will directly impact on patient treatment and rehabilitation.

THE HALSTEAD-REITAN NEUROPSYCHOLOGICAL TEST BATTERY FOR CHILDREN (AGE 9 TO 15)

The older children's or intermediate neuropsychological assessment battery is similar to the adult battery with the following changes being developed by Reitan:

1. The Category Test is reduced from 208 slides to 168 slides that are subdivided into six subsets (rather than seven). The fourth subset from the adult battery is eliminated and there are no colored slides.

2. The Speech-Sounds Perception answer sheet has been changed to reflect only three nonsense word choices per trial. The tape, correct responses, and number of trials (sixty) remain the same.

3. The TPT form board has only six cut-outs and blocks (four cut-outs and blocks were eliminated from the adult version).

4. The number of circles on the Trail Making Test for both Parts A and B have been reduced from twenty-five to fifteen, while the two tasks remain the same.

All other tests and all instructions from the adult battery are identical in the older children's evaluation with the exception of substituting the WISC-R for the WAIS and the elimination of the MMPI.

THE REITAN-INDIANA NEUROPSYCHOLOGICAL TEST BATTERY FOR YOUNG CHILDREN (AGE 5 TO 9)

The modification of the adult and older children's battery to meet the needs and level of understanding of young children required more extensive changes in specific presentation and instructions, as well as the elimination of several tests (Speech-Sounds Perception, Seashore Rhythm, and Trail Making A & B). The following changes have been made to the children's battery for application with five- to nine-year-olds:

1. The Category Test stimulus slides are reduced from 168 to 80 (in five subsets) and the numbers above the levers have been replaced with colors (blue, red, green, and yellow) since number concepts may not be developed in the five-year-old. The slides are all colored and the principles behind each subset of slide presentation involves different aspects of color (placement of color, quantity of color, uniqueness of color, and absence of color). The last subset of ten slides is a memory section consisting of previously presented slides.

2. The TPT utilizes the children's six block form board turned on its side so that it is within easy reach of a young child's short arms.

3. The Aphasia Screening Test has been reduced from thirty-two items to twenty-two items that essentially reflect evaluation of the same language processing and usage areas, but at a level that is appropriate for young children. For example, they are not asked to spell triangle; however, they are asked to name objects such as a fork.

4. The Sensory-Perceptual Examination is similar to the adult and older children's versions with the exception of fingertip number writing in which symbols (Xs and Os) are substituted for the numbers.

5. Age appropriate Wechsler Intelligence Scales (the WISC-R or WPPSI) are used.

Other tests such as the Marching Test, Color Form Test, Matching Pictures, Progressive Figures, Matching Vs, and Target Test, that are described by Reitan (1959) and Reitan and Davison (1974), have been recommended to supplement the young children's battery; however, few neuropsychology laboratories consistently apply these measures to their young, impaired populations. It is recommended that other developmental and academic tests be added to these core evaluation procedures in order to broaden the range of assessment of adaptive cognitive abilities.

In order to accurately administer and score the adult, intermediate, or young children's neuropsychological test battery, the examiner must take sufficient time to study the manual and practice the procedures under appropriate supervision. The manual and test procedures may be ordered from several sources.*

---

*Material can be ordered from Dr. Ralph M. Reitan, Dept. of Psychology, University of Arizona, Tuscon, Arizona, and Dr. Charles Matthews, Dept. of Neurology, University of Wisconsin, Madison, Wisconsin

INTERPRETATION

Interpretation of neuropsychological test data is predicated on the organization and understanding of assessment scores, the relationship of these data to normal and impaired functioning, the delineation of basic questions to be answered, the use of a variety of methods of inference, consideration of patient history and environmental variables, behavioral observations, and the development and use of hypotheses. Each of these issues is important in and of itself; however, there is a gestalt that must develop from the data for interpretation to be accurate and effective. Like many complicated issues and systems, it can be explained, but it is much more effectively learned and internalized through experience.

The organization of assessment data may be accomplished in many ways, however, the most straightforward is to transfer individual test scores to a summary data sheet such as that illustrated in Figure 10–3. From these scores, an Halstead Impairment Index must be calculated. The Impairment Index is a summary value reflecting general level of cerebral dysfunction computed from seven scores on the Halstead-Reitan Neuropsychological Test Battery for Adults including the Category Test, Speech-Sounds Perception, Seashore Rhythm, TPT Total Time, Memory and Localization (the Impairment Index is not computed for the intermediate or young children's battery). Each of these seven scores is evaluated against Halstead's cutoff scores for normal and brain-impaired subjects (see Table 10–2) to determine whether they will contribute to the Impairment Index. The greater the number of test scores falling in the impaired range, the larger the Impairment Index (see Table 10–3). An Impairment Index of 0.0 to 0.3 is considered to reflect normal functioning to mild cognitive impairment; 0.3 to 0.6, mild to moderate deficits; 0.6 to 0.8, moderate to severe impairment; and 0.8 to 1.0, severe dysfunction.

A comprehensive neuropsychological examination should be designed to answer a number of sequential questions that will contribute to an understanding of cognitive, behavioral, and neurological functioning to positively influence treatment and rehabilitation. These questions include:

1. Does the patient demonstrate cerebral dysfunction?
2. How severe is the impairment?
3. Is it a progressive neurological condition?
4. Is there a lesion that is lateralized to the right or left cerebral hemisphere or located in the anterior or posterior portion of the brain?
5. What is the neuropathological process and is this consistent with other medical data?

SUMMARY DATA SHEET
RESULTS OF NEUROPSYCHOLOGICAL EXAMINATION

Case Number:_____ Age:_____ Sex:_____ Education:_____ Handedness:_____
Name:_____ Employment:_____ IMPAIRMENT INDEX:____ *

WAIS (or WAIS-R)

VIQ [ ][ ][ ]
PIQ [ ][ ][ ]
FS IQ [ ][ ][ ]

Scaled Scores

Information [ ][ ]
Comprehension [ ][ ]
Digit Span [ ][ ]
Arithmetic [ ][ ]
Similarities [ ][ ]
Vocabulary [ ][ ]
Picture Arrangement [ ][ ]
Picture Completion [ ][ ]
Block Design [ ][ ]
Object Assembly [ ][ ]
Digit Symbol [ ][ ]

MINNESOTA MULTIPHASIC PERSONALITY
INVENTORY
(T-Scores)

? [ ][ ][ ]
L [ ][ ][ ]
F [ ][ ][ ]
K [ ][ ][ ]
Hs [ ][ ][ ]
D [ ][ ][ ]
Hy [ ][ ][ ]
Pd [ ][ ][ ]
Mf [ ][ ][ ]
Pa [ ][ ][ ]
Pt [ ][ ][ ]
Sc [ ][ ][ ]
Ma [ ][ ][ ]
Si [ ][ ][ ]

CATEGORY TEST [ ][ ][ ] *

TACTUAL PERFORMANCE TEST

                              Time -   # of Blks. In
Dominant hand: [ ][ ] . [ ] - [ ][ ]
Nondomin. hand: [ ][ ] . [ ] - [ ][ ]
Both hands: [ ][ ] . [ ] - [ ][ ]

        Total Time: [ ][ ][ ] *
        Memory: *
        Localization: [ ][ ] *

TRAIL MAKING TEST

    Part A: [ ][ ][ ] seconds [ ][ ] errors
    Part B: [ ][ ][ ] seconds [ ][ ] errors

SEASHORE RHYTHM TEST (correct)
    Raw Score: [ ][ ]   Rank: [ ][ ] *

SPEECH-SOUNDS PERCEPTION TEST
    Errors: [ ][ ] *

FINGER OSCILLATION TEST
    Dominant hand: [ ][ ] . [ ] *
    Non-dominant hand: [ ][ ] . [ ]

UNILATERAL SENSORY ERRORS
    Dominant hand: [ ][ ]
    Nondominant hand: [ ][ ]

SENSORY SUPPRESSIONS
    Dominant hand: [ ][ ]
    Nondominant hand: [ ][ ]

REITAN-KLOVE TACTILE FORM RECOGNITION
                        Errors   Seconds
    Dominant hand: [ ]   [ ][ ]
    Nondominant hand: [ ]   [ ][ ]

APHASIA SIGNS:

STRENGTH OF GRIP
    Dominant hand: [ ][ ] kilograms
    Nondominant hand: [ ][ ] kilograms

Figure 10–3 Is a sample summary data sheet used for the organization of assessment data.

Table 10–2 Halstead's Cutoff Scores for Calculation of the Impairment Index*

Tests	Impaired Range
Category Test	51 or more errors
Speech-Sounds Perception Test	8 or more errors
Seashore Rhythm (rank score)	6 or more rank scores
Tactual Performance Test:	
Total Time	15.7 or more minutes
Memory	5 or fewer memories
Localization	4 or fewer localizations
Finger Oscillation	50 or fewer taps (dominant hand)

The Trail Making Test does not contribute to the Halstead Impairment Index; however, it does have generally established cutoff scores:

Part A	32 or more seconds
Part B	90 or more seconds

*Reitan, R. M. *Manual for Administration of Neuropsychological Test Batteries for Adults and Children.* Seattle, Washington, privately published.

Table 10–3 Conversion of Impaired Test Scores to Halstead Impairment Index

Number of Tests in the Impaired Range	Impairment Index Score
0	0.0
1	0.1
2	0.3
3	0.4
4	0.6
5	0.7
6	0.9
7	1.0

6. What are the cognitive and behavioral strengths and weaknesses associated with this condition?

7. What are the implications for everyday functioning or prognosis?

8. What treatment and rehabilitation efforts should be made?

As stated earlier, the answers to the first five questions are secondary to the primary function of the neuropsychological examination as reflected in the last three questions. These first five questions are, however, an important foundation for developing a comprehensive assessment and establishing appropriate intervention.

These eight questions are answered through a systematic approach to the data and the use of at least four traditional methods of inference (interpretation) when evaluating these scores:

1. level of performance,
2. pattern of performance,
3. pathognomonic signs, and
4. right-left differences (Boll, 1978; Golden, 1978; Reitan & Davison, 1974).

Since these interpretive methods have been sufficiently reviewed in numerous other publications, they will be briefly defined and later their utility will be demonstrated.

Psychological assessment data are typically analyzed first to determine whether the patient has done well or poorly on the particular test measure. This simple, straightforward method of inference is the evaluation of *level of performance,* reflecting the degree of impairment or intact functioning. This interpretive schema allows for comparisons of individual test scores to normative and pathological populations (Boll, 1981). It is a limited interpretive method generally reflecting standard quantitative measurement in the absence of qualitative assessment. Cut-off scores developed from test analysis are employed that may not be sensitive to individual differences and variations. Although level of performance can be an important issue, it is not recommended to use only one method of inference to evaluate test results.

Pattern of performance is a familiar method applied to data evaluation for most psychologists, since it is studied when learning the Wechsler Intelligence Scales and Minnesota Multiphasic Personality Inventory interpretation. Pattern analysis involves evaluating relationships between and within tests and scores on the neuropsychological test battery to begin to answer the previously mentioned eight questions. Since the Halstead-Reitan Neuropsychological Test Procedures were developed to be a comprehensive battery of tests, many of the measures demonstrate related features that allow a dove-tailing and stepwise building of one result on another. The TPT, for example, provides right, left, and both hands time scores that can be analyzed all together to provide a pattern reflecting tactile-kinesthetic learning across trials (improvement in time score) if the patient exhibits normal functioning in this area. This pattern of scores within the TPT can then be related to other motor (Finger Oscillation) and sensory (Sensory-Perceptual) test findings to determine the probable interaction of these factors and how they affect the TPT results.

Neuropsychological test data must be inspected for specific symptoms of neuropathology and cognitive deficits. Such signs or evidence of pathology are referred to as *pathognomonic indicators,* and are usually quite specific to a particular disorder. Pathognomonic signs are usually found on the Aphasia Screening Test and include saying, "a spoon," when naming a picture of a fork, and responding, "red cross," when naming a black and white drawing of a Greek cross. These answers are considered pathognomonic for a type of aphasia or communication disorder referred to as dysnomia. This method of inference can be critical in the refinement of a diagnosis so that specific and appropriate intervention may be initiated.

The last method of inference, *right-left differences,* is directly related to pattern of performance and is usually applied to those tests measuring motor and sensory functions on each sides of the body. In most instances, upper extremity dominance implies approximately 10 percent more efficient motor functioning on the dominant side than on the non-dominant side (Finger Oscillation and Strength of Grip). This relationship does not generalize to sensory systems (Sensory-Perceptual Examination) where functions on both sides of the body should be intact and identical. If aberrant relationships between the right and left sides are discovered, impairment of cerebral functions in the contralateral cerebral hemisphere is suggested. Such information can help to clarify brain-behavior relationships as well as diagnostic issues.

Patient history, environmental variables, and behavioral observations are always gathered as part of a thorough neuropsychological evaluation by the clinician and technician throughout the testing process and interview. These are critical to the accurate interpretation of data and the development of appropriate intervention strategies. It is sometimes assumed that since technicians are employed to carry out many of the actual assessment duties, the clinician may never see the patient and that blind analysis of test scores is a typical clinical practice. This is neither true nor recommended since important clinical data may be lost if a comprehensive interview is not performed by the clinican to supplement the assessment data and behavioral notes gathered by the technician.

The interview and history gathering should include information regarding present circumstances (age, education, occupation, and family ties), level of success in school and vocational choices, family dynamics, relationships with individuals (friends) outside of the family, medical history, developmental history, recent cognitive, behavioral, psychological or physical changes or symptoms, past or present psychological or medical evaluation results, and other professionals the patient has been seeing (and for what purpose). These variables, combined with the extensive notes provided by the technician regarding behavioral observations during testing, have a significant effect on the interpretive process. For example, as in any other psychological assessment, age plays an important role in developing adjusted scores and in our understanding of level of everyday functioning. This is certainly quite clear in certain tests that have age-correction factors (or age appropriate scaled scores as on the WAIS and WAIS-R), indicating that our expectations are different for a sixty-five-year old, for example, than for a patient in his or her thirties. When evaluating level of impairment, it is important to use corrected scores if determining the difference between normal aging effects and neuropathology on an individual's cognitive functioning. Under similar circumstances, the same holds true for academic or vocational success as well as other variables. It is important to know from the patient and a significant other, the patient's school or job-related performance prior to neural trauma (premorbid abilities), so present assessment data may begin to address, for example, the issue of possible decline from a previously higher level of functioning and prognosis and treatment strategy determinations. Family ties and general relationships with others are important in understanding test data particularly if extended support systems appear necessary for rehabilitation success. Medical and developmental histories play a significant role in our understanding of impairment, since the past is often an accurate yardstick for the present and future, and can help to explain the etiology of symptoms. Finally, knowledge of previous evaluation results and professional intervention can clarify diagnoses, reduce redundancy in test procedures, assist in team-oriented treatment planning, and facilitate professional communication.

Halstead-Reitan neuropsychological test data can best be interpreted by attempting to systematically answer the previously mentioned eight questions by using the four methods of inference and rules or hypotheses for test analysis arising from these methods. Although every clinician has his or her own unique perspective and schema for inspecting data, the following outline is typical of the general process employed by many neuropsychologists.

1. First, review demographic information and history, and evaluate the scores on Halstead's four most sensitive tests of brain damage (in order of sensitivity). These tests are the Halstead Impairment Index, the Category Test, TPT Localization, and Trail Making B. Level of performance and cut-off scores are important here, and this step can help answer question 1, "Is there evidence of cerebral dysfunction?", and question 2, "How severe is the impairment?" If all or most of these test scores are signif-

icantly beyond Halstead's cut-off scores, cerebral impairment is highly probable.

2. Speech-Sounds Perception and Seashore Rhythm are often analyzed next to help determine basic level of concentration and attention and to aid in answering question 3, "Is this a progressive neurological condition?" Good scores (level of performance below Halstead's cutoffs) are usually not compatible with tissue destructive, space-occupying, progressive lesions. Poor scores usually indicate cerebral dysfunction; however, they are not always compatible with progressive conditions. Of course, the best method for determining whether a condition is progressive is to search the recent history for indications of acute, rapid, physical, or mental decline, and initiation of multiple longitudinal testings.

3. Lateralization and location of lesion (question 4) can be evaluated next through the inspection of test scores that lend themselves to pattern analysis and right-left comparisons, i.e., TPT time for dominant, non-dominant, and both upper extremities, Finger Oscillation (and Strength of Grip), Sensory-Perceptual Examination, and Wechsler Intelligence Scale Verbal and Performance IQs. Since TPT is a learning task, the expected relationship is one of improvement in test scores (less time) from trial to trial (dominant, non-dominant, both hands). Normal test scores for Finger Oscillation and Strength of Grip reflect 10 percent better performance on the dominant side of the body than on the non-dominant side. No sensory deficits should be found and in most cases Wechsler Intelligence Scale VIQ and PIQ scores should reveal less than a twenty-point differential. Deviations from these motor and sensory relationships suggest dysfunction in the contralateral cerebral hemisphere from the side exhibiting the impaired function. Impaired VIQ generally indicates left hemisphere dysfunction, while poor PIQ scores reflect deficits in right hemisphere function. If sensory test scores are more impaired than motor skills, posterior cerebral hemisphere dysfunction may be suspected, and if the reverse is found, anterior cerebral hemisphere deficits are likely (due to the locations of the sensory and motor strips).

4. The Aphasia Screening Test, Wechsler Adult Intelligence Scale subtests, and other allied procedures should finally be evaluated through the use of all of the methods of inference. A full analysis of all test scores and the responses to the previous four questions should enable the

examiner to develop certain hypotheses (see Jarvis &
Barth, in press) regarding pathological process (question
5). A knowledge of neuroanatomy and neuropathology,
along with the neuropsychological data, demographics,
history, etc., will help eliminate many neuropathological
entities and confirm the likelihood of others. A determination can then be made if the neuropsychological assessment is consistent with diagnoses that have been
made by neurologists or other related professionals.

5. The next step is the most important and is reflective of
the utility of a neuropsychological examination. All data
must be reevaluated to determine the cognitive and behavioral strengths and weaknesses and how these variables will impact on the patient's everyday functioning
(questions 6 and 7). This is accomplished by understanding the abilities and skills necessary to perform each of
the tasks in the battery (described in test procedure sections). A profile of strengths and weaknesses, along with
pathology prognosis, can then be developed and applied
to the individual patient's life situation to begin to speculate on the changes taking place in daily living skills
and on what interventions should prove useful (question
8).

It is quite obvious that the above outline for test interpretation
is extremely limited, particularly since it suggests that the clinician
is constantly developing and testing hypotheses concerning the integrity of neurological, cognitive, and behavioral functioning, yet the
reader is not exposed to all of these possible hypotheses. This ambiguity is intended since this chapter would develop into several volumes
if allowed to present to the reader the information, hundreds of hypotheses, and interpretive rules necessary to immediately begin independent evaluation of test data. It would, in fact, be misleading to
suggest that this chapter could sufficiently prepare the professional
for such data analysis; however, it is hoped that this simple approach
to the understanding and organization of test data can be an important
beginning to further study in the field of neuropsychological assessment.

INTERPRETIVE CASE EXAMPLE

To concretize the above interpretive procedures, the following
will systematically review one patient's data and attempt to clarify
the process of data analysis, hypothesis testing, and the basic infor-

mation to be presented in a report. Instead of illustrating results from an obvious and serious medical disorder, such as a neoplasm or major cerebrovascular accident which are certainly glamorous cases providing striking data, this case example will describe and analyze a more subtle condition where neuropsychological assessment can be most useful.

Mr. William G is a thirty-two-year-old corporate tax attorney who has been employed by a large tax consulting company for the past four years. He is married with no children, and he reports that his family life has always been a stable and happy one. He is an active, personable, and successful young man who is well liked in his community, and his past medical and psychological history (including that of his parents and family) is unremarkable.

The reason for Bill's referral for neuropsychological assessment was symptoms he was experiencing that appeared relative to a head injury he incurred three weeks earlier as a result of falling ten feet from a ladder he had been using to paint his house. He struck his head and experienced a period of unconsciousness that lasted approximately ten minutes. He was taken to the medical center emergency room where he was examined by a neurology resident who ordered a skull series. The x-rays were negative for concussion; however, Bill's pupils were slightly dilated and he complained of a headache. His speech and thought process appeared relatively normal, but he did demonstrate some mild dysnomia (word finding difficulty). These results convinced the medical staff to admit him, and an EEG and a CAT scan were obtained revealing no abnormalities. Within twenty-four hours, his headache had decreased, his pupils were symmetrical and normal, and his mild dysphasia had almost entirely disappeared. He was released that day and returned six weeks later as part of a routine follow-up. At that time, he complained of headaches and dizziness, difficulties in word finding, vague feelings of anxiety and depression, and memory problems. His wife reported a personality change characterized by his "losing some control over his temper," which was not typical of Bill prior to his accident. A repeat EEG and CAT scan were both within normal limits. Since subtle changes (at the histological levels) can occur in mild and moderate head injuries that will not show up on some of the most sensitive neurological assessment procedures, he was referred to the neuropsychology assessment laboratories for a comprehensive evaluation to delineate the cognitive and behavioral components of his present disorder and to relate these to cerebral functioning, prognosis, and treatment.

Bill was extremely cooperative throughout the test procedures, produced maximum effort, and was genuinely concerned about his test results. He informed the examiners that he was worried about these "strange symptoms" he was having since they were disrupting his work and family life. He clearly wanted to know what was wrong with him and how to correct it. His neuropsychological results are presented in Figure 10–4 and Figure 10–5.

Halstead's Impairment Index of 0.3 places him in the normal to mildly impaired range of adaptive cognitive abilities, and his Category score of 54 errors, TPT localization of 4, and Trail Making B of 105 seconds all indicate mildly impaired functioning when utilizing Halstead and Reitan's cut-off scores. These indicate some cerebral deficits, yet there are no indications of severe impairment in these data or from other scores. The Category score is of particular interest since 54 errors, even though just beyond the cut-off scores, can be considered indicative of moderate impairment (a bright, active attorney should be capable of obtaining less than 35 errors). Since both Speech-Sounds Perception and Seashore Rhythm performance are well within normal limits and the acute decline in abilities appears specifically related to mild to moderate head trauma, there is sufficient reason to believe that this is not a progressive disorder. There is, however, the possibility that even though the cerebral pathology should not increase in severity, behavioral and cognitive disruption may be exacerbated over time due to a rise in the level of frustration when impaired abilities are realized and work or family conditions require the use of such skills.

No lateralized deficits are noted on TPT, Finger Oscillation, Strength of Grip, Sensory Perceptual Examination, or WAIS VIQ and PIQ. Learning has occured on the TPT as evidenced by the decreasing time scores across hand trials and, as expected, there is approximately a 10 percent difference between dominant and non-dominant hands on Finger Oscillation and Strength of Grip (dominant hand being faster and stronger). The absolute speed of dominant index finger tapping is also within normal limits on Finger Oscillations; thus, it does not contribute to the Halstead Impairment Index. The Sensory-Perceptual Examination is unremarkable, except for one non-dominant side suppression when stimuli were presented in a bilateral, simultaneous fashion, and since there are no other indications of sensory or motor impairment, little significance will be attached to this finding. WAIS Verbal and Performance IQ scores were discrepant by 12 points, which may not be a significant difference; however, the Performance subtest scores are generally lower and less evenly developed (inter-test fluctuation) than the Verbal ones, which could mean impairment of abilities mediated by the right cerebral hemisphere (evidence for a lateralized finding), or, more probably, an indication of difficulty solving new problems (PIQ) as opposed to accessing over-learned and stored verbal knowledge (VIQ). It is important to note that his Performance subtest fluctuations may reflect premorbid conditions often associated with high verbal/analytic achievement in educational and vocational pursuits.

SUMMARY DATA SHEET
RESULTS OF NEUROPSYCHOLOGICAL EXAMINATION

Case Number: 001   Age: 32   Sex: M   Education: 20+   Handedness: R

Name: William G.   Employment: Attorney   IMPAIRMENT INDEX: 0.3 *

WAIS (or WAIS-R)

VIQ   1 2 4
PIQ   1 1 2
FS IQ

Scaled Scores

Information   1 5
Comprehension   1 5
Digit Span   1 0
Arithmetic   1 4
Similarities   1 4
Vocabulary   1 5
Picture Arrangement 1 0
Picture Completion 1 4
Block Design   1 0
Object Assembly   1 4
Digit Symbol   1 0

MINNESOTA MULTIPHASIC PERSONALITY

INVENTORY

(T-Scores)

?	0 0 0
L	0 4 0
F	0 5 2
K	0 6 9
Hs	0 6 5
D	0 7 0
Hy	0 5 6
Pd	0 6 2
Mf	0 5 1
Pa	0 5 4
Pt	0 6 8
Sc	0 5 1
Ma	0 6 9
Si	0 5 3

CATEGORY TEST   0 5 4 *

TACTUAL PERFORMANCE TEST

                          Time -   # of Blks. In
Dominant hand: 5 . 2 - 1 0
Nondomin. hand: 3 . 1 - 1 0
Both hands: 2 . 6 - 1 0

        Total Time: 1 0   9 *
        Memory: 0 7 *
        Localization: 0 4 *

TRAIL MAKING TEST

    Part A: 0 2 8 seconds 0 0 errors
    Part B: 1 0 7 seconds 0 0 errors

SEASHORE RHYTHM TEST (correct)

    Raw Score: 2 8   Rank: 0 2 *

SPEECH-SOUNDS PERCEPTION TEST

    Errors: 0 2 *

FINGER OSCILLATION TEST

    Dominant hand: 5 2 . 5 *
    Non-dominant hand: 4 7 . 2

UNILATERAL SENSORY ERRORS

    Dominant hand: 0 0
    Nondominant hand: 0 0

SENSORY SUPPRESSIONS

    Dominant hand: 0 0
    Nondominant hand: 0 1

REITAN-KLOVE TACTILE FORM RECOGNITION

                    Errors   Seconds
Dominant hand: 0   1 3
Nondominant hand: 0   1 7

APHASIA SIGNS: Mild dysnomia
                  Mild dysarthria

STRENGTH OF GRIP

    Dominant hand: 4 7 kilograms
    Nondominant hand: 4 2 kilograms

Using the summary data sheet as previously shown. **Figure 10–4** illustrates the results of the neuropsychological examination as completed by the case example, Mr. William G.

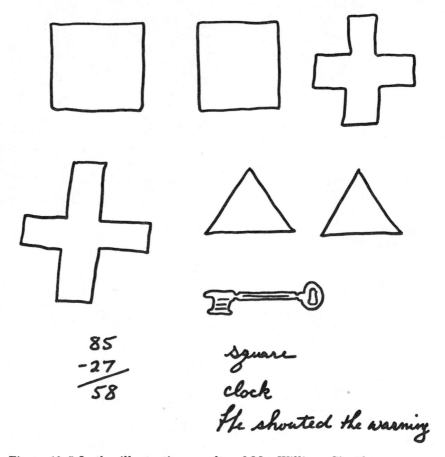

Figure 10–5 Is the illustrative results of Mr. William G's (the case
example) Aphasia Screening Test.

The Aphasia Screening Test was performed quite well, including
constructional items (Figure 10–5), yet there were mild indications of
dysnomia (in naming the cross, he first called it a "plus sign"), and
some mild difficulty repeating "Methodist Episcopal" (dysarthria). Such
findings cannot be considered normal for an individual with Bill's
education and profession; however, they are consistent with profiles
from similar individuals who have experienced mild to moderate closed
head injuries. The possible disruption of Performance subtest scores
on the WAIS, difficulties in abstract reasoning and concept formation
solving (Category Test), and deficits in two-step problem solving, and
attention and concentration (Trail Making B) in the absence of major
motor and sensory deficits are all typical neuropsychological test findings for such head trauma patients. The findings, then, would be

consistent with the medical history and indicate that most of Bill's present problems are related to his recent accident and his reaction to the associated cognitive deficits.

As said before, the analysis of data is important to understand the involved brain-behavior relationship and has little to do with neurodiagnosis. It is the foundation upon which the last three questions are answered.

To describe Bill's cognitive and behavioral strengths and weaknesses and determine their implications for everyday functioning, the examiner must again review the test data, focusing on abilities and skills necessary to successfully complete the tasks and then apply those findings to Bill's particular requirements for successful living. This necessitates a familiarity with the patient's life style and occupation as well as a thorough understanding of the relationships between the tests and cognitive/behavioral skills and abilities. In this particular case, the patient exhibits reasonably intact general cognitive abilities with his general fund of information and verbal skills being above average (WAIS Verbal) and his visuo-spatial new problem-solving abilities appearing somewhat unevenly developed (WAIS Performance). His mental flexibility, mental efficiency, abstract reasoning, and concept formation (Category Test) are mildly to moderately impaired, as is his ability to concentrate simultaneously on two aspects of a complex problem-solving situation (Trail Making B). Basic, single factor attentional skills seem well intact (Speech-Sounds Perception and Seashore Rhythm). Sensory and motor testing revealed no deficits in bilateral upper extremity motor speed and strength (Finger Oscillation and Strength of Grip), and no significant sensory deficits were noted (Sensory-Perceptual Examination). His abilities in the area of psychomotor problem solving were generally intact when tactile and kinesthetic cues were substituted for visual feedback (TPT); however, he demonstrated some difficulties in remembering spatial relationships when incidental memory was required (TPT Localization). Aphasia screening revealed no true aphasic symptomatology; however, Bill did exhibit mild deficits in naming common designs and in articulation.

Objective psychological assessment indicated a mild yet clinically significant level of depression and anxiety, as well as a concern with physical symptomatology, typical sequelae of closed head trauma. Follow-up memory testing (Wechsler Memory Scale and the Selective Reminding Task—not shown) indicated mild impairment of immediate and short-term verbal and visuo-spatial recall appearing at least partially related to attentional deficits.

The above information regarding cognitive and behavioral functioning should comprise the majority of the neuropsychological report with only a small section devoted to neurological implications, and the remainder focusing on how the deficits are affecting the client and what intervention will be necessary. In Bill's case, these deficits, although generally mild, are significantly disruptive to his everyday functioning. A corporate tax attorney undoubtedly requires a high level of concentration and attention, as well as new problem-solving skills, memory abilities, and mental flexibility to successfully compete and fulfill his vocational duties. Realizing impairment of such skills and reduced office efficiency will probably increase his level of frustration and anxiety, which may begin to strain his relationship with others. In all likelihood, his reported personality change and lowered frustration tolerance are directly related to these factors.

Since these results are quite common sequelae of head trauma, the examiner should expect a typical recovery curve that could range from six to eighteen months (for the majority of recovery to occur). Immediate benefits can certainly be realized by informing Bill and his family that his symptoms are quite normal and that he should see significant recovery over the next several months. He should also be informed that these specific deficits, although relatively mild, can become quite frustrating if they are not understood, and that it will be important for him, his family, and his employer to realize that recovery from such an injury is not immediate and that a reduction in work load and responsibilities is highly recommended. Finally, follow-up neuropsychological evaluation is suggested in six months to chart recovery and outpatient counseling is offered, if necessary.

ASSETS AND LIABILITIES OF THE HALSTEAD-REITAN NEUROPSYCHOLOGICAL TEST BATTERY

It has already been stated that the Halstead-Reitan Neuropsychological Test Battery is a comprehensive, well-validated, and reliable set of assessment procedures measuring a variety of cognitive abilities and behaviors. This battery has been used for years and, as such, a tremendous amount of data has been collected throughout the United States that adds to its clinical and research applications. Halstead-Reitan cut-off scores have successfully been applied to a variety of clinical populations and some limited age normative data have been developed, although little information is available concerning elderly patients (Price, Fein & Feinberg, 1980). The battery is most often criticized for its lack of extensive age norms, lengthy administration time, and equipment cost. More adequate age norms are certainly necessary, and it is understood that concerted efforts are being mounted to meet this challenge. It does take approximately six hours to administer the entire battery and allied procedures. There have been recent attempts to shorten the length of individual test procedures

(TPT individual trials reduced from fifteen- to ten- or five-minute trials and Category Test reduced from 208 slides to 100), but these attempts have met with varying degrees of success. The test equipment can be quite expensive, but development of card or booklet versions of the Category Test has eliminated an expensive slide projection apparatus. A final criticism is that the Halstead-Reitan Battery was not constructed based on a theory of brain function, but rather is atheoretical and empirical. Such a development of test procedures based on data reflects Halstead's original scientific concerns and Reitan's background in experimental and comparative psychology. Such an approach can also be viewed as positive, since it is not tied to one particular theory of brain functioning, and as such, may have broad applications.

SUMMARY

It is impossible to clearly demonstrate administration, scoring, and interpretation of a complex and comprehensive set of neuropsychological assessment procedures in one introductory chapter, but the chapter goal was to assist the reader in developing an interest in neuropsychology as well as provide exposure to the Halstead-Reitan Battery. Further readings are necessary, as are personal observations, test administration, and supervised experience, if one is to develop a proficiency with these procedures and begin to understand brain-behavior relationships.

REFERENCES

Barth, J. T. and Boll, T. J. (1981). Rehabilitation and treatment of central nervous system dysfunction: A behavioral medicine perspective. In C. K. Prokap and L. A. Bradley (Eds.). *Medical Psychology—contributions to behavioral medicine.* New York: Academic Press, Inc.

Boll, T. J. (1977). A rationale for neuropsychological evaluation. *Professional Psychology.* February, 64–71.

Boll, T. J. (1978). Diagnosing brain impairment. In B. B. Wolman (Ed.). *Clinical diagnosis of mental disorders.* New York: Plenum Publishing Corporation.

Boll, T. J. (1981). The Halstead-Reitan neuropsychological battery. In S. B. Filskov and T. J. Boll (Eds.). *Handbook of Clinical Neuropsychology.* New York: John Wiley & Sons, Inc.

Golden, C. J. (1978). *Diagnosis and rehabilitation in clinical neuropsychology.* Springfield, Illinois: Charles C Thomas, Publisher.

Halstead, W. C. (1947). *Brain and intelligence: A quantitative study of the frontal lobes.* Chicago: University of Chicago Press.

Hevern, V. W. (1980). Recent validity studies of the Halstead-Reitan approach to clinical neuropsychological assessment. *Clinical Neuropsychology, 2,* 49–61.

Jarvis, P. and Barth, J. T. (in press). *A guide to interpretation of the Halstead-Reitan Battery for Adults*. Odessa, Florida: Psychological Assessment Resources.

Lezak, M. D. (1983). *Neuropsychological assessment* (2nd Ed.). New York: Oxford University Press.

Ranseen, J. D., Macciocchi, S. N., and Barth, J. T. (in press). Neuropsychological assessment: Issues in its clinical applications. In J. R. McNamara (Ed.), *Clinical Issues, Developments and Trends in Professional Psychology 2*.

Reitan, R. M. *Manual for administration of neuropsychological test batteries for adults and children*. Unpublished manuscript. University of Washington, Seattle.

Reitan, R. M. and Davison, L. A. (Eds.). (1974). *Clinical neuropsychology: Current status and applications*. Washington, D.C.: V. H. Winston & Sons.

Russell, E. W., Neuringer, C., and Goldstein, G. (1970). *Assessment of brain damage: A neuropsychological key approach*. New York: John Wiley & Sons, Inc.

Swiercinsky, D. (1978). *Manual for the adult neuropsychological evaluation*. Springfield, Illinois: Charles C Thomas, Publisher.

Index